909

.F 58
1973

W9-DHF-883

The
Mexican War
Changing Interpretations

Edited by

Odie B. Faulk

and

Joseph A. Stout, Jr.

GOSHEN COLLEGE LIBRARY
GOSHEN, INDIANA

SAGE BOOKS

THE SWALLOW PRESS INC.
CHICAGO

Copyright © 1973 by The Swallow Press Incorporated
All rights reserved
Printed in the United States of America
    by Lorrin L. Morrison

First Edition
    Second Printing

Sage Books are published by
The Swallow Press Incorporated
1139 South Wabash Avenue
Chicago, Illinois 60605

This book is printed on 100% recycled paper

ISBN (cloth) 0-8040-0642-3
ISBN (paper) 0-8040-0643-1
LIBRARY OF CONGRESS CATALOG CARD NUMBER 72-94389

The

Mexican War

Changing Interpretations

Contents

(continued)

Maps

Introduction

ON APRIL 18, 1846, Mexican President Mariano Paredes y Arrillaga wrote the commander of his Army of the North, General Pedro de Ampudia, "At the present time I suppose you to be at the head of our valiant army, either fighting already or preparing for the operations of the campaign. . . . It is indispensable that hostilities be commenced, yourself taking the initiative against the enemy." Five days later, long before he could hear the result of this order, President Paredes issued a proclamation declaring "defensive war" against the United States. And the following day, April 24, Ampudia was superseded in command of the Army of the North by General Mariano Arista, a militant, who immediately issued orders for some 1,600 cavalry to cross the Río Grande and attack the American forces on the north side of the river. That same afternoon a large Mexican force came upon Captain William Thornton and about sixty American dragoons; following intensive skirmishing, Thornton was forced to surrender.

Thus began what many Americans have called the most disgraceful episode in American history. In fact, the Mexican War, as we have come to term this conflict, has been pictured as a case of American aggression, with the United States deliberately provoking a war in order to acquire the territory now labeled the American Southwest — a clear case of imperialism pure and simple. As a result, despite the many excellent books which have been written about the Mexican War proving that neither side was exclusively to blame for the conflict, most textbooks used in college survey courses of American history specifically charge the United States with starting the war for territorial aggrandizement.

We were recently sitting in our office discussing popular attitudes in the United States about war in general and the Mexican War in particular. We pulled out the first Instructor's Manual on the shelf and found this multiple-choice question: "President James K. Polk deliberately provoked war with Mexico in order to acquire (a) New Mexico (b) California (c) the entire Southwest." There was no asking *if* Polk had started the war; the only question was the amount of territory he intended to acquire. Yet a look at the hard facts reveals greater complexity than the standard textbook simplicism. The war that began on April 24, 1846, was the beginning of a conflict that would last almost two years, cost thousands of lives and millions of dollars, and would redraw the maps of the Southwest; but it was merely the last act, not the first, of a drama that had begun more than three centuries earlier.

The discovery of America had started a conflict among France, Spain, and England for possession of a continent. The French were eliminated in 1763, and then two decades later the United States established sovereignty over a large part of the British claim. Next came elimination of the Spaniards, to be supplanted in 1821 by the Mexican nation, while the United States purchased the territory known as Louisiana in 1803. The Anglo settlement of Texas and the subsequent revolution there brought a new element to this quest for territory, but it was erased in 1845 when the Lone Star Republic chose to join the Union. Thus by 1846 there were only three contestants left in this struggle for empire: England, which claimed part title to the Pacific Northwest; the United States, which shared the claim to the Oregon Territory; and Mexico, which claimed the territory from New Mexico westward and which still maintained — if ridiculously — a claim to Texas.

But it was not the Texas question which started the Mexican War, although many historians have argued this. True, it was this annexation which touched off the Mexican War, but Texas' joining the Union was not an act of hostility against Mexico. Rather it was the outgrowth of a series of events over the previous twenty-five years. In 1821 when Mexico won her independence from Spain there grew two major political parties, the Centralists and the Federalists. The Centralists were those favoring a strong central government, while the Federalists wished a government patterned in large measure after that in the United States. In 1822 the Centralists gained the upper hand and named Agustín de Iturbide emperor of Mexico — only to see him deposed in 1823 and the Federalists assume the upper hand and draft the Constitution of 1824 establishing a federal republic.

Stable constitutional government lasted only until 1829 when a series of revolutions began. These culminated in 1835 when Antonio López de Santa Anna overthrew this constitution and set himself up as a dictator (which, incidentally, caused the Texas Revolution). Chaos followed with coup and counter-coup, revolution and counter-revolution, pronouncement and counter-pronouncement. In 1845, when Texas sought annexation to the United States, the Federalists were in power, and the Centralists used this annexation to overthrow the Federalist government; in the process they worked the majority of the Mexican population into a war fever, asserting grandiosely that they would see the "Eagle and Serpent" of Mexico floating over the American White House rather than give up the Mexican claim to Texas.

Meanwhile on the northern side of the Río Grande, the question of Texas had been joined to the Whig Party's fight against the institution of slavery and the extension of this economic system to additional American territory. Thus the Whigs denounced the annexation of Texas as a "Slaveocracy Conspiracy" by Southerners anxious to extend their "peculiar institution" westward. To justify this thinking, some prominent Whigs proclaimed that Mexico maintained title to all of Texas, a claim so ludicrous that most Whigs contented themselves with asserting that Mexico owned at least that part of Texas between the Nueces River and the Río Grande (a claim, incidentally, which no Mexican ever advanced in print before this war began; Mexicans said they owned all of Texas, not just the Nueces strip). Thus when the issue of Texas joining the Union was before Congress, the voting was largely split along party lines — as was the American declaration of war on May 12. The Whigs saw the issue as a means of winning the next election and therefore charged the Democrats with motives which historians of a liberal leaning have since assigned to all the United States of 1846: expansionism, greed, and wrong-doing.

And once the war was concluded, the American acquisition of California was, and still is, cited as evidence of American imperialism. That President James K. Polk desired California cannot be argued. However, all impartial observers of the 1840s agreed that California already was lost to Mexico; the only question to be resolved at that time was who would get it: England, the United States, or possibly France.

California in the spring of 1846 had no schools or newspapers, no postal system, almost no police or court system, few books, and little protection from Indian raids from the interior. Even communication with Mexico was rare. Many Californians openly bespoke their desire to be annexed to the United States, while others favored English sovereignty. And there was virtually a civil war going on in the province at the time as Governor Pío Pico contended with Colonel José Castro for domination. Polk was well aware of these currents of intrigue and would have been derelict to U.S. national interest if he had not tried to offset British and French influence in this vital region. Thus he had the Pacific Squadron of the United States Navy standing by to intervene, just as he had Captain John Charles Frémont and a detachment of American soldiers operating in the region waiting for an opportune moment to interpose themselves on the side of American interests.

Finally there was the claims issue, which most American historians note, but which they dismiss as a cause for war. This concerned the payment of debts owed to American citizens by the Mexican Government — legitimate debts somewhat inflated, but which in the era of history under study constituted just cause for war (witness the French war against Mexico in 1838 over the claims issue alone). The claims issue had first been opened in 1829 but by 1846 had not been settled and showed little or no progress toward settlement.

Yet in 1846, when fighting started, the immediate cause was the Mexican desire to re-acquire Texas. President Paredes, for reasons of political gain, ordered his troops north of the Río Grande, insisting on a

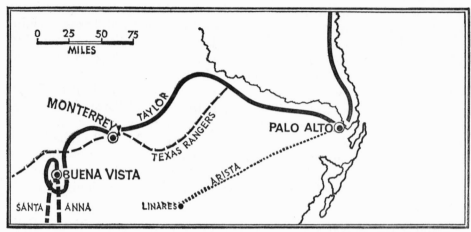

— *Map by Gilbert Drake Harlan*

TAYLOR'S ROUTE OF MARCH FROM PALO ALTO TO BUENA VISTA

war of aggression while proclaiming a declaration of "defensive war." Opposing General Arista in Texas was General Zachary Taylor, "Old Rough and Ready," as the troops called him. Polk had ordered Taylor to the mouth of the Río Grande, a position he assumed on March 23, 1846, with some 4,000 men. Once attacked on April 24-25, Taylor did not wait for Congress to declare war; he immediately began consolidating his position and preparing for battle — which came on May 8 at Palo Alto and the next day at Resaca de la Palma. Both of these battles he won easily, his artillery proving so devastating to the Mexicans that they broke and fled, leaving Matamoros open to Taylor without a fight.

The climate at the mouth of the Río Grande proved so hostile that Taylor moved his troops to Camargo, Texas. Despite the hundreds who sickened and died, recruits poured into Taylor's camp. Texans rushed to join the colors; to them this was a chance to avenge themselves against the Mexicans. "Here's to Old Zach! Glorious Times! Roast Beef, Ice Cream, and Three Months' Advance!" said one recruiting poster. In August, 1846, with 6,640 troops, Taylor advanced toward Monterrey, Mexico, guided by Texas Rangers. The fighting on September 21-24 was hard, but again superior American artillery broke the morale of the Mexican troops, and the town was surrendered to Taylor — who suddenly found himself the hero of the hour. Celebrations across the United States were held, while the Whigs talked openly of running "Old Rough and Ready" for President in 1848. Polk became so alarmed that he ordered Taylor not to advance further, to give up all but his volunteers to another command being formed by Winfield Scott, and to remain on the defensive.

Taylor chose to defy the President's orders, however. His troops advanced to capture Saltillo on November 16, and by mid-January he had a line, some 400 miles in length, of defense — and offense — stretching from Monterrey to the Gulf of Mexico. Yet this basic weakness was known to the new Mexican President, Antonio López de Santa Anna, who was hurrying north with approximately 20,000 hastily recruited troops to achieve a stunning victory, one that would make him once again dictator of Mexico. On February 22, 1847, the two armies came together at the Hacienda of Buena Vista, there to fight a two-day battle that saw Taylor's force saved yet again by superior artillery. During the night of February 23, as Taylor considered a retreat, the Mexicans broke and fled, leaving Taylor the victor — and a certain nominee for the Presidency in 1848.

At the same time that Taylor was winning his stunning victories in northern Mexico, a second major offensive was occurring in the American Southwest. At Fort Leavenworth, Kansas, Colonel (later General) Stephen Watts Kearny assembled a rag-tag army at the orders of the President. Designated the "Army of the West," it numbered some 2,700 men, most of whom were mounted. Also included in this number was a battalion of five hundred Mormons, enlisted at the request of Brigham Young, whose salaries were paid to the Mormon Church to help finance the sect's move westward from Illinois to the Great Salt Lake. When the major portion of Kearny's army marched toward Santa Fe on June 26, 1846, it was accompanied by a large wagon train of traders anxious to transact business in New Mexico. After a hot, thirsty march of 565 miles, the Army of the West reached Bent's Fort on the upper Arkansas River; there it rested while Kearny and his staff pondered reports that 3,000 Mexicans had marched north from Chihuahua to defend New Mexico.

At the same time in Santa Fe, Governor Manuel Armijo was aware of the approach of the Americans — and no doubt wishing that his 3,000 men were seasoned veterans instead of mainly raw recruits of little value, with no inclination to fight. He had at his command only two hundred regulars, mostly ill-equipped and poorly trained. Still he might have won a contest of arms with the Americans had he made full use of his geographical advantage. A short distance east of Santa Fe was Apache Canyon, a narrow pass in the mountains through which the American army had to pass. A handful of loyal Mexicans could have held off Kearny's army until heat, hunger, and thirst forced their retreat or surrender. But Armijo made no stand, thanks to the persuasions of James W. Magoffin, a Santa Fe trader accompanying Kearny by virtue of an order from President Polk. Magoffin went ahead of the Army of the West when it was at Bent's Fort; accompanied by twenty men commanded by Captain Philip St. George Cooke, he made his way to Armijo's headquarters. There Magoffin, an old friend of the New Mexican governor, was hospitably received. That evening the trader persuaded Armijo

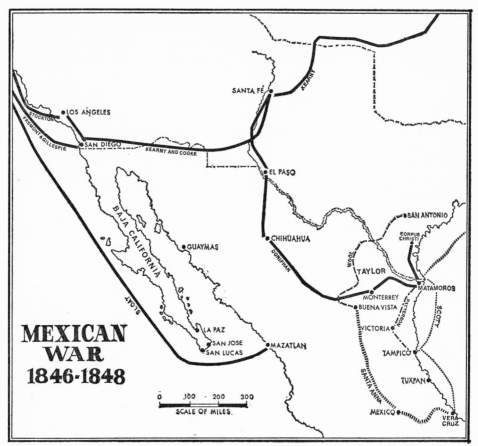

— *Map by Gilbert Drake Harlan*

MAJOR ROUTES BY LAND AND SEA

that resistance was useless (according to legend the persuasion was a satchel of gold). One Mexican officer, Colonel Diego Archuleta, wanted to fight anyway; to him Magoffin held out the promise of governing an area west of the Río Grande, either deliberately misleading Archuleta or not knowing that Kearny had orders to continue to California. As a result of Magoffin's persuasion, the American army encountered no resistance when it passed through Apache Canyon on August 17, for Armijo had fled southward. Santa Fe fell into American hands on the afternoon of August 18 without a shot having been fired.

At ceremonies in the capital city of the province on August 19, General Kearny tried to settle all doubts in the minds of the New Mexicans; he guaranteed them freedom of religion, recognition of their land titles, and full rights of American citizenship. Most local officials were left in office once they took the oath of allegiance to the United States. Kearny also organized a civil government, appointing Charles Bent governor and

Preston Blair, Jr. attorney general. Then, once the chiefs of the leading pueblos came to Santa Fe and took the oath of allegiance to the United States, Kearny no longer had any reason to remain in New Mexico, especially since he had orders to march to California. Accordingly he divided the Army of the West into four parts. Part of this force would remain in New Mexico under the command of Colonel Sterling Price as an army of occupation. A second portion, the Missouri Mounted Volunteers, were sent south under Colonel Alexander W. Doniphan; their role was to meet briefly with the Navajo Indians, then proceed south down the Río Grande to El Paso, cross the desert to Chihuahua City, and then move eastward to link up with Taylor. This Doniphan did, winning the battle of El Brazito just north of El Paso and the battle of Sacramento near Chihuahua City, finally linking with Taylor's army at Saltillo on May 21. In all, the Missouri Volunteers marched 6,000 miles, fought two major battles against superior forces, promoted commerce with the United States in Chihuahua, and inflicted heavy casualties on the Mexicans — all without government uniforms, supplies, commissary, or paymaster. It was a remarkable feat.

The third part of his Army of the West General Kearny would lead to California. This consisted of three hundred dragoons, while the Mormon Battalion under the command of Philip St. George Cooke, now a lieutenant colonel, was to follow from Santa Fe to California, opening a usable wagon road in the process. On September 25, after checking on a rumored uprising of New Mexicans in the southern part of the territory, Kearny departed for California. Down the Río Grande he marched to Socorro, then turned westward toward the Gila River Valley.

A short distance out of Socorro Kearny met Kit Carson, who was returning from California with dispatches from Frémont concerning the war on the Pacific Coast. Frémont and his party of explorers had been ordered out of California in the spring of 1846 by the governor and had moved across the boundary into Oregon at Klamath Lake. There on May 8 he was reached by Lieutenant A. H. Gillespie, whom President Polk had sent with secret instructions for Commodore J. D. Sloat, commander of the American Pacific squadron, Thomas O. Larkin, American consul at Monterey, and Frémont. According to Gillespie, the instructions he brought to Frémont from the President and Secretary of State were "to watch over the interests of the United States, and counteract the influence of any foreign agents who might be in the country with objects prejudicial to the United States."

Frémont immediately returned southward to the American settlements on the Sacramento River, while Lieutenant Gillespie went aboard an American warship at San Francisco where he was furnished arms, ammunition, and money which he took to Frémont on the Sacramento. On June 11 the Americans began an uprising against the Mexican forces

of Governor José de Castro. On July 4 Frémont addressed the revolution-
ists at Sonoma, advising them to declare their independence from Mexico
and to drive out Governor Castro and his adherents. This the group
attempted, proclaiming the existence of the "Bear Flag Republic" and
raising 150 men, among them Captain Frémont's sixty followers. Two
days previously, Commodore Sloat had received definite information that
the United States was at war with Mexico, and on July 7 he took Monterey and ran up the American flag. Two days afterward there were ceremonies at San Francisco and Sonoma, and on July 11 the Stars and
Stripes was raised at Sutter's Fort. Sloat's proclamation to the people
declared that he came as a "friend," that Californians would have full
citizenship and the right of free worship, and that their property rights
would be respected.

This action presaged a change in the Bear Flag Revolt. On July 15
Sloat was replaced by Commodore Robert F. Stockton. A few days later
the volunteers in the Bear Flag Revolt were enlisted as volunteers, under
Navy control, with Frémont as their major and Gillespie their captain.
On July 25 Stockton sent a warship, the *Cayane*, sailing south to San
Diego with Frémont and the volunteers, hoping to cut off the retreating
Castro. The Mexicans halted and encamped near Los Angeles, whereupon Stockton sailed the *Congress* to San Pedro and disembarked his
sailors and marines to do battle. Castro preferred to retreat southward,
however, and on August 13, accompanied now by Frémont, Stockton
entered Los Angeles, where he declared martial law and forbade the
carrying of weapons. Thus the war was over, they thought, and Kit
Carson was sent east with dispatches to that effect.

Upon receipt of this news, Kearny sent two hundred of his dragoons
back to Santa Fe and proceeded west with the remaining one hundred.
His orders specified that he was to continue from New Mexico to California, where he was to act as military governor. He persuaded Kit Carson to forego seeing his wife in Taos; the famous scout reluctantly agreed
to guide Kearny across the desert to his destination. Along the Gila they
met roving bands of Apaches who were peaceful but not friendly. In
central Arizona they entered the land of the Pima who were more than
friendly; when Carson tried to bargain for provisions for the soldiers,
the Pimas replied, "Bread is to eat, not to sell. Take what you want."
Near the Colorado River four prisoners were taken. These Mexican
herders, under questioning, told of a native California uprising at Los
Angeles against American authority. Kearny crossed the Colorado in a
hurry and pushed into the burning hell of the real desert. After a week
of hardship almost beyond description, his column entered the last range
of mountains — to be met by fog, cold, and heavy rains. One officer commented about the men after an inspection: "Poor fellows. They are well-
nigh naked — some of them barefooted — a sorry looking set."

8

Introduction

On December 6 and 7 at San Pasqual, Kearny's "sorry looking set" encountered the insurgent Mexicans, led by Andres Pico. Unaccountably the American dragoons had allowed their powder to get wet, and the Mexican lancers charged with devastating results. Eighteen Americans were killed — two by bullets, sixteen by lances — in the first onslaught, and as many more were wounded. The little force was surrounded and besieged on a hillside. Only with difficulty were Kit Carson and Lieutenant Edward Fitzgerald Beale able to slip through the lines and reach San Diego, where they called on Commodore Stockton for aid. In the early morning hours of December 10 help arrived and the Mexicans were routed. Other skirmishes followed in which Kearny acquitted himself more admirably, and on January 10 Los Angeles surrendered to him. The northern part of the province was also pacified, and the American conquest of California was complete.

Almost immediately a quarrel began among the victors to determine who was to govern California. Stockton claimed his orders entitled him to name the military governor of the area, and he chose Frémont. The thirty-three-year-old army captain — and major of volunteers — chose to side with Commodore Stockton against Brigadier General Kearny, and accepted the appointment. Kearny fumed and ranted, demanding the surrender of all documents and authority to himself, but Frémont stood adamant. The dispute was settled in February, 1847, by orders from Washington confirming Kearny as governor, whereupon the general humiliated Frémont, detained him in defiance of the President's order, and took him to Fort Leavenworth, where he arrested him on charges of mutiny and insubordination. From November, 1847, to January, 1848, Frémont's case was tried by court martial in Washington before a board of regular army officers; he was found guilty and given a disciplinary sentence. Although President Polk remitted the penalty (for bravery during the war), Frémont was so enraged that he resigned from the service.

Shortly after Kearny departed New Mexico, Lieutenant Colonel Philip St. George Cooke set out with his Mormon troops in accordance with his orders to open a wagon road to California. Cooke was a strong-willed commander, and only the fact that Brigham Young had enjoined the members of the battalion to remain obedient prevented a mutiny, for the Mormons were equally strong-willed and were distrustful of their gentile commander. Departing on October 21, 1846, they went down the Río Grande for one hundred miles, then southwest to a point near Janos, Chihuahua, and proceeded to the San Pedro Valley of Arizona. There they encountered wild cattle that attacked them (Cooke referred to the incident in his journal of 1846 as "the battle of Bull Run"). At Tucson a Mexican garrison threatened to prevent the American passage, but fled

9

at Cooke's approach, and he briefly occupied the city. Next the Mormons marched down the Santa Cruz River to the Gila, followed it to Yuma Crossing on the Colorado, crossed there, and went through the desert of Southern California. After toiling through the coastal Sierra, Cooke brought his command safely into San Diego on January 29, 1847. At the end of his report, Cooke commented: ". . . Marching half-naked and half-fed, and living upon wild animals, have discovered and made a road of great value to our country . . ." Indeed they had, for Cooke's Wagon Road, "The Gila Trail," became a principal route to California soon afterward.

Meanwhile, blood was being shed in New Mexico. Colonel Diego Archuleta was the principal instigator; his anger stemmed from his failure to gain political control of New Mexico west of the Río Grande as had been hinted to him by James Magoffin. He found supporters among those New Mexicans who felt that Governor Armijo's refusal to fight and subsequent flight southward had impugned Mexican honor. In secret the conspirators gathered an army and weapons and drilled their troops. At a secret meeting in Santa Fe, held early in December, 1846, plans for the uprising were formulated: Governor Charles Bent and Colonel Sterling Price were to be killed immediately; then all American soldiers would be exterminated or driven out of the province in the ensuing confusion. The date for the uprising was set first for December 19, then for Christmas Eve. The American authorities learned of the plot, however, and some of the conspirators were arrested, ending the planned rebellion — or so Governor Bent thought. On January 5, 1847, he issued a proclamation describing what had happened and asking the people to remain loyal to the new regime.

Thinking all danger past, Bent decided to visit his family and friends in Taos early in January. There on January 19 the uprising occurred. Led by Pablo Montoya, self-styled "Santa Anna of the North," the Indians at Taos Pueblo marched into town where they killed and scalped Governor Bent. Five others in the town, including the sheriff, the circuit attorney, and an army captain, were murdered. Seven other Americans were killed at Turley's Mill in the Arroyo Hondo, and about the same number died at the town of Mora. Colonel Price at Santa Fe heard of the outbreak the following day, and he quickly gathered troops to crush the rebels. Marching five hundred men northward through bitter winter cold, he met 1,500 rebels at La Canada on January 24, and won a decisive victory over them. Five days later another battle was fought with the same result. The rebels thereupon entrenched themselves in the Taos Pueblo. Price brought up his artillery to batter down the walls, but the thick adobe refused to give way before the shells. Ladders were employed, and the fortress was stormed. Seven Americans were killed and forty-five were wounded in the battle, but approximately 150 rebels died before the fighting ceased. Fifteen of the ringleaders of the revolt,

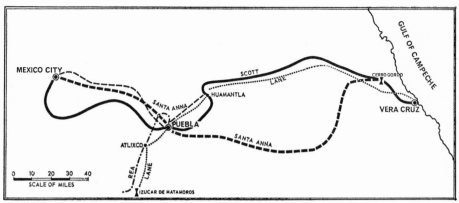

— *Map by Gilbert Drake Harlan*

FROM VERA CRUZ TO MEXICO CITY

including Montoya, were sentenced by a makeshift court and hanged. Archuleta, who was waiting in the south, heard of the defeat at Taos and fled the province, leaving it securely within American hands. A few other skirmishes were fought by the Americans, including a battle that saw the destruction of Mora, but the victory at Taos really marked the close of the Mexican War in the Southwest.

Meanwhile the United States Navy had been winning several spectacular victories off the coasts of California and northwestern Mexico. Most of the major ports of Baja California and Sonora, including La Paz and Guaymas, had been captured by elements of the Pacific Squadron, and these were held until May, 1848. And in the Gulf of Mexico the Home Squadron was performing equally well. In fact, it was victories by this unit at Tampico and Antón Lizardo (near Vera Cruz) which enabled General Winfield Scott to prepare his invasion of Mexico.

Scott was chosen to lead this invasion because President Polk feared, for political reasons, the growing popularity of Zachary Taylor. On November 18, 1846, Scott received vague orders from Polk ". . . to repair to Mexico, to take the command of the forces there assembled, and particularly to organize and set on foot an expedition to operate on the Gulf Coast, if, on arriving at the theater of action, you shall deem it practicable." Scott sailed to New Orleans, then moved to Brazos Santiago at the mouth of the Río Grande, and there assembled a force that eventually would number about 12,000 troops. With these men, he sailed aboard a motley fleet of ships to Tampico and then to Antón Lizardo; there he prepared to assault Vera Cruz, a heavily fortified city. His general staff, when consulted, argued for a frontal assault that would have resulted in heavy loss of life, but Scott chose to send his men ashore in whale boats some three miles downshore from Vera Cruz. This landing on March 9, 1847, was America's first amphibious landing — and

11

the Mexicans, when confronted with an American force coming toward Vera Cruz from the landward side where there were few fortifications, chose to surrender after a few days' bombardment. Scott's brilliant victory had cost just nineteen Americans killed and sixty-three wounded.

Leaving a token force behind to hold Vera Cruz, Scott next moved inland with 8,500 men — only to meet General Santa Anna and the Mexican army entrenched on the heights of Cerro Gordo, a narrow defile guarding the road to Mexico City. Again Scott's advisors urged a frontal assault, but again he outflanked the Mexicans and forced his way through Cerro Gordo with small loss of life. Brilliant victories followed until Scott was standing at the walls of Mexico City by August, 1847. He was receiving scant support from Washington as he fought his way inland; in fact, President Polk gave almost no help other than to send Captain Jack Hays and a detachment of Texas Rangers to Vera Cruz with orders to keep Scott's inland supply road open. The Texans took few prisoners, shot quickly, and fought ruthlessly so that soon the Mexicans were crying "*Los Diablos Tejanos*" at their appearance. Despite the meager help Scott received from Washington, he continued to supply his army by buying goods from friendly Mexican merchants with Treasury warrants which he simply signed. Without this aid from Mexicans, Scott would have been forced to surrender. Increasingly the Mexicans chose to do business with Scott, even to aid the Americans, because of the mismanagement, the exactions, and the forced loans, which Antonio López de Santa Anna had made so much a policy of the Mexican Government. The Mexican merchants preferred an occupation by Scott's American troops to their own government; Scott treated them fairly, taxed them equitably, and kept his troops from looting the country.

The battle for mastery of Mexico City began on August 20 with fighting at Contreras, followed by an engagement at Churubusco—both resulting in American victories. The invading general then granted a Mexican request for an armistice — which the Mexicans interpreted as an act of weakness and used to reinforce their position. No peaceful settlement could be reached, and fighting resumed on September 8 at Molino del Rey and Chapultepec, the Americans again winning. This time Scott did not hesitate after his victories, but hurried troops forward across the causeway into the city itself. Santa Anna tried to rally his men for one more fight; when he could not, he abandoned the city, and on the morning of September 14 Scott rode into the central plaza of Mexico City to raise the Stars and Stripes. In far-off London the Duke of Wellington, who had been following this campaign, later declared that Scott's feat in Mexico was "unsurpassed in military annals. He is the greatest living soldier."

Santa Anna and the Mexican Government withdrew northward to Guadalupe Hidalgo to try to regroup. Scott, meanwhile, used his men

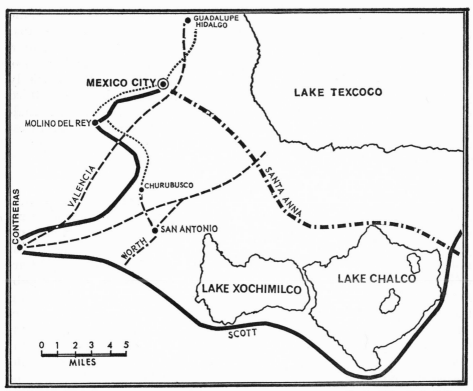

— *Map by Gilbert Drake Harlan*

THE CAMPAIGN IN THE VALLEY OF MEXICO

to restore order in Mexico City and to end the banditry that plagued the countryside. So effective was he that a delegation of leading Mexican citizens asked him to become dictator of Mexico. He refused. He had completed his task — and magnificently.

Now it was time for a State Department clerk named Nicholas Trist, who had accompanied Scott, to negotiate an end to the war, and on February 2, 1848, the Treaty of Guadalupe Hidalgo was concluded. This treaty of "peace and friendship" provided for an end to the conflict and, in theory, settled all matters of dispute between Mexico and the United States. By the terms of the agreement, Mexico gave up all claims to Texas; the new boundary would begin three marine leagues from shore in the Gulf of Mexico, proceed up the deepest channel of the Río Grande to the southern boundary of New Mexico, turn west at that point for three degrees of longitude, then run due north to the nearest branch of the Gila River, proceed down the Gila to its junction with the Colorado, and divide Upper and Lower California by a line running straight from the Gila-Colorado junction to a point one marine league south of the southernmost point of the Port of San Diego. For this cession of territory

13

the United States agreed to pay fifteen million dollars and to assume payment of all claims owed to American citizens (totaling $3,208,315). The United States Senate approved the treaty on March 10, 1848, by a vote of 38-14, and on May 26 ratifications were exchanged at Querétaro, the temporary seat of the Mexican Government. President Polk officially proclaimed the treaty to be in existence on July 4, 1848, the seventy-third anniversary of the independence of the United States. Except for a small slice of territory in southern New Mexico and Arizona, the Southwest had become American.

The chapters that follow are the result of recent scholarship from JOURNAL *of the* WEST. For this present volume, we have added introductory summaries to each original article. Most of these articles appeared initially in the Journal's April, 1972, issue, one of the topical numbers which the editors and publishers, Lorrin L. Morrison and Carroll Spear Morrison, initiated and which so distinguish this excellent publication. To them we owe a deep debt of gratitude both for publishing the topical number and for their cooperation in making this book possible. In addition we wish to acknowledge the support of the Library of Oklahoma State University and the Research Foundation of the same institution; without the help of these two organizations the present book could not have been concluded. Likewise the book obviously would be an impossibility without the contributions of each of the authors involved. We feel that their work constitutes a major addition to the historical investigation of this tragic conflict; no article is so pompous as to place sole blame on either of the combatant nations, but rather each takes a measured approach to the causes, events, and consequences of the war. In short, they give a balanced view of the Mexican War, one that allows students to draw their own conclusions. Therefore we are proud to have our names associated with this publication, which we feel does much to throw new light on the true events of 1846-1848.

ODIE B. FAULK

JOSEPH A. STOUT, JR.

Stillwater, Oklahoma
November, 1972

CHAPTER 1

California Ports: *A Key to West Coast Diplomacy, 1820-1845*

By Sister Magdalen Coughlin, C. S. J.

THE COLORFUL CALIFORNIA COAST from its discovery was coveted by men of all nations. Searched for the illusive and mysterious Strait of Anián, scoured for valuable beaver pelts, and ultimately settled in response to foreign intrusion, California was deemed a valuable prize by the commercially oriented nations of the world. First explored by Spaniards in 1542, California was not settled until 1769. Only then did Spain act to hold the area, for the Iberians feared encroachment by Russian explorers and trappers led by Vitus Bering.

Thus began nearly one hundred years of competition for the region. Significantly, no real decision would be reached about sovereignty over the area until merchants involved in the oriental trade enlisted the help of statesmen. But by this time only England and the United States remained in the race to control the vast area, for both knew that whichever nation controlled California might also dominate the trade with rich Far Eastern countries.

The American diplomatic effort to acquire the territory from Mexico began in 1819 when John Quincy Adams, as Secretary of State, attempted to include portions of that far coast in the Florida Purchase Agreement. When President in 1825, Adams again attempted to get California through diplomatic efforts. Always present was the English threat, and this country likewise utilized diplomatic techniques to halt any such American plan. Adams failed in his efforts, partly because of English efforts, but also because of the instability of the new Republic of Mexico. Andrew Jackson, when President of the United States, negotiated the claims issue and the Texas boundary question with the Mexicans, always with the thought in mind that some part of the coast of California might be included in any settlement. He also failed in his efforts, and in fact was unable to obtain anything from the Mexicans except a pledge to pay the claims over the next few years – and this only after he had threatened to collect claims from the deck of a battleship in Vera Cruz harbor. Thus diplomatic efforts to obtain California continued almost until the outbreak of the hostilities between the United States and Mexico in 1846. Sister Magdalen Coughlin has very ably presented an analysis of the role that diplomacy played in seeking control of the California Coast in the years from 1820 to 1845.

This chapter originally appeared in JOURNAL *of the* WEST in April, 1966.

THE THRUST TOWARD THE WEST was actually for the Far East. And by the time it became entangled in early nineteenth century diplomacy the thrust had become powerful enough to drive through the diplomacy and a war to the final possession of the ports necessary for the growing Far East trade.

Well into the nineteenth century both coasts of North America were scoured for a Strait of Anián, a Northwest Passage, a way through the land to the legendary wealth of the Orient. Thus, with Captain James Cook's accidental find that the sea otter skin had leverage of rare value in the China trade, one merchant after another challenged the "Spanish Ocean" and swarmed onto the Pacific Coast, thereby awakening keen competition. After the individual adventurer successfully exploited the coast, exposing a vulnerable Spanish control, his nation caught the excitement of this exceptionally profitable trade of seemingly infinite possibilities. And now a Pacific port became essential to a prosperous and stable Pacific-Far East commerce. It was for sea ports men now searched and it was in relation to this quest that the Pacific Coast first drew the attention of the world.

Yet all recognized the real decision of possession would not be made until the merchant could enlist the aid of the statesman — until the commercial banner was carried into the diplomatic arena. Thus the Pacific Coast, and eventually the Southwest Coast, with its choice harbor of San Francisco directly on the great circle route, became the object in a struggle of great moment — first a commercial and then a diplomatic battle for an area all recognized would give control of the opening Far East trade and eventually control of the Pacific. An inter-action of commercial interests and diplomacy established a cycle in which a constantly deepening economic interest created ever greater pressure for diplomatic action. The coast, therefore, gradually gained such importance that first Oregon and then Texas became pawns in the battle for California ports. While the diplomacy prior to the Mexican War was both circuitous and varied, then, ports were in sight every step of the way.

Russians were the first to cause international concern on the West Coast, but they were also first to be eliminated. For after being blocked by the Monroe Doctrine, the Russians withdrew by agreement to 54° 40'.[1] Thus with the removal of the extremely tenuous Spanish hold and the realization of the impotence of the Mexican, contestants for the Southwest Coast were further narrowed to three — the French, the English and the Americans — and to which of these the prize would go was, to the merchants and the world, a matter of conjecture right up to the moment Commodore John Drake Sloat raised the American flag at Monterey.

Of the three the French threat was actually the least powerful, although this was not fully recognized at the time. For the French were eliminated by their national instability in the period when claims were being established. Thus, although La Pérouse came to the Pacific in 1786, just when the race for trade was beginning, and reported that there are at present powerful political reasons . . . which may direct the attention of governments to this valuable part of America.[2] No attention was given for decades. And by this time the field was dominated by the Americans and the English.

French merchants did not concede, however. Duhaut-Cilly, arriving aboard *Le Heros* in 1827,[3] and the enthusiastic French agents and merchants who came during the next few years,[4] gave ample evidence that they dreamed the coast might be theirs, and they therefore contributed significantly to the growing tension. The ships sent by the French Government and merchants increasing from one or two a

16

decade to three or four a year, seemed a direct result of these visits,[5] and left no doubt of French imperialism in the minds of both native leaders and merchants of other nationalities. Vallejo wrote:

> The King of France . . . sent to Alta California an emissary well provided with money and letters of recommendation for the leading citizens of Monterey, San Diego, and Los Angeles . . . This emissary answers to the aristocratic name of Duflot de Mofras . . . [sent] with the purpose of preparing the animosities of the inhabitants for the project of the annexation of this department to the crown of France.[6]

And Captain Rosamel's[7] quick move to Monterey upon the arrest of a group accused of an attempted overthrow of the government evoked from an American sea captain the accusation that

> It is well known that the great powers of Europe have, for many years, sought every possible opportunity of getting a foothold in California. . . . The Frenchman, clothed with power and authority to obtain immediate redress, was much disappointed in not finding one of his own countrymen on the list of those sent away; had there been a single one claiming the protection of France, perhaps the flag of that nation . . . might now be floating over California. The Frenchman, with his broadside swung on the town, was only waiting for an excuse to open his battery; . . .[8]

Yet even the French, who caused the apprehension in their official reports, were forced to admit the futility of their dreams.

> As for the United States . . . the future is theirs . . . it will not be long before we shall see them marching with great strides toward the domination of these same shores where they seem so weak today . . . our policy must then be one purely tentative, as in the other distant lands of the globe. . . . As for England, dangerous adversary of France . . . it is necessary we keep a close watch on her on this coast . . . it might be possible that she would attempt to seize California, or at least one of the ports.[9]

It was these reports that sketched the lines official France would follow. For any actual evidence of official French interest is very vague. Enthusiastic pleas of individual Frenchmen, even officials, were unanswered from Paris. It is impossible, therefore, to prove that for all the loud French voices on the coast — voices of zealous individuals — Orleanist France was ever more than tentatively imperialistic toward California.

But the world neither read these reports nor was calmed by a knowledge of official French policy. These French visits were interpreted as a logical preparation to a growing French menace. And here lies a central factor in the diplomacy for the coast — the juxtaposition of the impression given by individual governmental or commercial agents and the reality of their government's policy. For when a Frenchman or an Englishman, sent to the coast by his government, offered to receive California as a protectorate, or when Americans began to boast of inevitable acquisition, strong commercial interests of other nationalities naturally became extremely concerned and demanded the protection of their governments. Diplomats throughout the entire period, therefore, show a vivid mutual apprehension — a conviction that the increasingly precious coast was in constant jeopardy. For although the historian can establish official positions in retrospect, these positions were not clear at the time, not even to the highest officials.

While the French continued to cause apprehension, then, their late start and lack of concrete claim diminished any real possibility of control. Therefore, it became increasingly clear through the 1830s and 1840s that the major competitors for the coast were the English and the Americans. For unlike the French, both of these had claims that they would not forfeit. But perhaps more significantly both had well established commercial roots which had begun early and gave exciting promise in this age of the opening Pacific.

Drake's thrust into the "Spanish Ocean" had been followed by countless English merchants who, in the light of the opening Far East, realized ever more clearly the value of this Pacific Coast they sailed along. And as their trappers moved across the continent to join them, these English merchants became deeply interested in the future of the California Coast.

But in the same period the other major contenders for the coast also arose. From the moment of independence the American, forced from former areas of trade by separation from England, had grasped the promise of the opening Pacific with an ingenuity and daring that would become associated with the image of the Yankee. New England sea otter traders[10] swarmed onto the coast in such numbers that for some time all Americans who came there were called "Boston men." And with the combination of the Napoleonic Wars and the East India monopoly system,[11] which momentarily removed competition, they almost immediately became firmly established. Boston traders not only continued to successfully challenge Hispanic control, thus establishing deep commercial interests, but in the 1820s, when the sea otter became nearly extinct, they began a new and extremely profitable New England venture on the Southwest Coast.[12] The hide and tallow trade and the whaling which now arose added the new penetration of resident agents to the regular coastal contact.

They also became quickly established in China. For although they met stringent competition there also, primarily from the established English merchants, the Americans came with the furs precious for exchange. And here can be glimpsed perhaps the first link between this Pacific trade and the United States Government. For the first Congress, on July 4, 1789, aware of both the need for commerce and the present barrier in· the Atlantic, passed a tariff and navigation act aimed explicitly at promoting Oriental trade. Taxes on tea, for example, were from six to twenty cents per pound if direct from China in American vessels, but eight to twenty-six if imported through Europe, and as much as fifteen to forty-five cents a pound if on foreign vessels, answering Thomas Randall's dictum to Alexander Hamilton that Americans definitely needed the help of "laying heavier taxes on tea imported from Europe."[13] The imports from China therefore, grew from $1,023,000 in 1795 to $5,745,000 in 1810,[14] driving the American interests in the Pacific deeper. A promising trade had begun.[15] The American merchants, as the English, therefore, also soon had deep roots both on the Pacific Coast and in the Far East, roots that would spread in the next twenty years to draw together such a combination of American interests that diplomacy for the coast became inevitable. And then, when diplomacy became hamstrung and final possession seemed threatened, these interests were willing to face war rather than jeopardize prize ports.

As Pacific commercial interests became more intense then, and as Hispanic control weakened, a diplomatic struggle was added to the commercial one. In the period before the 1820s all major diplomatic efforts of both England and the United States had naturally been toward the northern coastline, for here were the claims. But a combination of factors tended to shift first individual and then governmental interest to fasten on the choice ports of the Southwest Coast. For one thing, it became increasingly evident to the statesman what had long been clear to the seaman — that the Columbia River was, after all, not of great commercial value. Also, the monopolistic Spanish economic policy which had blocked any explicit diplomatic interest, was modified when the break up of the Spanish Empire resulted in an even weaker and more chaotic Mexican control of the coast. Constant rumors of possible insurrections, desires for independence and even aspirations for a protectorate gave both hope and excuse for diplomatic soundings. California ports, tenuously hinted at in the early period, as a result of growing economic pressure, assumed increasing diplomatic proportions until they became the dominant and primary objective in the major territorial negotiations of the period — the primary objective even in the negotiations for Texas and Oregon.

The first American diplomatic efforts to move down the coast began therefore as a comparatively slight side-issue of the effort of John Quincy Adams to readjust the unsatisfactory Southwest Boundary Agreement of 1819. By this time Adams had not only caught a vision of this coast, but seemed determined that the United States' possession of it was inevitable — if not yet to be publicly sought. In a cabinet discussion of the Spanish delay in ratifying the Adams-Onís Treaty, Adams sketched his continental vision:

19

. . . the world shall be familiarized with the idea of considering our proper dominion to be the continent of North America . . . the remainder of the continent should ultimately be ours. But it is very lately that we have distinctly seen this ourselves; very lately that we have avowed the pretension of extending to the South Sea; and until Europe shall find it as a settled geographical element that the United States and North America are identical, any effort on our part to reason the world out of the belief that we are ambitious will have no other effect than to convince them that we add to our ambition hypocrisy.[16]

And when in 1821 the Senator from Virginia, John Floyd, introduced a bill to establish forts at Astoria that came hard upon John B. Prevost's unannounced mission to the Pacific to receive the restoration of Astoria, the Secretary of State had an extraordinary session with the British minister to Washington, Stratford Canning, which Adams himself recorded with a good deal of relish. When Adams pointed out that "Britain surely did *not* have a claim at the Columbia River" and Canning questioned "And how far would you consider . . . this exclusion of right to extend?" Adams shot back "To all the shores of the South Sea . . . keep what is yours, but leave the rest of the continent to us."[17]

Convinced by both the need for Pacific ports and the misjudgment of the Columbia River, Adams' interest resulted not only in diplomatic relations being opened with Mexico within twenty days of his inauguration, but also in Clay's first instructions to the ambassador, Joel Poinsett, being to inquire into the advisability of a move into the Southwest.[18] Although nothing came of this first tenuous suggestion, a further effort was made on March 25, 1827, and this time the instructions were to buy Texas. Several alternative boundaries were offered. The most desired, but most extreme, began at the mouth of the Río Grande, went north to the Arkansas and thence to the 42° on the Pacific. Thus, in the opening diplomacy for the Southwest, the move down the coast was a definite, if only minor part, in the larger project of getting Texas. But this was to change, for a new direction in American diplomacy had been set. And thus the matter rested until Andrew Jackson became President.

In these first American steps toward possessing the coast it became evident that the instability of the Mexican Government and the English opposition to American control would be major obstacles. Mexican regimes seemed unable to transfer land for any consideration. An inherent imperial pride and an unrealistic assessment of the situation hamstrung every offer of purchase from Poinsett through Slidell no matter how desperate Mexican financial straits might be. Even when England, their only hope for assistance, begged the Mexicans to recognize Texas independence in an effort to save the rest of Mexico's possessions from the United States, Santa Anna was forced to refuse lest his control suffer from popular revulsion. This mentality echoed throughout the whole period.[19]

Another constantly recurring motif in this diplomacy for the coast was the ominous threat of England. Englishmen made it clear from the outset that if successful in Texas they would block American immigration to the Pacific, and if they failed in Texas their efforts would be redoubled in California. But the British policy was quite different in Oregon, Texas and California and this led to a confusion that was transformed into fear and then action under economic pressure. A fact of tremendous importance in this diplomacy, a fact missed by Washington and among Americans on the coast, was that the British Government never aspired to actually possess California ports,[20] but rather simply to block American acquisition. That from the beginning British governmental and commercial agents, as in the case of the French, so severely clouded this official policy accounts for much of the diplomatic anxiety throughout the period. Americans assumed this area they had come to prize so highly was desired by all. Therefore, while British diplomacy was often vibrantly active, the aim was consistently misunderstood.

It is significant to note also that even in these first steps of diplomacy for the coast, diplomacy which would prove so ineffective, the United States was at a distinct diplomatic disadvantage. The marked delay in the appointment of an American minister[21] was thrown into sharp relief by the contrasting alacrity of the British appointment of the envoy, Macki.[22] The British not only moved to open diplomacy immediately in 1822, but under the directions of the anti-American Canning[23] they both gained Mexican favor and further alienated American interests. From the beginning Poinsett keenly felt both this British advantage and the consequent threat to American interests on the coast, a threat which would haunt American diplomacy until the coast was finally possessed.

> It is manifest that the British have made good use of their time and opportunities. The President and three of the secretaries — those of state, treasury and ecclesiastical affairs — are in their interest . . .[24]

Added to this was another serious diplomatic disadvantage, the fumbling inefficiency of American diplomats. Poinsett, on a mission in 1822 to report on conditions in Mexico, seriously betrayed his hand and therefore put the Mexican Government on an understandable guard when, in an interview with Azcarate, an official in the entourage of Iturbide, he produced a map on which he not only pointed out the undesirable line of 1819, but also traced the desirable one which gave the United States sovereignty over Texas, New Mexico and California. Although the Mexican official concealed his rage at the moment, he was quick to make Poinsett's position clear to higher authority. Nor was the matter allowed to rest there. When Poinsett was returning to Mexico in 1825, this time in fact the official United States minister,

President Victoria received a letter from Azcarate concerning the incident just two days before Poinsett was to be officially received.[25] This only served to verify the fear of aggression which had arisen over a twenty-year period of American economic pressure in the Southwest.

Thus in the opening stage of diplomacy for the coast, American diplomats met several obstacles they would continually encounter — Mexican regimes too unstable to negotiate, constant moves by England to block American efforts and place the United States in a position of diplomatic inferiority. At the end of Adams' administration, then, in spite of growing economic pressures, the possibilities of concluding satisfactory American diplomacy for the coast were slight.

This already ineffective diplomatic relationship was only made worse by Jackson's first bid, an attempt in which Mexican national pride and crass American diplomacy were again predominant. And here, as in both Adams' and later attempts, the economic orientation of the diplomatic efforts is clear. Anthony Butler, an army acquaintance and old friend of Jackson's, seems to have instigated the move when he came to Washington in the summer of 1829 and urged both Jackson and Van Buren to do something about Texas — for Butler and other Americans had invested heavily in Texas land.

Jackson's first memorandum to Van Buren on the matter, August 13, 1829, directed Poinsett to renew the offer to adjust the border of 1819, still from the Río Grande to 42°, but this time for five million dollars rather than one million. The value was becoming more obvious. By this time, however, it had become clear Poinsett had created a situation in which he was doing more harm than good. He was therefore recalled in mid-October and Butler was named his successor. Only a few days after Butler's arrival in Mexico American negotiations were once more hamstrung when Mexican papers announced that he had come concerning the boundary adjustment and expressed the Mexican sentiment that territorial negotiations with the Americans marked submission, an extremely legitimate reason for the overthrow of a regime. Bustamonte's paper, *El Sol*, made this clear:

> . . . we presume that he does the new administration the justice to suppose it incapable of a transaction as prejudicial and degrading to the republic as it would be disgraceful to the minister who would subscribe to it.[26]

Jackson's periodic instructions during the next six years to make another attempt of purchase became a pattern, but accomplished little. But in 1835 a new dimension was added. Although his first move toward the Southwest had included a bid to move down the coast, it had essentially been a reiteration of Adams' offer with the main objective being Texas. But now Jackson seems to have caught a keener vision of the sea, for his eye seems to have moved from his original aim ". . . to secure forever to the inhabitants of the Valley of the Mississippi the undisturbed possession of the navigation of the river,[27] to focus more sharply on ports. This significant change in the official attitude was evident. John Quincy Adams wrote that it was a letter of August 1, 1835, from Lieutenant William A. Slacum that,

> . . . kindled the passion of Andrew Jackson for the thirty-seventh line of latitude from the river Arkansas to the South Sea, to include the bay of San Francisco, and was the foundation of Forsyth's instruction to Butler of August 6, 1835.[28]

That Jackson was deeply impressed by Slacum's views is true, and that Butler did receive important new instructions is also true. But that Slacum's letter of August 1 was the beginning of Jackson's new attitude is not clear. For as early as July 25 he had instructed Forsyth to enlarge the scope of Butler's negotiations. It would seem, therefore, this first explicit official move directly for the California Coast was rather rotation in the cycle — caused by economic pressures. The American whaling and commerce in the Pacific and Far East had grown rapidly in the administrations of Monroe and Adams[29] and the desire for protection and ports had grown proportionately. Also, the penetration of the fur men into the valleys of the Missouri had continued west and in cutting through previously unscaled mountain ranges into California valleys they had unwittingly opened paths that would be trampled into highways with the surge of an American invasion. It was these new economic pressures and the greater realization of the accessibility of the coast that caused the intensification of Jackson's efforts.

That the ports and not the land were now his primary aim was made clear in Secretary of State John Forsyth's instructions to Butler on August 6, 1835 — to offer $500,000 for San Francisco Bay and the area to the north.[30] The new emphasis on California ports is obvious.

> We have no desire to interfere with the actual settlement of Mexico on the coast and you may agree to any provision affecting the great object of securing the bay of San Francisco and excluding Monterey and the territory in its immediate neighborhood . . .[31]

The pace toward the coast had quickened now, for Jackson had made the acquisition of Pacific ports for commercial purposes an explicit aim of American diplomacy. His extreme anxiety that it be accomplished in his administration is clear right up to the end of his term. For when Antonio López de Santa Anna came to Washington in January, 1837, in an attempt to secure United States mediation between Mexico and Texas, Jackson wrote:

> If Mexico will extend the line of the United States to the Río Grande — up that stream to latitude 38 north and then to the Pacific including north calafornia [*sic*] we might instruct our minister to give them three millions and a half of dollars and deal then as it respected

Texas as a magnanimous nation ought — to wit — in the treaty with Mexico secure the Texians in all their just and legal rights and stipulate to admit them into the United States as one of the Union.[32]

After Jackson's failure, and with Van Buren's involvement in a financial crisis the move toward the coast seemed to slow down. But the financial crisis itself actually enhanced the move toward the Pacific and therefore, a further economic involvement in the coast once again laid the basis of more intense diplomacy. Fur trappers had not only opened routes but had touched the coast, and therefore suggested opportunities to farmers in need of markets.

By the late 1830s and early 1840s, therefore, it was obvious to all that the United States had not only started west, but was moving at a rapid pace by sea and now also by land. But as American interests both multiplied and became more intense the threat of English competition, which had always been a source of anxiety to American merchants, loomed even more distinct and therefore became a major catalyst to further diplomatic action.

Besides the more obvious economic and territorial claims on the coast the English land claims[33] was a major source of rumor that England was "securing the Bay of San Francisco" and "negotiating with Mexico for the purchase of California." This possibility assumed gigantic proportions when a request was added to the new land bond issued in April, 1837, that the region opened be one suitable for colonization and for trade.[34] The American fear this engendered was thrown into sharp relief when in 1839 James Alexander Forbes published in London his book, HISTORY OF CALIFORNIA, with the expressed purpose of backing this colonization plan.[35] By making this project known to the world just when American efforts for the coast were becoming intense, this book seems to have inspired the first serious fears that English aggression was imminent. The *London Times* reviewer expressed the opinion that Forbes' proposal of colonization was "well worthy the attention of the English politician."[36] And the episode was interpreted by the *Baltimore American* as a British plot to acquire California as a base for commerce with the East — this same charge was reiterated in the early 1840s by newspapers all over the country. Thus the conflict for the coast was sharply drawn.

This spectre that English efforts were to possess the coast was especially significant as a catalyst in American diplomacy in these crucial years in the early 1840s. But while agents urged England to take the coast, and Americans accepted this as an official aim, the British Government never moved in that direction. The first even semi-official British interest in California was elicited when, in connection with the Graham arrest of 1840,[37] American and British citizens were taken to Tepic by Castro and placed there under the protection of Barron,

24

the British consul. Barron's report inspired the British minister to Mexico, Pakenham, to investigate and realize more fully the tremendous value of California in the opening Pacific. It was at this same time de Mofras and Wilkes[38] came to the coast and that Americans were accused of instigating revolts. Therefore, Pakenham, swept up in the spirit of competition, and fearing that England would lose all, became extremely concerned about the coast. In reporting the Graham incident Pakenham, therefore, urged advantage be taken of the land claims to establish English settlements, for

> . . . I believe there is no part of the world offering greater natural advantages for the establishment of an English colony than the Province of Upper California; while its commanding position on the Pacific, its fine harbors, its forests of excellent timber for ship-building as well as for every other purpose, appear to me to render it by all means desirable, in a political point of view, that California, once ceasing to belong to Mexico, should not fall into the hands of any Power but England; . . .[39]

The reaction to this letter was a sharp definition of the British policy concerning the California Coast — a policy which would remain stable throughout the many negotiations in these crucial years of the 1840s. Stanley is clearly against

> . . . the formation of new and distant Colonies, all of which involve heavy direct and still heavier indirect expenditure, besides multiplying the liabilities of misunderstanding and collisions with Foreign Powers.[40]

And Aberdeen adds:

> Still less is Lord Stanley prepared to recommend the adoption of a plan whereby the Soil shall, in the first instance, be vested in a Company of Adventures, with more or less of the powers of Sovereignty and of legislation, and the Settlement so formed be afterwards placed under the protection of the British Crown; which as it seems to his Lordship is the position contended for by Mr. Pakenham.[41]

This British policy so significant in the formation of an American Far West is in part explained by the fact that the British Government to whom Pakenham addressed his letter had been replaced by the cabinet of Sir Robert Peel, with Aberdeen as Foreign Minister and Lord Stanley as the new Colonial Secretary. This change in British politics was to deeply affect the Pacific Coast, for the British Corn Law crisis brought to power a coalition whose success would be determined by results in an extensive program of proposed domestic reforms, and therefore, could not risk war by intervention in the Mexican crisis. Fortunately for the Americans, Peel's conservative lack of intervention was appealing to his time, for the same severe business depression which contributed to the American move west caused the manufacturing and merchant interests of England, which relied on trade, to dread international upsets which might delay the return of business confidence.

Thus the *Times* defended Aberdeen's lack of interest in California while accusing Palmerston of hampering British trade in America and the Far East — labeling him a "great anti-commercial diplomat," and *Punch* pictured him as a "God of War."[42]

This British conservatism not only restricted English intervention but also eliminated the possibility of a protectorate. For since the Canadian revolt of 1837 British statesmen had moved toward a "little England" policy,[43] and therefore Peel in no way favored the idea of adding a possession or protectorate of any kind to the British Empire. For all these reasons, then, the enthusiasm of Pakenham, Barron, Forbes and the others received this extremely cool and disinterested response which served to kill their zeal for some time.

The diplomatic exchange which shows this British policy in action most clearly, and one of the most significant and revealing diplomatic efforts of the period, was Webster's attempt at a tripatriate agreement. This incident throws light on several important facets of the situation in the early 1840s. It reveals that California ports had now become the key of American diplomacy in Oregon as well as in Texas, that the relative amiability of the British concerning the Oregon boundary starkly contrasts with their fierceness in Texas, and that the Mexican refusal to cede territory under any circumstances was a perpetual stumbling block to negotiations even in Oregon. But most significantly of all, this diplomatic exchange throws into sharp relief the great power Far East trade and consequently Pacific ports had assumed in American diplomacy. And as in all the major diplomatic efforts for the coast this one forms another rotation of the cycle, for the diplomacy emanated from economic demands. While Daniel Webster was involved in negotiations for Oregon and northern boundaries, he showed a willingness to exchange this very land for choice seaports.[44] His Massachusetts commercial orientation was never more clear.

Feeling the temper of the times Webster reïntroduced the claims issue originated by Jackson and launched into a bold attempt to use his negotiations with Ashburton concerning Oregon as a pawn for the infinitely more valuable California Coast — specifically for the port of San Francisco. Everett was instructed to inquire into possibilities of soliciting England's coöperation in a tripatriate agreement with Mexico

> . . . which should, as one provision, embrace a cession to the United States of the port of San Francisco on the Coast of California.[45]

The proposed plan was that Mexico would recognize Texan independence, Oregon would be settled at the Columbia River, and in return England would use her influence with Mexico to cede Upper California to the United States. The United States would pay several million dollars for California, part going to American claimants against

26

Mexico and the rest to the English bondholders.[46] There were obviously some advantages on all sides. Tyler, in full sympathy with this, never completely discarded Webster's idea. He later wrote:

> I never dreamed of conceding the country, unless for the greater equivalent of California, which I fancied Great Britain might be able to obtain for use through her influence in Mexico.[47]

The phrase "the greater equivalent of California" tells the tale.

The tone of the English reply to Webster's suggestion was consistent with Peel's conservation policy.[48] It seems that the Mexican aversion to giving up land was the sole block — until the hostility resulting from Commander Jones' seizure of Monterey brought the negotiations to an abrupt halt. But even the episode which ended the attempt, at first sight a fiasco, if examined more closely exemplifies the atmosphere on the coast. Jones' own explanation of his action reflects the tension.

> The Creole affair, the question of the right of search, the mission of Lord Ashburton, the sailing of a strong squadron from France under sealed orders, for the military occupation, as it now appears, of the Marquesas and Washington Islands; new difficulties between the United States and Mexico the well founded rumor of a cession of the Californias to England's naval force in that quarter, have all occurred since the date of your last order to me. Consequently I am without instructions [acting] . . . upon what I consider as a vital question to the United States — the occupation of California by Great Britain under secret treaty with Mexico.[49]

The source of the rumors upon which Jones acted was also indicative of the time. His information about the state of war came from a letter by Parrott, United States consul at Mazatlán. And in a Boston paper, containing an extract from the *New Orleans Courier*, Jones found a statement that Mexico had ceded California to England for $7,000,000.[50] Therefore, when in September, 1842, he saw Admiral Thomas take the British fleet from Callao under sealed orders, Jones, believing their destination was California, set out to arrive first.

After this episode it was clear to the United States Government that further direct efforts to obtain California at the moment were futile. But with the added pressure of those fleeing economic disasters[51] over routes established by economically significant fur men, desire for the coast had reached a new peak. And so, with even greater effort and determination, the focus of diplomacy for the Southwest Coast swung from Oregon back to Texas.

After United States-Mexican diplomatic relations had been severed as a result of Jackson's claims demand, no official move to acquire the Southwest Coast through Texas had been made until the vibrantly interested Tyler reöpened relations with the appointment of Waddy Thompson. The letter of Thompson to the Secretary of State immediately upon his arrival, and his letter to the President a few days later, reflect not only a distinct sharpening of the commercial motivation, but even more significantly, the extreme importance the Southwest Coast had by now assumed in United States diplomacy for Texas.

> As to Texas I regard as of very little value compared with California, the richest, the most beautiful and the healthiest country in the world. Our Atlantic border secures us a commercial ascendency there; with the acquisition of Upper California we should have the same ascendency on the Pacific. . . . France and England both have had their eyes upon it[52] . . . will reconcile the Northern people as they have large fishing and commercial interests in the Pacific and have literally no port there.[53]

The scales had shifted tremendously in California as they had in Oregon. While Adams, primarily concerned with Texas, had proposed the 42° as the most extreme of five possible boundary adjustments, and Jackson had with greater emphasis reiterated this proposal, now in 1842 diplomats, who in the same period were prepared to exchange part of Oregon for San Francisco, had become interested in Texas primarily as a gateway to the Southwest Coast. Webster himself wrote, "You know my opinion to have been and it now is, that, the port of San Francisco would be twenty times as valuable to us as all Texas."[54] As he had worked through Oregon for California ports, Webster's objective was clearly the same in Texas. For he answered the enthusiastic letter of Thompson with full permission to sound out the Mexican Government concerning an exchange of part of the Pacific Coast for American claims — essentially the same proposal as the tripatriate attempt except that the thrust was now from the South.

> . it is desirable that you should present the Port and Harbor of San Francisco as the prominent object to be obtained . . .[55]

But if American statesmen were dedicated to acquiring the coast through negotiations in Texas, the opposition of English statesmen was just as dedicated. British tacit consent to Webster's tripatriate plan, followed by frantic efforts to stop moves in Texas, may appear to pose a certain incongruity. But Texas was quite another matter. British efforts from the beginning had been strong here; obviously there was much more involved.[56] Britain had worked hard to establish a lucrative Mexican relationship, and the British investment, both economically and diplomatically, by this time was tremendous. Whereas it was a matter of an 8° adjustment in the Oregon boundary, the whole Southwest and the entire coast of the Gulf of Mexico as well as the Pacific were in jeopardy in the context of the Texas struggle. Also, the interrelationships of negotiations for Oregon, California, and Texas, and the key position of California ports in them all, was by now obvious. There was fear that the British would lose on all sides — the stakes were extremely high. The *London Times* noted:

. . . if any incident should lead to the declaration of war against Mexico, the seizure of Port Saint Francis and of Upper California, would be considered all over the Union as a sufficient pretext for adjourning the discussion of the Oregon Compromise.[57]

For a complex of reasons, then, in the spring of 1844, when it became apparent that Texas was moving rapidly toward union with the United States, Aberdeen, realizing Americans were aiming for the coast, launched a major diplomatic opposition campaign. It would be this campaign which would cause such economic and diplomatic tremors in the deeply involved United States that all pretense of restraint would be dropped and Polk's move to grasp the coast begun. Elliott, the British minister to Texas, was ordered to block annexation while Bankhead, minister to Mexico, pleaded with Santa Anna to recognize Texan independence[58] and thus remove the possibility of a war through which the United States could acquire the whole Southwest. At the same time, May 29, 1844, Aberdeen offered Tomás Murphy, Mexican minister to London, a suggestion to work for a joint English and French guarantee of the Mexican northern boundary — providing Mexico would recognize Texas. His offer went even further, indicating his awareness of the jeopardy of the coast.

> . . . *provided . . . England and France were perfectly agreed*, it would matter little to England whether the American Government would be willing to drop the question or not, and that, should it be necessary, she would go to the last extremity . . . in support of her opposition to the annexation; but that for this purpose it was essential that Mexico be disposed to acknowledge the independence of Texas.[59]

But this major British attempt was soon abandoned, for the French were at best luke-warm and both the French and English ministers to Washington warned that any hint of foreign intervention would defeat Henry Clay in the race for the Presidency and therefore lead to immediate annexation.[60] But the major source of Aberdeen's frustration was the now familiar refusal of Santa Anna and the Mexican people to see the logic of his plea. *La Voz de Pueblo* went so far as to publish a pamphlet lashing out at English intervention, charging a desire for a protectorate. But the charge itself is a further indication that California ports were the real issue.

> This power had discovered in the independence of Texas an efficacious means of advancing its interest . . . (Señor Henry Wheaton was shown that the new routes from northern Europe to central Asia will increase the importance of Austria and lessen that of Great Britain; and he had pointed out that in order to avoid ruin, England must establish somewhere in America a system of trade like that now flourishing in the East Indies). What better point can be found, say we, than Texas? (Firmly settled there, she will reach out to California, and use the magnificent harbor of San Francisco to establish direct relations with Asia . . . England would transform . . . as she transformed the Ionian Islands, into a *republic under her special protection*.[61]

29

When, on top of this, Pakenham, now the English minister to the United States, wrote Aberdeen on June 27, 1844, that once decided for annexation the United States would not change, even if it meant war, Aberdeen's course altered. On December 31, 1844, he sent word of the failure of the plan for Texas as well as new instructions to each agent involved. In his letter to Bankhead he added:

> But on the other hand you will keep your attention vigilantly alive to every creditable report which may reach you of occurrences in California, especially with respect to the proceedings of the United States Citizens settled in that Province, whose numbers are daily increasing, and who are likely to play a prominent part in any proceeding which may take place here, having for its object to free the Province from the yoke of Mexico.[62]

The highest point of American apprehension of foreign encroachment on a coast they, by now, considered their own was in reaction to this British diplomacy in Texas and it came between Polk's inauguration and his reöpening of diplomatic negotiations with Mexico.[63] It is understandable, however, why the Americans were extremely apprehensive. Surely after the burst of British diplomacy in Texas their official policy was not clear to the observer. In any case it would be difficult to convince an American in the atmosphere of the 1840s that the English actually were not out to possess the valuable California ports. With the strained relations over Texas, Oregon and Maine, and with the American migration meeting the Hudson's Bay Company, even the faintest rumor of a British move was still enough to create a furor both in official and nonofficial circles. Caution was, therefore, forgotten and blatant efforts for possession which might have been submerged in protracted diplomacy emerged starkly clear.

While Polk was pledged to get Texas and Oregon, then, it became obvious California was a very real and a very large part of his program.

> The conversation then turned to California on which I remarked that Great Britain had her eye on that country and intended to possess it if she could, but that the people of the United States would not willingly permit California to pass into the possession of any new colony planted by Great Britain or any foreign country, and that in reasserting Mr. Monroe's doctrine, I had California and the fine bay of San Francisco as much in view as Oregon. Col. Benton agreed that no Foreign Power ought to be permitted to colonize California. . . .[64]

That the fear of English intervention was the major catalyst in Polk's diplomacy was not new. Actually no really new element was introduced in the last few years of diplomacy for the coast. But the pace had quickened. The Americans who poured over the mountains onto the coast in the 1840s in ever-increasing numbers had proved the decisive factor, for now not only did the Americans possess the disputed territory, but an enthusiastic public gave weight to executive demands. The press swung all its powers to focus on the Manifest Destiny concept. Especially after the annexation of Texas the way seemed clear, for the people had lost respect for Mexican territorial integrity.

> The Río Grande has no more efficacy as a permanent barrier against the extension of the Anglo-Saxon power than the Sabine possessed.[65]

Therefore, with the joint resolution to admit Texas, Polk launched his well-known drive for the California Coast which ended in war. When Almonte, the Mexican minister, broke relations and sailed for Mexico April 3, Polk's agent, Parrott, was on the same ship, the *Anahuac*, to see if the Mexicans would accept a commissioner. When it was learned they would, Slidell was immediately dispatched with instructions that "The possession of the Bay and harbor of San Francisco is all important to the United States."[66] That California was a major objective was also boldly stated in Polk's letter to Slidell, sent on the same day as Buchanan's official instructions.

> I will say however that I am exceedingly desirous to acquire California, and am ready to take the whole responsibility . . . based on an intimate knowledge [Parrott's] of the public men and people of Mexico — that both New Mexico and California can be had for $15,000,000.[67]

But Polk's efforts to negotiate were soon replaced by preparations for force, and it was the new hints of English intervention that determined Polk to completely throw caution aside. This is pointed up when his decision to move beyond Slidell's mission was made in early October, when he received Larkin's report of a Hudson's Bay man supplying guns to Californians at the same time as he received a letter from Parrott in Mexico telling of the allegedly more vivid English interest in California.[68] A waiting policy was now replaced by thrusts in all directions — and in each the fear of England is evident. Slidell was sent new orders to

> . . . endeavor to ascertain whether Mexico had any intention of ceding it [Southwest Coast] to the one or the other power; and if any such design exists, you will exert all your energies to prevent [it] . . . From information possessed by this department it is seriously to be apprehended that both Great Britain and France have designs upon California.[69]

At exactly the same time Gillespie was sent to the coast with almost identical orders, "to watch over the interests of the United States in California, and to counteract the influence of any foreign or European agents."[70] Larkins' orders, sent in immediate response to his report, also contained an admonition to conciliate California toward union and block British and French designs in California. A capping proof that fear of foreign intervention was paramount in Polk's policy is his comment on the Treaty of Guadalupe Hidalgo.

> The immense value of ceded territory . . . [is] that it has become a part of the Union and cannot be subjected to European power, constitutes ample indemnity for the past.[71]

In those last frantic days there was one last desperate bid by the Mexican Government to crack the British policy and enlist her aid — and again California was the pawn. In May, 1846, right on the brink of a declaration of war, Paredes proposed to Bankhead that California be transferred to England as security for a loan. Bankhead immediately wrote Aberdeen, May 3, 1846,

> It is an indirect offer of sale, and it is the first time that any such offer has ever been hinted at from a responsible authority.[72]

Although the Admiralty was enthusiastic and even Peel seemed somewhat dazzled, Palmerston, again in the Foreign Office, knew that Mexico had lost control of California and could not really effect the transfer. While there was much discussion, in the end Commons upheld him in this, and thus, the same British official policy was maintained right to the end. This is further substantiated by Ashburton's statement at this time that

> . . . We certainly do not want colonies, and least of all such as will be unmanageable from this distance, and only serve to embroil us with our neighbor.[73]

It was this same policy that would direct British activity on the coast when the actual crisis came in the summer of 1846, disappointing both American apprehension and Californian hope. That the native Californians expected English protection against the Americans is clear.

> The undersigned is satisfied that Great Britain, being an ally of the Republic of Mexico . . . in view of such an outrage [American assault on Sonoma], will doubtless give her protection . . . as there is on the coast a war corvette, in the hope that this will be enough to stop the progress of the ambitions of the Americans. The undersigned feels that this step taken to save his country will be approved . . . that this petition will be granted.[74]

That Seymour, with the most powerful navy on the coast, delayed in coming to Monterey until after Sloat had raised the flag, seems only an execution of official instruction.

In retrospect there seems no question then that the frantic diplomacy before the war and the war itself were for the Southwest Coast. And both during and after the war the importance of California ports remained paramount. In mid-June of 1846, after having written through the last year of "personal interests" and many creditors "on the Coast of California as far South as San Diego,"[75] Samuel Hooper, the son-in-law and partner of the prominent Boston-California merchant William Sturgis, offered Secretary of the Navy George Bancroft, who was also related to Sturgis, several ships.[76] By the end of June, 1846, when actual movement to take the coast had already begun, the Secretary of the Navy was writing these leading Boston merchants to inquire exactly what arrangements on the coast would best serve their interests. And in their answer is etched the history of American merchants on the California Coast — decades of relentless Yankee merchant economic penetration of a lovely, undefended coast. "In your note of the 22d Inst.," Hooper wrote Bancroft,

> . . . you ask me to write you my views about California what order it would be for the Mercantile interest to give now and what line to insist on . . . The paralel [*sic*] you name if peace is made . . . includes the most important point, viz. the Bay of St. Francisco and the beautiful country watered by the principal streams that flow into it; . . . I see no reason why the American flag should not be hoisted at "St. Diego" & "Pueblo de los Angellos" — there is no force at "St. Diego" . . . "Pueblo los Angellos" has . . . no defense . . . It is important to the mercantile interest to have these two places taken as well as Monterey & St. Francisco as it would insure . . . and enable them to continue their trade as before along the whole coast and to collect their debts as they expected from the crops of this year.[77]

It was perhaps in direct response that Bancroft wrote Sloat to take and hold Upper California — and then to take San Diego and "Pueblo de los Angeles."[78] And by mid-August Hooper, in confirming that three of his company's ships were being sent to California for the government, added that it might be best for Bancroft to operate through their company agents. Send your letters to me, Hooper wrote Bancroft, and I will send them on — addressed in my usual hand so absolutely no one will know what is going on. I will address them, Hooper concluded, to "Capt. J. Sloat Care of H. Mellus, Esq., Monterey, California."[79]

But Bancroft was far from being alone in his concern that the California Coast and its ports be grasped. When in a cabinet meeting Buchanan urged a disavowal of territorial aggrandizement as a war aim Polk flatly refused. He assured the Secretary of State that if England and France disputed his policy regarding California he was prepared to

> . . . meet the war either England or France or all the Powers of Christendom might wage . . . and would stand . . . fight until the last man among us fell in the conflict.[80]

Therefore, after an economic and diplomatic struggle, conceived at the opening of the Pacific-China trade and waged in the context of a growing world trade, the California Coast became American. In retrospect one is inclined to agree with John Quincy Adams, that it was inconceivable any other nation should possess it. But this was not clear to his contemporaries — the consequent tension on the coast, therefore, encouraged ever greater economic investment and further diplomatic efforts. Thus a cycle, an inter-action of economy and diplomacy, set in motion by the magnet of Far East trade, evolved into a competition for control of the Pacific that led finally through a war to American possession of the California Coast.

CHAPTER 2

The Deterioration of Diplomatic Relations, 1833-1845

By Curtis R. Reynolds

CURTIS R. REYNOLDS has indicated that while diplomatic negotiations between the United States and Mexico over one problem or another continued from 1821 until 1846, these relations became more intense between 1833 and 1845 and led eventually to hostilities. During this entire period there was a steady deterioration in diplomatic relations between the two countries. The Americans had sufficient reason to act belligerently against Mexico, for the southern neighbor steadfastly had refused to settle the claims, and even had resented the pressure Americans were bringing for settlement. Thus both countries were angry over unsettled differences. Mexico was tired of the pressure to pay its debts; the United States was extremely upset over Mexico's refusal to discuss the Texas boundary question, or for that matter, any of the problems between the countries.

The discussion of boundaries began in 1819 when the United States ceded Texas, or at least claim to that area, in the Adams-Onis Treaty. However, Americans soon afterward realized they had made a mistake, and tried for the next twenty-five years to get recompense from the Mexicans. The Republic of Mexico refused to discuss any such changes, and therefore the Americans had to settle for a survey of the boundaries established in 1819. Finally, in 1839 Mexican officials agreed irrevocably to the conditions of an international tribunal, which set the amount of claims to be paid.

The inadequacies of the provisions worked out by that tribunal were clearly evident by 1842 — so evident in fact that both countries agreed to meet in Washington in 1843 to revise the entire agreement. Partly as a result of these meetings, Mexico agreed to pay its debts over a five-year period. Unfortunately Mexico would make only three of the twenty scheduled payments, and then refused to make any attempt to pay the balance. Thus over the years diplomatic relations between the countries further deteriorated, with each being offended at the other's actions.

Complicating the diplomatic difficulties was the status of Texas and California. As Mexico had never recognized the independence of Texas, Mexican officials reacted violently when the United States moved toward annexation of the Lone Star Republic. In addition, there was no agreement on the southern boundary of Texas. As a final blow to relations, the American desire for California surfaced again in 1845. Throughout much of this era, before its overthrow, Santa Anna's government was negotiating with England for the sale of California — long coveted by that nation. Finally, with the annexation of Texas in 1845, Mexico broke diplomatic relations with the United States. After a few months of futile attempts at negotiation, President James K. Polk prepared to draft a war message. It was not needed, however, for a Mexican attack on American troops stationed along the border provided the final impetus to war. Thus the thirteen years of deteriorating diplomatic relations ended in hostilities.

This chapter originally appeared in JOURNAL of the WEST in April, 1972.

THE LONG-STANDING CLAIMS[1] of the United States against Mexico were a principal cause of the Mexican War, a factor contributing to thirteen years of steady deterioration of diplomatic relations between the two countries. The final break that would result in war, however, was long in coming and by that time another issue — the annexation of Texas by the United States — was too much for either country to settle amicably.

The legality of the American claims against Mexico was well founded and an accepted fact not only to Spanish-American thinking but to the entire world as well. National and international tribunals formally acknowledged the claims as such.[2] The United States was as correct in the legal belief of its claims as it was in doggedly pursuing the adjustment and payment of these outstanding debts. More than once the claims of the American Government would result in a severe exchange of accusations which, in turn, would threaten the severance of diplomatic relations between the two countries. If the constant pressure of the United States over the settlement of claims angered Mexico, the continued refusal of Mexico to discuss the Texas territorial boundaries infuriated the North Americans.

The territory of Texas was added to the conterminous United States in 1803 as part of the Louisiana Purchase. But, in 1819 John Quincy Adams, the American Secretary of State, in order to acquire Florida and establish a favorable boundary in the Oregon territory, ceded Texas to Spain,[3] who, in turn, surrendered it to Mexico. The United States would have cause to rue that decision and in 1835 set about trying to recover the loss.[4] In 1825, President John Quincy Adams appointed Joel R. Poinsett as the first American minister of Mexico. Adams' Secretary of State, Henry Clay, outlined the conduct of the new minister and the goals of the United States in his instructions to Poinsett on March 26, 1825. Aside from the maintenance of the usual diplomatic protocol, Poinsett was to press the Mexican Government for a more specific delineation of the Texas boundaries[5] relative to the 1819 treaty. The negotiations failed.

In 1827, Clay revised his instructions on the boundary issue and bade Poinsett to sound out the Mexican Government's attitude toward "rectifying" the territorial limits in return for a direct money compensation, not to exceed one million dollars.[6] This new approach did not appeal to Mexico any more than had the first offer. The effort failed on two counts. Mexico simply refused to discuss the issue, emphasizing its adherence to the limits defined in the Adams-Onis treaty. On a personal basis, the attempt was doomed owing to the widespread unpopularity of Poinsett among Mexican government officials.[7] The Adams administration in the last year of its term finally contented itself with a treaty reaffirming the transcontinental boundary established in 1819 and providing for a new survey.[8]

President Andrew Jackson, in 1829, inherited the dilemma of the Adams foreign policy in Mexico. Jackson followed his predecessor's example but greatly intensified the effort. From March to October, 1829, Jackson worked through his minister in Mexico City, Joel Poinsett. On August 25, Jackson ordered Martin Van Buren, his Secretary of State, to modify Clay's earlier instructions to Poinsett, this time advising him to open negotiations for the purchase of the entire province of Texas. Jackson, however, was willing to pay as much as five million dollars for the area.[9] Poinsett never had an opportunity to present Jackson's plan; on October 19, 1829, Mexican President Vicente Guerrero requested his recall. Jackson replaced Poinsett with Anthony Butler, a man of dubious distinction who was professionally unfit for any such responsibility.[10] Butler proceeded with Van Buren's instructions given to Poinsett to buy Texas; but, working under considerable stress from the Mexican Government, his objective eluded him.[11]

After six years of futile negotiation, Jackson's patience to purchase Texas and endure Butler's incompetence was at an end. In 1836 Jackson removed Butler and Powhatan Ellis of Mississippi was appointed. Immediately the President ordered Ellis to abandon the Texas issue and press for payment of claims, by now long overdue. In the communique Jackson directed Ellis to set a deadline for a satisfactory adjustment of the debts within a fortnight, and if Mexico failed to comply he was to request his passports, break diplomatic relations, and return home.[12] This he did, and for the next three years the United States was without representation in Mexico. Thus, it was Mexico's intransigent attitude over the Texas boundary dispute that became the catalyst which eventually allowed the claims issue to ascend to one of primary importance in the formulation and execution of American foreign policy toward Mexico.[13] At this time, in 1836, the United States embarked on a vigorous and uncompromising policy to collect these outstanding debts. It is here that the real deterioration of diplomatic relations between the two countries over the claims had its beginning and took a decided turn on a course it would relentlessly follow until the outbreak of war in 1846. The claims were long in arrears when Jackson first began demanding their payment in 1836. Until 1836 Mexico recognized the validity of the claims, or at least most of them. But at best the claims were only quasi-legal regarding their obligation to pay them until the international tribunal was established under the claims commission of 1839. The United States then had the signature of the Mexican Government irrevocably obligating itself to pay its debts.[14]

Throughout the troubled era the United States was continually grieved over the numerous decrees, both oral and written, designed to curtail the commercial and individual activities of American citizens in the various provinces of Mexico. Charges and countercharges, real and imaginary, and with varying degrees of severity, were constantly being leveled at the other side and established a somewhat predictable pattern. Whatever the offense, it was generally considered as a violation of some article of some treaty. These not infrequent occurrences were seldom provocative enough to draw from one legation or the other more than a strong protest. The grievances were usually settled on the diplomatic level.[15] According to the established pattern during and after each successive crisis, the United States persistently reiterated its major foreign policy objective toward Mexico — to collect the unpaid and overdue claims.

The determination of the United States Government to collect the claims is best illustrated by reviewing its efforts during the last three years preceding the war. The United States, it could be said, persisted with commendable forbearance toward Mexico in its campaign to secure a final settlement for the claims. This forbearance was unexampled if compared to the French solution of attempting to exact payment for French claims against Mexico, although they were much smaller than those of the United States. The French took to arms and invaded the country in the "Pastry War" episode of 1838. Fortunately, President Jackson's words were more forceful than his actions for he might, as he declared to Congress in 1837, demand the next settlement for claims from the deck of a warship. Mexico's action, in his opinion, "would justify in the eyes of all nations immediate war."[16]

By 1843 the inadequacies of the 1839 claims commission were clearly manifest. Mexican officials vacillated, causing considerable delays which, in many cases, were understandable. Certainly they did not want to honor the claims and often found sufficient reason not to honor them. In 1842 the United States presented a ridiculous claim for payment. The claim by William S. Parrott was largely for the Mexican seizure of huge amounts of bottled porter. The total claim amounted to six hundred ninety thousand dollars. Waddy Thompson, the American minister who presented the claim, wrote to Secretary of State Daniel Webster saying that such claims, if they were not paid, could in no way be considered a menace sufficient to exact retribution if they were unpaid. He further stated that he was constrained to say that if they were referred to him as a judge he could not admit them, neither could he, with a clear conscience, assist in collecting the claim.[17]

Subsequently, both parties agreed that another convention was necessary on the grounds that the 1839 meeting was really more of a tribunal acknowledging the legal right of the United States to present the claims for payment and the Mexican Government's obligation to honor them. In the convention held in Washington in January, 1843, Mexico agreed to liquidate the adjudicated debts in quarterly instalments over a five-year period beginning the following April. In the end Mexico would make only three of the twenty payments under this agreement. To please the Mexican Government, the January treaty contained provisions to call another convention, to be held in Mexico City on November 20, in order that the Mexican republic could present its claims against the United States, although unofficially the latter denied that Mexico had any legal claims against the United States.

The Americans, having the most numerous claims, rightly insisted that the joint board of commissioners meet in Washington,[18] and Mexico agreed. This concession afforded the Mexican Minister of Foreign Relations, Juan de Bocanegra, another opportunity to delay the actual payment of the claims, as had become the custom. Ben Green, the American charge d'affaires at Mexico City, received the proceedings of the November convention on March 28, 1844. On that same day he addressed a letter to Bocanegra requesting an audience to discuss the convention results and the amendments attached by the United States Senate.[19] Bocanegra did not reply. Green summoned his attention to the matter again on March 30. In the second letter Green was as conciliatory as before but slightly more forceful, declaring unmistakedly that he and the United States Government confidently expected Mexico to accept the results with the amendments — the sooner the better.[20] Bocanegra this time replied. He insisted that to date he had received no official notification of the treaty modifications from the Mexican minister in Washington, General Juan N. Almonte. The American charge d'affaires pressed Bocanegra again on April 2, and again on April 6 and April 8. Each time the reply was the same.

Judging from the letters and correspondence of the American consular despatches at Mexico City, Ben Green apparently was not only the most able but also the most effective of all the consular diplomats during these distressing years. Green seemed better able to communicate with the Mexican officials and adjust to the revolutionary convulsions that frequently brought new ministers and administrations to power in Mexico. In addition, Green had considerable influence among other important circles in this uncertain environment, including the clergy. His advice to his superiors in Washington relative to the political conditions in Mexico apparently was seriously considered by them when formulating the strategy of their foreign policy.

Green's observations concerning the claims situation and the political pulse of Mexico were exceptionally valuable as shown in a long communication to Secretary of State John C. Calhoun on April 8, 1844. As concerns the claims, he said, the Mexican Government had made no pretentions to deny the justice of foreign claims nor did they sincerely object to having the grievances adjusted by a commission. However, the Mexican officials were hedging on paying any instalments by attempting to arouse popular public opinion against the validity of American claims.

In an informal conversation the Mexican Minister of the Treasury privately remarked to American Foreign Minister Waddy Thompson that his government, for the purpose of local consumption, must make the people believe that Mexico, too, had legal and outstanding claims against the United States Government. Employing the best use of this successful bit of propaganda, the Mexican Government was able to justify withholding payments for a while longer, that it might satisfy the demands of its people. Green warned that the next instalment, under a previous agreement, would probably not be paid as there was scarcely a dollar in the treasury.

The informative letter continued. Mexico was impressed with forceful tactics, as exemplified by the French diplomacy. The diplomat accordingly suggested that the United States assume a more forceful approach in diplomacy — the kind Mexicans best understood. This important communique contained enlightening insight about Mexico's most popular political enigma, General Antonio López de Santa Anna and some of his political ambitions which soon threatened to manifest themselves in the character of Mexican politics. Santa Anna had extemporaneously told Thompson that "Mexico needs a foreign war to develop her resources."

Green interpreted this audacious remark to mean that Santa Anna really hoped to involve his country in war and that he might restore his dictatorial powers and, worse, "that he seeks to place upon his own brow the imperial diadem which cost Iturbide his life." Finally, in this dispatch, Green, upon hearing rumors of British interest in the Californias, stated that "We have nothing to gain by quarreling with her [Mexico] unless indeed we should end by gaining possession of California, and thereby, secure a harbourage for our shipping on the Pacific and enhance our prestige abroad."[21]

This expression of expansionism reflected some of the popular political thinking of the day — that of Manifest Destiny. The importance of Manifest Destiny as an instrument of American foreign policy in conjunction with the settlement of claims appeared negligible at the time of Green's dispatch. Buchanan's instructions to Slidell possibly pointed to a juxtaposition of the two objectives for the first time.[22]

Throughout April and May of 1844 almost every letter of correspondence from the American legation addressed to the Mexican foreign office requested that payments for claims be honored. By April 25, the arrival of American newspapers, editorializing on the annexation of Texas, angered the Mexicans, causing debates and speculation that the event of war was near at hand. The furor of the Texas issue might bring about some changes in key ministerial posts that would be unfavorable to the United States, reported Ben Green to Secretary of State Calhoun.[23]

On May 23, 1844, the already strained relations between Mexico and the United States worsened. From this point onward to the outbreak of hostilities any real hope of ever collecting payment for the American claims was almost totally lost. Following instructions from President John Tyler, Green proceeded to inform the Mexican Government that the plenipotentiaries of the Republics of Texas and the United States had signed a treaty of annexation and had submitted it to the United States Senate for its approval.

Green's communication of May 23 to Bocanegra took care to insure the Mexican Government that the act of annexation was in no way meant to demean the honor and dignity of Mexico. He then explained the reasons why the United States took such a step. The United States Government, he said, was acting upon information that British efforts to abolish slavery in that territory were serious and abounding with intrigue. Second, he stated that in order to protect the continued harmony of the Union in those states adjacent to Texas, this step had become necessary. In addition, the Texas borders were left unidentified and open for further negotiations with Mexico. He concluded this reasoning by assuring Bocanegra that the United States' motives were sincere, and that it would be a circumstance of great regret if the Mexican Government were to think otherwise.[24]

This line of reasoning seems very curious to present to Mexico considering that in earlier years it had already abolished slavery in Texas.[25] Green's instructions from the President seemed to suggest that the Tyler administration was to sanction slavery as an instrument of national policy. With this kind of logic the forthcoming answer from Bocanegra should have been one that Green might have reasonably expected it to be.

In reply to Green's pronouncements, Bocanegra stated that the United States' reasoning for the treaty of annexation was unacceptable, and indeed that it appeared that official United States policy was to condone slavery. Bocanegra belabored the point enough to impress Green, saying that the Mexican Government looked upon slavery "with horror" and as a "relic of barbarous ages." In this correspondence Bocanegra officially informed the United States Government that if the annexation treaty were ratified by the Senate, Mexico must declare such an act as equivalent grounds for a declaration of war. Further, Bocanegra declared that once Texas was incorporated into the American Union, the Mexican Government would not convene to discuss the international boundary lines. These boundaries, he declared, were already fixed by treaty and under no circumstances were they to be adjusted.[26]

Green, on June 7, wrote to Calhoun to discuss Bocanegra's reply briefly and assessed the current situation in Mexico relative to the recent news of annexation. Green said that the Mexican Congress was in session attempting to muster another effort to reconquer Texas, and that Santa Anna probably would not attempt it again, and, therefore, would be reluctant to send another general to Texas who might succeed where he had failed. The money for such a conquest was, fortunately, not available and every effort to borrow it failed. The Mexican Minister of War privately told General Thompson that "Texas is gone from Mexico, it is impossible for us to reconquer her, and all we wish is to save the national decorum." Green continued discussing the influence of the several factions within the country — some wanted immediate action, while others wanted to wait until Tyler was out of office, hoping for a change. The situation, although uncertain at the time, was probably favorable because to date Mexico had shown much ineptitude in dealing with Texas, exemplified by eight years of inaction.

Santa Anna and the Mexican Congress were moving with caution because the powerful clergy seemed unalterably opposed to any action regarding the reconquest of Texas. Green's confidants had informed him of certain military troop deployments since the middle of May northward from two cities, San Luis Potosí and Jalapa. Finally, in his correspondence of June 7, Green warned that the success or failure of any definite plans of the Mexican Government might depend upon the success of a recent envoy sent to France and England to appeal for aid.[27]

From June to October the strained relations between the two countries continued without improvement. The two ministers, in their correspondence, maintained the requisite diplomatic protocols as they continued the two basic arguments — Texas and the claims.

If the diplomatic relations deteriorated in May, 1844, they turned sour in October of that year when Wilson Shannon succeeded Waddy Thompson as the American Minister in Mexico. This move did not improve the American position but a similar change in the Mexican Minister of Foreign Relations considerably improved Mexico's when Manuel Rejon replaced Bocanegra as the Minister of Gobernación. When Shannon was appointed, his instructions were the same as the other ministers — to press for the claims. Shannon, however, was not a subtle diplomat and had little tact in dealing with his skillful Mexican counterpart. From the beginning Shannon was given to the use of hard and abusive words which continually angered the Mexicans and seriously hampered his effectiveness. On the other hand, Rejon always maintained a remarkable diplomatic composure.

On November 12, 1844, Shannon wrote to Calhoun complaining of the grossly offensive language employed by Mexican officials (which was no worse than his own) against the United States, its government, and its people. The blustering and impatient Shannon was considering demanding his passports for this reason alone but demurred, thinking his mission was too important. Finally, he informed Calhoun of some of the methods of the Mexican Government to delay payment and declared, in his opinion, that unless the issue was certain to result in war, the claims would never be paid.[28]

For one pretext or another, the Mexican Government always found an excuse to avoid honoring payment of the claims. In September of 1843 the Mexican Minister of War issued decrees to the governors of the provinces of California, Sinaloa, Sonora, and Chihuahua instructing them to exercise their authority by judging for themselves when aliens, especially Americans, in their provinces were vagrants or otherwise dangerous menaces to the public laws. Those who were arbitrarily thought to be such were often arrested, incarcerated, fined, and expelled from Mexican territory. Those border regulations and other similar violations by Americans supplied the Mexican Government with additional reasons not to make their instalment payments or to discuss the Texas question.

In October, Mexico was still protesting the question of the Texas annexation. Rejon, in a letter to Shannon, reviewed the entire history of the province. In a letter, a masterpiece in diplomatic correspondence, Rejon skillfully manipulated the truth and any aspect of it clearly to the Mexican advantage. Basically, the argument set forth with amazing credulity all the legal aspects for the rightful ownership of Texas by Mexico as defined in the Adams-Onis Treaty of 1819, which was later confirmed by the 1828 treaty. He said, in essence, that the United States had seized the opportunity to recognize Texas' independence through the misfortunes of Mexico. Mexico, he asserted, had never recognized the independence of Texas and still retained, "in the eyes of all the world," legal and undisputed ownership of that province.[29] Shannon immediately expressed his indignation and demanded that the correspondence be officially withdrawn. Shannon, to his credit, did not attempt to debate the point with Rejon.

In early December, 1844, the Santa Anna government was overthrown in a revolution by General Mariano Paredes. In the midst of impending revolution, Calhoun, well aware of the political instability in Mexico, and knowing full well that the country was near bankruptcy, continued to press for payment of the claims. Green informed Calhoun of the present situation on December 17. He stated that the last three instalments had not been paid, and no prospect for their settlement was in sight. Green said that Mexico had borrowed enough money to satisfy all the outstanding claims but had used it for other purposes. The claims issue was a daily subject of vehement editorials in the Mexican Government's official organ, *El Diario*. These editorials were serving the purpose well, saying that American claims were totally unjustified and, in consequence, should not be paid. Evasively, the present government placed the obligation to pay the claims on the old Bustamante government, which, of course, absolved the present government of any blame.[30]

At the beginning of 1845, in addition to the Texas and the claims disputes, California became a part of American foreign policy. On January 9, 1845, Shannon advised his superiors in Washington of new events relative to British efforts to buy the two Californias. Santa Anna, although out of power, was negotiating with the British Minister for the sale of California. The negotiations were based on the English claims against Mexico which amounted to $26,000,000 in mortgages. Shannon assessed the English to be seriously interested in the project, but for the moment it looked as though it might fail because public opinion in Mexico was not favorable to Santa Anna or to the British. This unpopularity came about because Santa Anna, acting on British advice, dismissed the Congress and declared himself a dictator.[31]

That the United States became more interested in obtaining California might have been the result of developments contained in Shannon's communication to Washington on the subject. President James K. Polk, once in office, stepped up activities in California because he feared that Great Britain or even France might acquire California before the United States could.[32] By September, 1845, the President was ready to pay from fifteen to twenty million dollars for the purchase of Upper California and New Mexico. The matter must have seemed of paramount importance to Polk, for he readily became willing to pay upwards to forty million dollars for that territory if the situation demanded it.[33]

The period from January to March, 1845, was uneventful. The exchange of letters and correspondence between Mexico and the United States was characterized by short notes and short tempers. The notes were straightforward and to the point, concerning only trivial matters, such as consular appointments, permission to hold public auctions, and some minor grievances.

Shannon felt that the United States could not convince Mexico to reconsider its position on Texas, especially with the introduction of the California question. In this position the American minister pursued the only issue on which he had legal ground—that of the payment of claims, which since 1825 was never allowed to lay idle for any length of time. The Mexican Government made no genuine effort to pay the claims but it did adopt a policy to keep the question from getting out of hand. The government would issue notes through the foreign minister but the Treasury would not honor them.

On March 28, 1845, the final break in diplomatic relations took place. Luís Cuevas, the next Mexican Foreign Relations Minister, informed the United States Government and Mr. Shannon that, owing to the recent ratification of the treaty for annexation of Texas by the United States, all diplomatic relations between the two countries were thereby severed.[34] When notified of this decision, Shannon attempted to get the Mexican Government to reconsider. The Mexicans, however, were adamant and declared that they would stand on their decision. Shannon, in reluctant acquiesence, requested his passports on May 8, 1845, saying he regretted that Mexico had refused the extension of the "olive branch" and the desire to discuss further the distressing problems between the two countries.[35]

Wilson Shannon was not the last United States Minister to Mexico before the war, but was the last one to reside in Mexico City. The Polk administration had decided on another attempt to re-establish diplomatic relations with Mexico. Accordingly, it was decided that Mr. John Slidell of New Orleans would be appointed as the new minister.[36] Slidell's commission was explicit in its instructions. He was directed to take up the subject of the claims issue. This time, however, the United States, hoping to appease Mexico on the issue, decided to make an offer. The proposition, in essence, stated that in return for acknowledging the limits of the United States territory to the Río Grande, the United States would release Mexico from the obligation to pay the remainder of those American claims still outstanding. If this agreement could have been made, the United States Government would have taken on itself the responsibility of payment of the old debt.[37]

However, Mexico availed itself of a technicality in the wording of Slidell's commission, saying that Mexico would be willing to receive only a commissioner for preliminary discussions before restoring formal diplomatic relations, not a full-fledged minister, as was Slidell. Accordingly, the Mexican Government rejected Slidell, his credentials, and his mission.[38] The United States had said and done all it could do.

The United States had exercised considerable forbearance in its relations with Mexico during these trying years. Although the United States had lawful grounds for declaring war to exact its claims, it chose rather to negotiate its grievances and avoid war if possible. In the previous decade President Jackson had recommended war; however, by the time Polk became President relations between the United States and Mexico had reached such a point that he was willing to actually declare war over the issue. On May 9, 1846, with the consent of his cabinet, Polk made plans to draft a message to present to Congress requesting a declaration of war, basing his reasons chiefly upon the unpaid claims. On the same day, Providence would dictate another reason[39] — the Mexican attack on American troops north of the Río Grande. After thirteen years the ever-deteriorating diplomatic relations between the two republics finally ended in war. The unresolved claims and the Texas issue would have to wait another two years.

CHAPTER 3

A. Butler: *What a Scamp!*

By Joe Gibson

SEVERAL FACTORS made diplomacy increasingly difficult between the United States and Mexico. The Centralist-Federalist struggle, the periodic presence of Antonio López de Santa Anna, and the constant appointment of poor diplomatic agents by both countries made stability of government in Mexico and a solution of general problems nearly impossible. Joel Poinsett was sent to Mexico in 1825 as United States Chargé d'Affairs, and for the next four years so involved himself in Mexican internal problems that he was asked to leave in 1829. President Andrew Jackson had an opportunity to appoint a qualified man to the Mexican post, but he chose instead a close friend, Anthony Butler. Butler functioned as poorly as the American representative before him. Furthermore, he obviously entertained a "flagrant" disregard for Mexican rights — and had almost no respect for Mexicans. His political and diplomatic activities only widened the gap between the two nations, a gap already plainly characterized by suspicion, distrust, and unfriendliness.

Butler was instructed to regard the Mexican nation as an equal, and to negotiate secretly for the purchase of Texas if there appeared any possibility that the Mexicans would sell. Mexico not only refused even to consider selling, but also became alarmed about Butler's ambiguity concerning the boundary. When Mexican officials refused to talk of Texas, Butler worked silently to create difficulties within the country that would benefit the United States. Likewise, Butler was instructed to protect American citizens living in the Mexican territory, and in pursuing this task he increased Mexican animosity toward Americans. The claims issue also came in for its share of bungling, for Butler antagonized, misunderstood, and misconstrued Mexican officials and their intentions. Thus Butler resolved no real problems while in Mexico, and in fact hindered the settlement of pressing diplomatic issues. He was obsessed with trying to acquire Texas, and even after his dismissal, still in Mexico, he tried unsuccessfully to get Texas. Because of his unofficial efforts, the Mexican Government became even more distrustful and negative toward Americans and their diplomacy.

This chapter originally appeared in JOURNAL *of the* WEST in April, 1972.

MEXICAN POLITICS during the period of 1829-1836 were in a chaotic turmoil of revolution. The results of the national election in 1828 were overthrown by force of arms. During the brief Spanish invasion a Centralist coup, planned by Lucas Alamán and executed by Anastacio Bustamante, seized the government. Immediately the Federalists organized a revolt that swept across Mexico and succeeded in ousting Bustamante in 1832. The Federalists returned briefly to power in the election of January, 1833. However, this change from Centralism to Federalism did not markedly affect Mexico's foreign policy, which remained Centralist and anti-American in nature. There were two reasons why Mexico's foreign policy maintained a Centralist outlook, even while the Federalists controlled the Presidency: one was that throughout this period, the Mexican Congress was Centralist or was sympathetic with Centralist ideals concerning foreign policy;[1] and second, the predominant political philosophy during this period was dictated by Santa Anna.

Although professing Federalism when the political winds blew in

GOSHEN COLLEGE LIBRARY
GOSHEN, INDIANA

that direction, Santa Anna's sympathy was with the Centralists.[2] It must also be remembered that each administration in office during this period was there at Santa Anna's discretion. Even though Valentín Gomez Farías, acting president in 1833-1834, was a true liberal, it was obvious that the political bureaucracy maintained the conservative philosophy that had been established during Bustamante's tenure from 1830 to 1832.[3]

In 1829, when the Centralists were in complete control of the political apparatus in Mexico City, Lucas Alamán and Santa Anna were in the cabinet as Premier and Secretary of War, respectively. One of the first acts of this administration was to request the pro-Federalist American Chargé de Affairs Joel R. Poinsett to leave the country. There is no doubt that Poinsett had engaged in political activities which were completely out of his official capacity and, in some instances, clandestine in nature.[4] However, the abruptness of his dismissal indicates a radical shift in Mexican sentiment towards the United States. J. Fred Rippy best describes the situation at the time of Poinsett's dismissal:

> . . . Not only had the early apprehension and bitterness in Mexico become more widespread and intense, but the unprecedental [sic] treatment accorded Poinsett had left the United States piqued and somewhat angry. . . . To handle this situation much sagacity, patience, and tact would be needed.[5]

Instead of appointing a man with diplomatic experience to undertake the delicate mission of Minister to Mexico during this critical period, President Andrew Jackson chose an old friend and comrade-in-arms, Colonel Anthony Butler. A native of South Carolina, Butler had settled in Mississippi where he had served in the legislature. Why Butler took the appointment in 1829 is debatable; perhaps he sincerely believed that he could better relations between the United States and Mexico.[6] Yet, through his activities and by his flagrant disrespect for Mexicans, Anthony Butler succeeded in widening the gap of unfriendliness, suspicion, and distrust that already existed between the two nations.

Why Jackson sent Butler to Mexico is not clearly understood. Perhaps friendship played some part in the decision, but Jackson was influenced more by Butler's first-hand knowledge of the Texas political situation and his familiarity with the "geography and productions of Texas."[7] Whatever the reason for the appointment, it perhaps was one of Jackson's biggest political blunders. Robert Remini, a Jackson biographer, states that "Jackson had made some pretty ghastly appointments in his time but perhaps few were as spectacularly bad as Butler's."[8]

When Butler received his appointment to Mexico, he was given official instructions stating explicitly that he was to be completely amicable toward Mexico and regard the young republic as an equal.[9] Secretary of State Martin Van Buren also impressed on Butler that one of the most important duties of his mission was protecting the interests of American citizens in Mexico. However, Van Buren revealed his lack of respect for the Mexican Centralist administration by authorizing Butler to forego normal diplomatic channels and go directly to the Mexican Government when presented with a grievance by an American citizen.[10] How could Van Buren expect Butler to regard Mexico as an equal when the administration did not?

Butler also had other instructions. President Jackson secretly authorized him to approach Mexican officials on the possibility of purchasing part or all of Texas.[11] Jackson well understood the sentiment of Mexicans concerning the ticklish question of Texas. He made it clear to Butler that while he was to "conduct the negotiation for the purchase of Texas, which is very important to the harmony and peace of the two republics," he also was to consider constantly the jealousy that the Mexican Government had toward the American desire to purchase that area.[12] Jackson believed the summer of 1829 was the most opportune time to conclude the purchase of Texas. He believed Mexico's financial straits, compounded by a threat of Spanish invasion, gave the United States a chance to relieve Mexico of her "embarrassments."[13] With his official, and supposedly secret, instructions, Anthony Butler in October, 1829, accepted the duties of Chargé d'Affairs in Mexico City.

Butler did not arrive in Mexico City until late in December, 1829. Thereupon he quickly learned the attitude and sentiment of the predominantly Centralist Foreign Office. He had scarcely set foot in the American embassy when he was presented with a copy of the government-controlled newspaper, *El Sol*. In a letter to Van Buren, Butler professed shock and dismay that *El Sol* not only asserted "that the object of my mission is the purchase of Texas, but they also state a price to be paid for the cession."[14] The article to which Butler alluded left no doubt as to the Mexican Government's view on the subject of Texas, and it asserted that Butler had come to Mexico for the sole purpose of negotiating

> . . . for the cession of the province of Texas for the sum of five million dollars. As we are not informed that, so far, the colonel has made any overtures on the subject, we presume that he does the new administration the justice to suppose it incapable of lending itself to a transaction as prejudicial and degrading to the republic as it would be disgraceful to the minister who would subscribe to it.[15]

It is evident from the above quotation that the hostility and bitterness of the Mexican Government which had plagued Poinsett before his recall had been instantly transferred to Anthony Butler.

By March the knowledge of Butler's mission regarding Texas had become common knowledge among Mexican officials. Butler wrote freely on the subject in his dispatches to Washington, and in these communiques he blamed his initial diplomatic failures on the radical shift to Centralism in the Mexican Government and on the activities of

British agents in Mexico City.[16] However, the ineptitude of Butler's diplomacy with the Centralists, combined with his inflated ego, assured his failure far more than did British agents.

Butler purposefully created anxieties and apprehensions in Mexican officials by his ambiguity concerning the boundary. Butler informed Van Buren that he "more than once had been approached on the subject [boundary], but always found means to evade it, leaving them under the influence of whatever their imagination might create to awake suspicion or alarm their fears."[17] Such remarks indicate that Butler had little sense of diplomacy and that he did not understand the Centralist government in Mexico. However, he was successful in one sense: he awakened Mexican suspicions about the desire for Texas.

Lucas Alamán, the Mexican Secretary of State, obviously frustrated and confused by Butler's activities, addressed the Mexican Congress on the subject of Texas. His report was the first official statement concerning Texas by the new Bustamante government. Alamán accused the American Government of encouraging Anglo immigration to Texas for the sole purpose of eventual acquisition. He made it clear that Mexico could not "alienate or give away the smallest department without affecting the integrity of the republic"[18] and he proposed to stop such Anglo immigration into Texas, by force if necessary. Evident throughout this report was a sense of futility concerning Mexico's ability to keep Texas.

However, the innate Mexican pride was the predominant tone, which Alamán best exemplified in his final remarks. He wanted it known "that the Executive will sustain at last, both in diplomatic discussions, and with military measures, this honor of the nation and integrity of its territory."[19] The Centralist Congress responded with the law of April 6, 1830, which closed Texas to American immigration, cancelled all empresarial contracts, and established a stringent, quasi-military supervision over Mexican colonies.[20] Because of the obvious hostility of the Mexican Government on the subject of Texas, Butler did not revive the subject until July, 1832. However, there is ample evidence to indicate that Butler used this time to work privately with other Mexican officials to achieve his goal.[21]

In the interim, when the Texas controversy subsided somewhat, a more open — and not less sensitive — situation concerning the treatment of American citizens in Mexico arose. Although Butler's primary concern was Texas, his official instructions had impressed on him the importance of protecting American citizens from illegal and prejudicial treatment by Mexican authorities.[22] And, naturally, this problem of mistreatment was closely tied to the claims question. The claims of Americans against the Mexican Government had increased rapidly after 1829. One of the first instances of concern for the treatment of Americans in the Mexican provinces came in December, 1829, when two Americans were imprisoned in San Diego with no charges given. Representative Nicholas D. Coleman demanded that Van Buren secure their release and, "what is equally to be desired, to prevent a recurrence of similar and outrageous conduct toward the citizens of this country."[23] The two Americans eventually were released, but more significantly, Coleman's attitude was a reflection of the attitude which permeated the United States Government, newspapers, and the populace in general. Yet such threats accomplished little except perhaps to strengthen the Mexican resolve to do nothing.

One claims question, that of Dr. John Baldwin, illustrates the difficulties of the total question of claims. Although Baldwin's case is an individual one, his claim was typical. Moreover, the communications between Mexican and American officials in this case were similar in tone and wording to practically all claims presented; and the time element involved in settling such a case also was typical. Baldwin was an American physician living in the colony of Goazacualcos. The first accounts of his case appeared in documents in January, 1832.

Butler received a letter informing him that Baldwin had been jailed for malpractice and for charging exorbitant prices to his clients. Butler also understood that Baldwin had his leg broken while being arrested. Despite such scanty information — and so far as he knew the charges were totally legitimate — Butler immediately notified Alamán that the Baldwin situation "details the circumstances of an outrage committed on the person of a citizen of the United States, which, from its violent, lawless, and aggravated character is without parallel in the history of civilized nations."[24] In the same note he demanded Baldwin's release and punishment of the offenders in the case.

Butler did not hear anything concerning his protests or his demands until two weeks later. At that time Alamán notified him that Baldwin would not be released, but promised additional information on the case soon.[25] Alamán then used what became the favorite tactic of the Mexican Government when deliberating a case involving claims, i. e., long periods of silence interrupted by a polite "I'm sorry," an ambiguous "I don't know," or a vague promise that "Something will be done soon." This type of communication infuriated and frustrated Butler more than a rebuke or a threat would have done — as the Mexicans doubtless knew it would.

Butler's next move was to insist on seeing the formal charges against Baldwin. On February 18, 1832, Alamán finally submitted a copy of the charges and an account of Baldwin's capture. This wordy document was filled with accounts of Baldwin's alleged crimes against the people of Vera Cruz, and with it came a promise that "the truth shall be sought by legal means and the guilty most certainly punished."[26] Realizing that his demands accomplished nothing, Butler temporarily dropped the issue — while Baldwin remained in jail without trial.

Not until more than a year later did Butler make another attempt to help the imprisoned doctor. This came after a change of Mexican administrations; the Federalist, Gómez Farías, had become President. Yet this change did not aid Butler's cause. The new Secretary of State, Carlos García, although more communicative than Alamán, was as adamant — or more accurately, as lethargic. Butler threatened that the United States would make the Baldwin case a national issue if his demand for action was not answered.[27] García feigned offense at this threat, and Butler was forced to apologize for his "energetic" phraseology.

Obviously, Butler and the United States Government by this time were becoming extremely irritated about the number of claims of American citizens not adjusted. In October Butler was instructed by the American State Department to exert his energies toward clearing up all claims, yet Butler's attempts met with the same failure as before. After a strong exchange between García and Butler concerning Baldwin, Butler received a letter in December, 1833, on the progress of Baldwin's case. In a letter from the governor of Vera Cruz to García, the governor stated that nothing new had been learned on the subject.[28] This meant that as of December 8, 1833, no progress had been made since the initial report of February, 1832. Although communication between the American minister and García continued, Butler met the same evasive tactics he always had encountered. Secretary of State Louis McLane finally instructed Butler that, if confronted with more delaying tactics, he was to break off relations and return home.[29]

Evidently, a fear of broken relations excited the Mexicans for Baldwin was brought to trial, and by March 19, 1835, a verdict was finally reached. The irony of this trial was immense. After charges and countercharges were made, the court learned that Baldwin's only crime was exporting cochineal by the River Malpaso without paying duties on it — and as the trial unfolded and the evidence was submitted, Baldwin's lawyer, who apparently was competent, proved that the doctor had paid the customs to the receiver of the district who had stolen the money and departed, never to return. Thus Baldwin was acquitted and awarded a judgment.[30] Most ironical was the magistrate's final statement that Governor Ortigora and previous governors of Oaxaca, through their "influence and improper interference, prevented the executive and decrees of the supreme judicial power of this state in favor of Baldwin."[31] Obviously, this was an attempt by the magistrate to justify the unorganized and pitifully slow Mexican judicial process.

Although Baldwin had been acquitted and awarded a judgment, he never received payment. In September, 1837, two years after Baldwin's trial, Mexican Secretary of State Francisco Pizarro Martínez sent a letter to United States Secretary of State John Forsyth in which he discussed claims of American citizens against Mexico; accompanying this letter was a list of sixty-eight names of Americans who had claims against the Mexican Government. John Baldwin was number forty-six on the list.[32]

The Mexican Government had declared that in many instances some American claims were justified, but in February, 1836, the Centralist government drastically altered its view concerning the legitimacy of American claims. In an article in the official government newspaper, *The Nacional*, the editor denied that Mexico owed any claims to *Norteamericanos*,[33] implying that Americans had forfeited any right to claims because of the superfluous smuggling by Americans and because of the aid extended by the United States to rebels in Texas. The paper also stated that Mexicans were "aware that the whole nation [the United States], particularly New Orleans, is a haunt of all the villains in the world."[34] Butler suggested that the United States should adopt "some decisive measure for convincing the Mexican Government not only that they must give ample satisfaction for the wrongs that we have suffered at their hands, but that our rights shall in the future be respected."[35]

Although no strong decisive measures were taken, the relations between the two countries were dealt a severe setback because of the claims issue. The exasperation of the Unitd States State Department in 1836-1837 concerning this question seemed justified. Jackson, in his address to Congress early in 1837, when he cited Mexico's continued failure to adjust the claims as a plausible excuse for military action, nevertheless recommended further efforts at negotiation.[36] Thus the claims question, which had its infancy in the 1820s and 1830s, helped compound the antagonism between the two countries and was important in bringing them into conflict in 1846.

Butler, realizing in 1830 that for a time he would have to suspend negotiations for the purchase of Texas, directed his attention to the claims. Moreover, he was under pressure from the Jackson administration to secure ratification of the treaty of amity, commerce, and navigation which earlier had been negotiated by Joel Poinsett. Although Poinsett had successfully negotiated this treaty in 1828, the allotted time for appointing commissioners to mark the boundary of 1819 had lapsed, thus voiding the earlier negotiations.[37] Butler entered into new negotiations with his characteristic exuberance, but was faced with the same vacillating tactics he had undergone in negotiating for the claims.

Mexican politics were in such disarray during this period that delay was unavoidable, but Butler was totally unsympathetic with, and completely frustrated by, the Mexican Congress.[38] Under pressure from Washington to secure compliance with the treaty of amity, Butler sent Alamán a private note containing an ultimatum for its ratification; he wrote that he had "but one course to pursue — a termination of my mission to the Mexican Government, and a return to my own."[39] Butler then sent President Jackson a message justifying the long delay of rati-

fication; more important, the letter revealed Butler's opinion of the
government with which he was negotiating:

> I have no language to describe the vexation, mortification, and per-
> plexity I have suffered from the ignorance, vacilliating conduct, and illib-
> eral prejudices displayed by the present Mexican Congress, before whom
> this subject has for nine months been pending; and I am not sure that it
> would have been concluded 12 months hence, but for the decisive stand
> I made, and which was communicated to the Secretary of Foreign Affairs
> by private note.[40]

Regardless of Butler's justification for ire, his overt disgust with the
government with which he was negotiating explains why he was beset
by the many difficulties and blind alleys he confronted while in Mexico.
Yet his threat to sever diplomatic relations did accomplish its goal; the
treaty was concluded on April 5, 1832.[41] In essence this instrument regu-
lated the use of the ports of each country for purposes of trade, but primarily it was designed to assure equality between the two nations and
their citizens.[42]   And, an article was inserted by Butler that extended
the time for a boundary settlement.[43]   All of Butler's plans and schemes
for Texas would have been negated completely with the ratification of a
boundary.   Once this treaty was ratified, Colonel Butler therefore could
turn his attention to his "secret" mission, the purchase of Texas.

In July, 1832, in an effort to reopen negotiations for a boundary settlement, Butler approached Alamán on the subject.[44]   The American representative was prompted to make such a move at this time because he
had been informed earlier in the year that Mexico was on the verge of
national bankruptcy.[45]   He thus felt the moment was right to tempt the
Mexican Government with a lucrative offer, as did Alamán's changed attitude toward him.[46]   Their first discussion was conducted on July 2, 1832,
with the conversation surprisingly cordial and frank.   Butler's main arguments were that most of the territory under discussion was populated
by Americans; that if the boundary line of 1819 was observed, Mexico
must compensate Americans west of that line; that because of its fiscal
situation, Mexico could not pay Americans living west of the boundary
of 1819; that Texas was on the verge of revolt and Mexico would lose it
anyway; and that even if Mexico should suppress the revolt, it could not
afford the expense of continuing to hold Texas without costs that would
drain the Mexican national treasury.[47]   Alamán replied that he concurred with many of Butler's thoughts, but considering the embarrassing
character of the question and the ambiguity concerning a more westerly
boundary he must decline to commit himself at the moment.   Thus he
requested another meeting on the tenth of the month whereat they could
trace a boundary appropriate to relieving all jealousies and suspicions of
their two governments.[48]

At the second meeting between the two, the discussion centered on
the Mexican desire to decide which branch of the Sabine River was ap-

propriate and the American's contention that the question of the Sabine was so complicated that an entirely new boundary farther west should be established.[49] Examining a map, Butler "pointed to the Desert or Grand Prairie, as a spot that seemed designed by nature as the boundary between the two nations. . . . Its great width and uninhabitable character . . . made it useless as a part of the national domain of either party."[50] Much of the area Butler thus would annex to the United States, Alamán politely pointed out, was purely Mexican in settlement; nevertheless he said that he and Butler were not too far apart, that Butler should send an official communication on the subject to Alamán's office, and that such a communication would receive immediate consideration.[51] Butler's expectations were thus heightened — but were never to be realized.[52]

Shortly after this discussion with Alamán, the Federalists succeeded in a revolution, President Bustamante was overthrown, and a new cabinet under a different administration was appointed. Under the administrations of Pedraza and, later, Farías, Butler met total rejection whenever Texas was mentioned — perhaps because Santa Anna was the actual master of Mexico. Although he was disappointed with the new Federalist administration, Butler sent assurances to Andrew Jackson in January, 1833, that he would "succeed in uniting Texas to our country before I am done with the subject or I will forfeit my head."[53] By September, Butler's expectations and efforts had met so many failures that he was urging Jackson to occupy the territory between the Sabine and Neches Rivers; he believed Farías impossible to deal with and urged Jackson therefore to use this move to show the Mexicans that the United States meant business.[54] Jackson rejected Butler's advice and chided him somewhat by saying that he hoped he did not die before Butler finally negotiated a treaty.[55]

Butler seemingly had exhausted every diplomatic avenue in his effort to reach a boundary settlement with Mexico, one that would transfer part of Texas to American ownership. Thus he tried the last method open to him, perhaps in desperation: he proposed bribing Mexican officials. According to him, this was not his own idea; in a letter to Jackson dated October 28, 1833, he informed the President that he had been approached by a gentleman of high rank, one with influence with President Santa Anna, who said that for "200 or 300 thousand dollars" Butler could "gain" the man needed to achieve his goal.[56] This mysterious person also stated that an extra "3 or 4 Hundred thousand" may be necessary to distribute to other nameless but influential Mexican officials.[57] Butler had responded to this gentleman of high rank that he could not get the money. And in closing this letter, Butler informed Jackson that he believed the prospect of acquiring Texas was at least fair — much better than at any time since the departure of Alamán.

Jackson's reply to Butler in November was eloquent. He made it very clear that any treaty signed by Butler must be obtained "without any just imputation of corruption."[58] He also said that Butler surely had misinterpreted his instructions, for although he had discretion as how best to effect his mission, corruption was not allowed.[59] The only thing the President would allow Butler was some discretion in the disbursement of funds to clear fraudulent grants in Texas.

Butler apparently never lost hope that Jackson would allow bribes to be employed. As late as February, 1835, the American diplomat wrote that the President must remove the "one stumbling block" and within three months a treaty would result.[60] Yet Jackson was adamant; no evidence survives to indicate that the President ever authorized Butler to bribe Mexican officials. Moreover, when Jackson earlier had received a note of March 7, 1834, from Butler asking permission to employ bribes and if this was not granted that American troops occupy "that part of Texas which is ours [between the Sabine and Neches Rivers] and placing me at the head of the country to be occupied."[61] The President endorsed the note, "A. Butler: What a Scamp. Carefully read. The Secretary of State will reiterate his instructions to ask an extension of the treaty running the boundary line, and then recall him."[62] Jackson obviously wanted no advice from Butler.

At this juncture Butler became certain he could persuade his old friend Jackson of the merits of his plans to purchase Texas if he could only see him personally. In April, 1835, he therefore departed for Washington, arriving in June. And in person he again tried to explain to Jackson that Texas could be had simply by allowing discretion in the disbursement of the money to be paid.[63] At this conference Butler produced a letter from a Father Hernández, Santa Anna's personal agent, dated March 21, 1835. This letter indicated that Santa Anna indeed was ready to forfeit Texas — for a price:

> The negotiation which you have so long desired to effect is, as I have often told you, perfectly within your power; nothing is required but to employ your means properly. Five hundred thousand dollars judiciously distributed will conclude the affair, and when you think proper authorize me to enter the arrangement depend upon my closing it to your satisfaction.[64]

Jackson was not impressed with this information. Perhaps he thought Mexico was going to lose Texas very soon; more likely, he did not want to be party to bribery. At any rate, he preferred not to be associated with Butler's scheme. Thus in November, 1835, Secretary of State John Forsyth recalled Butler from his post, giving him until December 1 to close out his affairs.[65]

At the end of Butler's tenure in Mexico City, the same problems that had plagued American-Mexican relations since 1825 were still evident. And there was increased anxiety in Mexico because of the infiltration of armed Americans into Texas.[66] José Tornel, the Mexican Secretary of

War and Marine, at this time issued a warning that Americans entering Texas would be considered pirates and would be executed if captured.[67] This was more than an idle threat; on January 26, 1836, twenty-two Americans captured during a filibustering expedition were shot at Tampico on direct orders from Tornel.[68]

Butler's major problem as a diplomat was his obsession to acquire Texas. And subsequent to his dismissal, he remained in Mexico City to work toward the same goal; he informed Forsyth that "although my mission as a representative of the United States might be at an end, yet I should not return until the object had been attained for which I had been so long laboring."[69] In this same correspondence Butler intimated that he had a personal interest and plans involving Texas and its ownership.

It was while Butler was staying in Mexico City unofficially that he did his greatest damage to Mexican-American relations. In the months following his dismissal, he developed a personal feud with Tornel. Why or how this feud began is unclear; perhaps Tornel rejected Butler's overtures concerning Texas, or perhaps Butler became incensed with Tornel because of the execution of the Americans at Tampico. Whatever the origins of this quarrel, it progressed to the point where Butler publicly challenged the secretary to a duel.[70] Tornel refused — and Mexican honor was impugned.[71] Butler thereupon issued a second challenge, this one in writing, informing Tornel that he intended to

> . . . insult you in terms so direct and gross as might excite you to resent them. Your dastardly spirit has disappointed me in the last, and shown you equally destitute of the honor of a gentleman and courage as a soldier. No courage remains for me but to inflict upon you the chastisement appropriate for your character. This lesson will be given by me on the first occasion of meeting you . . . you are now apprized of my intentions . . . you will receive the discipline of my cane and whip.[72]

Butler also stated that should Tornel elude him until his departure, he would hold the secretary up to "public gaze" as "an object of scorn and contempt," thus showing "how completely the fable of the ass in the lion's skin is realized in the person of himself."[73] Ironically, it was José María Tornel, serving as a special envoy to the United States in 1829, who had lobbied for Butler's appointment to Mexico so that Butler could negotiate a treaty of boundary and amity.[74]

The Tornel incident caused an international crisis of sorts. Secretary of Foreign Relations José María Ortiz Monastero demanded satisfaction of Butler because a high Mexican official had been insulted, and through him the entire Mexican nation.[75] The result was an order for Butler to leave the country within eight days. Not until October, however did Butler finally depart Mexico City — and then he had the audacity to demand from Monastero a guard of no less than twelve men to escort him to Texas.[76]   This was refused, whereupon Butler departed Mexico by way of Vera Cruz.

The Butler escapades left the Mexican Government more distrustful than ever of American diplomacy.   The newly appointed chargé d'afaires, Powhatan Ellis, along with succeeding ministers after him, were to experience the same Mexican tactics of delay and obstruction — and even wrath — which had confronted Butler in 1829.   The result of the years of failed diplomacy, of misunderstandings, and of differences of national temperament would finally be realized in 1846 — in the form of war.

CHAPTER 4

The Santangelo Case: *A Controversial Claim*

By Lowell L. Blaisdell

DIPLOMATIC PROBLEMS between the United States and Mexico increased steadily until the outbreak of hostilities. Much of the difficulty arose because of American claims against the Mexican Republic. Commissions were set up to dispose of the problems, but these never brought a solution. In fact, discontent grew and emphasized the inability of the two governments to resolve the issues. Moreover, so many individual claims existed that no one was able to determine which actually were fair and valid. Lowell Blaisdell investigates one of the many claims problems, the claim of Orazio de Santangelo, which individualizes the difficulties between the two countries.

Santangelo was a former Italian revolutionary who immigrated to the United States, and during two stays in Mexico, so angered the Mexican officials that twice he was expelled from the country. Throughout his lifetime he assumed that his mission was to lead people to a more democratic and, hence, better society. In 1826, while briefly in Mexico, he wrote an unfavorable treatise about Mexicans and their volatile political situation; soon thereafter, he and his family were expelled. He traveled to the United States and lived here for two years. Then in 1833 he packed all his belongings and set sail for Vera Cruz, insisting that he had been treated unfairly in his earlier visit and plainly indicating his desire to live in Mexico. For two years he operated a boarding school, only to be expelled again in 1835. This time eight trunks of his belongings were "lost" en route to the United States, and he accused the Mexicans of confiscating his library and other belongings.

For twenty years after his last expulsion, Santangelo tried to collect for his losses. First claiming nearly $400,000 in damages, he was forced to bargain for a "paltry" $50,000 — and that he had to take mostly in scrip. Thus his case was typical of those that may have been exaggerated, were first scaled down, paid with scrip, and not actually resolved until after the Mexican War. Such cases created animosity both on the part of Americans and Mexicans, and doubtless influenced the continued deterioration of relations between the two countries in the years immediately preceding the war.

This chapter originally appeared in JOURNAL *of the* WEST in April, 1972.

A FAMILIAR CAUSE of the Mexican War was the claims dispute growing out of injuries in property or person suffered by Americans resident in Mexico. Though in 1840-42 a Joint Commission disposed of many of the actions, discontent continued to fester because many of the litigants and, indirectly, some of the public felt short-changed by the commission's dispositions. Of the claims processed, probably the most politically significant was that of Orazio de Santangelo, an Italian revolutionary who had immigrated to the United States and then spent two intervals in Mexico, only to be twice expelled. Because Santangelo had a talent for publicizing his grievances, actual and exaggerated, his case illustrates the prolongation of the claims problem and, in retrospect, clarifies the two governments' inability to resolve the issue.

Santangelo's early life in the Old World is the clue to his behavior in the New. Born heir to an aristocratic Neapolitan family on October 23, 1774, he received an excellent classical education, as well as training in law, literature, and linguistics. However, the military was his career choice. The French Revolution inspired him to apply its libertarian ideas to the Italian peninsula. Yet there was an aristocratic slant to his republicanism, for he assumed that he was entitled to lead the populace to a better life, as in another age his ancestors had commanded them to accept a humble one.

From 1790 to 1815 Santangelo fought in several Italian and French armies. He saw duty in Spain, North Africa, and up and down Italy. He served in Napoleon's legions in two of his most memorable campaigns, the passage of the Alps in 1800 and the disaster in Russia twelve years later. Over the years he was repeatedly decorated and several times wounded. At the close of his military life he had become adjutant general and chief-of-staff of the gendarmerie of King Joachim Murat of Naples, Napoleon's brother-in-law.

Between military assignments Santangelo immersed himself in republican political activities, sometimes at no small risk. To objectify his liberalism he joined the Masons and for a time became a French citizen. In 1796, as secretary of a legation from Lombardy to Paris, he participated in a premature scheme to convert that northern Italian state into a republic on the French model. Three years later, involved in a plot in Italy, he drew a death sentence, which was later commuted to life imprisonment. Confined on Elba, he contrived a daring escape. Years later, after Napoleon's downfall, Santangelo, finding the Restoration regime in the Kingdom of the Two Sicilies to be intolerable, participated in the 1821 revolt against King Ferdinand I. When it was crushed, he had to leave, on pain of a death sentence should he return. Crossing over to Spain, he joined in the 1821-22 revolt against Ferdinand VII. Its failure forced his exit to Gibraltar and then to the United States in 1824.

Santangelo supplemented his actions as an engagé with a spate of theoretical propositions and personal opinions. In 1801 he authored a pamphlet, *La repubblica italiana in idea.* In the last year of Murat's rule he offered that monarch a memorial on a related theme. After the Neapolitan revolt collapsed, he published from Barcelona *L'ottimestre costituzionale delle Due Sicilie.*[1]

While the Neapolitan's actions amply demonstrated the sincerity of his beliefs, it was less politics than certain peculiarities of personality that shaped the course of his life. Officiousness, ambition, and *amour propre* were the mainsprings of his character. He loved to offer advice, solicited or not, and felt injured if it were not adopted. He expected, and felt entitled to, high places for himself. Frequently he suffered injury to his feelings or honor, leading to an excessive expenditure of energy in the airing of grievances, and the settling of grudges. Finally, there was in his make-up an element of quixotry which rendered him oblivious to the inappropriateness of some of his political actions and recklessness in money matters.

These traits were prominent in his European days, as they were to be later in America. At the time he penned his *Repubblica italiana* pamphlet he had had the temerity to exasperate Napoleon by the insistence with which he called the great man's attention to its import. He had also annoyed Murat, for his memorial advised that shaky Napoleonic satellite on how he might save his throne and simultaneously free Italy. In his opinion the Neapolitan revolt of 1821 would have benefited appreciably by a greater role assigned to himself. Similarly, he attributed the failure of Rafael Riego and the Spanish rebels of 1820-23 in no small measure to their failure to heed his advice, and accordingly held them in contempt.[2]

In the spring of 1824 Santangelo arrived in the United States as a fifty-year old widower with a teen-age son. After obtaining introductions from Napoleon's brother, Joseph, Murat's predecessor as King of Naples, and declaring his intent to become an American citizen, Santangelo took up residence in New York City. There he dabbled in literature, published a brochure offering advice on business and commerce, and tried to establish a language-oriented private school. However, only a year after his arrival, restless, and with his several ventures not having panned out, he decided to escort his son, who had been offered a position with a mining company, to Mexico.[3]

In the neighboring country the expatriate found prospects much more to his liking. No language difficulty obtruded and in the largely elitist-led new country he found it much easier to make the acquaintance of the top political leaders. Soon he was airing his views on policies, associating himself with the more liberal Yorkist-Masonic faction in the government, and extolling the value of a treaty of amity between Mexico and the United States which minister Joel Poinsett was negotiating.[4] Notwithstanding his earlier desire to acquire United States citizenship, he now actively sought Mexican naturalization.[5]

At this point Santangelo managed to convert a seemingly harmless development into a bundle of troubles for himself. With the possibility of a Panama conference in the air, the minor philosophe Abbé Dominique de Pradt published a treatise on the subject in January, 1826. Encouraged by Mexican friends and confident that he had more cogent comments than de Pradt, Santangelo began to publish a multi-part analysis of the situation. Personally acquainted with the Restoration powers' intervention in Italy and Spain, he felt absolutely certain they would attempt to restore Mexico to Spain. Thus the visiting writer warned the Latin Americans to unite for their own protection. Much less to his hosts' taste, he urged Mexico to draw under the protective mantle of England and the United States, and wrote in glowing terms of the Monroe Doctrine.[6] As he had formed a very low opinion of Mexican political judgment, he so far forgot himself in his second lesson as to refer to the country's national dignity as merely "absurd vanity" and its courage as only "imprudent and blind contempt of all dangers."[7]

Santangelo's opinions antagonized the political leadership, more particularly the politicians of conservative hue. In a trice he found himself *persona non grata* and was allowed only a short time to remove himself from Mexican terrain. The vehemence of his protest and the public insult he heaped on liberal Minister of Justice Miguel Ramos Arizpe at Poinsett's Fourth of July, 1826, reception foreclosed any possibility of redemption.[8]

In the strict legal sense the visitor had done nothing to justify expulsion. The Constitution of 1824 guaranteed free speech and press. A visitor from a friendly neighboring country was supposed to be able to exercise the rights that natives had. Yet, on a more realistic level, how could anyone expect to insult a sensitive, insecure host with impunity? Moreover, since Mexicans were themselves far from possessing the rights assured in the 1824 document, and Santangelo was not even a United States citizen, his faith in the abstractions of international comity was quixotic in the extreme.

During the course of their removal, the Santangelos, father and son, improved an acquaintanceship with the inimitable General Antonio López de Santa Anna, who expressed agreement with the elder Santangelo's Panama writings, regretted his expulsion, and intimated that he ought to return. This episode excepted, the Santangelos' midsummer leavetaking *via* the Vera Cruz passage was a harrowing one. It ended in stark tragedy on shipboard when yellow fever deprived the widower of his only son.[9]

The bereaved father at first settled in Philadelphia. There he met the daughter of a local banker, and in 1827 re-married. He improved his English, but an attempt to establish a language school failed. At the invitation of Mozart's librettist, Lorenzo da Ponte, he moved to New York City to re-establish himself. There he and his American wife lived for six years, doing reasonably well in operating a boarding school for girls from families with means.[10] In May, 1829, he achieved United States citizenship.[11]

However, Mexico continued to dominate the new citizen's thoughts. Santangelo desired to return to obtain full redress for his 1826 ouster. Furthermore, he felt, as he had before his first sojourn, that the ambience would be more receptive to his scholarly, literary, and pedagogic skills than was the case in the United States. Most important, the possibility of political eminence continued to appeal to him. He corresponded with several Mexican leaders, and kept abreast of the frequent factional changes. In particular, he cultivated his ties with Santa Anna. In their different ways, both he and the Napoleon of the West desired to use the other, but, as it turned out, only the latter reaped any return. The European had in mind to become a behind-the-scenes wire-puller. In view of Santa Anna's apparent receptivity to his ideas and wishing to maintain their long-range friendship, Santangelo assumed, despite several indications of the general's wiliness, that he could become the force who would guide Mexico's rising political star. Accordingly, at Santa Anna's request, he got busy puffing that worthy's name in the Spanish and French language press and, where possible, in the English journals, for his friend's prestige in his homeland rose at news of his high regard in the northern republic.

After he had been rebuffed in several earlier soundings, Santangelo decided by the spring of 1833 that he could safely return. He disposed of his boarding school, and set forth with his wife, maid, and an enormous luggage, consisting of equipment for a new school, private library, literary endeavors, and personal papers. However, Santa Anna now in power, directly or indirectly, no longer found the Italo-American's friendship convenient. Santangelo, upon arrival at Vera Cruz, refused to interpret a protracted delay as a hint that he should turn back, and after an uninvited call on Santa Anna at his nearby hacienda, secured a reluctant acquiescence to proceed to Mexico City.

Resident in the capital for two years, Santangelo and his wife established an exclusive school for the children of prominent families. Its most noteworthy pupil was a natural son of Santa Anna, who in the schoolmaster's opinion, had been sadly neglected.[12]

Though chances of redress for his 1826 expulsion were nil, and his relations with Santa Anna continued to be cool, Santangelo, if not exactly loved, might have been tolerated indefinitely. However, his penchant for blunt words in times of tension undid him again. Having heard and observed that an independent periodical was badly needed in the capital, Santangelo only too willingly obliged by founding the *Correo atlántico*. Shortly thereafter, the simmering discontent in Texas boiled over. The Santa Anna press, in anticipation of the general's campaign to suppress the Anglo-Saxon Mexicans, featured planted stories of the northerners' misdeeds. Piqued by the inaccuracies and doubtless resentful, too, of Santa Anna's cold shoulder, Santangelo took up the cudgels for the "Texians." He asked that tales of cruelty not be printed without verification and pointed out that, contrary to reports, the Texans had made no move to declare independence — which through 1835 was true. Also, using various news items he implied that Mexico suffered from undue influence of the Catholic Church, criticized Santa Anna's centralism, and ridiculed the demagogue's passion for cock-fighting.[13]

Punishment awaited in the form of a second quick expulsion. The Santangelos had to close down their school, the *Correo atlántico* ceased publication, and considerable financial loss inevitably resulted. Again he and his companion had to make a summertime departure by way of tropical Vera Cruz, though this time both survived. Eight trunks were to follow, but enroute they toppled into a torrent, or, according to Santangelo, were plundered by Santa Anna's hired brigands. In any case, most of his personal effects and private papers were ruined. While it is not at all improbable that Santa Anna was responsible for the injured trunks, there was not a particle of evidence other than the victim's own assertion.[14]

On this occasion the expellee was an American citizen, and his expulsion was in manifest violation of Clause XIV of the United States-Mexican Amity Treaty of 1831 specifying that Americans resident in Mexico were entitled to the same rights and protections that Mexicans had.[15] Yet, with liberty still only an abstraction for Mexicans, could he expect to enjoy freedoms the natives themselves did not in reality possess? Furthermore, since he had once earlier been banished and he was already unpopular with the vainglorious ruler, had it not been the height of folly for him to criticize so freely?

For five years Santangelo and his wife lived in New Orleans, where they operated another boarding school for girls. For a short time he revived the *Correa atlántico* on behalf of the Lone Star cause. In revenge for his hardships, he had become an ardent Texan independist and Mexico disintegrationist, favoring a federation by the northeastern states of Mexico.[16] After Texas won her independence he petitioned the congress of that nation for some form of compensation, pointing out that his unsolicited moral support had, in his opinion, been distinctly beneficial. The legislators chose to view the request of so warm a friend with favor and awarded him a grant of land.[17] Oddly, it seems likely that the Texas polemicist never set foot on her soil, for in his numerous writings he never made reference to it.

Otherwise, the double expellee kept a close eye on the United States Government's efforts to negotiate the claims disputes with Mexico. Through articles and at open meetings he publicized his own and others' grievances, as this became increasingly a serious source of difference between the two countries. Since Americans, in Santangelo's opinion, had been so patently mistreated and insulted, their government, rather than accept arbitration, ought immediately to chastise Mexico by war![18]

In 1839 the disputants signed a treaty creating a Joint Claims Commission consisting of two members each, with the addition of an umpire from a neutral country to render decisions in cases in which differences between the two sets of commissioners precluded settlement. The commissioners would "impartially . . . examine and decide upon claims," Mexico was to provide documents necessary to claimants' cases, and, in disputes referred to the arbiter, his decision was to be final.[19]

The commission met from 1840 to 1842. The umpire was the Prussian ambassador to the United States, Baron Roenne.

Because observers' standards of judgment have varied so widely, opinions on the commission's performance have likewise varied.[20] The treaty objective of impartiality was much easier to approximate for the American commissioners, sharing the nationality of the aggrieved parties, than for the Mexicans, who acted largely as their country's diplomatic representatives aiming to concede as little as possible to claimants. The ground rules turned out to be what the Mexicans desired, because there would have been no procedures, and therefore no awards, had not the Americans reluctantly accepted theirs, for there was no way of resolving a tie vote, and the Mexicans invariably voted as a pair. These regulations worked to the maximum disadvantage of those advancing claims: they or their attorneys could not be present to put forth their cases, Mexico was extremely dilatory about forwarding documents, and, between some petitioners' tardiness in gathering their evidence, and the commissioners' extended disputes over procedure, quite a few cases were not even taken up before expiration of a time deadline.

That complainants had to bear with these rules was in Santangelo's opinion the climax to the government's appeasement of Mexico. He had originally protested the treaty of arbitration and, worse, the acceptance of an umpire, contending that the United States, like France, ought to settle the matter by armed chastisement of Mexico. Beginning with President Martin Van Buren and his Secretary of State, John Forsyth, he kept up a drumbeat of criticism of succeeding presidents and their foreign secretaries in the public print and in letters directed to officials.[21] When in 1840 the need to press his case in the nation's capital necessitated abandonment of the New Orleans boarding school, his wrath peaked.

It seems highly probable that despite the forms of legal procedure, personalities, and especially that of the claimant, had much to do with the disposition of his case. As luck would have it, the acting Mexican Foreign Minister in 1840 was Sebastian Camacho, while the chief clerk was José Monasterio; the first had signed the order for his 1826 banishment and the second had done the same for his 1835 expulsion. When Santangelo requested original doucments, there were interminable delays.[22] Of course these two had something to do with the appointment of Mexico's commissioners and the latter, in turn, voted against this complainant's case, "differing wholly [from the American commissioners] as to its merits" in every particular. They would not even concede that in the second expulsion there had been some miscarriage of justice against an American citizen, while for the the first they simply stood on the position that since no claim of citizenship could be made, there was no issue. No doubt Santangelo's bent for clamorous protest did not help, for at one point one of his complaints was dismissed as "impertinent," while separately his lawyer urged the members to overlook any "excessive zeal" displayed by his client.[23]

By comparison, the plaintiff offered a strictly legalistic compilation of evidence and analysis of grievances. Though conceding that his various publications in Mexico were political, he maintained that under the Mexican Constitution of 1824, international comity and the United States-Mexican Amity Treaty of 1831 he was entirely within his rights. Unmentioned, but surely on the minds of all the commissioners and, later, the umpire, was his conduct which twice had rendered him guilty of officious meddling in the internal affairs of another country, a political felony, if not a legal crime. Interestingly, too, Santangelo and his attorney, in presenting the case of an outraged American, carefully disguised his active solicitation of Mexican citizenship in 1825-26. In their opinion the victim's hardship entitled him to the immense sum of $398,690.75 for damages, with interest, a little more than two-thirds of which was to be due for the second banishment.[24]

Though some aspects of the case must have made them wince, the American commissioners solidly backed their countryman in principle, though not on the astronomical reimbursement sought. Doubtless, aware of the unreality of Santangelo's figure, Henry Brackenridge, one of the American commissioners, through the plaintiff's lawyer, urged him to scale down his claim drastically, leading the victim to conclude that his own nation's representatives were part of a cabal against him.[25] However, they did uphold Santangelo's contention that he had a valid claim for his first ouster, recommending $24,592,.50, principal and interest, as compensation. They fixed upon $54,588.00 for the second, for a grand total of $79,180.58.[26] With the Mexican commissioners unwilling to concede a penny for either, the case was then referred to the arbiter.

In addition to the treaty clause specifying that the decision of the arbitrator would be final, there was an unwritten rule that he could render verdicts without having to issue a précis of the reasons for his decisions. This had a bearing on Santangelo's situation. The Mexican commissioners held that the repeated references in the arbitration treaty to American citizens meant that a non-citizen had no claim. Umpire Roenne agreed with them that this was a reasonable inference. This disposed of Santangelo's first expulsion. Roenne, however, as was his privilege, did not choose to make this known as part of his verdict. He took the American commissioners' estimate for the second expulsion, revised it downward to $50,000, and simply let that figure stand as his decision in the Santangelo case.[27] Many others had their claims scaled down, though usually not quite so steeply, a few had theirs dismissed, others had theirs drag on, and some found theirs unattended to. Thus, though in some respects the commission did as well as the difficult circumstances permitted,[28] the dissatisfied claimants and their sympathizers in the press and the public were able by their complaints to keep the issue simmering.

Frustrated and outraged, Santangelo found that he had to accept the "pitiful" $50,000,[29] for no avenues were left open save a to-be-hoped-for appeal to some potential tribunal for redress for his first dismissal. Very soon, even the $50,000 was in jeopardy. The beneficiaries reluctantly accepted scrip which was to be later exchangeable at no less than par value for hard currency. After the signing of the payment treaty, the impoverished Mexican Government was able to meet its obligation only by a forced loan at the expense of its overtaxed merchant class, making continued payment improbable. Coincidental with the imminent annexation of Texas, Mexico discontinued its disbursements, due either to that probability or to bankruptcy.

These developments added to Santangelo's personal difficulties. As a consequence of the frequent changes of residence and occupation as well as his own extravagance, the elderly complainant was almost entirely without funds. Therefore, he sold $2,200 of his scrip at a fourth of its face value, due to the lack of confidence it inspired, to U. S. Senator Samuel McRoberts of Illinois, with whom he made an honorable arrangement for re-purchase, should he be able later to obtain ready cash. McRoberts proceeded to refuse to re-sell, which meant a $1,650 loss for the former owner. Santangelo denounced the senator in a pamphlet which he took care to have widely circulated, thus putting McRoberts in a dubious light with colleagues and constituents. When the senator sued for libel, Santangelo had to pay out more money for an out-of-court settlement.[30]

By the mid-'forties, with prospects for war with Mexico visibly increasing, the persistent complainant, so long insistent upon a showdown, began to urge caution. He observed that Mexico might take much longer to defeat than anticipated. His change of mind stemmed from his realization that warfare might have the effect of still further delaying the reimbursement due to the recipients of awards. In the election of 1844 he strongly favored Clay and opposed Polk, because the latter was so plainly in favor of annexing Texas, and, therefore, probably, war.[31]

In yet another publication at his own expense he argued that Texas ought not to enter the Union, because that would only make her subservient to the Southern slave interests. In it he pointed out that this was his view even though his Texas land grant would be likely to appreciate, should she join the United States.[32] As to Mexico's default on the claims payments, he propounded a theory identical with his own self-interest, which, if adopted, would have provided him with his money: as long as Mexico would not or could not pay, it was incumbent on the federal government, pressed by the states, to reimburse the claimants.[33]

When Polk indeed did move toward conflict with Mexico and simultaneously made no move toward rescuing the claimants, Santangelo's disillusionment with the United States was complete. He outdid himself in his denunciations of Polk. In his opinion the political foundation of the nation had rotted away with "the elective franchise [having been] extended to idiots, vagabonds, servants, criminals, bankrupts, minors [and] beggars," and the country shortly would be at the mercy of a militarist. Polk was an advance model to whom he gave no more respect than "in other times and in other regions [he had given] to crowned tyrants or military despots."[34] His two decades in America had brought him no more than a certain notoriety derived from his pursuit of his claim against Mexico and his harrying of the government of the United States.

The close of Santangelo's life had an odd *déjà vu* note to it. By the 1840s his surviving relatives had died, and, since the ban against him in the Kingdom of the Two Sicilies had long since been removed, he decided to return in order to claim family property. In September, 1847, after disposing of his remaining $35,000 of Mexican scrip for $25,000 the septagenarian and his wife left for Italy.[35] He arrived just in time to witness the Revolution of 1848, a recrudesence of the libertarian spirit of which had been a part of his young manhood forty years before. Even in his old age he was not without opinions to offer, which he incorporated into a final pamphlet of advice to Charles Albert of Savoy,[36] the foremost royal liberal in 1848. He also, in his wife's words, "'squandered the sum we brought from America *with the so-called patriots* of Italy." In this setting Santangelo fell ill and died on January 10, 1850.[37]

His wife was left with the problems of trying to establish ownership of his property at Naples, the disposition of a very generous Texas land grant of 4,605 acres,[38] and the lingering claim concerning his ouster from Mexico in 1826. As for the latter, in the aftermath of the war with Mexico, the American Claims Commission, set up subsequent to Article XV of the Treaty of Guadalupe Hidalgo, decided the matter. On March 19, 1851, the commissioners disallowed the claim, on the ground that the 1839 treaty specified that the decision of the arbiter was final, and, since umpire Roenne had agreed with the Mexican commissioners that Santangelo's claim was invalid because in 1826 he was not an American citizen, there was nothing for the new commission to decide.[39] In this fashion finis was written to an individual complaint which in its day had contributed significantly to the misunderstandings between the United States and Mexico arising out of the claims issue.[40]

CHAPTER 5

Sectionalism and Political Fragmentation

By John R. Collins

DIPLOMATIC ISSUES clearly occupied the minds and efforts of Americans during the decade before the Mexican War. Involved in the diplomacy, and even overshadowing relations with other countries, was the sectional dichotomy existing in the United States. This sectionalism was emphasized by dangerously different philosophies in the North and South on such issues as slavery, tariffs, and states' rights. With the possible addition of new territories to the United States, the controversy over slavery became even more heated. Yet with the affirmation of the Missouri Compromise in 1820, differences appeared resolved. Despite this settlement, however, sectional problems emerged again when Texas sought and obtained independence in 1836. These sectional biases were so strong from 1836 to 1845 that Texas existed as a republic, for it had no opportunity to be annexed to the United States. In 1845, as Texas entered the Union, diplomacy with Mexico became involved in the sectional feelings of Americans, further complicating the question of acquisition of new territories. Mexico clearly warned that if the United States did annex Texas, it would consider such action as grounds for war.

The war with Mexico, the sectional issues with all their controversial aspects, and general differences in political philosophy brought a fragmentation in American politics. When the war began, there at first appeared some widespread concensus approving the hostilities, but as the struggle progressed, Whigs seeking to increase their party's national power began speaking of "Jimmy Polk's War." Some even hinted that America had little — or no — moral justification for fighting the Mexicans. Even some Southern statesmen such as John C. Calhoun of South Carolina expressed fear that the war would further antagonize the sectional conflicts already so serious in the United States.

After the war the seriousness of the problem increased for almost no one agreed on just what to do with the newly acquired territory. However, territorial problems were temporarily resolved in 1850 when Henry Clay's last great effort to save the Union resulted in the Compromise of 1850 — and thereby postponed the Civil War for a decade. Thus John Collins, the author of this chapter, contends that the issue of war with Mexico not only involved diplomacy with that country, but also became even more entangled as the sectional conflict in the United States began to dominate the minds of Americans and to obstruct the channels of government both on the state and national level.

This chapter originally appeared in JOURNAL *of the* WEST in April, 1972.

THE HOUSE CHAMBER was filled as the clerk read the message of President James K. Polk. Congress was meeting in joint session to hear this message calling for war with Mexico. The hush was broken only by an occasional cough and by the voice of the clerk reading President Polk's words:

> We are called upon by every consideration of duty and patriotism to vindicate with decision the honor, the rights, and the interests of our country.[1]

Following the reading of the request, the congregation of Senators and Representatives returned to their respective chambers to consider what the President had asked. The next day, May 12, 1846, Congress had concurred with the President and had given him his declaration of war with Mexico.

Thus the Mexican War was begun officially, a war which has been over-simplified, and consequently, misunderstood. For many, the only needed explanation for the war's existence was summed up in a single word — "sectionalism." Some historians have dismissed it as a Southern war, created by and sustained for the sole benefit of that section of the country. Such generalizations, while perhaps convenient, do not entirely do justice to the facts. An analysis of Congressional roll-call votes proves that the Mexican War was more the promoter of sectional discord than the product of sectional interest.

The first Congressional vote to create problems with Mexico and at the same time provide Congress with a sectional issue was the annexation of Texas. The Mexican Government had ominously warned that the annexation of the Republic of Texas by the United States would be considered a hostile act. Yet, despite this warning, the Lone Star Republic was added to the Union in 1845. In the fall of 1843, President John Tyler's administration had begun negotiations with the administration of President Sam Houston, completing a treaty of annexation on April 12, 1844. However, the treaty failed to receive the required two-thirds majority for ratification, owing its rejection in large part to the activities of Northern abolitionist Senators. The "re-annexation of Texas" and the "re-occupation of Oregon" were major points in James K. Polk's platform. Polk won the election of 1844, indicating to him the nation's desire to see Texas become part of the Union. President Tyler was likewise convinced and, prior to leaving office, introduced a joint resolution of annexation requiring only a simple majority of both Houses of Congress. After long debate, Congress passed the measure, and the President signed it on March 1, 1845. Mexico for its part lived up to its threat and broke diplomatic relations with the United States five days later.

Aside from the threat of war with Mexico, there were other factors which entered into the debate on the annexation of Texas. Of these additional issues, it was the question of slavery which proved to be the crux of the argument. If brought into the Union, the Lone Star State would bring with it a vast expanse of territory — slave territory. Many Northerners were resolutely opposed to the addition of more slave states. The debate, therefore, assumed sectional characteristics. Many states, both North and South, passed their own resolutions giving opinions on the advisability of annexing Texas. As would be expected, many Northern States, such as Massachusetts and New Jersey, passed resolutions against annexation, while nearly every Southern state expressed its opinion in favor of such a move. However, sectional unity on this matter was not absolute. The General Assembly of the State of New Hampshire passed a resolution in favor of adding Texas to the Union. Sounding remarkably like those of its Southern neighbors, the resolution declared:

> That we regard it as an insult to the people of Texas, who have gallantly achieved their liberties by the sword of revolution, to make the con-

sent of Mexico a prerequisite to their reannexation to the United States; and that an attempt to procure the assent of Mexico, now convulsed with insurrection and torn with contending factions, each claiming to wield the powers of government, would be as fruitless, as unnecessary, and uncalled for by the justice and law of the case.[2]

On January 25, 1845, the House of Representatives passed the joint resolution of annexation by a vote of 120 to 98. The previous day, Senator A. P. Stone of Ohio had remarked that Texas must inevitably join the Union because "our republic is to be an ocean-bound republic. Providence intended this Western Hemisphere to be an asylum for the oppressed, and that our institutions should be their guardians."[3] Such was the moralistic tenor of many remarks, be they pro or con. However, the vote in the House of Representatives revealed that the more pragmatic concerns of party politics were also of great importance.

TABLE 1

THE ANNEXATION OF TEXAS — HOUSE VOTE[4]

	YES		NO	
	Democrat	Whig	Democrat	Whig
Northeast	7		9	15
Middle Atlantic	22		17	23
Northwest	24		4	13
Border	16	4	1	9
South	42	5		7
TOTAL	111	9	31	67

TABLE 2

THE ANNEXATION OF TEXAS — SENATE VOTE[6]

	YES		NO	
	Democrat	Whig	Democrat	Whig
Northeast	4			8
Middle Atlantic	3	1		4
Northwest	5			3
Border	2	1		5
South	9	2	1	4
TOTAL	23	4	1	24

The Democrats under Polk had been elected on an expansionist platform, and some Whigs were not particularly eager to help the Democrats fulfill their campaign pledges. Thus, despite much of the sectional nature of the debate, the vote was surprisingly partisan.

Party cohesion in the Senate on the issue of annexation was even greater than in the House. However, like the debate in the House, the oratory which filled the Senate Chamber had a decidedly moral tone. Senator W. T. Colquitt of Georgia urged his fellow Senators to "bid them [Texans] welcome, as brethren, to share with us the common heritage; and by passing the resolution on your table, paint another star on our flag, under the wings of that proud bird which is the emblem of the nation's glory."[5] On February 27, the Senate narrowly approved the resolution by a vote of 27 to 25.

For some, sectional loyalties were secondary to other concerns as is evidenced by five Southerners voting against annexation. Furthermore, in both houses of Congress there were Northern Senators and Representatives who voted for annexation, fearing an increased British influence in North America if Texas remained an independent republic.

On April 24, 1846, Mexican troops crossed the Río Grande, attacked an American patrol, and killed or wounded sixteen Americans. Polk had considered asking Congress to declare war before he heard of the Mexican raid. However, the news of the attack (received by Polk on May 9) made his war message more forceful and assured him of Congressional support. He wrote, "the Mexican Government . . . after a long-continued series of menaces, have at last invaded our territory, and shed the blood of our fellow-citizens on our own soil."[7] Polk's words appealed to the emotional; the national honor had been impugned. The House quickly took up debate on the issue and later the same day voted a declaration of war by the overwhelming margin of 174 to 14.

TABLE 3
DECLARATION OF WAR — HOUSE VOTE[8]

| | YES | | | NO | |
	Democrat	Whig	Native American	Democrat	Whig
Northeast	8	7			7
Middle Atlantic	27	17	3		2
Northwest	28	5			5
Border	17	12			
South	43	7			
TOTAL	123	48	3		14

Opposition to the declaration of war came from a small group of Whig abolitionists who viewed the war as a "slavocracy conspiracy." Some Northern Whigs voted for the declaration fearing possible political consequences if they did not. However, the majority of Representatives were motivated by nationalistic concern and believed at the time that war was imperative.

The debate in the Senate was considerably more lengthy. John C. Calhoun of South Carolina urged a closer examination of the facts. Thomas Hart Benton of Missouri believed that the message concerned two matters, one of which was diplomatic, while the other was military. The message, at Benton's request, was divided and sent to the appropriate Foreign Relations and Military Affairs Committees. The next day the debate continued. Senator John Davis of Massachusetts agreed with Calhoun and wanted more time to examine the question of an existence of war. He stated that "if it turns out that this territory [between the

Nueces River and the Río Grande] is debatable ground, a serious responsibility rests somewhere, and presents the question of war in a very different aspect from what it would have possessed had the invasion been made within the acknowledged limits of this country."[9] Yet, despite the hesitancy of some of these Senators, the declaration of war was passed by a vote of 40 to 2 on May 12, 1846.

TABLE 4
DECLARATION OF WAR — SENATE VOTE[10]

	YES		NO	
	Democrat	Whig	Democrat	Whig
Northeast	3	2		1
Middle Atlantic	3	2		1
Northwest	5	2		
Border	3	4		
South	12	4		
TOTAL	26	14		2

The two dissenting votes were cast by Whigs: Thomas Clayton of Delaware and John Davis of Massachusetts. John C. Calhoun, a Democrat, plus George Evans of Maine and John M. Berrien of Georgia, both Whigs, were present *but did not vote.*

The news of the war was received at first enthusiastically. Americans — both North and South — rushed to volunteer for military service. Citizens meeting in Detroit, Michigan, affirmed their loyalty to the cause saying, "that Michigan will cheerfully respond to the call of the general government, and furnish her quota of men and means, and hold herself in readiness to defend the honor and soil of our common country."[11] A public demonstration outside city hall in New York City was attended by 50,000 people calling for vigorous measures in prosecuting the war.[12] Some members of the Catholic Church in America regarded the war as a possible means of adding large numbers of Catholic Mexicans to their fold, while several Protestant groups eyed Mexico as a fertile ground for the conversion of poor deluded papists.[13]

However, as the war progressed it became increasingly more unpopular. Whigs, hoping to recapture the White House and increase their party's power, soon labeled the conflict "Jimmy Polk's War." Northern "Conscience" Whigs attempted to cast doubt on America's moral justification for fighting Mexico. And not all religious groups supported the war; Quakers were actively involved in anti-war activities. Nor was all the dissatisfaction located in the North; Calhoun became a bitter opponent of the war. Should the United States win the war and thereby gain Mexican territory, the possibility existed that such alien territory would threaten the South's prominent position in national politics. Furthermore, Calhoun feared increased sectional and class conflicts should any Mexican territory be added to the Union.

71

John C. Calhoun's fear that the Mexican War would lead to additional sectional antagonisms was well founded. The war posed one basic problem. If Mexican territory was added to the United States, would it be free or would it be slave, and who would decide such an important issue? Most Americans wanted California, and many wanted yet more of Mexico. But the question of slavery complicated the issue.

In August, 1846, just prior to the adjournment of Congress, David Wilmot, a Representative from Pennsylvania, introduced an amendment to the "Two Million Bill," a general appropriations measure. It quickly became known as the Wilmot Proviso. In short, it forbade the introduction of slavery into any territory the United States might gain as a result of the war with Mexico. Despite the South's strenuous objections, the proviso was added to the appropriations bill which was also passed. However, the bill reached the Senate only an hour before the set time for adjournment of the first session of the Twenty-ninth Congress, and as a result died in the Senate.[14]

Wilmot remained persistent. In February of the next year he reintroduced the proviso as an amendment to the "Three Million Bill," a replacement for the never-passed "Two Million Bill." The debate in the House was long and passionate. Jacob Brinkerhoff of Ohio declared that "there is no danger of the dissolution of the Union; but if . . . the arms and the blood of this nation shall be used to propagate slavery over free soil — why, let dissolution come!"[15] The vote on the Wilmot Proviso came on February 15, 1847, approving the amendment by a vote of 115 to 106.

TABLE 5

THE WILMOT PROVISO — SECOND HOUSE VOTE[16]

| | YES | | | NO | |
	Democrat	Whig	Native American	Democrat	Whig
Northeast	10	20			
Middle Atlantic	31	23	3	5	1
Northwest	17	11		11	
Border				18	13
South				48	10
TOTAL	**58**	**54**	**3**	**82**	**24**

The vote was overwhelmingly sectional as could be expected. It was a sectional issue, and as such elicited a sectional response.

There were those within the Senate who wished to avert what seemed to be an impending crisis. Senator John Berrien of Georgia proposed an amendment of his own to the "Three Million Bill" stating that the war should not be conducted for the purpose of gaining additional territory from Mexico. Voicing the concern of Calhoun, Berrien warned that "the acquisition of territory must bring before us . . . a question which now menaces the permanence of this Union."[17] Senator James T. Morehead of Kentucky agreed and asked, "Have we not land enough to satisfy any American citizen? Or is there such a pressing necessity to have more, that we will endanger all that is dear to us in the pursuit of this policy?"[18] However, the pleas of these and other Senators were in vain; the amendment failed and the Senate was faced either with accepting or rejecting the proviso of David Wilmot.

After much debate on the advisability of acquiring Mexican territory — and the fate of any such territory that might be acquired — the Senate rejected the proviso by a margin of 31 to 21 on March 1, 1847.

TABLE 6

THE WILMOT PROVISO — SENATE VOTE[19]

| | YES | | NO | |
	Democrat	Whig	Democrat	Whig
Northeast	4	8		
Middle Atlantic	3	3	1	
Northwest		1	3	
Border	1	1	4	5
South			13	5
TOTAL	8	13	21	10

Like that in the House, the vote in the Senate was non-partisan but sectional. The Northeastern Senators voted unanimously for, while Southern Senators voted unanimously against the proviso. Senators from the Northwest and Border states gave most of their votes to the opposition and thereby assured defeat of the amendment.

David Wilmot made one last attempt to add the proviso to the "Three Million Bill" when the House of Representatives reconsidered it. This time the House narrowly rejected the amendment by a vote of 97 in favor to 102 opposed on March 3, 1847.

TABLE 7

THE WILMOT PROVISO — THIRD HOUSE VOTE[20]

| | YES | | | NO | |
	Democrat	Whig	Native American	Democrat	Whig
Northeast	9	20			
Middle Atlantic	25	19	1	12	
Northwest	13	10		10	
Border				18	11
South				42	9
TOTAL	47	49	1	82	20

As had been the case in the Senate, the crucial votes came from Representatives from the Middle Atlantic and Northwestern states. In the second vote the Middle Atlantic states doubled their opposing votes (from six to twelve) with the State of Pennsylvania providing the largest number of "no" votes. Thus the Wilmot Proviso had been rejected, but not until it had greatly polarized Congress and had caused deep resentment in the South.

The next major vote concerning the war was on the Treaty of Guadalupe Hidalgo, negotiated by Nicholas Trist, the chief clerk of the State Department. He had been sent along with General Winfield Scott's army to negotiate a peace settlement with the Mexican Government. Trist's performance did not please the President and, in October, 1847, the State Department sent a note recalling him. Trist ignored the note and continued negotiations without authorization, which shocked and infuriated Polk. On February 2, 1848, in the Mexico City suburb of Guadalupe Hidalgo, Trist signed a treaty of peace with Mexico. The treaty called for Mexican recognition of the Río Grande as the southern boundary of Texas and for a vast cession of land which included California, New Mexico, and points in between, for which the United States agreed to pay Mexico the sum of $15,000,000. Also the United States agreed to pay all American claims against Mexico, which eventually amounted to the sum of $3,208,315.00.[21] The treaty included a provision for the establishment of a separate commission to survey the boundary lines between the two countries.

President Polk decided to submit the treaty to the Senate for ratification even though it had been negotiated without official American sanction. The Senate dutifully ratified the treaty on March 10, 1848, by a vote of 38 in favor to 14 against.

TABLE 8

THE TREATY OF GUADALUPE-HIDALGO[22]

| | YES | | NO | |
	Democrat	Whig	Democrat	Whig
Northeast	4	4		3
Middle Atlantic	4	2		1
Northwest	4		3	1
Border	1	4	2	
South	13	2	2	2
TOTAL	26	12	7	7

The vote was basically non-sectional and non-partisan, although a larger percentage of Whigs than Democrats voted against the treaty. Justin Smith, the war's chief historian, sarcastically pointed out that:

> The inefficient and shameless war was now brilliant and most creditable. Indeed, the Whigs chose for standard-bearer a man [Zachary Taylor] who represented professionally the military spirit they had raised pious hands against, who belonged to the slave-holding order so plainly viewed askance by the New Commandment, who had recommended the advance to the Río Grande, who had aimed the cannon at Matamoros, who had advised appropriating Mexican territory by force of arms, and who owed in fact all his prominence to playing a leading role in the "illegal, unrighteous, and damnable" war.[23]

Clearly, most Northern Senators were not unhappy with the treaty. On the other hand, four Southern Senators, fearing the addition of alien territory, voted against the treaty.

The years which immediately followed the Treaty of Guadalupe Hidalgo were trying ones. By 1850, the nation was threatened with disunion. Some of the troubles had been caused by the Mexican War; others had not. In 1849, California, New Mexico, and Utah (Deseret) applied for statehood. The question of slavery in these areas loomed large; the North wanted slavery prohibited while the South wanted it permitted. To further complicate matters, Texas had attempted to organize New Mexico County (the part of present-day New Mexico east of the Río Grande) only to be spurned by New Mexicans, as well as Presidents Zachary Taylor and Millard Fillmore. The problem reached such grave proportions that Texas, unwilling to give up a large part of her territory without some sort of compensation, threatened to organize the area by force if necessary. In addition, the North wanted the slave trade abolished in the District of Columbia, while the South wanted a strong fugitive slave law. Neither section favored the other's proposal.

Congress was badly divided and talk of secession was not rare. Into this impasse stepped Henry Clay, returned to the Senate for his last great effort. Clay proposed a series of compromises. California would be admitted as a free state as it had requested. Texas would not exercise jurisdiction over eastern New Mexico but would be compensated for its loss (Texas was eventually paid $10,000,000). New Mexico and Utah would be made territories, and they would choose (according to the doctrine of free sovereignty), upon admittance to the Union, whether they wished to be slave or free states. A fugitive slave law would be enacted and the marketing of slaves in the District of Columbia would be forbidden. Congress agreed to these terms in an omnibus bill which has since been labeled as the Compromise of 1850.

The Senate, on August 15, 1850, passed the bill making New Mexico a territory with the right of popular sovereignty. The vote was 27 to 10 in favor. It was primarily sectional, but not as rigidly as with the vote on the Wilmot Proviso. Opposition to the measure came from Representatives in the Northeast, Middle Atlantic, and Northwest regions who

TABLE 9

The New Mexico Bill — Senate Vote[24]

| | YES | | NO | | |
	Democrat	Whig	Democrat	Whig	Free Soil
Northeast	2		2	4	
Middle Atlantic	2	2		1	
Northwest	7		2		1
Border	2	1			
South	7	4			
TOTAL	**20**	**7**	**4**	**5**	**1**

were opposed to the concept of popular sovereignty. The South voted unanimously for the bill.

Senators Daniel Dickinson of New York, a Democrat, and Truman Smith of Connecticut, a Whig, were paired with other Senators and therefore their votes were not recorded. However, both acknowledged that they would have voted for the bill.[25]

On September 7, the House passed the bill organizing the Territory of Utah with the provision for popular sovereignty. The bill was approved 97 to 85.

TABLE 10

THE UTAH BILL — HOUSE VOTE[26]

| | YES | | NO | | |
	Democrat	Whig	Democrat	Whig	Free Soil
Northeast	5	2	4	9	4
Middle Atlantic	10	10		28	2
Northwest	15		10	8	5
Border	15	11			
South	17	12	15		
TOTAL	62	35	29	45	11

The vote was non-partisan and non-sectional. In essence, each man voted as his conscience dictated. There were those who put sectional considerations aside and voted to preserve the nation. There were also those who could not morally justify a vote for popular sovereignty, be it a Northerner who saw it as a sanction of slavery, or a Southerner who saw it as a betrayal to his cause.

The Mexican War began on a nationalistic note and ended on a sectional note, mirroring the complexities of its age. Partisan politics and sectional strife combined to fragment Congress and the nation as a whole. The war served as the vehicle to party power and as an unfortunate contributor to sectional unease. The question of slavery in the territories gained as a result of war with Mexico greatly strained the nation and sewed the seeds of disunion. It made the Compromise of 1850 necessary, a compromise which only tenuously held the nation together. The decade which it had helped to usher in would, in the final analysis, prove to be more than the Union could bear.

CHAPTER 6

The Whig Abolitionists' Attitude

By Cheryl Haun

THE FRAGMENTATION in American politics, of the formal political parties, was considerable during the years before, during, and after the war with Mexico. The Democratic and Whig parties, which had shown some degree of internal harmony for many years, began to experience considerable difficulties. The Whig party, with its many factions, exemplifies the internal struggles of this day. Cheryl Haun has presented an analysis of the Whig Party from 1844 to 1848, the era when its members sought to maintain unity and avoid a sectional split.

Unfortunately, the war with Mexico prompted Whig abolitionists to pressure the party to oppose the annexation of Texas, to withdraw support of the war, and to fight the presidential nomination in 1848 of General Zachary Taylor. When the party proved unresponsive to such changes, abolitionist Whigs joined with Liberty men and formed the Free-Soil Party. The basic problem was that the entire party organization was loosely tied together with no real platform, and during elections it campaigned with no issues, instead choosing to nominate popular heroes or statesmen whose positions were not easily defined. Thus dichotomies in the Whig party reflected the general mood of sectionalism in the United States. The struggle over control of the Whig and the Democratic parties provided enough dissenters to form first the Free-Soil Party and later the Republican Party, which in turn would elect Abraham Lincoln in 1860.

This chapter originally appeared in JOURNAL of the WEST in April, 1972.

THE AIR in the town hall of Worchester, Massachusetts, was exceptionally warm on June 28, 1848; the emotional fervor of five thousand free-soilers[1] had made it so. Because of the large crowd, the convention was adjourned to the Common where the hot sun blazed down upon the heads of an assemblage of disaffected Whigs, Democrats, and Liberty men. Toward the afternoon they sought protection in a shadier place called the Grove, which adjoined the Worchester Lunatic Asylum. (To the Taylor Whig press the afternoon location seemed quite appropriate.)[2]

These Whigs who gathered on this scorching summer day were the protesters of their time. Years before, on July 4, 1845, in the Boston City Hall, Charles Sumner, a leading Whig abolitionist, had warned that the greatness of nations lay, not in warfare, but "in moral elevation, enlightened and decorated by the intellect of man."[3] According to the dissenting Whigs, neither the Whig nor the Democratic national parties were aware of their moral duties. Both parties were too concerned with practical politics rather than this idealistic form of "moral elevation." From 1844 to 1848 the Whig protesters tried to work within their party. Their presence fostered sectionalism in both parties at a time when the Democrats and the Whigs were attempting to prevent sectional divisions. In 1848, after the Democrats and Whigs had committed their final *faux pas* with their Presidential nominations, the dissenters within both parties joined with Liberty men to give birth to the Free-Soil Party. However, it was the display of courage by the abolitionist Whigs in opposing their own party's position from the annexation of Texas and the Mexican War to the Whig Presidential nomination of the Mexican War hero, General Zachary Taylor, which instigated the movement towards this new third party.

Had the Whig national party not been such " a coalition of the most diverse elements of political life" the abolitionist Whigs might not have felt forced to abandon the Whig party.[4] Nevertheless the Whigs clung steadfastly to no particualr platform and in Presidential nominations they either popularized war heroes or statesmen whose positions were not clear. Between the years of 1844 and 1848, the Whig party had tried consistently to maintain party unity, to avoid a sectional split, and to attain domination of the federal government. When the Southern Whigs were not bowing to their Northern brethren, the Northern Whigs were paying obeisance to their Southern counterparts. To the men assembled at Worchester, moral principles were more important than party politics. The storm between these two elements of the Whig national convention in Philadelphia on June 7, 1848, was heartily welcomed across the nation by disillusioned sections of all parties. A grand convention with an anti-slavery platform could then become a reality.

The tension began in the halls of Congress when, by joint resolution, Texas was invited to become a state in the Union. On March 1, 1845, three days before James K. Polk's inauguration, President John Tyler signed the resolution. Comparing the election of 1844 to the election of 1840, the Southern Whigs had cut their majority in the black belt and did not appeal to the Democratic back-country either.[5] The Democrats in Congress forced Southern Whigs to face the necessity of deciding between sectional interests and party politics. The party line weakened and annexation was accomplished. Previously, the Southern Whigs had followed the policy of Henry Clay, Whig Presidential nominee in 1844. He maintained, in his "Raleigh letter," that annexation at this time was a danger to the national character and would force the nation into a war with Mexico. This would endanger the integrity and financial condition of the Union.[6] Many Whigs thought Clay had abandoned the annexation of Texas in this letter. In order to alleviate these fears, the Great Compromiser wrote two more letters in which he established that he would be glad to see Texas annexed without dishonor or war and with the consent of the States on fair and reasonable terms.[7] If elected, he would judge annexation on its own merits. His position was endorsed by many Southern Whigs who claimed annexation would endanger the old slave states by rendering slavery unprofitable.[8] Slavery would not be profitable in the semi-arid Texas land, thus it could only become a refuge for runaway slaves. Still some others argued that Eastern Texas, with its virgin soils, might prove to be a strong competitor with the old slave states and their rapidly depleting soils. Economics was a major consideration as was politics.

In the election Southern Whigs were the champions of the Union; their slogan, "Union without Texas rather than Texas without Union," rang pleasantly in Northern ears. However, Henry Clay was not elected. The election revealed the Whig's strength in the North. The numerical decrease in Whig votes in the black belt convinced many Southerners to abide by sectional interests. The Texas issue had cut their majority.

Alexander H. Stephens of Georgia and Milton Brown of Tennessee agreed it was necessary for Southern Whigs to support annexation of Texas. With the assistance of eight other Southern Whigs the resolution was carried in the House of Representatives. Simultaneously, in the Senate, Ephraim H. Foster of Tennessee presented the joint resolution. Later, he refused to support it when it was amended to permit President Tyler to secure annexation by treaty if he so desired. Most of the Whigs concurred with Foster's refusal. They felt the amendment failed to recognize the control of their legislative body over the treaty-making power. Nevertheless, three Southern Whigs enabled the enactment of the resolution on the final ballot.[9]

The passage of the resolution by Congress posed a dual challenge to the Whig party and its abolitionist allies. In domestic national policy a contest was being waged between the agrarian West and South and the industrialized East and Great Lakes regions.[10] Joshua R. Giddings, a Whig abolitionist from Ohio, had spoken of it in 1844 in the House.[11] The West was reminded by Giddings that, with Texas annexed, the North not only would lose its protective tariff, but the West would lose its internal improvements. He suggested Texas annexation would prove to be a financial burden in the form of paying Texas' debts and providing an army to protect Texans from Mexico. Furthermore, he asserted the United States Constitution contained no guarantee in regard to slavery. Giddings' argument presented the second challenge to the North: the expansion and strengthening of slavery.[12]

Whig journals were cautious not to offend the South on this matter. Meanwhile, the abolitionist newspaper, *The Liberator*, soundly thrashed the South. Appealing to the pecuniary interests of the North, the organ assailed the "wantonly disrespectful acts of the South with regard to the rights and feelings of free states."[13] By illegal maneuvering the South had legislated a burden upon the North. Texas was a state with a population equal to only three or four of the largest counties in Massachusetts. Yet, through its newly acquired legislative powers, Texas could swallow the North. Texas was the land of little money. Money scarcity would not promote importation of Northern products. If the Texas population grew, markets would not increase, they would only shift. Nothing could profit the North by annexation of Texas, argued the newspaper. Texas was the

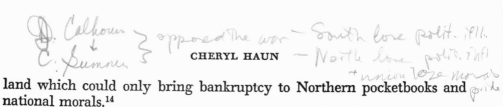
land which could only bring bankruptcy to Northern pocketbooks and national morals.[14]

The Whigs, for differing reasons, were just as dismayed at the calamity called Texas annexation. Charles Sumner wrote in his memoirs, " . . . History records no baser transaction than the annexation of Texas."[15] Failing to prevent the incorporation of Texas into the Union, a small number of Whig abolitionists began to campaign against admission of Texas with a pro-slavery constitution. The majority of the Whigs shuddered at this movement. In New England the influence of manufacturers and capitalists was dominant, and for them the issue of paramount importance was the maintenance of the protective tariff of 1842 — and not Texas. To them, Whig success was essential and depended upon party unity with their Southern neighbors. The slavery issue could only embarrass the Southern Whigs and perhaps prevent a Whig restoration to power in the up-coming election. With these men material questions strived for the triumph of moral duty over party politics.

Massachusetts was the model state for the experiment on consciences. In an open invitation Massachusetts conscience men called for a meeting on annexation. Gathering at Faneuil Hall on November 4, 1845, were such well-known men as Charles Francis Adams, son of John Quincy Adams, John Gorham Palfrey, Sumner, and George S. Hillard, representing the Whigs; Wendell Phillips, William Lloyd Garrison, and W. H. Channing, speaking for the abolitionists; and H. B. Stanton, agent for the Liberty party. Garrisonian men proposed disunion resolutions which the Whigs labored to prevent. The true course for Massachusetts was marked through the Texas resolutions proposed by the Texas committee. Their recommendations ranged from exclusion of slavery in any acquired territories to absolute termination of the internal slave trade. Although the meeting had Daniel Webster's attendance and sanction, it was conspicuously lacking in the participation of other prominent Whigs from Massachusetts. Abbott and Amos Lawrence, Nathan Appleton, Levi Lincoln, and Leverett Saltonstall believed nothing had been accomplished by the meeting, and their absence was widely noticed.[16]

This meeting stimulated similar gatherings in rapid succession throughout 1845. Speeches were made; pamphlets were written; and editorials printed on behalf of the anti-slavery cause. Palfrey and his friends frequented many of these meetings. They fidgeted uncomfortably when abolitionists damned the Constitution and countenanced disunion.[17] Soon the Texas Committee appeared to be dominated by the extreme adolitionists' ideas. On December 29, 1845, Texas was admitted to the Union with a pro-slavery constitution. The next day the Texas Committee had its final meeting.

The dissolution of the Texas Committee left the Whig activists in a quandary. How could they continue to play a role in the anti-slavery question? The abolitionist factions had many journals to present their views to the public. Yet the Whig activists had none. Whig journals clearly ignored the slavery issue. Early in 1846 Charles Francis Adams negotiated for a daily means of public expression for the newly dubbed "Conscience Whigs." The *Boston Whig* had come under the ownership of Adams, Palfrey, and Stephen C. Phillips, a Salem merchant and shipowner. Adam's first editorial stated that existing Boston newspapers were not true to Whig principles and, herein, the *Whig* would deal more on the question of human rights than of property rights.[18]

The *Whig* soon had a great issue on which to expound its theories. On May 11, 1846, a week after the purchase of the *Whig*, Congress was requested by President James K. Polk to recognize that a state of war existed due to a Mexican invasion of United States territory. Robert Winthrop, a Massachusetts Whig in the House, asked for the official correspondence to be read. The supporters of the administration rejected this proposal. They supported a bill which contained, in its preamble, the President's statement on the Mexican invasion. A motion to strike the preamble was sustained by nearly every Whig member,[19] but it was overruled. In the flurry which ensued, the bill with the controversial preamble was swiftly passed. It contained a provision for fifty thousand men to be raised and appropriation for ten million dollars to prosecute and quickly terminate the war.[20] John Quincy Adams headed the list of those opposed to the measure in the House. Thirteen Whig abolitionists concurred with this opposition.[21] The Senate had only two Whigs who rejected it. Except for these sixteen, the mass of Whig members voted for the bill. Even though they thought the war had begun unjustly and unconstitutionally, they construed their votes to mean only a direct aid to those soldiers who were engaged in battles. Their actions were not formally condemned by the party. However, Henry Clay, then in private life, said that "no earthly consideration would have ever tempted or provoked me to vote for a bill with a palpable falsehood stamped on its face."[22]

Disapproval was also expressed by the national Whig organ, the *National Intelligencer*. It foresaw the day when the Whigs would regret their actions.[23] Many excuses were made. Thomas Corwin, Senator from Ohio, voted for the bill to save "our little army from its perilous position."[24] He had no idea the "little army" would invade Mexico. Later, he regretted his vote. Robert Toombs, a Representative from Georgia, reasoned that if the Whigs did not vote for the bill the President and his party would make political capital of it.[25] He did not want to be on the wrong side of what appeared to be a popular war. Even though Giddings voted against it, he said that the first vote was given under "peculiar circumstances," for the Whigs had no time to compare views or to discuss the propriety of the matter. They were told the United States troops had been cut off so they responded on first reactions.[26] The *Na-*

tional Intelligencer stated, "Congress went to war on deficient information."[27] The paper questioned the details which it felt the Executive had not given the Congress or the people, and it asked what might have been the result had the Mexican Government immediately resolved war without information or avowal or disapproval from the United States when Commodore Thomas ap Catesby Jones, in 1842, moved on the Mexican town of Monterey, California, on the Pacific Coast.[28]

Having acknowledged the war, the Whigs began to question the President and his objectives. The Twenty-ninth Congress was volatile. Numerous versions for Polk's purposes were made . The *National Intelligencer* challenged them. If Polk were sincere when he said in his Proclamation to the People of Mexico that the object of the war was to overthrow tyrants, why did he want to negotiate with President Paredes? Polk had stated in the same proclamation that the object of the war was to obtain indemnity for claims. The Whig journal derided Polk for spending money to obtain money. In a speech on May 11 to Congress the object was to repel invasion and defend United States territory. But Congressmen from both parties questioned if this were indeed United States territory.[29] The Whigs were in the precarious position of bombasting the President for the war and continuing to vote for appropriations to sustain it.[30] A few Whigs stood with Giddings when he stated that this was a war of conquest. Therefore, if they voted for war appropriations, they would certainly have a wicked part in it.[31] The split between abolitionist Whigs and the Whig party was apparent. Nowhere was this division more apparent than in Massachusetts.

One-half of that state's delegation had voted against the war, while Winthrop and one other colleague had voted for it. Winthrop was held responsible for the breaking of the unity of the Massachusetts delegation.[32] He was defended by Whig politicians and capitalists who apologized for him by saying that the peculiar and difficult circumstances justified an honest difference of opinion.[33] They did not shield his vote by patriotism and public duty, for this would have reflected upon his Conscience colleagues. This would have harmed party harmony. Sumner reluctantly criticized Winthrop's vote. Based on moral grounds, he challenged the right of a representative to affix his name to legislative falsehood. Although Sumner had always cherished a high personal regard for Winthrop, the abolitionist implied Winthrop feared "to be found alone in the company of truth."[34] Later, Sumner wrote, "Blood! blood! is on the hands of the representative from Boston."[35] Greatly incensed by this assailment of his public morality, Winthrop declared Sumner would not ever have to have the service of the blood-stained hands. Aside from the question of slavery, the two elements of the Whigs were directly opposed to each other on the war. Presentation of appropriation bills made this fact apparent. The two factions radically disagreed on questions of morals, politics, and national honor.[36]

When David Wilmot, a Pennsylvania Democrat, rose in the House in August, 1846, and attached a rider to an appropriations amendment, he gave the abolitionists a cause upon which they could nail their anti-slavery sentiments. In this proviso, Wilmot moved that slavery be for-ever barred from all the lands acquired from Mexico. Sectional differ-ences became more noticeable in the Whig and Democratic parties. Southern Whigs united solidly with Southern Democrats to oppose the measure, and with the help of Northern men with Southern principles, they succeeded. The Whig party danced awkwardly on its tip-toes trying to attain some form of party unity because of the approaching mid-term elections.

To avoid the issue, many Southern Whigs declared their hostility to the acquisition of any territory as a result of the war. In the House, Alexander Stephens, with Toombs' support, offered a resolution to this effect.[37] The Senate rallied around John M. Berrien of Georgia who called upon national patriotism to exclude this question. The Northern Whigs cooperated to ensure order, but they did not succeed.

In 1846 the "Conscience Whigs" fought their battles in Congress and in state conventions. The Conservative Whigs in Massachusetts sought to keep the supremacy of the former issues, such as the tariff, while the young activist Whigs pushed questions on slavery and the Mexican War. A conference was held before the state convention in Massachusetts. The conservatives decided they needed a platform which was broad enough to offend no one in the national Whig party.[38]

On September 23, the convention met in Faneuil Hall. The friction was apparent between the Conservative and "Conscience" Whigs. The managers of the assembly were of the former class. They had arranged their business so that anti-slavery sentiments could be eluded. Scattered throughout the hall, the anti-slavery Whigs called loudly for Sumner, and, without formal permission, Sumner marched to the platform. There he demanded the Whig Party sustain the fundamental principles of human rights and duty by amending the United States Constitution to allow further aggressive action against slavery. Cheers rose as the young Whigs applauded this idea. However, they were not in the position to win unanimous approval for Sumner's suggestion as the Conservative Whigs found it repugnant.[39] After Sumner stepped down, Winthrop spoke. He dwelled upon the measures on which the Northern and South-ern Whigs agreed. The two speeches vividly showed that sympathetic ties no longer existed between the two divisions.

When the platform was being considered, the anti-slavery forces pro-posed that it be based on resolutions upholding their position on the "pe-culiar institution." The small "island of Conscience Whigs" was fur-ther isolated by the request of Stephen C. Phillips. He asked for amend-ments which would make opposition to slavery the prime political duty of the Whig party. Support would only go to men who promoted that principle and purpose.[40] Of course, this would offend the National Whigs for it reeked of sectionalism. As Phillips spoke, sullen countenances and angry retaliations were exchanged. No one knew what would happen to Phillips' amendment. Then the door in the back of the hall flew open. Heads turned. Voices hushed. Everyone rose, with a loud cheer and prolonged applause. Daniel Webster entered Faneuil Hall, led by a Conservative Whig, Abbott Lawrence. Slowly, he walked the length of the hall, delegates parting as he advanced. Webster's very presence had decided the fate of the amendment, for it was well known that his escort, Lawrence, was unfriendly to Phillips' motion. After the vote was taken and the amendment failed, Webster spoke briefly to inspire party unity and enthusiasm.

In spite of Whig differences, the party triumphed over the administration in the election, gaining a solid majority in the House. Robert Winthrop was elected Speaker of the House much to the dismay of many "Conscience Whigs." Congress got little done with "Proviso" men from both sides upsetting the plans of party managers. Anti-slavery speeches were frequent, and "Conscience Whigs" found themselves agreeing more and more with "Proviso Democrats." Southern Whigs cooperated in restraining their violent utterances. The year 1847 quickly passed. Polk commented on the Thirtieth Congress in his diary when he noted that after half-a-session it had accomplished nothing but arguments on "politics and slavery."[41]

By March 10, 1848, Conscience men had been deprived of one of their main arguing points — the Mexican War. The status of slavery was left undetermined. The Treaty of Guadalupe Hidalgo was not ratified on party lines. However, upon the resolution of thanks to the officers, Giddings declined saying the war was unconstitutional and that he would not thank murderers.[42] Most Whigs "trimmed their sails for public sentiment."[43] They were thinking of the Presidential election in 1848. The Mexican War had made Zachary Taylor a possible candidate. "Conscience Whigs" knew they would have to block his nomination. They would give their support when they found a candidate who would agree to the Proviso.

The issue of freedom or slavery for the new territories acquired by the treaty was the most important issue for the Thirtieth Congress. Previously, a proposition had been made in the Senate by Berrien that no land be acquired as a result of the war with Mexico. This allayed Northern and Southern Whigs. Winthrop presented this proposal in the House. The vote was along party rather than sectional lines, and Berrian's request died. In July, 1848, a compromise committee, headed by John M. Clayton, a Whig Senator from Delaware, left the question of slavery to the Supreme Court and prohibited territorial legislatures from acting on the subject. Most of the Northern Whigs in the Senate rejected the Clayton Compromise, however, Southern Whigs cooperated, and it passed.[44] In the House the compromise was shelved by Southern Whigs. Stephens, leader of this movement, knew the Supreme Court could only recognize the continuance of Mexican laws against slavery. Northern Whigs helped defeat the bill because the Democrats could make political gains from it in the next election.[45]

And 1848 was above all, an election year. The Democratic National Convention met in May, 1848, and nominated Lewis Cass for President. His was the party favorable to the annexation of Texas and to the Mexican War. Because the convention's resolutions had been dictated by the South and because of a variety of tensions in New York politics, a group of Democrats known as the "Barnburners," organized a revolt in the Democratic Party in New York.

Meanwhile, the Whigs were aligning their possible nominees along pro- and anti-slavery bases, too. Clay seemed a logical candidate for the Whigs. Yet Southern Whigs recalled his "Raleigh letter," while Northern Whigs remembered his subsequent letters. Taylor's name was frequently mentioned. The Southern Whigs reasoned that Taylor was not only popular with the public but also was a champion of the Southern cause. During the 1848 campaign, efforts were made to establish a Taylor bloc in New York City. Earlier attempts had been disrupted by Clay Whig "roughs." Alexander Stephens arranged for Isaiah Rhynders, "captain among toughs and shoulder hitters in New York" and, a Taylor man, to ensure an uninterrupted speech given by Toombs in a hall in the city. The price for this was $200.00.[46] At Rhynders' suggestion, Toombs met with some of the Rhynders boys at a favorite saloon to establish camaraderie the night before his speech. The next evening Toombs' speech was interrupted by shouts of "slaveholder" and "a hurry for Clay." Toombs continued speaking. Again the cries erupted in the hall. The speaker began to question his success at establishing camaraderie in the saloon the night before. Then, a great row broke out, and the hall was cleared of forty trouble-makers in two minutes. Later, Toombs discovered that during the initial heckling Rhynders' men had circulated and chalked the backs of the hecklers. Then, on order, they were bodily ejected.[47]

Other speeches were made on behalf of Taylor by Northern Whigs as well as by Southern Whigs. Before the Whig National Convention in Philadelphia, Henry Wilson, a Whig abolitionist, suggested to Charles Francis Adams that a few "Conscience Whigs" should assemble to decide what to do if Taylor were nominated by the Whigs. As a result of this meeting on May 27, 1848, they concluded that the "Conscience Whigs" would bolt the national convention if Taylor were nominated. Yet there was no need of a convention, for no platform was adopted, and Taylor had virtually won the nomination before the convention. When the Whigs placed in nomination for Vice-President the name of Abbott Lawrence, the Massachusetts delegation was not silent. Charles Allen stated he felt the Whig Party was dissolved, and Wilson declared he would return to Massachusetts to help defeat the Whig nominee.[48] Millard Fillmore was nominated for Vice-President, but the "Conscience Whigs" had already made up their minds. Horace Greeley aptly described the Whig convention as "the Slaughterhouse of Whig Principles."[49]

On June 10, a call for a convention was made in Massachusetts for all who were opposed to the nominations of Cass and Taylor to meet in Worchester on June 28. A few days before the Worchester convention, anti-slavery meetings were held in Ohio and New York. The Ohio men did not propose a Presidential nominee, however, the "Barnburners" in New York nominated Martin Van Buren for the job. At Worchester speakers were enthusiastically received. Remnants from all parties were present. Although the "Conscience Whigs" had no declared nominee, they questioned Van Buren's sincerity, but they realized that he was all they had. He was sure to be the nominee at Buffalo in August. During July the "Conscience Whig Speakers' Bureau" sent speakers to various states urging rebellious elements to come to Buffalo, New York.

The popular upheavals against Taylor and Cass seemed overwhelming when, on August 9, anti-slavery factions from all parts of the free states flocked to the Buffalo City Park. Meeting under a spacious tent, their numbers estimated at between ten and forty thousand, these men adopted a clearly stated platform.[50] They accepted constitutional limitations which excluded interference with slavery in national territories and to relieve the government from all responsibilities for extension and continuance of slavery wherever governmental power extended.[51] A bargain was made concerning the platform and the nominee. Liberty Party leaders agreed to back Van Buren if the "Barnburners" would support a Liberty Party platform. After the platform was approved, amidst much waving of hats and handkerchiefs, Van Buren was unanimously nominated as the Free-Soil candidate for President. To balance the ticket, Charles Francis Adams was selected to run for Vice-President.

Sentiment against slavery was highly diffused and many Whigs were offended by the nomination of Taylor because he was not a statesman of the Whig tradition. However, Taylor won the election while Van Buren received only one-tenth of the popular vote. The Free-Soilers elected nine members to Congress which gave them the balance of power in the House. Large numbers of anti-slavery Whigs had given Taylor their votes, because he had stated that he was against the executive use of the veto power. Later, they favored his policy of allowing territories to settle the slavery question for themselves without executive interference. At his death on July 9, 1850, there were no more sincere mourners than the anti-slavery men of the free states.[52]

The "Conscience Whigs," although unsuccessful in 1848 under the

Free-Soil banner, did accomplish some major feats between 1844 and 1848. During this period they were the only element of highly respected men who fought the annexation of Texas and its result, the Mexican War. They gave their support and sympathy to revolutions within both the Whig and Democratic Parties. Had the "Conscience Whigs" not existed, the question of slavery might have died with the Liberty Party in 1847. Political expediencies were placed so highly in the minds of the parties that moral principles could have been easily forgotten. Sectional differences within the parties would not have occurred without the influence of abolitionist Whigs. Because the Northern Whigs were so stubborn in their insistence on party unity, they tried to appease simultaneously both the Southern Whigs and the "Conscience Whigs." Upon doing this they repelled both divisions. The "Conscience Whigs" served as an example for the "Barnburners" in the Democratic Party. Thus, as a result of the existence of the activist Whigs, the Free-Soil Party was capable of being formed. Twelve years later many of these men would be involved in the American Civil War. Only then would they finally be satisfied at the triumph of moral principles over political savagery.

CHAPTER 7

Jones at Monterey, 1842

By James High

As early as December, 1841, American warships were sent to the Pacific area in anticipation of problems with Mexico. Actually the threat to American security came not from the Mexicans, but from the English and French, both of whom had strong interests in Latin America. To prepare for anticipated difficulties in the Pacific, Secretary of the Navy Abel P. Upshur sent Commodore Thomas ap Catesby Jones to the area as commander. In this position Jones committed a serious blunder, which served to heighten Mexican hatred and to forewarn them of American intentions. While on a cruise off the coast of South America, Jones stopped briefly at a port and heard that the United States and Mexico were at war. He had standing orders that should such an event occur, he was to sail at once to Monterey, California, and occupy the port. This he accomplished, advising the Mexican officials there that he was taking over, as he raised the American flag. Soon thereafter he learned of his mistake and tried to make amends to the Mexican governor. That proved to be an impossibility.

Diplomatic correspondence protesting the illegal American invasion was sent to Washington as Mexican officials expressed their anger at the commodore's action. The American Navy quickly sent another officer to replace Jones, but the erring commodore had departed the coast for a cruise on the Pacific. He sailed to Hawaii and then to South America; there he learned that the officer sent to replace him had died in 1844. In 1845, rather than being disciplined, Jones was lauded by the new President, James K. Polk, who renewed the commodore's command in the Pacific.

James High contends here that many questions remain unanswered about the occupation of Monterey. Was Jones given verbal orders, as he claimed, to take the Mexican port? For that matter, why was the commodore publicly censured for his actions, but never officially disciplined, and in fact even commended by President Polk? Answers to these questions must be largely conjecture, but doubtless much of the confusion and resulting actions were brought about by the embarrassing position in which the action placed the United States Government as far as its relations with Mexico were concerned. Jones' act was a prelude and a rehearsal for the hostilities that would break out in 1846, when General Zachary Taylor's troops were attacked along the international border.

This chapter originally appeared in JOURNAL *of the* WEST in April, 1966.

Commodore Thomas ap Catesby Jones commanded the Pacific Squadron at the end of the Mexican War in 1848. He was a colorful, trusted and competent officer sharing military responsibility in California with General Persifer Smith of the U. S. Army. It was not, however, Commodore Jones' first tour of duty on the faraway West Coast of North America.

On December 4, 1841, the Secretary of the Navy, Abel Upshur, announced that an increased naval force was needed on the Pacific and he dispatched Jones in command of a squadron. Thus began a game of naval hide-and-seek among the Americans, the British and the French which lasted until the United States held undisputed sovereignty over California. During the three years preceding the outbreak of war with Mexico a policy developed which came to have the quality of a standing order in the United States Navy. It was to maintain a force in readiness in the Pacific to take advantage immediately of any war to seize California. France and Britain were to be kept out at all costs.

Finally the policy bore fruit. In 1845, just before the war, Marine Lieutenant Archibald Gillespie traveled to the West Coast bearing a momentous dispatch from President James K. Polk and Secretary of State James Buchanan to their special agent, Thomas O. Larkin, in Monterey. The key words in the dispatch said that the government "would vigorously interpose to prevent [California] from becoming a British or French colony." With such support from the administration California was almost sure to fall to the Americans. Commodore John D. Sloat, on July 7, 1846, sailed into Monterey just ahead of Admiral Seymour of the British Navy, took the town and thereby assisted John C. Frémont's Bear Flag Revolt which just preceded the Mexican War.

But all of this was after the readiness policy of the United States Navy had paid its dividends. There was much mischance and there were many slips between the time when Secretary of the Navy Upshur established a squadron in the Pacific and the time when Secretary of State Buchanan dispatched Lieutenant Gillespie to Monterey.

Commodore Thomas ap Catesby Jones, on his cruise to California in 1842, made a spectacular blunder. As the ranking United States naval officer in the Pacific he seized Monterey, California, from its Mexican sovereigns during peacetime. True, he held the Mexican provincial capital for only thirty hours, and then realizing the error of his judgment he dusted off the disgruntled *oficionados* and tried to restore their dignity. As it turned out, restoration to office was somewhat easier than calming the Mexican gasconade and soothing the wounded pride of Governor Micheltorena.

An explosion of diplomatic and private letters detonated in Washington and Mexico City. Newspapers as far away as Hawaii added editorial fuel to the comic opera fire. Daniel Webster, Secretary of State, directed the ambassador in Mexico to extend an apology and the promise of adequate reparations. He, at least in public, was convinced that Commodore Jones had acted in good faith. The Mexican Government accepted the apology, but proceeded to insist on Jones' recall and punishment. One of the official papers describing the affair bore the ludicrous title, *Agresion en Californias por el Comodoro de los Estados-Unidos, Thomas Ape Jones.* It would appear that every Mexican official from Washington, D. C., to Mexico City, and back to Monterey tried to claim credit for having scared off the United States Navy and Marines when in actuality Commodore Jones had simply made an understandable mistake and upon discovering it he had rectified the error as best he could. No lives were lost and very little property was damaged. What damage there was had more than ample compensation — except for the wounded pride of the Mexican officials.

Jones was immediately relieved and ordered to return to the United States which he did — two years later. Commodore Dallas was sent to Callao early in 1843 to take over Jones' command, but there is no record that he ever caught up with the "disgraced" commander. Jones had been ordered independently to return home "in such mode as may be most convenient and agreeable" to himself. It was "most convenient" for him to sail from the California Coast to Hawaii followed by a leisurely cruise in the Pacific. He finally put into Valparaiso, but in the meanwhile Dallas had died in Callao in 1844, never having met his predecessor. One gets the ridiculous picture of Commodore Dallas in the *Erie* chasing Commodore Jones in the *Dale* all over the Eastern Pacific in order to take over his command. One observer wrote: "And so, snapping his fingers at Dallas, he sailed away around the Horn for Old Virginia." Jones told the consul at Valparaiso that he had brought the ship to the Pacific, and he would "be damned if he wouldn't take her home."

John Quincy Adams, in the House of Representatives, attempted to get through a resolution making provision for the "signal punishment" of any officer invading the territory of a nation at peace with the United States. He was unsuccessful. Jones was never given a trial. In fact, he was lauded indirectly in 1845 by the new President, James Knox Polk:

> Ample atonement having been made to Mexico for your acts complained of, there has been no disposition to visit you with punishment of any description for conduct actuated by such elevated principles of duty. The department has been and still is anxious to give you employment; in this the president concurs, and it will give him the greatest pleasure to see you speedily placed in a situation corresponding with your rank and merits.

On March 1, 1845, the navy officially exonerated Jones and his forces of any blame in the incident and promised him a new command.

It is a commentary on the time, only a little more than a century ago. Communication was slow and faulty. National policy might be one thing, but if the men in the field did know what was happening they had to do the best they could with the materials at hand. It is impossible now, in this age of radio and fast aircraft, to envisage an amphibious assault mounted by mistake against a distant shore belonging to a nation at peace with the United States. But one hundred years can make a lot of difference, and Commodore Jones, with three ships and a few marines did make an amphibious attack on Monterey, a Mexican provincial capital, when the United States and Mexico were not at war.

Very little really new can be added to the basic story of Commodore Jones' premature assault on Monterey, but the episode continues to be of interest. It still poses some unanswered questions. For example, what were the verbal instructions given to Jones before he left the United States for his Pacific mission? Why was he publicly censured in the press by his government but not punished? Why was he rewarded after the Mexican War by a responsible command in California? Attempts to answer these questions, along with descriptions of the action have been regularly made almost since the conclusion of the episode.[1]

In 1842 the Far West was huge, ill-defined and without firmly established sovereignty under any national state. Great Britain and the United States disputed possession of the Oregon country. Hawaii was a degenerating kingdom, port-of-call for all nations. Even the Russians had a claim on the Pacific Coast in the ownership of Alaska. California was part of a huge and barren appendage to Mexico, dumped on the Mexicans as a result of their successful revolution against Spain in 1825.

California was nearly unpopulated, having only a string of Franciscan missions up the coast and a few drowsy seaports from San Diego to San Francisco. Cattle, Mission Indians and a few *rancheros* and *cabildos* populated the huge land. The largest settlement was Monterey, the capital. It consisted of a customs house, presidio, the governor's palace and a few adobes. It was the center of whatever administration there was. This was mainly connected with supporting a small contingent of barefoot soldiery and a handful of civil servants. Life went on in a leisurely fashion, the cattle in the hills content to subsist on the plentiful grass and render up their hides at the end of a short life to foster the economic mainstay of life in California. Indians did what little work was required, and the few members of the upper social group lived in leisurely luxury substantially isolated from the rest of the world.

Life in California for the Mexican administrators and estate owners may have been carefree and pleasant, but they were not to be left in that state of bliss. Manifest Destiny in the United States was beginning to work its way. William Henry Harrison was elected President in 1840 as a Whig. He was against all further expansion, but he lived only a few weeks. His vice-president, John Tyler, bolted the party of peace and resumed his Democratic allegiance to the idea of filling up the country from sea to sea. It was Tyler, as the last act of his tenure, who signed the joint resolution making Texas a state. With the mid-century Democrats in office it was only a matter of time until California also would be brought into the Union, fulfilling the dictates of Manifest Destiny: America for Americans. The "Texas game" had to be played out in California to keep that Mexican province out of the hands of Great

Britain, or so thought enough Americans to make the nation the size it has become today.

During the 1840s international tension steadily increased over power in the Pacific and concerning the sovereignty of California. Great Britain, France, Russia and the United States variously accused each other of launching nefarious schemes to deprive Mexico of her rightful claim to the Spanish legacy. Each nation attempted to establish righteous friendship with Mexico, while, at the same time, doing what she could to undermine the flimsy hold that Mexico had in California. Americans came out and established themselves in increasing numbers as individual business men on the Pacific Coast. Often they took Mexican citizenship. Mexico was suspicious, but too lethargic to enforce regulations. British warships and merchantmen had a way of appearing unexpectedly in the Pacific, and finally the mutual feeling emerged in England and in the United States that if one of these nations did not seize California the other would. Mexican rights seem pretty much to have been forgotten.

Under the heading of "The Outrage of 1840" the following tale was typical of what Americans liked to believe in the 1840s:

> While lying at Mazatlán, Mexico, with his ship, the *St. Louis,* Commander Frence Forrest received information of some outrageous proceedings on the part of the California Government toward British and American citizens residing in Upper California. Over sixty American citizens and British subjects had been arrested, robbed of their arms and other property, their houses forced open, and they were fired at while in their beds, and, without any attempts at defense, were dragged to a loathsome jail and there incarcerated for about twenty days. Some of the prisoners were subsequently discharged, while forty-seven of them, strongly ironed, were transported to San Blas, *via* the sea, a distance of over 1,200 miles. All this was done without any civil process, conviction, or trial whatever. One of the prisoners, an American by the name of Duger, died at San Blas. All were charged "with an intent to revolutionize California." The outrage unquestionably had its origin in a disposition or conspiracy, on the part of some of the Government officers, to expel the foreigners from the country, and to possess themselves of the fruits of their industry; at the head of this conspiracy was one José Castro, the prefect or head police magistrate of California.

> "These atrocities," as Secretary of the Navy James K. Paulding called them, committed on the foreign residents at Monterey and its neighborhood, by the Mexican authorities, did not pass without notice from the Navy. Commodore French Forrest, in command of the *St. Louis* anchored his ship at Monterey on June 15, 1840, at 3:15 p. m. By his prompt and spirited interposition he vindicated and secured the rights not only of American citizens, but of British subjects resident in Upper California. For these services Commander Forrest received a formal expression of the thanks of the American and English residents, and on July 5th sailed from Monterey for the East Coast via Cape Horn.[2]

Naval altruism toward British subjects was short-lived. On September 30, 1841, the *New Bedford Mercury* published an item reflecting probable American attitudes.

> California must in time become a place of vast importance, the land, harbors and climate, being the best in the world; San Francisco being the very best. Should John Bull obtain this country, the owners of American whalers may bid farewell to their ships in the Pacific, in case of war between England and America.

This opinion was apparently based on the United States Naval expedition's findings on the California Coast and up the Sacramento River which had been made in the summer of 1841. It is more understandable, with this background in view, how Commodore Jones could have made the fantastic "mistake" that he did the next year.

It was in this atmosphere that Commodore Jones arrived in the Pacific with somewhat ambiguous orders. War with Great Britain or Mexico was a constant possibility, and in either case Jones was to seize whatever objective he thought would best serve the interests of the United States. If he had any secret orders to do a more specific thing — to capture a Mexican capital — there is no record. Ever since 1842 there has been a persistent feeling among observers and historians that perhaps a verbal agreement had been reached between Jones and some of the politicians before he left the United States, but this is apparently without foundation. Jones was not ordered to commit war-like acts, but, on the other hand, he was not forbidden to seize foreign territory if circumstances warranted such a thing. "Jones knew," as one historian put it after the Mexican War, "the programme of the politicians, that Texas was to be annexed, that Mexico was to go 'on the rampage,' that the Americans were to discover unparalleled outrages on the part of Mexico, that finally war was to be proclaimed, and then California would be fair game for the American squadron in the Pacific."

On December 10, 1841, under orders from Secretary of the Navy Upshur, Commodore Jones took command of the Pacific Squadron of five ships mounting one hundred sixteen guns. The ships were the frigate *United States*, the sloops *Cyane*, *Dale* and *Yorktown* and the schooner *Shark*, as well as the store-ship *Relief*. Jones was told that because of

> . . . increasing commerce of the U. S. within the gulf and along the coast of California, as far as the bay of St. Francisco, together with the weakness of the local authorities, and their irresponsibility to the distant government of Mexico, renders it proper that occasional countenance and protection should be afforded to American enterprise in that quarter. You are therefore directed to employ either a sloop of war or a smaller vessel, as may be most convenient, or both if necessary, in visiting occasionally or cruising constantly upon that line of coast.

The order seems legitimate enough, and it certainly had enough

93

latitude implied so that the commander's judgment could be exercised. If taken, however, in conjunction with the known tensions and published aspirations of several nations to own California, such broad instructions appear to be less innocent. Also it must be remembered that Great Britain had a fleet of four ships on the coast, all superior to the American vessels although mounting only one hundred four guns, and that the French fleet in the same waters consisted of eight ships of war with two hundred forty-two guns. The chances for some kind of confrontation were very great.

In May, 1842, almost as soon as Jones arrived in Callao, he was alarmed at the report of a French squadron setting sail from Peru in "great secrecy," bound for a destination "altogether conjectural." He reported that

> I might have considered it my duty to follow this expedition and to propound certain interrogatories to the French commander touching the object of so formidable an expedition fitted out with so much secrecy as to have eluded the observation even of Great Britain, her ever-watchful rival.

He called for instructions and announced that

> . . . it is not impossibe but that, as one step follows another, it may be necessary for me to interpose by the assertion of our national commercial rights in case they are infringed by any power within the limits of my command.

The commodore might better have followed the American policy of watchful waiting in the Pacific, because it turned out that the French fleet was on its way to the Marquesas — not California; but events conspired with the slowness of communication to goad the American commander into an embarrassing action. British Admiral Thomas suddenly appeared in September with secret orders and three men-of-war from Great Britain. United States Counsul John Parrott at Mazatlán announced the imminence of war between Mexico and the United States, and a copy of the *New Orleans Advertiser* showed up carrying the news that Mexico had ceded California to Great Britain for $1,000,000.

After consulting with United States Charge d'Affaires Pickett at Lima, Jones put to sea on September 7, 1842, with the *United States*, *Dale* and *Cyane*. He submitted to his three captains the opinion that the United States and Mexico were probably at war, and that it was their "bounden duty" to seize and hold every tenable place in California in order to uphold the Monroe Doctrine. The captains concurred, but suggested sending the *Dale* to Panama for late news and further instructions. The other two ships made all sail for Monterey, to be joined there later by the *Dale*.

Jones at Monterey, 1842

As the *United States* and the *Cyane* approached the California Coast, after the long voyage across the equator, during which they had touched at no port nor sighted any sail, Commodore Jones issued a special order against disorderly conduct and looting in the coming engagement.

> During the battle and strife every man must do his utmost to take and destroy; but when the flag is struck, all hostility must cease, and you must even become the protectors of all, and not the oppressors of any.

Monterey was sighted at dawn on October 19, 1842, and Jones saw that, at least, the British squadron had not beat him to the punch. Only one Mexican ship was active in the anchorage.

The Americans, convinced that Mexico and the United States were at war, and fully believing that England had seized California, Jones raised British colors on his flagship, seized the Mexican ship coming out of the harbor and proceeded into Monterey Bay. The master of the Mexican ship swore that he knew of no war, but Commodore Jones approached as near as the depth of water would permit — now flying the *Stars and Stripes* — and cast anchor in front of the fort.

Commodore Jones later asserted:

> The time for action had now arrived. Whilst nothing had occurred to shake my belief in the certainty of hostilities with Mexico, the re-iterated rumored cession of California to England was strengthened by what I have already related. Hence no time was to be lost, as another day might bring Admiral Thomas with a superior force to take possession in the name of his sovereign; General Micheltorena, or the new governor-general of California, might appear to defend his capital, within less than three days' march he was then said to be. If I took possession of the country and held it by right of conquest in war, and there was war with Mexico, all would be right; then if the English should come and claim it under a treaty of cession, as such treaties do not give title until possession is had, I should have established a legal claim for my country to the conquered territory, and at least have placed her on strong grounds for forcible *retention* or amicable negotiations, as after circumstances might dictate. If Admiral Thomas should afterwards arrive and attempt to supplant our flag on shore, the marines of the squadron to man the guns of the fort without weakening our ships would insure us the victory, and the responsibility would rest on the English commander. On the other hand, if it should turn out that amicable relations had been restored between the United States and Mexico, that Mexico had not parted with the Californias, and that at the time I demanded and took possession of Monterey there was no war, the responsibility of the act at first might seem to rest on me, certainly not on your government, who gave no orders upon the subject. But if I am right (of which there can be little doubt) in assigning to Mexico the attitude of a nation having declared conditional war, Mexico is the aggressor, and as such is responsible for all evils and consequences resulting from the hostile and menacing position in which she placed herself on the fourth of June last. But I may be wrong, *toto caelo*, in all my deductions and

conclusions. If so, I may forfeit my commission and all that I have acquired in seven and thirty years' devotion to my country's service.

At 4:00 p. m., on October 19, 1842, Captain James Armstrong of the *United States* went ashore under a flag of truce to demand surrender of the town and presidio "to avoid the sacrifice of human life and the horrors of war." The Mexicans were given until 9:00 a. m. the next day to capitulate, but by two hours after Armstrong landed Captain Pedro Narvaez and José Abrego, representing military and civil authority, came aboard and signed articles of capitulation. They surrendered the territory from San Luis Obispo to San Juan Bautista, and gave up all their military personnel and supplies. The force reported was twenty-nine soldiers, twenty-five militia, and eleven cannon, nearly all useless and lacking ammunition, and one hundred fifty muskets. Captain Mariano Silva, the comandante, commented on the state of readiness for defense as being of "no consequence, as everybody knows."

Thomas O. Larkin served as interpreter in the affair. Larkin had come to Monterey from Boston in 1832 and had become a successful business man during the intervening decade. He was appointed United States consul in 1843, and subsequently served very usefully in bringing California into the Union.

At 11:00 a. m. on October 20, 1842, Commander Stribling, captain of the *Cyane*, was ordered ashore in boats with a force of one hundred fifty sailors and marines under First Lieutenant George W. Robbins[3] to secure the town and the fort. As he touched the beach the garrison marched forth "with music, and colors flying," and surrendered their arms in front of the government house. The *Stars and Stripes* were raised over the abandoned *castillo* in place of the Mexican flag. Salutes were exchanged between the guns of the fort and the batteries of the two American ships of war riding at anchor in the harbor. Cabildo Alvarado conveniently retired to his rancho some miles away, and no one was deprived of liberty, even temporarily. Not a shot had been fired in anger, no property was damaged, and a territory the size of Connecticut and Rhode Island combined was transferred to the American flag. A proclamation was issued "to teach the people how great a blessing had been vouchsafed to them in the change of flag."

Such blessing, as it was, lasted only a few hours over one day. Larkin, aboard ship on the nineteenth, had expressed great doubt that there was actually a war, but Jones had remained convinced that he was a legal belligerent. When the commodore came ashore in person on the twenty-first he was shown papers and dispatches from Mexico as late as the middle of August which proved conclusively that Mexico and the United States had amicable relations. Cession of California to Great Britain was publicly denied at that time, and one of the reasons given for its impossibility was the Monroe Doctrine itself.

Commodore Jones found himself in an embarrassing position, because he had been counting on an infringement by England of the Monroe Doctrine and on a state of war with Mexico. Neither condition was present, and he had seized a piece of foreign territory completely without justification. "This change in the aspect of international affairs," wrote Jones, "called for prompt action on my part. The motives and only justifiable grounds for demanding a surrender of the territory were thus suddenly removed, or at least rendered so doubtful as to make it my duty to restore things as I had found them, with the least possible delay."

On October 22, 1842, the events of October 20 were re-played — in reverse. The American flag was hauled down, the Mexican soldiers were given back their arms and the force of marines and sailors returned to their ships in the harbor as the batteries ashore exchanged salutes, and apparently all was as it had been before the ill-advised seizure of Monterey.

That same day Commodore Jones wrote a long explanation to Waddy Thompson, United States minister in Mexico City, in which he tried to put as good a face as possible on the episode. He wrote:

> It is a great source of satisfaction that, notwithstanding what has happened, no angry words or unkind expressions have been used by either party; and that, although we had 150 seamen and marines on shore 30 hours, not one private house was entered, or the slightest disrespect shown to any individual; nor was any species of property, public or private, spoiled, if I except the powder burnt in the salutes, which I have returned twofold.

Regardless of what was said, however, the Americans had committed a serious breach, and the Mexican Government was not slow to try to take advantage of it. Colonel Vallejo called it a "violation of the rights of hospitality, the law of nations, and the trust with which [Jones] had been received." Vallejo was a little disappointed that Jones withdrew so soon, because he probably wanted to raise a personal revolutionary army to try to overthrow Governor Micheltorena. Vallejo disliked his own governor considerably more cordially than he did any of the Americans. It will be remembered that a similar situation arose a few years later when General Frémont staged the Bear Flag Revolt in California, but Vallejo was then in the office of governor.

The chief outcry on the part of the Mexicans came from Governor Micheltorena who, when Jones arrived at Monterey, was at San Fernando, more than three hundred miles away. He blustered from a safe distance and ordered his troops at Monterey (a total of fifty-four men) to fight to the death. He, himself, quickly repaired to Los Angeles, ordered the batteries removed from San Diego and San Pedro and brought to his headquarters in the pueblo of Los Angeles. He barricaded himself with all available defenses and proceeded to roar and write letters, most of which were never sent. He apparently hoped to get all of Mexico's outstanding debt to the United States cancelled as salve for wounded dignity, because even he could not show any real damage to Mexican property.

As soon as Micheltorena heard that Jones had restored Monterey he issued bombastic orders to conduct war "so just, so holy, and so national." This was followed next day (when everyone knew that all danger had passed) by a public announcement designed to humiliate the commodore. He wrote that "the multitude of persons now surrounding me will not be content with such satisfaction as you can give me in a single official dispatch." He insisted that Jones come to Los Angeles for a public conference and disavowal of his actions at Monterey. Nothing less would have satisfied the pride of the Mexican, and what he wrote was more calculated for its effect in Mexico than to overawe his adversary. As a matter of fact, when Jones did go to San Pedro, aside from having to refuse to sign any binding treaty or article of capitulation, the visit was mainly devoted to celebration and parties.

Micheltorena's demands were extravagant and couched in florid language, but he made no demur at their refusal. His point was to get a proper transcript of "evidence" in the hands of his superiors in Mexico, and to insure that he would get recognition for having properly dispatched his duty. As soon as the conference with Commodore Jones was concluded the Mexicans invited the Americans to a grand ball. Micheltorena could not overlook *punctilio* any more than he could avoid bombast. The American officers attended the ball, probably at the old Domínguez Rancho about half-way between San Pedro and Los Angeles. It must have been a picturesque sight, the Mexican officers and ladies in their best European finery and the American officers in their dress uniforms. There was a certain incongruity because there was a drenching rain on that night, on one of the rare occasions of rainfall in Southern California when the whole countryside became a sea of mud. There were no decent roads, and a trip of ten miles in such a downpour must have rendered the guests more uncomfortable than happy.

Although Jones and Micheltorena exchanged complimentary addresses at San Pedro and most of the American officers departed bearing gifts of California wine, the affair was not settled so easily. Micheltorena submitted a list of expenses incurred by the invasion included the cost of fifteen hundred uniforms spoiled by the necessity of marching in the rain (actually directly away from the scene of invasion and after the withdrawal of Jones' forces), fifteen thousand dollars in cash and a set of musical instruments alleged to have been destroyed. As the days went by, mostly through dint of writing to Mexico City, the list of grievances and expenses gradually grew until finally the bill exceeded thirty thousand dollars.

As a comment on the slowness of communication and movement in those days, immediately after Jones' evacuation of Monterey he had sent one ship to Hawaii for supplies and another to Mazatlán carrying dispatches for Washington. The ship returned from Hawaii before the dispatches reached Washington. Lieutenant H. T. Hartstene departed from Monterey October 26, and by January 13, 1843, he had crossed Mexico and arrived in New Orleans, still several days from Washington. Since Mexico City was a little closer, on December 19, 1842, José María de Bocanegra, Mexican minister of foreign relations, addressed a letter to United States Minister Waddy Thompson expressing surprise and grief at "the greatest outrage that can be done to an independent and sovereign nation." He officially asked the United States to disavow the acts of Commodore Jones and to see that he received punishment "corresponding to the magnitude of the offense." Because there had not been enough time to send and receive communications between Mexico and Washington, Thompson had to act on his own. He did so by disclaiming any national responsibility for Jones' acts.

Bocanegra insinuated that the United States had authorized the invasion, and that Jones was only carrying out his orders. There is some mystery, as has been said, concerning the exact nature of the verbal orders which Jones had when he departed the United States. The Mexican request for his punishment was designed to embarrass the United States if there actually had been such an order. John Quincy Adams, in the House of Representatives, representing opposition to the administration, was inclined to the view that Jones had not entirely misjudged his responsibility and authority. He pressed very hard for summary punishment.

Toward the end of January, 1843, Secretary of State Webster (who had remained loyal to President Tyler) had become aware of the public fiasco, and he wasted no time in directing Thompson to inform the Mexican Government that Jones had acted entirely on his own, without authorization from the United States. He issued a public and complete apology to the Mexican Government. General Almonte, Mexican Minister in Washington, demanded the exemplary punishment of Commodore Jones whose delinquency was "so serious, so obvious, and so notorious that it would be superfluous to particularize its enormities." It was at this point that Jones was recalled and Commodore Dallas sent to relieve him.

Public statements were made so that Mexican officials would believe that Jones was to be disgraced by a trial and conviction, and so that such supporters of non-expansion as John Quincy Adams would be satisfied in their political activities. In reality, however, the forces of expansion were at work, the President and a majority of the American people felt that the demands of Manifest Destiny were inevitable and righteous, and that Americans should fill up the West. Because of this, and despite the public announcements, Secretary Upshur sent Jones orders to proceed home "in such mode as may be most convenient and agreeable to yourself."

It was most agreeable to Commodore Jones and to the United States for him to delay his return for almost two years. By then the Mexican War was only a matter of a few months away in which the doughty commodore's services could be quite legitimately used.

CHAPTER 8

The Superiority of American Artillery

By Donald E. Houston

COMMODORE THOMAS AP CATESBY JONES' premature seizure of Mexican territory may have forewarned the Mexicans of American intent. Nevertheless, the Republic of Mexico, whose army on paper was far superior to that of the United States at the beginning of the war, needed more than a warning to prepare its forces for defeat of the American Army. Several reasons account for American superiority; perhaps as significant as any single reason was the American superiority in artillery. A devastatingly effective concentration of artillery fire saved the Americans from defeat in more than one major battle. Don Houston clearly shows how and why American soldiers had the advantage in any battle involving an artillery duel. Utilizing both fragmentation and solid shot, American troops could break up enemy troop concentrations or batter down enemy barricades, thereby making the infantryman's job easier. No quirk of fate made American artillery and tactics better than those of Mexico, for the United States Army for years had studied the results of the Napoleonic Wars and the use of field artillery in those engagements. In 1838 Brevet Major Samuel Ringgold suggested that new light weight guns might be used to support and keep pace with dragoons and other fast-moving troops during an attack. So effective were his arguments that Joel Poinsett, then Secretary of War, authorized one light-mounted battery per artillery regiment — providing the instrument and tactics for General Zachary Taylor to win several battles that otherwise would have been disastrous.

In addition, the Mexican War also served as "a laboratory for the testing of artillery theory, material, and officers and men."

This chapter originally appeared in JOURNAL *of the* WEST in April, 1972.

AMERICAN ARTILLERY in the Mexican War saved the United States Army from destruction on several occasions and provided the overall basis for victory in the conflict. The Regular Army redleg,[1] a name given to artillerymen derived from the red stripe down their uniform trouserlegs, played two fundamental roles in the war. First, using fragmentation shot, grape, canister, and spherical case,[2] they could rake or spray an area, breaking up enemy fortifications and pave the way for friendly troops in their attack, or if necessary, retrograde movements. Second, utilizing solid shot, the gunners could batter fortified positions or drive the defenders from those positions, subjecting them to infantry and dragoon attacks.

From the 1820s to the 1840s the American Army studied the results of the Napoleonic Wars, especially the utilization of field artillery.[3] Cannoneers riding horses could employ a weapon faster than those who were riding the limbers of the gun. In 1838 Brevet Major Samuel Ringgold, after receiving new lightweight guns, demonstrated that his battery could keep pace with and give fire support to infantry and dragoons. This feat so impressed Secretary of War Joel Poinsett that he authorized one light-mounted battery per artillery regiment.[4] That one decision was perhaps the most beneficial affecting the artillery, for it would be those light batteries that would dramatically serve under Brevet Brigadier General Zachary Taylor.

Artillery has traditionally been and still remains a small, elite branch of the Army. In the fall of 1845 there were four regiments of ten batteries each, or a total of forty batteries, in the United States Army. The branch had an authorized strength of 2,340 officers, enlisted men, musicians and artificers, but an actual strength of 2,303.[5] Of this, sixteen batteries and 932 officers and men were with Taylor in Texas.[6]

In the fall of 1845, Taylor was ordered to Corpus Christi; in March, 1846, he proceeded to the Río Grande. Although Taylor was repudiated to have a "low opinion" of artillery, he spaced his cannons so that each brigade would have artillery support,[7] and he continued this practice throughout the war.

The first decisive actions of the Mexican War were fought on May 8-9, 1846, when the Mexicans attempted to prevent Taylor's return to Fort Texas from Point Isabel, where he had gone for supplies and two 18-pounder siege guns.[8] Seeing the deployed Mexican Army, commanded by General Mariano Arista, the Americans prepared for battle by placing their infantry on the flanks and the artillery toward the center of the line.[9] When the Mexican cannon began firing, directing their cannonade against both the heavy guns and Ringgold's light battery, Ringgold was ordered to advance to the right front, occupy a position about 700 yards from the Mexicans and return their fire.[10] The Mexican fire was ineffective, while the American guns cut the enemy ranks apart. In the maneuvering phase of the battle, Arista ordered Mexican lancers, under General Anastasio Torrejon, to attempt a turning movement around the American right flank, apparently trying to capture the American supply train. At approximately the same time, the American Fifth Infantry, on the extreme right flank, was ordered to turn the left flank of the Mexican Army. The Fifth advanced about one-half mile to the right front, where it came upon the Mexican force supported by two pieces of artillery. The infantry formed a square, advanced on the cavalry, halted about fifty yards from them, and fired.[11] A section of two guns from Ringgold's battery, commanded by Lieutenant Randolph Ridgely, was sent to help. The guns fired canister, and in the words of their commander, "frustrated the enemy," and drove him off.[12]

In the center of the line, the Mexicans attempted to capture or destroy the 18-pounders of Lieutenant William H. Churchill. When the Mexican cavalry launched a concerted assault on those guns, the cavalry was repulsed by Brevet Lieutenant Colonel Childs' artillery battalion, which was fighting as infantry, and by the heavy cannons firing canister.[13] After a shift of position, caused by a grass fire, Captain James Duncan spotted an enemy force of cavalry and infantry moving against the

American left flank. He moved forward, causing the enemy to halt even prior to his going into action. He fired and drove the enemy back, but the Mexicans regrouped, attacked a second time, and again were repulsed. All this was done, according to Duncan's brigade commander, before infantry support arrived to aid the artillerymen.[14]

The following morning, May 9, the Mexicans occupied a strong defensive position at Resaca de la Palma. This forced Taylor to use his infantry instead of his hard-hitting artillery. Another problem for the Americans was the single road into the Mexican position protected by their artillery.[15] Taylor, with approximately 1,700 men,[16] advanced some five miles from where he had left his supply train and found the Mexicans in position. He sent Lieutenant Stephen Decatur Dobbins forward to draw the Mexican fire and then deployed his infantry to either side of the road.[17] Lieutenant Ridgley, who had replaced the mortally wounded Ringgold, was ordered to advance and blast the Mexican battery out of the road.[18] As Ridgley moved forward to within approximately four hundred yards of the enemy, the Mexicans opened fire. He kept moving, returning the enemy's fire. Finally, although he was only some one hundred yards from the enemy, he was yet unable to silence the Mexican guns.[19] Taylor, knowing that the Mexican artillery had to be quieted, ordered Captain Charles Augustus May and the dragoons to charge the guns, but the dragoons could not silence them. The guns were finally captured by American infantry,[20] and the Mexicans fled from the field.

Palo Alto was essentially an artillery victory. The cannoneers demonstrated mobility, a capability to deliver counter battery as well as anti-personnel fire, and almost the flexibility of cavalry. Sometimes the guns were in the line with but, for the most part, they were in front of the infantry.[21] The American redleg protected his troops, delivered effective fire against the enemy, and did it with only ten guns. Resaca de la Palma, however, was primarily an infantry success, made possible by the unorthodox tactic of having a battery charge into the fire of a defensive battery. Duncan's battery, which chased the fleeing Mexican Army, showed that it could keep pace with the dragoons, and fire while pursuing its enemy.

Taylor's advance on Monterrey showed that he was to have trouble. His artillery, one ten-inch mortar, two 24-pound howitzers, and four light batteries, nineteen pieces in all, was inadequate for seige operations, and the Mexicans occupied a strongly fortified position.[22] The American commander devised a plan that had a portion of the Army swing to the west, cut the Saltillo Road, capture the commanding heights, and attempt to force its way into the city. This task was given to Brevet Brigadier General William Jenkins Worth,[23] who started moving on the morning of September 21. Mexican cavalry and infantry attacked his movement.

Immediately after the firing started, Duncan's battery and a section from Lieutenant William Whann Mackall's command arrived, fired grape into the Mexican ranks, and drove them back.[24]

After interdicting the Saltillo Road came the hard assignment: to attack and capture the hills overlooking the road and the western wall of the city. Federation Hill was taken, along with an enemy 9-pound gun, which some of the redlegs turned on Soldada, aiding in the capture of that strong point, and another 9-pounder.[25] Next was the Bishop's Palace on Independence Hill. Both captured guns, along with a 12-pound howitzer that Lieutenant John Frederick Roland had managed to bring up and place about four hundred yards from the palace, were used. They produced immediate results. The Mexicans abandoned their position, along with two more guns.[26] Meanwhile, Duncan and Mackall brought their batteries to Independence Hill in time to aid the infantry in repulsing a Mexican cavalry counter-attack.[27] Taylor's diversionary attack on the northeast corner of the city greatly eased Worth's move. Taylor began with an artillery barrage from his heavy guns, but they did little damage to the strongly fortified position.[28] In what appeared to have been a desperate move, Taylor brought his light batteries close to the walls of the houses and fortified positions in an effort to breach them. Brigadier General David Emanuel Twiggs summarized the results as having "annoyed the enemy's advanced works."[29]

The Mexican decision to surrender came unexpectedly, and was directly influenced by artillery. In Worth's sector, the artillerymen managed to bring their guns to bear, after placing them on roof tops, on the plaza and market place, which was crowded with civilians, soldiers, and animals, and on the cathedral where gunpowder was stored. Near dusk on the evening of September 23, a mortar shell landed close to the gunpowder. This alarmed General Pedro de Ampudia, who asked for and received surrender terms from Taylor.[30] What was essentially another infantry victory had been directly caused by fear of the cannons. Whether the Americans would have fired into the crowded marketplace and plaza is unimportant. The Mexican command thought that it would happen, and acted accordingly.

At Buena Vista the only regulars, in a force of 4,759 men under Taylor, were two squadrons of cavalry and three batteries of artillery, or approximately 476 men.[31] Opposing him were about 20,000 Mexicans.[32] Taylor and General John Wool placed the American troops where they could most advantageously be utilized. Major John Macrae Washington's eight-gun battery was placed to guard the road from Buena Vista to San Luis Potosí.[33]

Antonio López de Santa Anna, commander-in-chief of the Mexican forces, feinted to the western side of the American line in an apparent move to force Washington out of his position.[34] The first attack came on

104

the American southeastern front. To meet this threat, two regiments of infantry and three guns from Washington's battery under Captain John Paul Jones O'Brien were sent to plug the hole.[35] Brigadier General Joseph Lane ordered the regiments forward; O'Brien, receiving enemy fire, moved to within musket range of the enemy, began firing, and drove the Mexicans back.[36] For unknown reasons, one regiment, the Second Indiana, retreated, exposing the American artillery to continued and reinforced enemy attacks. Finally, O'Brien had to retreat. He lost one gun, a Mexican 4-pounder, but he did manage to save his two larger guns.[37]

During the night of February 22-23, the Mexicans shifted positions. Eight guns were brought up to fire on Washington; eight 8-pounders were emplaced to fire on O'Brien. The San Patricio battalion brought up 18- and 24-pounders for use in attempting to break the American lines. In the battle, Captain Braxton Bragg and O'Brien were many times in front of the American infantry, blasting away at the Mexican guns, which failed to take advantage of their extra range.[38] During the cannonade, the Americans pulled in to shorten and straighten their lines; causing the artillery to consolidate, and for once all the guns were firing in something resembling a co-ordinated pattern.[39]

Following the lancer attack against Colonel Jefferson Davis and the Mississippi Riflemen, Brevet Captain John Fulton Reynolds was sent to aid in the defense of the ranch buildings, which were being used as a supply depot and hospital. The Mexican lancer attack against them was broken by artillery fire and May's dragoons. Not content with stopping the enemy, the American artillerymen limbered up their guns and pursued the Mexicans over terrain that was considered impassable. The Americans might have achieved a victory at this point, had not a white flag been displayed and the fighting ceased.[40]

After the momentary lull, Santa Anna launched a final, desperate attack against the American center, which had been stripped to send men elsewhere. To meet this threat, Wool ordered the Second Illinois and the Second Kentucky Regiments, O'Brien, and one gun under Lieutenant George Thomas to that part of the line. O'Brien advanced, fired, and halted the enemy attack, but his infantry support was routed, and again O'Brien faced the possibility of losing his guns.[41] He later wrote that sometimes an artillery officer has to sacrifice his guns for the safety of the army. He knew that the guns could be saved, but to retreat at that time, in his opinion, would have caused an American defeat. The young artillery officer decided to stay in position, fighting until the reinforcing artillery arrived or until the enemy reached the muzzles of his guns. He did finally withdraw, but not until Bragg arrived to challenge the Mexicans.[42] Bragg, in a pretentious report, claimed that victory or defeat depended on the successful stand of his battery, and since no aid was available, he loaded and fired as rapidly as possible and broke the final attack.[43]

The opening phase of the battle against Major Washington came on the morning of February 23, when the Mexicans launched infantry, lancer, and artillery attacks against him. At the same time that the Mexican artillery was attempting to blast him from his position he reported that General Santiago Blanco's attack was repulsed by the "rapidity and precision of our fire."[44] This fire, according to his infantry support commander, caused wide gaps in the ranks of the enemy.[45] O'Brien's supporting infantry which had been routed, tried to find its way to safety through the many gullies in the area. They soon came under lancer attack, and Major Cary H. Fry, commanding officer of the Second Regiment of the Kentucky Volunteers, said, "At this time I had come to the conclusion that we were all lost."[46] But lost they were not, for they soon came within range of Washington's battery, which drove off the Mexicans and was credited with saving the day.[47]

The artillery at Buena Vista demonstrated its shooting and moving capabilities, but, more, it also showed capacity to fulfill its mission, even without infantry support.[48] In their after-action reports, both Taylor and Wool had high praise for the cannoneers. Taylor saw the guns at the right place at the right time, dealing destruction to the enemy.[49] Wool was even more straightforward, saying, "Without our artillery we would not have maintained our position a single hour."[50] The Americans began the battle with fourteen guns available; later one more returned from detached duty. Four stayed emplaced with Washington, and one was captured from O'Brien immediately in the first action. The moving and much of the shooting was done with only ten guns, and Bragg's final stand was made with but four.

The operations of Major General Winfield Scott illustrated the second fundamental role of artillery: to conduct battering or destructive operations. For this use, heavy weapons are needed, and if properly utilized, could force a city or fortress to surrender. The capture of Vera Cruz demonstrated that point. Seige operations began March 22, 1847, with seven ten-inch mortars firing on the city. The next day, the Army emplaced four 24-pound guns along with two eight-inch Paixhan guns. The Navy landed and manned three 32-pound guns and three eight-inch Paixhan guns.[51] The Army, experimenting with rockets, fired several on Vera Cruz. Their use seemed to cause some "stampede amongst the Mexicans,"[52] but was probably not as influential in causing the surrender as the naval gunfire, whose speed and accuracy seemed to amaze the Army and which breached the city walls,[53] causing the Mexicans to capitulate.

Scott then moved inland. The march began on April 13, led by Brigadier General David Twiggs, who had 2,600 men and two dissimilar batteries of artillery. The first was composed of heavy guns — 24-pound guns, eight-inch howitzers, and ten-inch mortars; the second was comprised of mountain howitzers and rockets.[54]   The march proceeded smoothly until the enemy was found entrenched astride a road at Cerro Gordo.   Twiggs pulled back, awaiting reinforcements and orders.   He launched his attack on April 17, and made limited progress after fighting all day,[55] for his light batteries could not be brought rapidly into the conflict.[56]   What seemed an advantage was achieved when Captain Robert E. Lee and Lieutenant George H. Derby found a route around the Mexican position and were able to emplace, after working all night, three pieces of artillery on the flanks of the Mexicans, which could enfilade their ranks.   The value of this accomplishment has been debated.   Silas Bent McKinley said that it made victory possible,[57] while George B. McClellan wrote that the guns did "little or no damage" for they were badly served.[58]   However, once the enemy had been forced from his position, the Americans turned the captured Mexican guns against them, and along with the dragoons, pursued the fleeing Mexicans.[59]

The Army continued inland, progressing smoothly despite occasional sniping and guerrilla action.   The next series of battles occurred in the bitter struggle for Mexico City.   While there were predominately infantry victories, they were greatly assisted by the artillerymen who tried to make the infantrymen's job as painless as possible.   The Mexican position at Contreras was organized in depth, utilizing a forward line of eight thousand men and two cannons, while about a thousand yards to the rear, was the main force of five thousand to eight thousand men and twenty-two more guns.[60]   The terrain — lava flows on one side and bogs on the other — greatly favored the defenders.   Only a costly frontal attack against superior forces, beyond the supporting range of American cavalry and artillery, seemingly would pry the Mexicans out of their positions.[61]

Scott decided to put two artillery batteries in a position to fire on the Mexican defenses.   Major John Lind Smith, Corps of Engineers, told Twiggs that the two units would be sacrificed to the heavier enemy guns.[62] However, the two batteries, one of 6-pound guns and 12-pound howitzers, commanded by John Bankhead Magruder and the mountain howitzers and rocket battery, under Lieutenant Franklin Dyer Collendes, Ordnance Corps, held their positions and repulsed all efforts to dislodge them.[63] Their major contribution was to fire and thereby screen a scouting force which was attempting to find a route around the enemy flanks.   This job the batteries did with success,[64] but they suffered heavily from enemy fire.[65]

The bright spot for artillery was Captain James Duncan's attack on the Church of San Pablo, which was the key to Mexican defenses in the First Division sector.   Duncan advanced to within two hundred yards of the enemy and in five minutes drove the enemy from his guns and the infantry from their entrenchments. They fled to the church. A few rounds forced that strong point to surrender.[66] Another artillery achievement was that of Captain Simon Henry Drum, who captured two 6-pounders which were the same guns lost by O'Brien at Buena Vista. After their capture, the guns were formed into a battery under the captain.[67]

The final battles of the Mexican War were the most expensive for the Americans. The enemy had to be blasted out of his positions, which most often were defended with artillery. The First Division, commanded by Brevet Major General William Jenkins Worth, with attached units, was to take El Molino Del Rey, a foundry which was thought to be manufacturing cannon. American heavy guns, two 24-pounders, were emplaced about six hundred yards from the foundry, fired about twenty rounds, and then moved to take up supporting positions. One gun, under Lieutenant Charles Pomeroy Stone, was placed to fire on enemy troops advancing to aid the foundry, while the second, under Captain Benjamin Huger, was to fire on the fleeing defenders.[68] On the right of the American line, an infantry attack supported by Drum's two-gun battery, drove the Mexicans from El Molino Dey Rey. On the left side of the line, Duncan and his four-gun battery assisted in the attack on Casa Mata, and drove off Mexican infantry and cavalry who were going to their countrymen's aid.[69] With the capture of the foundry, the way was open for the attack on Chapultepec.

To capture the fortress guarding the Mexican capital, guns had to be emplaced to fire on the road and flat areas, the Mexican artillery, and the stronghold itself. During the night of September 11-12, Lieutenant George Pearce Andrews and his battery fired a few rounds of canister down the road and prevented reinforcements from reaching the fortress, which was isolated from support.[70] The fortress of Chapultepec would probably have stood had it not have been for the heavy siege guns that battered it for two days. In spite of that pounding and its isolation, however, infantry, supported by light artillery, had to storm and take it in bloody hand-to-hand fighting. Lieutenant Jesse Lee Reno pushed his mountain battery forward until it was almost muzzle-to-muzzle with the Mexican guns.[71] Duncan's battery circled the fortress, came to within four hundred yards of the escape route, and fired on the retreating Mexican troops.[72] With Chapultepec taken, the Mexican capital fell with only a few shots fired by the artillery, along with vigorous pursuit of the fleeing Mexicans by the infantry.

Within the two broad areas defined by the type of shot used, artillery served two other purposes. It was both an arm of preparation and an arm of succor (or aid). As a preparatory force, it was to protect deploying troops, disrupt enemy formations, force the enemy from his positions, and continue firing until its fires were masked. As an aiding or assisting branch, the redlegs were to give impulse to the attack, arrest enemy offensive movements, protect avenues of approach, and if necessary, cover friendly retrograde movements.[73] All of these the American artilleryman did with outstanding success. The campaigns of Zachary Taylor demonstrated that Ringgold's concept of light, highly mobile guns was not only possible, but desirable and needed. Had it not been for the horse or "flying" artillery as it was most often called, Taylor and his army would most probably have been defeated at Palo Alto or Resaca de la Palma and surely would have been at Buena Vista.

Taylor's use of siege artillery was poor. He had only three guns with which to work, and against thick adobe they were ineffective. His attempt to use light guns was even more futile. Scott, on the other hand, showed that with careful preparation and by emplacing his guns where they would be most useful, siege operations could be conducted effectively. Scott used his heavy guns to batter and force the enemy into open areas, where they could be attacked by infantry, dragoons, cavalry, and light artillery.

These campaigns together revealed that in effect the Mexican War was a laboratory for the testing of artillery theory, material, and officers and men. Unlike the infantry, dragoons, and cavalry, artillery units needed professionally trained officers and men. Except for the Missouri Artillery Battalion, all the units were regular army and, except for one battery commander, all other officers were graduates of West Point. One can only speculate what the results would have been had the artillery been composed of volunteers. But the artillerymen, by delivering timely and accurate fire on the enemy, saved the American Army from destruction, and paved the way for victory in the Mexican War.

CHAPTER 9

Soldiering, Suffering, and Dying

By Thomas R. Irey

AMERICAN ARTILLERY AND TACTICS may have been superior and crucial, but the war was won by the blood, labor, and lives of the fighting man on the front lines. By portraying the hardships of the soldier, Thomas Irey has effectively shown that "war is hell." Especially was *this* war hell, for the soldier had to contend with filthy camps, rampant disease, and constant exposure to the elements. In fact, so serious was the problem of sickness and death from non-combatant causes that nearly 11,000 Americans died from disease, while only about 1,500 died as a result of battle wounds.

The blame for such statistics rested on most all parties concerned, for the soldiers and their commanders were not careful about sanitary procedures; officials in Washington took no action to supply needed commodities; and for that matter the United States was not prepared for fighting under a semitropical environment. Amoebic dysentery, diarrhea, yellow fever, and many diseases not identifiable at the time plagued the American soldier. Knowing nothing of the causes for the diseases, men blamed the water – which often as not was the culprit – but they continued eating fruits, vegetables, and other Mexican delicacies carrying contamination which the American soldiers' systems could not tolerate.

Officials in Washington supplied tents that were inadequate for the different types of climate encountered, clothing that was designed for colder temperatures; and those officials made little effort to educate the raw recruits to what they would face. Significantly, the fighting ended in 1848, but many soldiers who had contracted some malady during their days in Mexico continued to die for years afterward. Unfortunately, the United States Army learned little from its experience in Mexico, for this suffering was only a prelude to what lay ahead during the Civil War. Yet, in over-all casualties, the Mexican War remained the most deadly in United States history.

This chapter originally appeared in JOURNAL *of the* WEST in April, 1972.

AN OLD cliché holds that "war is hell," and the American soldier who served his country in the Mexican War found an extra special kind of hell — a hell in the form of filthy camps, disease, and exposure to the elements. Fighting the enemy was the least dangerous task which confronted the soldier during this war. Of a total force of 100,182 soldiers,[1] 1,548[2] were killed in action while 10,790[3] died from disease and exposure. Statistically, the Mexican War was the deadliest war the United States ever fought. The mortality rate from disease in the war was 110 per 1,000 per annum as compared with a Civil War rate of 65; a Spanish-American War rate of 27.79; and a World War I rate of 16.[4] The army dead in World War II represented about three percent of its ranks.[5]

The reasons for the unusually high mortality rate of the soldiers in the Mexican War are many and varied. Some of the reasons rested with the soldiers, some with their commanders, and some with the persons directing the war from Washington, D. C. In 1846 the United States was essentially unprepared to fight a war so far from its major centers of supply. The army was small, slightly over seven thousand men, and with the opening of hostilities there was a desperate need to expand it rapidly.[6] This was accomplished with poorly trained and undisciplined volunteer regiments and the formation of ten new regular army regiments. Medical science was still in the pre-bacteriological era, and the sanitary conditions in the camps were dreadfully inadequate for the general welfare of the troops.[7] It was in this climate of unpreparedness, filfth, and ignorance that the naive young American soldier was sent into the war zone in Mexico.

The American soldier, especially the volunteer, generally arrived at one of the staging areas such as Corpus Christi, Matamoros, or Camargo half-equipped, poorly trained, and improperly clothed.[8] Ignorant of even the more basic rudiments of military discipline and routine, the volunteers quickly transformed the camps into miasmic sink-holes of filth and squalor.[9] Amoebic dysentery, compounded with diarrhea and served with a touch of yellow fever, became the soldier's lot. The more the diseases drained the precious life-giving fluids from the sickened soldier, the more he replenished with contaminated brackish river water. At an unnamed camp at the mouth of the Río Grande, Lew Wallace, of the First Indiana Volunteers, was in a quandary whether the tepid, brackish river water or the steady diet of spoiled salt pork was the culprit;[10] others blamed the sudden change in the weather. Most, however, continued partaking of the succulent samples of Mexican fruit.[11]

The patterns of disease varied little from command to command. The American soldier could find sickness and suffering with equal ease in General Zachary Taylor's camps along the Río Grande, General Winfield Scott's army in the south, or with Colonel Alexander Doniphan's regiment ont he road. Although the specter of death accompanied diarrhea and dysentery into camp most often,[12] commanders could always count on yellow fever, catarrh, small-pox, and cholera to increase the death rate among their troops.

Any examination of the soldier's plight in the Mexican War must, by necessity, begin with Taylor's death camps along the Río Grande. The first such camp of infamous distinction was the site of Corpus Christi, Texas. It was located near the Gulf Coast and the troops during the late spring and summer months enjoyed the soft, cool breezes that frequently enveloped the camp. Petty annoyances such as insects and rattlesnakes often frustrated the leisurely disposition of the troops. Despite the removal of scrub trees to eliminate the covert presence of the snakes, they were, on occasion, found in pairs, resting quietly in a soldier's tent.

The winter months drove the pests out of camp and brought in the blue "northers"[13] which ushered in the cold, wet season and, for the soldiers, untold amounts of suffering. Chilled and wet bodies were the price the soldiers paid for the privilege of sleeping in paper-thin government issue tents. While these tents provided excellent, well-ventilated coverage during the summer months, they were of dubious value during the cold, rainy, wintery nights. It was not uncommon for the soldier to wake and find several inches of water rising in his quarters. Consequently, troops frequently plodded about camp on the freezing mornings in damp and musty clothing.[14]

During the seven-month encampment at Corpus Christi, the number of troops increased from 1,500 to almost 4,000.[15] By late autumn the entire camp took on the atmosphere of a huge medical ward with ten percent of the officers and thirteen percent of the enlisted men bed ridden; while throughout the camp, about one-third of the troops suffered from dysentery and catarrh fever.[16] Corpus Christi, for all its disease and frustrations, proved to be excellent conditioning for preparing the troops to face even greater privations at a later date.

On February 3, 1846, orders reached Taylor to move his troops to the Río Grande. Fifty-three days and 196 miles later, Taylor's force of 3,100 men rested ont he banks opposite Matamoros. Somewhere between eight or nine hundred weak, sick, and demoralized troops were unable to march and were left in Corpus Christi.[17]

Taylor's Matamoros mudhole possessed all the frustrations common to most camps: sand flies, spiders, mosquitoes, steaming heat, and muddy water. Violent thunderstorms frequently leveled acres of tents and left the camp a veritable quagmire.[18] The Congressionally designated "epauleted loafers" and "wasp-wasted vampires" were no longer hanging about in high places, but were generally "wading about low places, halfway up to their knees in mud and water . . . with an absolute fear of being drowned out of their positions."[19] To coincide with the atmosphere of the camp the menu no longer featured the delicious oysters, fish, fowl, venison, beef, and mutton of Corpus Christi, but instead included such standard items as beans, pancakes, and saltpork.

The sticky climate coupled with the prevailing camp boredom generated formidable numbers of discontented and ill-tempered troops. Their attention easily was drawn to the numerous gambling halls, barrooms and brothels that provided the main-street decorum for the City of Matamoros. Before long these pent-up troops began brawling among themselves and pillaging the city. Their relationship with the women shifted from love to rudeness to rape.[20] It was, therefore, without regret, that Taylor received orders to shift his headquarters up-river to Camargo.

Camargo was a horrible place plagued with heat, mud, disease, and death. An estimated 1,500 troops[21] died from various diseases, although not all these deaths can be credited to the conditions at Camargo, as a good number of the death cultures owed their incubation to Matamoros.

It was noted by one writer that "sickness killed so many new recruits in unsanitary camps all the way to Camargo that mocking birds learned from the band how to trill the death march."[22]

Taylor arrived at Camargo at an unfavorable time of the year. During the early days of August, Camargo, walled in by limestone rock, lay sweltering in an envelopment of hot, humid, motionless air. Tents were pitched too near the camp's only supply of water — which also served for potable water and for waste disposal of animal and troop bathing area.[23] The blistering heat and primitive sanitary conditions of the camp created even more disease and death among the sick and feverish troops. The grotesque repetition of sickness and dying, day-in and day-out, prompted young Lieutenant George B. McClellan to lament, "I have seen more suffering since I came out here than I could have imagined to exist. It is really awful. I allude to the sufferings of the volunteers. They literally die like dogs."[24]

Soldiers died elsewhere during the summer of 1846. An unnamed camp at the mouth of the Río Grande served as a funeral home for the First Indiana Volunteers. "I cannot recall another instance of a command so wantonly neglected and so brutally mislocated," wrote Lew Wallace.[25] The drinking water was a colloidal suspension of thirty percent sand; the rest was a half-yellow mud. The troop's diet consisted of beans, pickled pork, flour, and bug-infested biscuits. Dysentery deaths became so numerous that customary military honors had to go unobserved. Bodies were interned in the shifting sand and when the supply of lumber, gunboxes, and cracker barrel staves was exhausted in making coffins, the bodies were then buried in blankets.[26] It was at this camp that Lew Wallace described the appearance of a person stricken with diarrhea:

> His cheeks have the tinge of old gunney-sacks; under the jaws the skin is ween and flabby; his eyes are filmy and sinking; he moves listlessly; the voice answering the sergeant is flat; instead of supporting the gun at order arms, the gun is supporting him.[27]

When the sick could no longer muster the energy to make roll call, they were lumped together with as many as six others into the suffocating enclosure of a nine-by-nine-foot tent.

The history of disease and death among the troops under Taylor's command goes on and on. In Monterrey, Mexico, Taylor appealed to Washington for medical officers — his regimental strength, due to disease, had been reduced to five hundred effectives.[28] Taylor's command, however, was not the only command to experience death, disease, and exposure during the war.

On another front, Scott prepared to make an amphibious invasion near Vera Cruz. After a flawless landing on March 9, 1847, Scott's forces encircled Vera Cruz from the landward side and established a classic set-piece siege. Vera Cruz was occupied by March 29 in accordance with the general's plans to reduce the city before the arrival of the dreaded yellow fever season. With the arrival of late spring, conditions among Scott's troops in Vera Cruz worsened. By mid-April the hospitals were filled to overflowing with troops stricken with diarrhea.[29] On May 25, several fatal cases of yellow fever were reported and, over-all, seventy-seven soldiers died from disease during the month of May.[30]

Scott wisely moved his main force out of Vera Cruz early, but logistics for his campaign into the interior demanded stationing a formidable quartermaster corps in the city. As a preventive measure against yellow fever, the quartermasters were detailed to the wharf area. This measure proved fruitless and hundreds of quartermaster troops and other soldiers died from yellow fever, dysentery, and infected wounds.[31]

Scott had moved his force seventy-four miles north to Jalapa to avoid yellow fever and to plan his march into the interior. The march would have to be made through burning, sandy, desolate, waterless, chapparal-infested areas. Scott, like Taylor, was confronted with Mexico's paradox: "if you come with too few, we will overwhelm you; if you come with too many, you will overwhelm yourself."[32] The troops were without greatcoats and blankets and badly in need of clothing.[33] Wagons were lightened and only included items which Scott deemed indispensable; medical supplies, clothing, salt, ammunition, horseshoes, coffee, and commissary stores.[34] Baggage was cut to a minimum to compensate for transportation deficiencies with each company being alloted three tents for the sick and protection of the weapons. Each man carried full equipment and four-days' personal provisions in his haversack.[35]

According to Scott, "Rigid discipline, exact obedience to orders, is . . . the first and great want of this army, of valor and patriotism there is no deficiency."[36] The general's "wants" were not realized as Brigadier General David E. Twiggs and his force of 2,600 menu straggled out of Jalapa toward the national highway leading to Puebla. This distance could be measured in discarded equipment, arms, and mutilated bodies. Four-fifths of Twiggs' force fell behind, unable to keep pace in the intense heat and encumbering deep sand leading out of town. Many met a horrible fate at the hands of guerrilla bands that waited in the chapparal to interdict soldiers who had become separated from the protection of the main force. Even the knowledge of possible mutilation at the hands of the guerrillas could not spur the badly fatigued from straggling.[37]

The dearth of tents and blankets had an adverse impact on the health of the troops. Exposed to the burning sun in the daytime, the troops discarded what little heavy clothing they wore in hopes of enjoying a few moments of comfort, but, suffered long hours during the night when the temperature would drop to the extent of requiring at least two good blankets as covering.[38] As the force moved into the higher regions of Mexico the more pronounced climate caused fevers and disease. By June 4, Scott informed Secretary of War William L. Marcy that one thousand men were bed-ridden in Vera Cruz, one thousand were reported sick and wounded in Jalapa, while 1,014 of his immediate force were on sick report at Puebla.[89] It was Scott's opinion that the prevailing sickness induced by chills, fever, and diarrhea was brought on by either the contrasting climate, insufficient clothing, or the want of salt meats.[40] By August, Scott's force of 11,000 men stationed in Puebla contained 2,000 sick and incapacitated troops.[41]

In addition to disease, the want of proper food, and exposure to the elements, Scott's men faced other afflictions such as mental anguish incurred upon hearing rumors of the poisoning of the water supply or of plots to assassinate the officers. There were, of course, numerous false alarms of enemy attacks with which the tired and sleepy soldiers had to contend throughout the campaign. To the utter annoyance of the exhausted soldiers, troop movements sometimes commenced as early as three o'clock in the morning, fair weather or foul.[42]

In Mexico City, Scott was plagued with trouble brought about by undisciplined troops' drinking, gambling, and brawling. Scott met these outbursts of dissipation with stern measures ranging from confinement to lashings and, in some instances, hanging.[43] Notwithstanding disciplinary and morale problems, Scott would carry about twenty-five percent[44] of his force continually on the sick rolls and by the end of the campaign was confronted with the fact that he lost a third of his force to disease and exposure.[45]

In yet another theater of war the American soldier could count on one-half rations, hard marches, and no clothes with which to overcome the necessary hardships so prevalent in this war. Colonel Alexander Doniphan and his Missouri Volunteers had been on the road since departing from St. Louis on June 22, 1846. From St. Louis they journeyed westward to Bent's Fort and onward to Santa Fe. From Santa Fe the troops moved temporarily to clear up Navajo Indian trouble, and then snaked their way southward to their primary destination, Chihuahua.

Most of the time Doniphan's men were half-faint with thirst and hunger, subsisting for the most part on half-rations.[46] After months of bivouacking on the rocks and sands of Mexico, their buckskin apparel was torn to tattered shreds. The march extended through barren and rugged territory, sometimes crossing deserts stretching for one hundred miles or more. Marches of fifty miles in one day were not uncommon. Mud holes became the determining factors between life and death and at times Doniphan's "boys" had to fight the Mexicans for the use of those mud holes.[47]

At Chihuahua, Doniphan's force of slightly more than nine hundred defeated a Mexican force of more than four thousand while losing only one man. The occupation of the city became another matter. For Doniphan's volunteers, "Any form of manly dissipation was to their taste, as a rule; and they despised all carefulness, all order, and all restraint."[48] Some thirty percent of the force was soon on sick report and unfit for duty — a significant percentage of the sick had venereal disease.[49] It was under these deteriorating circumstances that Doniphan appealed to General John E. Wool at Saltillo for permission to depart Chihuahua.[50] Doniphan and his regiment completed their duty assignment and returned home to Missouri by way of New Orleans. They had been in the saddle for nearly thirteen months and, in that time, had travelled some 5,500 miles.

In the course of the war 100,000 troops were engaged at one time or another, but not more than 14,000 were assembled for battle at any one time.[51] The total number of troops killed in battle was 1,548. The volunteer force of 73,260 lost 613 killed in action; the new regulars' force of 11,186 suffered 143 battle deaths; while the old established regulars[52] lost 792 of their 15,736-man force. Thus, the mortality rate for the volunteers killed in action was 9.96 per 1,000 per annum as compared with a new regulars' rate of 10.2, and an old establishment regulars' rate of 23.3. The higher rate for the old establishment regulars is attributed to the longer period of time spent in the war zone; an average of twenty-six months, as compared with fifteen months for the new regulars, and an average of ten months for the volunteers.[53]

On the field of battle the volunteer carried superior firearms. Although badly in need of proper clothing, he generally brought with him the latest in new weapons. The variety of weapons carried among the volunteer forces included an impressive array of percussion rifles and Colt six-shooters.[54] The rate of fire for percussion rifles was somewhat slower than the conventional flintlock musket of the regulars but, with the "sugar-loaf bullet,"[55] the rifle's accuracy was increased to five hundred yards as compared with the effective range of one hundred yards for the musket. The regulars' flintlocks were the improved model, 1841-42, some of which had been converted to use the percussion bullet, and a few had been rifled.[56] Lieutenant Ulysses S. Grant was not overly impressed with the performance of the flintlocks, "At a distance of a few hundred yards a man might fire at you all day without your finding it out."[57] The Mexicans, on the other hand, were armed with the hundred-year-old Tower muskets of London which had an effective range of about fifty yards.[58]

Whereas the volunteer had it over his regular counterpart in firearms, the volunteer usually went into battle with clothing much less impressive.[59] Initially, the volunteers arrived in Mexico wearing uniforms of various shades and hues, the style of which had dressed the troops of previous wars. Some states did not furnish their men with uniforms at all. Head covering included the stovepipe with pompoms, tri-color with plumes, flat oil-cloths and sombreros (battle trophies).[60] Each volunteer had been granted, by an act of Congress, a clothing allowance of three and one-half dollars for every month for which he signed.[61]   Most volunteers tried to skimp on the allowance, usually a total of forty-two dollars, and purchased inexpensive and inferior clothing which wore out long before their obligated service expired.[62]   Some resorted to making footgear out of rawhide in order to avoid going into battle barefooted.

Although the purchase of inexpensive clothing caused the soldiers a great amount of suffering, his indifference toward all things military brought him even more misery.   The American soldier, and especially the volunteer, had joined the service for the purpose of enjoying a picnic and a turkey-shoot south of the border.   Once in camp he ignored the seemingly unimportant details of the camp routine, and displayed an absolute abhorrence to military drill and discipline.   The old establishment regulars were noted for their superior cleanliness and military discipline in camp and field, and the death rate from disease bears this out.[63] The mortality rate for the old establishment regulars was 76.8 per 1,000 per annum, as compared with a volunteer rate of 103.2; and 148.8 for the new and inexperienced regulars.[64]   Better personal hygiene and improved sanitary conditions in camp could have prevented many deaths from disease and illness.

In addition to turning the camps into sinkholes, the inexperienced soldier ran afoul of army regulations.   Infractions of military rules were met with harsh punishment; disobedience of orders netted confinement or lashing on the bare back with a leather whip; more serious violations such as rape and murder usually resulted in death by hanging.[65]   From May, 1846, through December, 1847, thirty-two soldiers were executed for various offenses.[66]

As the glamor of war wore off, the enthusiasm among the troops diminished proportionately.   Very few volunteer units were willing to re-enlist once their short period of obligated duty expired.   Moreover, the rigors of war and camplife drove many soldiers to desertion;[67] some of which returned to the United States, others joining the Mexican cause. There were 6,725 American deserters during the war.   The greatest percentage of deserters came from the ranks of the old establishment regulars which had 2,247 desertions, or 14.2 percent.   The new regulars lost 602 from desertions or 5.3 per cent, while 3,867 volunteers deserted for 5.3 percent[68]   Deserters, if captured, were usually hanged, although those who deserted prior to the outbreak of hostilities were lashed on the back fifty times and branded on the cheek bone near the eye with a "D."[69]

Beyond the privations and hardships the American soldier endured during the Mexican War, there were factors beyond his control that played a leading role in contributing to his suffering and dying.   The theater commanders and medical departments must share a good deal of the blame for the unsanitary conditions which prevailed in camp.[70] Moreover, the War Department in Washington compounded the problem by ordering thousands of troops to Taylor's command during inopportune times — and then failed to provide adequate measures with which to supply these troops.

Generally there were too few medical officers to properly administer aid to the sick and wounded,[71] and many of the volunteer regimental doctors were of questionable competence.[72] For the soldier who lay wounded on the field of battle it became a race as to whether a doctor would dress the wound or the flies would blow it. Treatment for wounds ran the gambit from amputation to milk and bread poultice,[73] and medicines included quinine, calomel, laudanum, tincture of Cayenne pepper, spirits of camphor, essence of peppermint, and Hoffman's anodyne.[74] The care of food and water, disposal of waste, and other functions were carried on in a primitive manner or generally ignored.[75]

Logistical support for the major commands was erratic and often found wanting. "The task of beating the enemy is among the least we encounter," wrote Taylor, "The great question of supplies necessarily controls all the operations in a country like this."[76] The general staff had not planned adequately for providing supplies to areas so distant from the major centers of supply.[77] To further complicate matters, the Quartermaster Corps was continually in need of manpower to maintain an army over supply lines ranging up to 275 miles in length. Few of the extra personnel hired, mostly from the ranks of discharged volunteers, would agree to serve more than six months, and even fewer were willing to renew their contracts.[78]

Steamboats were used as much as possible to funnel supplies into Mexico *via* the Río Grande, since major railroads had not been constructed in Mexico or even west of the Mississippi River before the war.[79] Wagon supply trains sent over the plains were often interdicted by Indian raiding parties with great loss of life to the teamsters; and in Southwest Mexico, west of Vera Cruz, guerrillas preyed heavily upon the line of supply supporting Scott's army. The merchant marine fleet which was the major umbilical cord nourishing the American troops in Mexico was often intercepted by "acts of God."[80] Overall, the problems inherent in provisioning the American forces during the war subjected the soldier to additional suffering and privations for want of medicines, food, blankets, and other supplies.

Congressional support for the welfare of the soldier left much to be desired. It was known in Washington that a large amount of suffering was brought on by the want of proper clothing.[81] The various field commands had sufficient supplies on hand to distribute to the volunteers, but lacked the authorization to do so. A week before the war ended, Congress enacted legislation giving field commanders authorization to issue clothing to the volunteer; but the war was over before Congress earmarked funds necessary to implement the legislation.[82]

Although hostilities formally ended in February, 1848, soldiers continued to die from lingering effects of disease long afterward. On June 30, 1849, the Surgeon General of the Army reported that for the year ending, the ratio of deaths to the number of men in the army was an unusually high rate of 1 to 12.46, or 8.02 percent. The high mortality rate of the troops in the peace time army was attributed, in part, to the significant number of fatal dysentery cases which could be traced to exposures of those who served in the Mexican War.[83]

The American soldier endured a great amount of suffering and dying in the Mexican War but, unfortunately, it was only a prelude of what lay ahead in less than fifteen years. The war taught the United States little in regard to sanitation and prevention of disease, and it went into the Civil War as unprepared and ignorant in these matters as it was fifteen years before.[84] This unpreparedness once again exacted a heavy toll in death and suffering. And, although the Civil War diminished the memory of the experiences south of the border, it did not alter the fact that the Mexican War was the deadliest, percentage-wise, in United States history.

CHAPTER 10

Los Diablos Tejanos: The Texas Rangers

By Stephen B. Oates

SUFFERING, DYING, AND FIGHTING was not confined to the battlefield nor was it caused entirely by Mexican troops or disease; men quartered closely and suffering from disagreeable conditions often vented their wrath on whomever happened to be nearby. The behavior of the Georgia Rangers and the Texas Rangers testifies to this. D. E. Livingston-Little, in his "Mutiny During the Mexican War: An Incident on the Río Grande" (JOURNAL *of the* WEST, July, 1970), records the first-hand account of a Private Thomas D. Tennery, Illinois Volunteer Infantry Regiment, who helped put down a riot among Georgia Rangers aboard a steamer on the Río Grande.

Texas Rangers were equally, or more, unruly during the Mexican War. These *Tejanos* hated Mexicans with immeasurable passion. They had waited long for the opportunity to shoot and kill Mexicans legitimately, and nothing or no one was going to stop them — not even Army discipline or General Zachary Taylor. The Texas Rangers were veterans at fighting. Even General Taylor admired their bravery, but he was chagrined at their wild and utterly uncontrollable actions both in battle and in camp. The Rangers raided settlements in Mexico, hanged civilians, and generally wreaked havoc on the Mexican countryside. Taylor tried unsuccessfully to direct the Rangers specifically toward the Mexican Army; once he even threatened to jail the entire regiment if they did not obey his orders, but almost to a man the seven hundred Rangers refused to listen to his pleas and threats. Taylor was vexed, but he knew well that the Rangers were the "eyes and ears" of his army — a valuable adjunct that he could not do without.

Stephen B. Oates, in this chapter from his book VISIONS OF GLORY: *Texans on the Southwestern Frontier*, has shown the more unsavory side of the activities of the Texas Rangers. These men have been venerated and presented to posterity as the symbol of chivalry and bravery for all Texans to admire; yet Oates feels that that part of their nature which caused them to take reprisals on innocent civilians has been overlooked and seldom discussed by historians. Here he clearly shows the Rangers as they were, brave men whose contribution to Texas and the country was considerable, but also as men who plundered and killed indiscriminately under the pretext of revenge for earlier acts of violence committed by Mexicans.

This chapter appeared originally in JOURNAL *of the* WEST in October, 1970, simultaneously with its appearance in the book mentioned above. (See Editors' Note below.)

IN THE SWELTERING TWILIGHT of May 22, 1846, a company of sunburned, grim-faced Texas Rangers, the advance unit of a newly organized Texas Regiment, rode into Fort Brown, the southernmost outpost of Anglo-American civilization in Texas and combat headquarters of General Zachary ("Old Rough and Ready") Taylor, commander of the Army of the Río Grande. The war with Mexico over the annexation of Texas and ultimate control of the American Southwest had begun only nine days before, but Taylor's troops had already won two decisive victories over a demoralized Mexican army and sent it in headlong

EDITORS' NOTE: This article is chapter two in a recent book, VISIONS OF GLORY — *Texans on the Southwestern Frontier*, by Stephen B. Oates (Norman: University of Oklahoma Press: 1970). It is reprinted here by special permission of the copyright owners, the University of Oklahoma Press, Norman, Oklahoma. Reproduction of the work in these pages, in any form, format, medium, or quantity, without permission of the copyright owners, is expressly forbidden.

retreat for Monterrey, some 175 miles southwest of Fort Brown. The possibilities of crushing this army and ending the war in northern Mexico were bright indeed, and Taylor was already moving his veterans across the river to Matamoros when the Rangers reached Fort Brown.

Captain Ben McCulloch, company commander, reported to the general that night while the men themselves made camp and oiled their guns, hoping to see action at once. They were not disappointed. Taylor promptly ordered McCulloch to scout the arid land between Matamoros and Monterrey and find a good route for his army to follow. The next morning, as the Texans crossed into Mexican territory, they broke into their celebrated "Texas Yell." At last — at long last — they could shoot Mexicans legitimately — and shoot to kill.

It was not long before the rest of the Texas Regiment, under the overall command of a convivial, boy-faced colonel named John C. "Jack" Hays, arrived at Matamoros and also started scouting for Taylor's army.[1] The general no doubt expected a great deal from the Hays outfit. The Texas Rangers were veteran Indian fighters, known for their extraordinary courage and endurance. As individual fighters they were virtually incomparable: almost no one could fire a six-shooter with more accuracy; almost no one could move quicker and use a bowie knife with more skill in close-quarter combat. But as soldiers who had to respect rank and order, these Rangers were beyond hope; they soon proved themselves so wild and tempestuous and utterly uncontrollable that even Taylor, as spirited and independent as any man, came to regard them as barbarians, as "licentious vandals."[2] For no sooner had they arrived in Mexico than they began to commit shocking atrocities. They raided villages and pillaged farms; they shot or hanged unarmed Mexican civilians. On one occasion Taylor lost his temper altogether and threatened to jail the lot of them. The occasion was a Fourth of July celebration at Reynosa in which the Texans stole two horse buckets of whiskey to wash down a meal of Mexican pigs and chickens which they had killed "accidentally" while firing salutes to honor the day.[3]

What could Taylor do with such men? He could not put all seven hundred of them in the guardhouse — no matter how much he might like to — because the Rangers would be indispensable as scouts once the army began the advance on Monterrey. As one of their own put it, the Rangers "were not only the eyes and ears of General Taylor's army, but its right and left arms as well."[4] Nevertheless, the general had to do something, for on August 2 he received a report that the Rangers were at it again. While encamped at Matamoros, they attended theaters, jingling spurs on their boots, with rifles in their hands, Colt revolvers in their holsters, and pistols and bowie knives tucked in their belts. They not only frightened the citizenry but also picked fights with regulars in the United States Army and shot at makeshift targets in the middle of town.[5]

"What," Taylor kept asking, "made these men do such things?" "Was it simply inherent in their nature?" "Were they criminals?" "Were they mad?" Or had it something to do with the wild frontier beyond the Río Grande whence they came, that land whose revolution some ten years earlier had finally let to this war which Taylor was committed to win? For Texas in 1846 was indeed a hard, cruel frontier whose soil was thin and dry, whose commerce was slight, whose Indians were belligerent and, if Tonkawas, were man-eaters — a land where pioneers, if they lived at all, lived by their own cunning and granite will. The Rangers themselves came from the fringe areas of frontier Texas, from the thickly- wooded and red-hill districts in the east, from the twisted mesquite country in the west, and the swelering brush regions in the far south. They came from a land whose civilization was divided into little remote pockets of settlers who had gathered together out of a common fear — a fear of coming violence, a fear of the unknown. Such isolated communities had only a trace of civil organization, almost no law, and one over-riding justice: revenge. Yes, vengeance was the moving spirit — a spirit of passion — by which men enforced their rights in frontier Texas. Avenge the horses which renegade Indians had stolen by moonlight; avenge those stout, red-necked women whom Comanche bands had roped and dragged through prickly pear until they were mangled beyond recognition as human; avenge the insults which a neighbor had shouted in moments of cold fury; avenge the friend who had died in the metallic blaze of some stranger's gun; and now, for the Texas Rangers fighting with Taylor, avenge the fathers and brothers, uncles and cousins, whom the Mexicans had slain at the Alamo and Goliad, at Santa Fe and Mier and the Hacienda Salado in the infamous "black bean" episode. Yes, if Taylor was looking for an answer, this was it: this persisting compulsion to avenge atrocities committed upon their people now moved the Texans to commit atrocities themselves — to hang Mexican civilians, to gun down peon farmers in the moving sand south of the river, to fire over the heads of the little brown boys running barefoot through the Matamoros streets.

Somehow, though, Taylor had to discipline them, or President James K. Polk, who did not like the general for political reasons, might reprimand him in public for waging an uncivilized war.[6] The trouble was that the Rangers were beyond discipline, and Taylor knew it. It was impossible to control hard-boiled frontiersmen who liked to drink and swear and who were in Mexico to settle a score and were not to be bothered by rules and regulations in going about it. Except perhaps for Colonel Hays, who was mild-mannered when he was not in battle, their officers had the same attitude: veteran fighters like Ben McCulloch, cold and austere in features, who had hunted bears in Tennessee before coming to Texas, and Samuel Walker, whose hatred for Mexicans was as famous as the six-shooters he carried strapped to his legs. These men had become officers not because they could give orders or click their heels but because they could out-fight anyone in their commands.[7]

Because of their attitude about fighting, Taylor had some misgivings in sending the Rangers 130 miles southwest to scout the area between San Fernando and China when the army, after nearly a month of final battle preparations, at last set out for the Mexican stronghold at Monterrey. On this scout the Rangers lived up to Taylor's positive and negative expectations: they were indeed the eyes and ears of his main column, but they were also "licentious vandals" who committed further outrages. A glaring example was the time they caught a poor wretch trying to steal one of their horses and decided to show the people of that region how Texans administered justice. They tied, gaged, and shot him dead, leaving the corpse in the blowing sand as they mounted and rode on toward Monterrey.[8]

The Rangers overtook Taylor at Marin on September 17, and the combined force then marched through light and darkness to a group of tree-shaded springs known as the Bosque de San Domingo (the Americans called it the Walnut Springs), about two miles northeast of Monterrey. It was here that the Texans' vandalism gave way to something even more annoying: a persistent refusal to follow orders. When McCulloch's Rangers, followed by Taylor himself and his immediate staff, made a reconnaissance the next day, the Texans kept looking at a black fort about half-way between the American camp and the city. Taylor warned them not to try anything, but the Rangers ignored him, let out an ear-splitting yell, and charged the fort without order or organization. "Like boys at play," said a regular who watched them in awe, "those fearless horsemen in a spirit of boastful rivalry, vied each other in approaching the very edge of danger. Riding singly, and rapidly, they swept around the plains under the walls, each one in a wider and more perilous circle than his predecessor. Their proximity occasionally provoked the enemy's fire, but the Mexicans might as well have attempted to bring down skimming swallows as those racing dare-devils."[9]

Taylor, looking on in disbelief, at last called them back, but there was little he could do except order them back to camp. There the general prepared the whole army, 6,230 strong, for attack the next day. For better or worse, the Rangers had precipitated the crucial five-day battle for Monterrey. On Sunday, September 20, 1846, as Taylor's main column struck the northeastern section of the city, General William J. Worth's division, led by the Texans, under Colonel Hays, flanked Monterrey and approached it from the northwest along the Saltillo road.[10] With the Texans still in front, Worth's contingent flung itself against the forts that protected the rear of town; Federation Hill and Fort Salado fell on September 21, then Independence Hill and the Bishop's Palace, which McCulloch's men, shrieking like Comanches, captured almost single-handed.

On the third day of the battle, September 23, a storm broke with rolling thunder and lightning that danced across the tops of the buildings. While the rain fell and fell harder still, Hay's Rangers and light infantry drove into the city proper, shooting at enemy soldiers in windows and on roof tops, tunneling through adobe walls with crowbars and picks, sprinting through narrow streets that the rain had converted into small streams full of debris and corpses. Hand-to-hand fighting in the streets continued through the night and most of the next morning when the Ranger captains received an order from General Worth to withdraw so that Taylor's artillery could shell the city before the main attack began. Outraged, the Texans sent back a note that they had carried the lower part of the city by themselves and that they would not budge. In a few moments the bombardment commenced with the Texans still in the target area, but as if by a miracle none of them were hurt. They soon received another message to hold their positions while the commanding general and the Mexicans had a talk. By nightfall an understanding had been reached, and the Mexicans began to evacuate. Soon after, on October 2, 1846, the Rangers, whose six months' enlistments were over, set out for Texas in pairs and groups; Colonel Hays and his staff were the last to go in mid-October, and regulars who watched them leave praised them for their extraordinary fighting abilities. "Had it not been for their unerring rifles," one volunteer remarked, "there is no doubt we would have been whipped at Monterrey."[11] Others recalled the Texans fiercely "charging on the guns which swept the slippery streets," but Colonel Hays had been heard to admit that the Mexicans "were damn poor shots or not a mother's son of us could have got them."[12]

General Taylor also grudgingly commended them for gallant action, even if they had disobeyed orders, and watched them ride off with unmitigated relief: the prospect of having seven hundred idle Texans in Monterrey now that the fighting was finished was a foreboding thought, even for "Old Rough and Ready."[13]

Taylor, however, had not seen the last of the Texas Rangers. Captain McCulloch and twenty-seven of his most pugnacious Texans returned to Mexico when they heard that Santa Anna himself was leading an army over the desert with a ringing promise to drive the "gringos" from Mexico or perish in the attempt. Taylor received the Texans cordially enough, putting them to work as scouts and couriers. On February 16, with the American army entrenched at Agua Nueva, the general sent the Texans across the desert to scout Santa Anna's position at Encarnación, about thirty-five miles south of Monterrey.[14] Beneath a sliver of moon, the Rangers slipped inside enemy lines and came finally to a low ridge overlooking the Mexican army, encamped on a vast plain. It was a chilling sight: tents and huts as far as the Texans could see and thousands of men and wagons moving about in the flickering shadows of orange watch fires. In a few moments a party of Rangers slid down the ridge and crawled from fire to fire counting bedrolls and cannon and occasionally knifing a careless sentinel; at last they rejoined the others on the ridge, then all the Texans rode under the noses of Mexican pickets and raced back to report. Santa Anna, they concluded, had over twenty thousand men and a far superior field position for the forthcoming battle.[15] Knowing then that he was heavily outnumbered, Taylor ordered a withdrawal from his exposed position at Agua Nueva to an almost impregnable one behind the Angostura Pass near Buena Vista where he could not be flanked. That afternoon, with blare of trumpet and tuck of drum, Santa Anna's legions attacked, but Taylor's army turned back assault after assault and at last forced the Mexicans to withdraw. Had the Rangers not been there to scout for him, Taylor might have engaged the Mexicans at Agua Nueva and gone down to defeat.[16]

As it was, Taylor had won a brilliant victory, a victory that ended the war in northern Mexico and made him popular enough in the public eye to become a serious Presidential possibility. He would have thanked the Texas Rangers for their good work had they not become exasperatingly troublesome. With inactivity, they took to brawling and to committing "extensive depredations and outrages" on Mexican civilians. "The mounted men from Texas," Taylor complained, "have scarcely made one expedition without unwarrantably killing a Mexican," and they had indulged in practically every other "form of crime" as well. When their enlistments ended and they set out for home, the general declared that because of the "constant recurrence of such atrocities," he urgently requested that no more Texans come to help his army.[17]

The Texans, however, were not yet through fighting. Between April and July, 1847, Jack Hays recruited a second regiment of Rangers, many of whom had already seen action with Taylor, and prepared first to serve on the Indian frontier and then, under new orders, to reinforce Taylor, whose rear echelons were under constant harassment from Mexican guerrillas.[18] The officer corps of the second regiment was made up of tough, battle-hungry captains like Alfred Truitt, Isaac Ferguson, Samuel Highsmith, Gabriel M. Armstrong, Jacob Roberts, Alfred Evans, and staff officers like Major Michael Chevaille and Adjutant John S. Ford, a tall, restless frontier doctor who would keep a record of Ranger action throughout 1847 and 1848. Many of the five hundred enlisted men were jobless adventurers and would prove more violent and uncontrollable than those of Hays' first regiment.[19]

In mid-August, 1847, the command rode to Mier, Mexico, where "our entrance caused some excitement among the Mexicans," who nursed "bitter recollections" of the battle of Mier fought there some four years earlier. As the horsemen passed through the streets, one "good looking" señora shouted to them: "I had rather see every relative I have dead, here, before my eyes, than to see the Texians enter Mier unresisted."[20]

The Rangers did not remain there long, however, for orders arrived from the War Department that they were to reinforce General Winfield Scott, who had led an invasionary force into the Valley of Mexico in the spring of 1847.[21] There the Rangers were to have a special assignment, one which would test their fighting prowess and their pugnacity.

In mid-May the Rangers rode down the Río Grande to a place called Ranchita, where they waited for transportation to Vera Cruz. While they waited, they probably learned what Scott had done in the Valley of Mexico. The general's advance divisions, moving swiftly through the valley, had driven into Mexico City on September 13 and gained control of the capital by the next morning. Two days later Santa Anna, renouncing the presidency, had fled into the mountains with 5,000 men and another ringing promise to return and drive the Americans back into the sea. The presidency had then devolved on Manuel de la Peña y Peña who set up an emergency government at Querétaro, some 150 miles northwest of Mexico City. Peña, though a moderate desiring peace, was afraid to sign a treaty because a powerful political faction, opposed to any kind of peace talk, threatened to desert him if he did. Mexican leaders would neither treat nor fight. Many of them promised to prolong the war through endless guerrilla operations.[22]

While Scott and American envoys tried to negotiate with Peña, guerrilla bands stepped up attacks on Scott's long, thin supply line that extended more than 260 tortuous miles from Mexico City to Vera Cruz on the eastern coast. Protecting this supply line from Mexican terrorism was to be the special assignment of the Texas Rangers, who were to proceed to Vera Cruz at once and "disinfest" the valley of every Mexican bandit and irregular they could find. This was the kind of challenge the Texans loved best (both Scott and President Polk, who had conceived the idea of sending the Rangers against Mexican guerrillas, understood the Texans' temperament better than Taylor did), and they vowed that before they were through, the valley would be littered with dead *guerrilleros*.[23]

In the first week of October four companies of Rangers, along with Adjutant Ford, boarded troop transports at Brazos Santiago and prepared to sail down to Vera Cruz and locate a regimental campsite. Colonel Hays and the rest of the Ranger force would join them in Mexico on October 17.[24] On board the transports some of the Rangers started making trouble before they were out of sight of the Texas Coast. One or two of them provoked sailors into fist fights; others — most of whom had never been on a boat in their lives—went exploring like mischievous adolescents. Irate ships' captains demanded that Ranger officers control their men. But the officers were causing their own trouble. Even the Rangers' horses were causing trouble. One of them pitched at an Irish sailor, took the man's ear off as "clean as it could have been done by a pair of shears; then chewed it up, and swallowed it." It was so hilarious, said one Ranger, that the Texans could not help but laugh.[25]

After a few days on the rolling, churning sea, the Rangers had little at all to laugh about. For the rest of the voyage the decks were packed with horsemen leaning desperately over the rails or stumbling about trying to comfort one another. "Landsmen do not enjoy being cooped up on a sea-going craft," Horseman Ford said, speaking for all. "There was rejoicing when our feet touched on land."[26]

The Rangers did not rejoice for long, though. General Robert Patterson, in command of Vera Cruz, ordered them to set up camp at a virtually uninhabitable place called Vergara, some three miles away on the road to Jalapa, along with another regiment of his "Yankee" division — the Ninth Massachusetts Infantry. Apparently the Massachusetts troops had heard about the Texans' propensity to fight their own countrymen if Mexicans were not available: the Ninth Infantry sent over half-a-barrel of whiskey along with a peace offering.[27]

Regardless of how much whiskey the Rangers consumed, it did not mitigate the nasty conditions at Vergara. A hot, dry wind blew constantly, stirring up loose sand and dust. It was amost impossible to cook or eat there or to keep tents up since the sand would not hold the stakes; the wind kept blowing the tents down anyway. To make matters worse, water was scarce, soon there was no tobacco or whiskey, and a rumor was going around that General Patterson did not think the Rangers could fight the *guerrilleros* in the jungles around Vera Cruz and that the Texans might have to remain in Vergara until Patterson was ready to march for Mexico City. The Rangers were, of course, bitterly disappointed. It might be a month before the general was prepared to move, and a month in Vergara was worse than a month in hell. With nothing to do except sit around and take pot shots at things, the men became extremely restless. "We were anxious to sustain the reputation of Texas Rangers and not lie around in idleness," the adjutant said, speaking for all.

At length Captain Truitt, Captain Ferguson, and Adjutant Ford called on General Patterson and asked that he send the Rangers against a Mexican guerrilla contingent allegedly operating out of the hacienda of San Juan, about thirty miles away. Although the general doubted that the scout would accomplish anything, he knew that if the Rangers remained idle much longer they might start their own war in the streets and saloons of Vergara or Vera Cruz. Reluctantly, he permitted them to undertake an expedition.

It was still dark when the Ranger column moved out of camp "at the trot." About mid-morning the horsemen entered a sweltering jungle with parasitic vines that had to be chopped away with bowie knives before they could advance. The Rangers at last reached a waterhole at the edge of a rolling prairie and stopped to rest. Suddenly Adjutant Ford shouted something, then leaped on his horse and galloped away with his pistol blazing. Barely visible on a rise several hundred yards away was a party of guerrillas moving at a killing pace. Mounting on the run, the rest of the Rangers followed the adjutant, shooting recklessly, yelling, spurring their horses faster and faster. On they rode, the guerrillas alternately disappearing and reappearing in the tall grass and ravines, with Ford, not far behind now, trying desperately to draw a bead on the last rider; then came the other Rangers who fired their revolvers and fired again. Suddenly the galloping figure between the two clusters of riders seemed to come apart as the horse stumbled and sent the Ranger flying over its head and into a painful heap on the ground. Captain Truitt, thinking one of the Texans had accidentlly killed Ford, started cursing and whipped his wheezing horse toward the fallen rider. But in a moment the adjutant was up cleaning himself off. Signaling to Truitt that he was all right, he leaped on his horse, which apparently was not hurt, and rejoined the chase.

Over the prairie and through the woods the wild riders raced. At last the guerrillas' horses gave out and they had to take shelter at an abandoned ranch. From its buildings they fired at the yipping Texans, who galloped past at full speed while returning the fire, then rode back and dismounted to fight the Mexicans hand-to-hand.

In a few moments the guerrillas were in complete rout and the skirmishing was over, except for a fist fight two Rangers were having over a dead Mexican's sombrero. When that was settled and all the loot had been fairly divided, the Rangers mounted and set out to find more *guerrilleros*.

A short ride brought them to a fine-looking hacienda where another party of guerrillas was hiding. The Mexicans opened fire, but the Rangers shot several of them dead and chased the rest into the woods where they mysteriously vanished, like Indians. The Texans were disgusted about that, but the rich hacienda made up for the Mexicans they had lost. As they pillaged the place, though, they found some shocking things piled on the marble floor — bloody clothing, forage sacks, and other American articles. Outraged, the Rangers chased the family outside and set the building on fire. Then with their loot they mounted and headed toward Vergara at a fast trot, fearing that a larger enemy force might soon come to overwhelm them. The ride back soon became a race, for "two things are considered uncomfortable by mounted men of pluck," Adjutant Ford mused, "to be in the rear in a charge, or behind in a retreat."[28]

The next day, October 17, Colonel Hays arrived in camp with encouraging news: all the American troops in the Vera Cruz vicinity were finally going into action. Their orders were to proceed to Jalapa and Puebla, dispersing any guerrilla bands they happened upon, and then to

128

join General Scott in Mexico City. On November 2, 1847, with Adjutant Ford and his newly organized spy company leading the way, the Texas Rangers set out for Jalapa, followed by the Ninth Massachusetts Infantry, then by regular cavalry and artillery. Like a long, black snake, the United States column crawled through the Mexican sand and dust; thirsty and tired, still following Ford's spy company, it forded rivers that were treacherous with quicksand and shifting mud, hacked its way through humid jungles of vine and bush, and finally reached Jalapa on a warm, sticky afternoon in early November.[29] Regular troops of General Joe Lane's brigade, stationed in the area, aligned themselves along the road to give the Texans "three cheers" as they rode by. "They are a fine body of men and well mounted, with six-shooting rifles," remarked a Pennsylvania volunteer. All the Pennsylvanians believed that the Rangers were "the very men" for Santa Anna's "rascals," who were reported to be holding the town of Izúcar de. Matamoros, some 100 miles southwest of Jalapa and about twenty-five miles south of Puebla.[30]

At Jalapa the Texans found a company of independent "Texas mounted riflemen." These men had a sad and bitter story to tell. It was about the death of their commander, Samuel H. Walker, a "short slender, spare slouchy man" with fiery red hair and a red beard.[31]

Many of Hays' Rangers had known Walker personally, having fought with him in the Monterrey campaign, and they listened tight-lipped as a man told about his death. The captain and his company had come to Mexico in May, and General Scott had ordered them to stay at Perote to protect American supply convoys from guerrilla attacks. Severals months later General Lane's brigate arrived at Perote on its way to garrison duty at Puebla. Lane and Walker planned a joint operation against a Mexican force at Huamantla, said to be under the command of Santa Anna himself. On October 9, Walker and his Texans led some 1,800 regulars down the quiet, shadowy streets of the town. Suddenly Mexicans opened fire from roof tops, and mounted lancers charged in from side streets. The fighting was long and desperate, but the Americans prevailed, driving the Mexicans away to Izúcar de Matamoros. When the smoke had cleared and the men had regrouped, the Texans found Walker lying in the dust, face down, with bullets in his head and chest. The sight of their captain, dead, caused them to "burst into tears" and swear revenge. During the next month, across the Valley of Mexico, they had fought with bitter hatred and would continue to do so as long as the war lasted. And the Rangers, under Hays, hearing this, were also moved to tears, and they too swore to avenge Walker's death.[32]

For some of them the chance came the next day. Colonel Hays hand-picked 135 of his best fighters and rode on to Puebla. There General Lane joined him with cannon and a detachment of Louisiana dragoons, and the combined columns, moving by night and resting by day, reached Matamoros on November 24. On the plain outside of town there was a brief engagement between the Texans and a regiment of Mexican Lancers, brilliant in their glittering armor and snapping colors. But the Rangers charged them fiercely, and the Lancers, out-fought and out-flanked, soon fled.[33]

On November 25 the other Ranger companies under Ford and Chevaille joined Hays near Puebla, and the next day the entire American column, with the Texans in the lead, resumed the march for Mexico City. A regular officer who was most impressed with the Texans wrote in later years that "they certainly were an odd-looking set of fellows, and it seems to be their aim to dress as outlandishly as possible. Bobtailed coats and long-tailed blues, low and high-crowned hats, some slouched and others Panama, with a sprinkling of black leather caps, constituting their uniforms; and a thorough coating of dust over all, and covering their huge beards gave them a savage appearance. . . . Each man carried a rifle, a pair of . . . Colt's revolvers; a hundred of them could discharge a thousand shots in two minutes, and with what precision the Mexicans alone could tell."[34]

The Mexican could tell all right; any Mexican in Matamoros — any soldier who tried to fight these Texans since the war began — could tell with what precision they killed. The Mexican soldier himself believed they were uncanny marksmen who could pick a man off at full gallop more than 125 yards away, while he had to shoot one of them at least five times to kill him. The Mexican would not, of course, admit that he was an extremely poor shot, that his cartridges contained twice as much powder as was necessary, and that this caused his musket to kick bruisingly, which in turn, spoiled his aim. Nor would he admit that he feared the recoil of his gun so much so that he often closed his eyes and flinched while firing. No, the explanation lay with the Rangers themselves who were supermen, aparently knowing neither fear nor death. But worst of all, the Texans had six-shooters. "The untutored greaser," according to one Ranger, had a "holy awe and superstition . . . in regard for the 'revolver.' They understood the term to mean a turning around and about — a circulator; and were led to believe the ball would revolve in all directions after its victims, run around trees and turn corners, go into houses and climb stairs, and hunt up folks generally."[35] Consequently, Mexican officers had found it next to impossible to keep their men in line when the Rangers, firing their terrible revolvers and crying the "Texas Yell," came flying down on them.

That yell was another thing. It was awful to hear, even more terrifying in sound than the celebrated "Rebel Yell" of the Civil War. The Texas Yell consisted of a series of wildcat screeches followed by a blood-curdling yip-yip. "Such yells," said one Texan, "exploded on the air" and "have been heard distinctly three miles off across the prairie, above the din of musketry and artillery.³⁶

This hideous yell, the revolver with its ubiquitous bullets, the enormous horses, the tall, bearded supermen from beyond the Río Grande who defied Mexican *escopetas* — no wonder villagers along the road to Mexico City bolted their doors when the Texans rode by. And no wonder citizens in Mexico City were nearly frightened to death when, on December 6, Colonel Hays led his Rangers into the heart of the city well ahead of the main column. *"Los Diablos Tejanos! Los Diablos Tejanos!"* cried the Mexicans as they crowded along the streets, like moths drawn to fire, to get a look at the "Texas Devils."³⁷

The Rangers had been in town scarcely an hour when they began making trouble. While they waited on the Grand Plaza to get their camp assignments, a Mexican came along with a basket of candy; a Ranger leaned over from his horse and took a handful but refused to pay. The nervous old man shrieked at him, but the Ranger only laughed, so the Mexican hurled a stone at the Texan's head. Almost instantly there was a resounding roar as a revolver appeared in the Ranger's hand, and the Mexican leaped back as if from a powerful blow, dying before he struck the ground. "There must have been ten thousand people on the Grand Plaza," another Texan recalled. "They were desperately frightened; a stampede occurred. Men ran over each other. Some were knocked into the filthy sewers, all were frantically endeavoring to increase the distance between themselves and *Los Tejanos Sangrientes* — the bloody Texans."³⁸

Los Diablos Tejanos. What made them so vicious? They came to Mexico for revenge, they said, but revenge soon became a pretext for acts which transcend human understanding. One evening two Rangers, with bright red bandannas hanging from their hip pockets, started to enter a theater. A Mexican boy ran up, grabbed one of the bandannas, and ran off. The Ranger yelled at him in Spanish, but the boy kept running. So the Texan drew his revolver and killed him. "The Ranger," Adjutant Ford wrote later, "recovered his handkerchief and went his way as if nothing had happened."³⁹

There was hatred in Mexico City after that, a growing hatred for those *Diablos Tejanos* who brawled in Mexico City's saloons and beat up her men and made violent love to her women. Finally, as the weeks passed and the number of outrages increased, the Mexicans had taken enough. One moonless night a large band of them caught a lone Texan in the street and stabbed him until "his heart was visible, and its pulsations were plainly perceptible." When the Texans saw his slashed body the next day, they cursed and swore to avenge this ugly deed. That night some twenty-five of them walked deliberately into the "cut-throat" section where the slaying had occurred and murdered an estimated fifty to eighty Mexicans, including young toughs called *léperos.*[40]

This was too much for the Mexicans. A number of businessmen called at army headquarters and demanded that General Scott keep the Texas Devils off the streets, and the *léperos* themselves swore they would fight any Americans they encountered. If the Rangers were not restrained, the war was going to start up again in the streets of Mexico City, just when the Americans were about to consummate a peace treaty that would permit them all to go home.

When the Rangers shot several more Mexicans in another "affair," General Scott called Colonel Hays to army headquarters. The general was in an ugly mood. "I hold you responsible," he told Hays, "for the acts of your men. I will not be disgraced, nor shall the army of my country be, by such outrages."

"The Texas Rangers are not in the habit of being insulted without resenting it," Hays replied. The Mexicans had thrown rocks at his men, had murdered one of them in cold blood, had attacked others. In his judgment, they had "done right." And he was "willing to be held responsible for it."[41]

But after the general had dismissed him with a stern warning to keep his men in line, Hays was not so sure. What the Texans really needed was to get out of the capital, away from the saloons, the liquor, the hated Mexicans. They needed a campaign, with full-fledged battles in which they could kill Mexicans legitimately. Only that could satisfy them. Only that could keep them out of trouble.

Hays went back to Scott's headquarters and proposed an expedition against one of the tougest bands of *guerrilleros* in Mexico, that of Padre Caledonio de Jarauta, which was hiding out somewhere in the valley east of Mexico City. Over the months this elusive band (along with others led by Juan El Diablo and General Mariano Parades) had ravaged American trains coming from Vera Cruz, had ambushed cavalry detachments and burned outposts. The Texas Rangers would welcome a chance to prove themselves against the padre's force, Hays declared, and any other guerrillas they could find. Scott was so anxious to get the Texans out of Mexico City that he approved Hay's plan of operations on the spot.

On the early morning of January 10, 1848, the Rangers left their camp on the southern edge of the city, near San Ángel, and rode into the valley with high hopes of obliterating the infamous *guerrilleros* in a Texas-style fight. First, however, the Rangers had to find them, and that in itself was a formidable task.[42]

The *guerrilleros* were clandestine marauders, but it was no secret that they lived freely among the peons and *léperos* in the villages all across the great valley, gorging themselves and dancing in fiestas that sometimes lasted for days. They made the law in the region, and the law was the bullet. They fancied themselves indomitable fighters and dressed in resplendent costumes that kept in awe the pauper youths who idolized them, who lied and stole for them. To the youths they were not men but gods, these *guerrilleros*, in their great sombreros, their velvet jackets so elaborately embroidered by their special señoritas, their skin-tight trousers that were slit open at the sides and fastened by dazzling gold buttons, with tiny silver bells on their boots that jingled as they walked, and huge spurs, and their swords, and the *escopetas* in their hands, and their lassos swung over their shoulders, which they could use with deadly dexterity in close-quarter combat. Yes, they were fighters without equals, they said, and the poor who sheltered them and kept their secrets, the youths who worshipped them and the señoritas who loved them, knew in their hearts that no one, not even the Texas Devils coming down the valley, could ever really defeat them.[43]

Yet the Texans, riding in a two-column front behind Hays, with the Lone Star flag and the Stars and Stripes whipping about in the wind overhead, were coming now with every intention of defeating the *guerrilleros* once and for all. Throughout January, 1848, the Rangers searched the whole valley for Padre Jarauta; they skirmished with his detachments at Otumba and San Juan Teotihuacán, but could never capture the padre himself with his main column, said to be 450 strong. Then, in mid-February, riding with a column of United States dragoons under Joe, "Old Gritter Face," Lane, the Rangers swooped down on a town called Tulancingo where another guerrilla chief was supposed to be hiding. They found no enemy to fight there, but that evening they were given a clue to the whereabouts of the infamous padre: Zacualtipán, they were told, a village about two days' ride from Tulancingo, was Jarauta's secret headquarters. Moments later, the Rangers, followed by Lane's dragoons, mounted in the streets and moved at a gallop into the Mexico night.

The second morning out, they reached the outskirts of Zacualtipán just as the sun was coming up over the mountain peaks. They charged down the streets, taking the *guerrilleros* almost completely by surprise. While the main force under Colonel Hays and General Lane stormed the plaza, a dozen other Rangers leaped from their horses to engage a large body of partially dressed Mexicans who had gathered in an open lot. The Texans fought deftly with revolver and bowie knife in a fast-moving, hand-to-hand fight that lasted about fifteen minutes before the Mexicans broke and fled over the walls and away into the mountains beyond. The Texans, yelling like animals, then ran up the street to the plaza where a heated battle was raging. Americans and Mexicans were wrestling and slashing at one another with long knives, were firing into one anothers' faces and stomachs at point-blank range. The killing finally ended at mid-afternoon, with the *guerrilleros*, following their padre down the valley in headlong flight. Adjutant Ford, who saw the smoking streets littered with corpses, recorded that at least 150 Mexicans "had ceased to feast on *tortillas*" that day.

The Texans were proud of the victory, even if the padre had gotten away. The next morning they led the dragoons back toward Mexico City, convinced that with this victory their service in Mexico had only begun, that on the day they caught the padre again or any other guerrilla chief they would fight a battle Mexico would not forget.

As it turned out, Zacualtipán was the last battle in Mexico for the Texas Rangers. On February 2, 1848, a peace treaty had been signed between Mexico and the United States, and when the Rangers reached the capital, the Americans were beginning to evacuate. The Texans' orders were to ride to Vera Cruz, where transports were waiting to take them home. The order produced a variety of sentiments among the men. "Some felt the full fruition of success had rewarded their labors," a Ranger remembered. Others adopted "the devil-may-care feeling of letting tomorrow take care of itself." But many of the Rangers, believing that they had not achieved a full measure of revenge against Mexico, regarded the armistice as a tragic turn of events and were extremely bitter about having to return home.[44]

On March 18, 1848, the Texas Rangers rode out of Mexico City and headed for Vera Cruz. Some ten days later they reached Jalapa, when they heard news that cheered them considerably: General Santa Anna would pass through Jalapa on his way out of the country into exile. The men became quite excited; they would kill Santa Anna; they would. . . . But Colonel Hays warned them that they could do nothing to Santa Anna now, for the war was over and the fallen emperor was, according to the colonel's reports, traveling under a safe-conduct pass from General Scott himself. Hays made them promise to pitch camp nearby and to stay there, then left them under Adjutant Ford and rode over to an estate some miles away where Santa Anna was expected to take supper; the colonel, Ford was told, wanted to have "a few words" with his old enemy.

Hays had been gone barely an hour when the Rangers became quite uncontrollable. The entire regiment was "in a white heat," Ford recalled; "revenge was the ruling passion of the hour" as the Texans started calling for Santa Anna's head.

Adjutant Ford did not know what to do. Colonel Hays was probably the only man who could dissuade the Rangers from their plan to murder Santa Anna when he passed over the road near their camp. It was not that Ford had had a change of heart about Santa Anna. The adjutant would have liked to get a shot at the Mexican himself, but under the circumstances he had to think of the consequences. For should the Rangers gun down Santa Anna when he was leaving the country under a safe-conduct pass, they would all get into serious trouble. Ford explained this to them; he pleaded and reasoned with them and somehow — he would wonder how for years to come — managed to convince them that if they did kill Santa Anna, they would not only dishonor Texas but all would go to prison. Grudgingly they agreed not to harm him if Ford would at least let them get a look at the general as he passed. To this Ford finally consented.

Grumblng about their missed opportunities and bad luck, the Rangers aligned themselves on each side of the road and waited. Presently, Santa Anna, whose "face blanched a little at the sight of his enemies of long standing," approached in an open carriage, his wife and daughter with him, followed by a Mexican guard of honor brightly dressed in plume and sash. As the carriage passed by, the Texans glared at the Mexican leader with cold hatred, looking as if they wanted more than anything to be turned loose on him or to at least shake their fists at him. Santa Anna seemed to sense their hatred. "He sat erect," a Texan observed; "not a muscle of his face moved; if his final hour had come he seemed resolved to meet it as a soldier should." But the Texans did nothing, nothing at all, and after the carriage had disappeared in the trees, they filed back to camp more bitter now than before.[45]

The next day the Rangers joined Colonel Hays at Jalapa and rode on to Vera Cruz, where on April 29, 1848, all of them except the colonel and Adjutant Ford were mustered out of the service in a sad and solemn ceremony.[46] A few days later they boarded troop transports and sailed north for Texas, no doubt spending the humid days at sea reminiscing about the war and their part in it and how much more they could have done had it lasted longer. According to their officers, according to Texans back home, some already gathering at Port Lavaca to give them a rousing welcome reception, and according to contemporary writers already assiduously at work recording their deeds of derring-do, the Rangers had done all that was humanly possible: they had helped whip a nation given to political coercion and persecution, to all those passions of despotism which so violated their Anglo-American heritage of freedom and the natural rights of man. And they had helped give the United States control of the entire American Southwest, including prosperous California. In the short two years the war lasted, the Texans had "waged hostilities upon a scale they deemed legitimate" and had proven themselves "good citizens and meritorious soldiers."[47]

Yet, what about the many outrages they had perpetrated on the Mexican people? Said Adjutant Ford:

> It was sometimes difficult to restrain these men, whose feelings had been lacerated by domestic bereavements and who were standing face-to-face with the people whose troops had "committed" such "bloody deeds" as massacring Texan prisoners at Goliad and in the ill-starred Santa Fe and Mier expeditions. If the Rangers themselves had indulged in a few

excesses, it was because they were an intensely proud band of fighting men who wanted revenge; even if revenge became a cloak for pillage and murder, the Rangers were still honorable men — "good citizens and meritorious soldiers" — who had a "high grade of patriotism for Texas."[48]

So the Texas Rangers have been presented to posterity. No writer has dared to challenge this traditional image, to take them to task for their vainglory and unpredictable violence. Even the venerable Walter Prescott Webb, whose TEXAS RANGERS has clearly become a classic study, refused to say much about their worst crimes — their propensity to hang and stab civilian men and ransack their homes, to kill boys under the pretext of revenge for a slain comrade, to fight their own countrymen when Mexicans were not available.[49]

The same is true of virtually every other study of these men; they may be scolded occasionally for a minor misdemeanor, such as stealing pigs and whiskey, but their demonic deeds are either entirely ignored or played down or explained away as the inevitable results of militant patriotism. Nobody has dared any other explanation. The Texas Rangers could not have been sadists. *Surely* they were not that. *Surely*, as pioneer volunteers representing a democratic nation, they had killed for something beyond a mere love of violence. *Surely*, as frontiersmen imbued with the republican principles of tolerance and Christian love — for they all, according to Ford, knew the historic meaning of their own revolution and professed to believe in the Bible — *surely*, then, they had been moved to kill civilians by something other than an indigenous racial hatred of Mexicans. *Surely*, unlike the citizen soldiers of revolutionary France, the Texas Rangers had not succumbed to that intoxicating passion of killing just to kill.

It is difficult indeed to consider the possibility that these heroes of the Republic, whose courage and fighting prowess we still revere, regarded war as did the barbarian hordes of Genghis Kahn — that war was one occupation in which man could strip himself of all compassion, all diplomacy, and fight with uninhibited fury, as the violent nature of his soul dictated.

CHAPTER 11

Governor Armijo's Moment of Truth

By Daniel Tyler

D ECISIVE MILITARY ACTION during the Mexican War was not confined to present-day Mexico, but occurred also in the northern Mexican possessions. In New Mexico and California considerable action characterized the American conquest of the new territory. Much of this action was not a result of armed hostilities, but rather of decisive troop movements at opportune times and diplomatic parlaying to avoid needless casualties. New Mexico fell to the "gringo" invaders without a shot, although armed conflict did break out later between Mexican patriots in the area and the American Army of the West. Daniel Tyler investigated the surrender of New Mexico in an attempt to understand why the Mexicans gave up so easily. Tyler indicates that the answers to Governor Manuel Armijo's capitulation have been well hidden in Mexican records, and that rather than scrutinize these records carefully to find the real causes of surrender most historians, both American and Mexican, have chosen to denigrate Armijo for his actions.

In truth, Armijo acted to secure the support of citizens of New Mexico, and even warned them of the approach of the Americans. He made preparations to fend off the American attack and agreed to lead the troops in battle. However, after talking with James Maggoffin, Armijo decided to avoid a struggle and leave the area. Soon thereafter he arrived in Mexico with a large amount of trade goods, and therefore it has been suggested that the Americans bought his surrender. Although this cannot be proved, there is some evidence that a bribe factored in the retreat. Nevertheless, the fact was that Armijo knew there was no chance of ultimately defeating the Americans because the Mexican Government was in a state of chaos. It may be that history has censured him too severely for a course of action that was unavoidable.

This chapter originally appeared in JOURNAL *of the* WEST in April, 1972.

E VERY STUDENT OF THE MEXICAN WAR knows that General Stephen Watts Kearny occupied Santa Fe in the summer of 1846 without firing a shot. It is also common knowledge that New Mexico's Governor Manuel Armijo dispersed his forces, retired from the battlefield, and enabled Kearny to accomplish the bloodless conquest.

A host of questions have been raised by Armijo's actions. Did he feel that New Mexicans were less capable of defending their homeland in 1846 than in 1841 when they had won a day of glory against the hated Tejanos? Did the governor make any real effort to arouse his countrymen, or did he assume that the Department was too weak to unite against a disciplined army? Did Armijo take a bribe? Was his patriotism purchased by the American trader James W. Magoffin, who arrived in Santa Fe one week before Kearny's forces? And is it fair, therefore, to conclude that Armijo was both coward and traitor, that he deserves the villification heaped upon him by Anglo and Mexican historians, and that he lived only by a code of opportunism singularly directed at promoting his own interests?

Answers must be found in the Mexican records. Here there is evidence of the governor's many quandaries: Indian hostilities, bankruptcy, internal dissension, lack of support from Mexico City, and numberless deficiencies in New Mexico's military capability. Here, too, can be found a relatively complete record of Armijo's efforts to arouse the citizenry. At some point he lost the will to resist. Convinced that his people could not defeat Kearny's forces, he decided to retreat. Publicly he re-iterated his willingness to lead in battle, but he made careful arrange-ments to leave the Department at the most opportune time. Why he risked his reputation instead of his life, and what his countrymen thought of him for making this choice are the central questions to which this essay responds.

Ute and Navajo hostilities were incessant in 1846. As described by Donaciano Vigil, one of the Department's leading citizens, Indian un-rest was a result of the increasing number of foreigners who settled within the limits of New Mexico.[1] These interlopers sold firearms to the Indians, depleted the buffalo herds, and forced the ubiquitous na-tives to raid Mexican ranchos. Lacking horses and weapons, frontier residents were essentially defenseless. The presidial garrison in Santa Fe was occupied in numerous administrative duties. So long as the rest of the nation was politically unsettled, no military assistance could be expected from the central government. Though Vigil expressed confi-dence that Armijo would do all in his power to prevent further Indian pillaging, he was afraid that without a great increase in military sup-plies, New Mexico would remain in its present decadent condition.

Vigil's estimate of the situation was hardly overdrawn. Reports from all three districts in the Department pointed to the intensification of Indian attacks in the spring of 1846. No one felt safe; but it was il-legal to leave the frontier without risking the loss of granted lands.[2]

Armijo relied on the militia to repel Indian attacks, but when their efforts proved deficient he requested permission from the War Ministry to lead a campaign against the pesky Utes. Approval for this mission was received in July, but by that time Armijo knew that Kearny's army had left Missouri.[3] Rumors of enemy movements were so confused with those of Indian and militia forces that the governor suspended all op-erations against the Utes and suggested that district prefects sue for peace.[4] Armijo also warned his prefects not to expect help against the Navajo. But with increasing evidence that his people were more con-cerned about the Indians than the Americanos, he designed a new militia system in which the people could respond more rapidly to Na-vajo attacks.[5]

There were Apache problems too, particularly in the lower Río Grande Valley; but even if Armijo had troops available to protect all frontier settlers, he lacked the funds to pay them. In January Com-andante Principal Juan Andrés Archuleta reported that his presidial regulars had suffered too long without pay. Armijo questioned the De-partment treasurer, who replied that demands on the national treasury so far exceeded the availability of money that even he had not been paid a salary for three years.[6] By April, when Armijo had been named commanding general of New Mexico forces, he informed the War Ministry that his soldiers were in a desperate condition owing to the miserable state of affairs in the national treasury.[7] This was no exaggeration. Extant financial statements for civilian and military agencies in the spring of 1846 reveal little more than funds for petty cash. Armijo needed more troops, but his realistic appraisal of the Department's financial plight led him to recommend to the central government that if auxiliaries were going to be sent, they would have to come with their own funds and supplies.[8]

Armijo considered every money-raising tactic. He appealed to New Mexico's vicar for three hundred pesos from the Pious Fund; he asked the prefects to make contributions from their municipal treasuries; and he begged the Assembly to consider the consequences of not paying men who soon would be asked to defend their homeland.[9] But the appeals failed. In previous years leading citizens had been called on too often to contribute to New Mexico's treasury. By the spring of 1846, investment in the government appeared even more unwise.[10] Armijo could understand this. In 1845 he had refused to pay an assessment of one thousand pesos. Now, a year later, he declared himself bankrupt. Since rumors abounded that the annual caravan from Missouri was delayed, no one wanted to make loans against the promise of tax revenue that might never be collected. Armijo could only appeal to New Mexican national pride, stressing his reliance on the pecuniary resources of each person to overwhelm the invading Americans.[11]

But the patriotic spirit was muted by a strong undercurrent of dissension. Frontiersmen were angry at Armijo for not providing protection against the Indians. Government officials were in arrears in their salaries. Influential merchants were suspected of profiting in the Santa Fe Trade, while the majority of citizens lived a life of grinding poverty. From Taos, Armijo encountered criticism from the powerful priest, José Antonio Martinez. The governor was faulted for his business dealings with Charles Bent, whose interests were represented by the self-righteous Manuel Alvarez, unrecognized American consul and commercial agent in Santa Fe. Alvarez defended the rights of all Americans in New Mexico, directing a stream of protests at the governor in a way which implied criticism of every aspect of Mexican administration. Armijo's patience was worn thin by the summer of 1846.[12]

Declining morale was particularly noticeable among presidial soldiers, some of whom were deserting their posts. Of the fifty-eight men attached to the presidial company of Santa Fe, only twenty-five were available for immediate action, the others being scattered across the frontier or assigned to administrative jobs. For the troops stationed on the frontier, records reveal a shocking shortage of weapons and horses. Without pay and supplies, regular and militia soldiers bickered with each other and speculated more in local commerce than on the approach of enemy forces.[13]

Armijo might have abdicated his post on this evidence of internal strife, but he felt an allegiance to the new President Mariano Paredes y Arrillaga, whose successful revolution against José Joaquín Herrera in December of 1845, now needed support from Mexico's leading civil and military officials. Armijo was flattered by the personal attention he received from Paredes, and he worked hard to secure the allegiance of all local authorities in New Mexico.[14]

By March it was plain that Armijo's efforts were recognized. The Fifth Division in Chihuahua was abolished after refusing to declare in favor of the new President. In consequence, New Mexico was no longer dependent on Chihuahua for approval of military decisions, and Armijo was given full control of his Department by being appointed commanding general.[15] Now he had a freer hand to prepare the necessary defenses.

On April 3 Armijo proclaimed that each district would field two companies of militia, all of which were to report to him directly. No citizens between the ages of eighteen and fifty were exempted from service, and all soldiers were to receive a salary and military privileges normally accorded the regular troops.[16] Armijo worked hard at his new responsibility but soon complained to the Minister of War that as both governor and commanding general he was losing sleep because of the excessive work load.[17]

In May Armijo asked for and received permission to leave for Albuquerque in order to bring his family to Santa Fe. By June 2, the Armijo's were installed in the governor's palace.[18] Immediately, by proclamations and circulars, the governor alerted New Mexicans to the danger of imminent invasion. Reminding them of their success against the Texans in 1841, and promising to lead them personally to another victory, he made clear the American intention of occupying the left bank of the Río Grande.[19] In succeeding weeks Armijo organized reconnaissance parties to patrol the frontier and ordered that no one would be allowed to leave the Department without a passport he had personally signed.[20] Basic military preparations were completed by early August — about the time that Armijo decided to abandon both his family and the Department he governed.

Though war between the United States and Mexico was declared on May 13, 1846, it is doubtful that the governor heard anything but rumors until June. Even then he was not sure whether they would be invaded by "Texans or Americans," but he urged those on the eastern frontier to remain alert.[21] During July Armijo entertained a variety of rumors about the size and strength of Kearny's Army. Everything he heard convinced him that Kearny had no less than 2,500 troops, well-supplied and well-mounted, who brought with them twenty-four pieces of heavy artillery.[22]

He was by no means alone in his trepidations. At a meeting called in Santa Fe in early August, a majority of persons present expressed a desire to surrender. But a small clique favored armed resistance. Armijo had no choice but to go through the motions of leading his countrymen. His lack of enthusiasm alarmed some of the more bellicose regulars, who suggested he resign his command; but Armijo refused.[23]

Dejected by this ill-considered resolution to fight, Armijo worried about the careful scheme he had concocted for departing the territory honorably. Since early in July, when it was evident that the American army was advancing, Armijo had made known his desire to welcome the desperately needed Missouri caravan while holding the army at Las Vegas.[24] The governor's motives were unquestionably personal and pecuniary. Among the traders expected in the 1846 caravan was his partner in business, Albert Speyer. Armijo was greatly relieved when Speyer's wagons arrived ahead of Kearny's army, and when the import duties were paid, a *guía* was made out enabling Speyer to travel to Chihuahua and beyond with 15,000 pesos worth of trade goods.[25] By the end of July, and certainly no later than August 3, Armijo had decided to abandon New Mexico in favor of his business interests. By then he had evidence to support his suspicions that a military victory against the Americans would be impossible. On August 3, therefore, he carefully directed a letter to "Don Manuel Armijo y Mestas" authorizing himself to lead the annual caravan to Chihuahua.[26] On the following day Armijo drew up a power of attorney authorizing a trusted friend to settle his private affairs in the future.[27] Because of these plans, Armijo was noticeably upset by the citizens' decision of August 7 to stand and fight. As a soldier of more than twenty-five years, he was reluctant to abandon the men he had been chosen to lead. Fortunately, James Magoffin and Philip St. George Cooke arrived as Kearny's advance emissaries to help Armijo compromise his military honor.

Magoffin arrived in Santa Fe with Cooke and twelve dragoons on August 12. He was greeted warmly by the governor, and after delivering a letter from Kearny, Magoffin explained that the only object of the United States Government was to take possession of that part of New Mexico which the state of Texas recognized as its western boundary — the left bank of the Río Grande. Armijo's second in command agreed not to resist the Americans, but after further private talks with Magoffin, Armijo replied to Kearny indicating his intention to oppose the American advance with six thousand troops.[28]

It is now abundantly clear that Armijo was bluffing. Circumstantial evidence suggests that he was bribed. An El Paso laborer returning home from Santa Fe, testified that before he left New Mexico he heard Donaciano Vigil state publicly that he had proof of Armijo's purchase of 24,000 pesos worth of trade goods. Vigil further charged that this merchandise was being carried south by Albert Speyer and that Armijo was in possession of five hundred ounces of gold which Captain Cooke had brought with him to Santa Fe.[29] If the laborer's report is accurate, and there is every reason to think that it is, Vigil had turned on his friend.[30] But sufficient evidence is still lacking to prove unequivocally that the governor accepted a bribe from the Americans. It can be argued that he needed the incentive to overcome his military obligation and that Magoffin's later claim to the United States Government for $50,000 was based on expenditures made in Santa Fe in 1846.[31] But there is no positive proof of deliberate collusion.

Whatever the truth, Armijo gave every appearance that he was finalizing defense preparations in the five days following Magoffin's visit. Militiamen, presidial troops, and a squadron from Vera Cruz were assembled at a point fifteen miles east of Santa Fe in Apache Canyon. On August 17, the day before Kearny arrived, Armijo rode out to join his troops, emptying the prisons on the way. After ordering the militia to disperse, he started south with two hundred regulars, hoping to catch the trade caravan he had assigned himself to lead.[32] What became of him?

The records are sketchy, but they reveal a course of march which brought Armijo almost directly to the city of Chihuahua. Here he wrote a report to the Minister of Foreign Relations explaining his actions in New Mexico.[33] He did not stay long in Chihuahua. At some point he joined Speyer and continued south to San Juan de los Lagos, where the partners sold their trade goods.[34] By the end of 1846, Armijo was in Mexico City . He remained in the capital until the spring of 1847, during which time his enemies in Chihuahua charged him with treason and cowardice. The accusations made Armijo angry, and he requested permission to leave the city while the Supreme Court deliberated.[35] The request was granted, but Armijo's wanderings for the next year are obscure. He was in and out of Chihuahua, but the relentless accusations of General Angel Trias finally succeeded in having Armijo demoted. Trias also kept alive the treason charges by sending a barrage of reports to the War Ministry.[36] When Armijo's reputation seemed all but ruined, Trias finally clamped him behind bars. But both the Supreme Court and Congress failed to act on the available evidence, and Armijo was free by January, 1850.[37] He returned to New Mexico.

By then Armijo was *persona non gratis* in his own country. Testimony of travelers seemed to confirm the suspicions of most Mexicans that the governor had acted out of cowardice when he retreated from

New Mexico. One Albuquerquean went so far as to accuse Armijo of being not only a coward but a real Mexican bastard, totally lacking in virtue, common sense, and patriotism.[38] From Santa Fe to Chihuahua, Armijo had made enemies who reveled in the chance to strike back at their former oppressor.

On the other hand, some were more understanding. Captain D. Rafael Chacón, a young soldier at the time of the Kearny invasion, spoke of the chaotic conditions that prevailed at Apache Canyon. He concluded that Armijo had no other choice but to flee, since the army was without leaders, without commissary supplies, and without military training.[39] Armijo was also praised immediately after his death in 1854 by the territorial legislature of New Mexico, which resolved that the late governor had been one of the territory's great benefactors.[40] Obviously, Armijo had made as many friends as enemies during his long career of public service. One Mexican historian was so impressed by Armijo's exploits in 1841 against the Texans, that he dedicated a volume of history on the Mexican War to Armijo.[41] For these and other acts of bravery Armijo was awarded the Mexican National Cross. If the Mexican Congress failed to find him guilty of treason in 1846, perhaps his past record of achievements balanced favorably against the accusations of personal enemies.[42]

Reflecting on his own behavior, Armijo never failed to remind his own critics that one mistake should not be allowed to destroy his career, particularly when it was not in his power to deter the aggression of the United States. He refused to be a dead hero. Bravery and patriotism to him were always measured against the probability of success. He departed Santa Fe and later El Paso and Chihuahua, because he did not want to be governed by the conqueror. For this he was considered a coward and a traitor. Yet it is evident in his official and unofficial correspondence that Armijo was deeply attached to the Mexican Republic. Had he felt otherwise, there would have been no reason to make the trip from New Mexico to Chihuahua in 1849 to face the accusations of his detractors. Before leaving he wrote Manuel Alvarez in Santa Fe saying he was returning to Mexico. He hoped that he might be considered a Mexican, who, having been a coward at one time, could at least show his gratitude to the fatherland.[43]

Armijo was no paragon of bravery, virtue, or honesty. But he never pretended to be so noble.[44] His instinct for self-preservation was strong and uncompromising, and when the scenario called for retreat, he moved with celerity. He recognized the unfavorable odds at Santa Fe in 1846, and he retired. If he took some American coin with him, so be it. Undoubtedly he would have withdrawn anyway. Having done everything possible to rally his meager force, the only feasible course of action was to follow his business interests south. One can only wonder if he deserves the censure which history has heaped upon him.

CHAPTER 12

The Pacific Squadron off California

By Oakah L. Jones, Jr.

WHILE GOVERNOR ARMIJO in New Mexico was surrendering to the Army of the West, the United States Navy was not inactive. In fact, the Navy was a critical factor in the conquest of California. Unfortunately, the role of the Navy has been largely overlooked by historians who have concentrated on the better-known events and men of the era. Oakah L. Jones, Jr., has carefully scrutinized numerous documents pertaining to naval action, and here presents an analysis of the United States Pacific Squadron and its role in the conquest of California. The United Sttaes Navy did not have to contend with a large Mexican fleet, and therefore quickly closed all California ports, leaving the army to deal only with those forces already in the area.

Commodore John D. Sloat, commander of the Pacific Squadron during the first few weeks of the war, did face a potential British threat, for there were reports of British warships nearby. Nevertheless, Sloat and his men systematically sealed off the coastal towns and also delivered supplies to Americans fighting in the area. Commodore Robert F. Stockton, who took command in July, was more aggressive than his predecessor — and perhaps more decisive in his actions.

The Pacific Squadron did make possible the American conquest of the Pacific Coast. Especially significant was the part played by the Navy in supplying John C. Frémont and his forces. In fact, without naval help all along the coast many important harbors could not have been held continually after July of 1846. Likewise the squadron must be credited with playing a critical role in the fulfillment of the American dream to occupy the country from coast to coast.

This chapter originally appeared in JOURNAL *of the* WEST in April, 1966.

THE HISTORY OF THE UNITED STATES during the nineteenth century records many stirring naval battles which have been studied and analyzed in detail. These engagements have become an integral part of the nation's history from the wars against the Barbary Pirates to the Spanish-American War. Yet, a very unusual episode in the history of the naval service pertains to the conquest of California during the war with Mexico, and this has received comparatively little attention. Although the Navy played a prominent role in the seizure of California from the Republic of Mexico, its importance has been largely ignored in favor of concentrating upon the more colorful figures of the era, such as John Charles Frémont and Stephen Watts Kearny. Strangely enough, the conquest of California by the United States could not have been accomplished when it was had not these naval forces been present. Of special note is the fact that these naval contingents were largely successful because of their operations on land rather than at sea.

Since there was virtually no naval opposition from the small Mexican Navy, the United States Pacific Squadron was able to concentrate its manpower in a unique land campaign against the disorganized and poorly-supplied enemy forces in the province of California.

Marines and sailors formed the nucleus of the makeshift army of the United States in that region. Together with the California Battalion, led by Major John C. Frémont, and the Army of the West, commanded by Brigadier General Stephen Watts Kearny, this array succeeded in occupying California after the Navy had closed all of its seaports.

The support furnished by naval vessels enabled land troops to conduct their campaigns, and the mobility of sea transportation allowed United States units to be moved rapidly to strategic locations to oppose Mexican forces wherever they might be located. While the Mexican troops and loyal native Californians were forced to move slowly and over great distances, causing exhaustion, desertion, and poor utilization of limited manpower, the naval vessels enabled United States contingents to move freely without fear of interception. This mobility factor, and the supplies in men and materiel which could be provided by naval vessels were important in determining the ultimate success achieved by United States forces in California.

During the decade of the 1840s the government of the United States had become increasingly aware of the importance of the West Coast of the North American Continent, particularly in the necessity of possessing the harbors at San Francisco and San Diego.[1] Realizing that war with Mexico was a distinct possibility, President James K. Polk and Secretary of the Navy George Bancroft decided to issue tentative instructions to naval forces in the Pacific. Secretary Bancroft sent orders on June 24, 1845, to Commodore John D. Sloat of the Pacific Squadron, presently anchored at Mazatlán, Mexico. If Mexico should declare war, Commodore Sloat was to strike vigorously along the West Coast with his Pacific Squadron, and "at once possess . . . the port of San Francisco, and blockade or occupy such ports as . . . [his] force might permit."[2] He was further instructed to be careful to preserve "the most friendly relations with the inhabitants" and to "encourage them to adopt a course of neutrality," if possible.[3]

Nothing significant occurred for almost a year, and Commodore Sloat had no need to take action on the instructions he had received. Meanwhile, the United States forces on the West Coast were augmented by the arrival of a sixty-man topographical and military expedition under Captain John C. Frémont. He arrived in California in early 1845, antagonized Mexican officials by menacing the northern settlements, and finally withdrew to the vicinity of Klamath Lake in Southern Oregon to await developments. Thomas Oliver Larkin, U. S. Consul at Monterey, received instructions to act as a confidential agent of the United States and to promote the establishment of an independent republic in California. These orders were transmitted by President Polk's personal messenger, Lieutenant Archibald H. Gillespie, a Marine Corps officer who also had been ordered to recall Frémont to Sutter's Fort and to aid American citizens in the event of war with Mexico.

Meanwhile, Commodore Sloat remained in the vicinity of Mazatlán with the entire Pacific Squadron except for the sloop *Portsmouth*, which he sent to Monterey at the request of Consul Larkin. By 1846 this fleet consisted of the frigates *Savannah*, *Constitution*, and *Congress*, each of forty-four guns, the sloops *Warren*, *Portsmouth*, *Cyane*, and *Levant*, each of twenty guns, and the transports *Relief* and *Erie*.[4] This unusually large force was maintained in the Pacific in view of the possibility of a war with Great Britain over the Oregon country. The British were also prepared for hostilities on the West Coast, since a squadron larger than that of the United States, commanded by Admiral George F. Seymour,[5] remained in the Pacific ports of Mexico. But, the British fleet ultimately withdrew from the scene since it had no instructions to force hostilities in the event that the United States and Mexico should go to war.

Sloat was awaiting either a declaration of war or the commencement of operations in the Gulf of Mexico before moving his fleet northward. The commodore was then sixty-six years old, in failing health and had already asked to be relieved of his command.[6] Sloat displayed a desire to avoid responsibility and possible censure by not taking any definite action toward the seizure of California ports in spite of the fact that he was constantly being informed of the impending conflict and even actual engagements after May, 1846. He was particularly hesitant to act for fear that haste in seizing California would expose him to the same censure that had been directed against his predecessor, Commodore Thomas ap Catesby Jones, who had mistakenly seized Monterey in 1842.

On May 17, Commodore Sloat received news of the outbreak of hostilities in Northern Mexico and on the Gulf of Mexico, but still he had not been advised of a formal declaration of war. The Secretary of the Navy sent him instructions two days earlier to execute his previous orders. San Francisco, Monterey, Mazatlán, and Guaymas were to be taken immediately, and blockades must be established where there were insufficient forces to possess the territory effectively. On June 8 these instructions were repeated, but Commodore Sloat did not receive any of these orders until mid-July, when most of the activity had subsided.[7] Even though Sloat had determined to act when he heard news of naval activity in the Gulf of Mexico, he did not proceed immediately to California. Instead he forwarded a letter to Larkin, announcing his intent to "visit" Monterey right away. This letter was sent on the sloop *Cyane*,[8] but Sloat remained in Mazatlán until June 7, when he received news of the blockade of Vera Cruz.[9]

The Pacific Squadron reached Monterey, the former capital of the

146

province, on July 2, but its commander still delayed taking decisive action. Commodore Sloat learned that the *Portsmouth* was now at San Francisco, and he received information about the outbreak of hostilities in the Bear Flag Revolt at Sonoma the previous month. Some of his men were allowed to go ashore the next day, but on July 4, 1846, all were retained on board for fear of causing a disturbance in the quiet Mexican town.[10] Dispatches arrived from the *Portsmouth's* launch July 5, and the next day, Commodore Sloat, urged by Larkin, determined to take possession of Monterey. He drew up a proclamation, formed his orders for the landing forces, and sent the *Portsmouth's* launch back to San Francisco immediately with copies of the papers he intended to promulgate on the following day.[11]

At seven o'clock on the morning of July 7, Commodore Sloat sent Captain William Mervine of the *Cyane* ashore with three other officers. They went to the house of Don Mariano Silva, the military coman-dante of the town, and demanded the surrender of Monterey. Silva explained that he had no orders to give up the property and flag of the town in the absence of the military comandante of Northern California, General José de Castro.[12] There were no effective military forces in the town as the Mexican army was concentrated in two locations. The first, under General Castro, was near San Jose, and the second was near Los Angeles, the present capital of the province, under the general command of the Mexican governor, Pío Pico. Prior to the arrival of the American forces a virtual state of civil war existed in the Mexican province between the northern and southern departments, but the presence of a foreign armed force had caused temporary and uncertain unification.

Two hours after Silva's apparent refusal to surrender the port of Monterey, Commodore Sloat dispatched a force of 256 seamen and marines from his naval vessels. This contingent was commanded by Captain Mervine and Commander Hugh N. Page. Sloat's orders were very detailed. His men were to maintain strict discipline while ashore, weapons could not be fired without the express orders of the officer commanding the party, boats must be maintained in readiness offshore should evacuation become necessary, the men would remain in ranks, they were not to insult any of the town's inhabitants, particularly the women, and plundering was strictly forbidden.[13] The landing force was organized on the beach and marched to the customs house where Commodore Sloat's proclamation was read to the Californians. This document stated, in part, that

> ... henceforth California will be a possession of the United States, and its peaceful inhabitants will enjoy the same rights and privileges they now enjoy, together with the privilege of choosing their own magistrates and other officers for the administration of justice among themselves, and

the same protection would be extended to them as to any other states in the union.[14]

After reading and posting the proclamation, Captain Mervine decided to hoist the United States flag as a formal act of possession, but it was first necessary, according to established custom, to lower the colors of the surrendering nation. Since there had been no Mexican ensign on the flagpole for more than two months, a search of the town was conducted to find a suitable one.[15] After raising the newly-found banner to the top of the pole, it was immediately lowered, and the United States flag was raised and saluted by a twenty-one gun cannonade from the ships in the harbor. A courier was sent to General Castro, demanding the surrender of his forces and munitions.[16] The occupying "army" was then quartered in the customs house which had been refitted to accommodate one hundred men. The entire occupation of Monterey was conducted in an orderly manner, without military or civilian opposition, and on July 8 the populace witnessed a colorful parade of the conquering forces, including a band. This peaceful demonstration was greeted with apparent enthusiasm by the native Californians.[17]

Meanwhile, Captain John B. Montgomery, in command of the sloop *Portsmouth*, had arrived in San Francisco Bay on June 1, 1846. Enroute from Mazatlán he had stopped for nine days at Monterey, where the Californians displayed their friendship with a gala picnic the day before the ship sailed.[18] Montgomery anchored near the little pueblo of Yerba Buena,[19] and proceeded to watch developments all around the area while awaiting further instructions from Commodore Sloat. He remained there, isolated from all official contact, while the surrounding countryside was ablaze with activity.

While Montgomery rode at anchor in San Francisco Bay, Captain John C. Frémont marched from Sutter's Fort, the Bear Flag Revolt occurred at Sonoma, General Castro marshalled his forces at the southern extremity of the bay, and Lieutenant Gillespie arrived with his message for Frémont. Since Gillespie was an authorized government agent, Montgomery furnished him with supplies and one of the ship's launches to take him to Sutter's Landing on June 12 in pursuit of Frémont.[20]

Montgomery was personally delighted with the capture of Sonoma by the small rebel force under William B. Ide on June 15,[21] but he declined to furnish the supplies requested by Ide for a further campaign north of the bay. Montgomery maintained that he was in San Francisco Bay as a "representative of a government at peace . . . with Mexico and her province of California," and that he had "no right or authority to furnish munitions of war, or in any manner to take sides with any political party, or even indirectly to identify . . . [himself], or his official name with any popular movement . . . of the country. . . ."[22] In reality Montgomery was under Sloat's orders to maintain neutrality awaiting further developments. Still, he sent Frémont carbines, cutlasses, two pistols, powder balls and caps on June 28.[23]

Still uncertain as to the official relations between his government and that of Mexico, Captain Montgomery wrote to Consul Larkin on July 2:

> Were I enlightened respecting the future designs of our government or concerning the actual condition of affairs with Mexico; I could probably do much. . . . My neutral position, while all is stirring and exciting about me, renders us quiet spectators of passing events.[24]

This letter was taken to Monterey by the ship's launch, which returned with the news of Sloat's arrival and his papers concerning the intended occupation of Monterey. These documents also contained orders for Montgomery to take immediate possession of the San Francisco Bay area. The directions reached Montgomery late in the evening on July 8, and were acted upon at seven o'clock the following morning.[25]

Captain Montgomery landed peacefully on July 9, 1846, with seventy men to take possession of the town of Yerba Buena, but there were no Mexican officials present for an official surrender. The United States flag was raised over the customs house and Commodore Sloat's proclamation was read to the inhabitants. Most of the sailors and marines returned to the ship, leaving a small garrison of fifteen or twenty marines and sailors under Lieutenant H. B. Watson to perform soldierly duties and to control the town.[26] Some field pieces were located on the side of what is now Telegraph Hill to protect the newly occupied region,[27] and the male residents of Yerba Buena were enlisted into a company of thirty-two men to assist United States forces in the event of an attack by the enemy.[28] Stores and munitions amounting in value to $2,199 were dispatched to Captain Frémont at Sutter's Fort.[29]

On the afternoon of July 9 a portion of the volunteer force from Yerba Buena under the command of Marine Lieutenant T. S. Mosroon seized the fort at the entrance of San Francisco Bay, and on the same day Lieutenant Joseph W. Revere, a descendent of Paul Revere, with a small detachment of marines and sailors, landed near present Vallejo, marched to Sonoma, raised the United States flag, and again read Commodore Sloat's proclamation to the Californians.[30] By July 11, the United States flag was also flying above Sutter's Fort and at Bodega Bay.[31]

Northern California was occupied without opposition. General Castro, on hearing of the seizures, marched his small force southward to join Governor Pico at Los Angeles. Not a shot was fired by the United States naval forces in the acquisition of the population centers above Monterey.

Commodore Sloat, still reluctant about proceeding further since he had not received any news of a formal declaration of war, organized a company of thirty-five dragoons, and sent this group northward to keep communications open between San Francisco and Monterey. While searching the area between San Jose and San Juan Bautista, this force encountered Captain Frémont, and the two "armies" returned to Monterey together.[32] On July 19 Frémont met Sloat on board the *Savannah*. Both feared that the strong British force of naval vessels in the Pacific might be used to proclaim a protectorate in California,[33] but Sloat was considerably upset when he discovered that Frémont did not possess any official orders from the United States Government to justify his hostile actions. The naval officer had hoped that Frémont would possess the authority for commencing hostilities, but when he ascertained that this was not so, Sloat became certain that his own movements had been accomplished too hastily. Now he refused to proceed further, and he considered withdrawing completely.

Fortunately, the solution to his problem was at hand. The United States frigate *Congress*, commanded by Commodore Robert F. Stockton, arrived on July 15. Stockton had been ordered to join the Pacific Squadron upon completion of his primary mission to deliver government officials to the Sandwich Islands. He was ready and anxious to take command of the naval forces in the Pacific. On July 23 Commodore Sloat turned over his squadron to Stockton, and sailed in the *Levant* for Panama six days later, unaware of the severe reprimand he would receive in Washington for his hesitation and lack of initiative.[34]

The new naval commander and Frémont became immediate friends, and on the same day that he assumed command, Commodore Stockton took Frémont's men into the naval service as an unofficial unit, naming it the California Battalion. Captain Frémont was appointed a major and Lieutenant Gillespie was made a captain in this organization.[35] The following day Consul Larkin suggested that Commodore Stockton send an armed force to the south to oppose the remaining Mexican forces in that region. On Sunday, July 26, the *Cyane*, now under Commander S. F. DuPont, sailed with the California Battalion aboard.[36] The ship reached San Diego three days later after a stormy passage in which most of the newly-organized group were seasick.

Commodore Stockton sailed on August 1 with the *Congress* and *Savannah*, stopping at Santa Barbara to take formal possession there with a flag-raising ceremony after an unopposed landing. A small garrison of ten men, commanded by Midshipman William Mitchell, was left there,[37] while the main force proceeded to San Pedro, arriving on August 6.[38] A makeshift army of three hundred fifty sailors and marines landed on the same day. Their armament consisted of muskets, carbines, pistols, swords, boarding-pikes, and a few cannon from the ships.

The force presented a very ragged appearance because there were so many representatives of various groups and since shoes and clothing supplies were beginning to run short.[39] Some who had muskets had no bayonets and others who had bayonets had no muskets; some had carbines and no ammunition; one had a musket with no lock; and one Irishman had only a handle off a shipboard squeegee.[40]

Thomas Larkin had accompanied the naval force in an effort to arrange a peaceful capitulation, if possible. All attempts to force Governor Pío Pico to declare California independent under United States protection failed, and the Mexican forces, aware of the superior strength of the invading "army," secretly retired from Los Angeles on August 10.[41]

While Stockton organized his force at San Diego, the *Cyane* seized the Mexican brig *Juanita*, which attempted to escape after the arrival of the enemy. This obsolete vessel was captured without a serious engagement, and the forty thousand percussion caps on board were appropriated for the use of the American "army."[42] So ended the only actual naval encounter during the acquisition of California.

Commodore Stockton, with some two hundred fifty-nine eager men, left San Pedro for Los Angeles on August 11. The "army" marched under strict rules and was kept under arms at night. The band, strangely enough, proceeded first, followed in order by the marines, sailors, and a battery of four quarterdeck guns, mounted on carts.[43] They reached Los Angeles the next day and entered the city unopposed the following morning, looking more like "a parade of home guards than an enemy taking possession of a conquered town."[44] Frémont's California Battalion arrived on the same day from San Diego. Not an armed soldier was found in the provincial capital to oppose this formidable conquering force.[45]

Commodore Stockton appointed himself provisional governor of California, proclaimed the territory a part of the United States, and established military law. He organized the newly-acquired land into three military districts: one in the south, commanded by Captain Gillespie, another in the north, under the leadership of Frémont, and a third for the entire province under his jurisdiction with headquarters at Monterey. Laws were drawn up and promulgated by Stockton alone, a schoolhouse and a newspaper were established, and postal facilities were begun. In September Stockton arranged for regular municipal elections,[46] then embarked in the *Congress* to return with the major portion of his forces to Monterey. Captain Gillespie and fifty marines were left in Los Angeles to maintain control in the south, and the garrison at Santa Barbara was withdrawn.[47]

Soon after the departure of Commodore Stockton, Gillespie demonstrated that he was not capable of effectively governing the Californians. He arrested suspicious persons, treated the natives as inferiors, and aroused disaffection by making haughty and restrictive laws. Discontent spread among the Californians, and a revolt occurred, led by Lieutenant Colonel José M. Flores. This ultimately resulted in the expulsion of Gillespie and his force of marines. Flores was now elected provisional governor and comandante general by the legislature of Californians, but he was content to confine his military efforts to the southern section of the province since he had inadequate supplies and munitions.[48]

When Captain Mervine arrived at San Pedro on October 7, and landed a force of sailors and marines, he was repulsed by the newly-formed Mexican army, which had managed to find one ancient and serviceable piece of artillery.[49] After the United States forces were re-embarked and the ship sailed northward the Mexican and loyalist Californian forces were left in control of all Southern California. However, discontent mounted within this army as there were neither funds with which to pay the troops nor supplies to continue the war. Flores was imprisoned by a mutiny of his own soldiers, and the army disintegrated into small, disorganized bands.

Disturbed over the defeat of Captain Mervine's contingent near Los Angeles, Commodore Stockton resolved to reconquer the area in person. While he proceeded with the naval and marine forces by sea, he ordered Frémont to take his California Battalion overland to Los Angeles to dispose of resistance along the way. Meanwhile, the Army of the West, under Brigadier General Stephen Watts Kearny, was approaching the Southern California border in its westward march from Santa Fé.

Kearny and his Army of the West had conquered New Mexico by August 19, 1846, whereupon the commander of the expedition had divided his troops. He commanded one unit of approximately three hundred dragoons on its march down the Río Grande and across the southern sections of present New Mexico and Arizona *via* the Gila River route to California. While en route, Kearny met the famous scout, Kit Carson, who had been dispatched earlier from California by Stockton to advise the United States Government that California was safely under U. S. authority. Since he had departed prior to the initiation of the counter-revolution, Carson had no knowledge of the threat that now existed in Southern California. Upon hearing the news that all was quiet in California, Kearny persuaded Carson to join him and then ordered two-thirds of his troops to return to Santa Fé.

With scarcely one hundred dragoons, Kearny and Carson reached California on November 25 after fording the Colorado River near Yuma. Kearny's command arrived at Warner's Ranch, some sixty miles from

San Diego on December 2. After resting for two days the command proceeded toward San Diego.[50]

The naval force under Commodore Stockton sailed from San Francisco on December 5, reaching San Diego four days later,[51] but the *Congress* ran aground at the entrance of the harbor and was in danger of capsizing. After considerable effort the ship was floated again and anchored in the bay. All the marines and sailors that could be spared were landed from the *Congress* and *Savannah*, and a military organization was established ashore while extensive training was conducted. Sailors were formed into companies and drilled in field maneuvers. All turned to their new duties on land conscientiously, believing that the honor of the flag and the navy demanded that they retake what had been lost, proving to the Mexicans that sailors, like marines, would stand on a battlefield and fight.[52]

General Kearny suffered a serious setback at San Pasqual, where approximately eighty insurgents surprised his command and carried out a devastating attack upon his troops, killing eighteen and wounding fifteen, including Kearny, in the first and only serious charge. The survivors fell back to San Diego, greatly impressed with the unexpected might of the enemy. Here they found the *Congress* and reinforcements of more than four hundred sailors under Stockton's command. This force frightened the Californians from the field, enabling the resumption of the United States advance toward Los Angeles.[53]

On December 29, 1846, Commodore Stockton and General Kearny, with their combined force of some sixty dragoons and more than four hundred sailors and marines, began their move along the sandy road that led to Los Angeles.[54] This motley "army" deserves intensive examination because of its naval composition, its unusual organization, and its heterogeneity of weapons. The artillery company, commanded by a navy lieutenant, consisted of one hundred men and five cannon. Its personnel were armed individually with pikes and pistols. The marines from the naval vessels, numbering about one hundred muskets, constituted the most efficient body, but all efforts to form them into a group of Horse Marines failed in a humorous episode after they had been given the command to mount. There was also a contingent of fifty-seven dragoons, armed with carbines. Since they lacked horses, they became foot soldiers, discarding their sabres, and adopting boarding pikes as their principal armament. In addition there were some volunteers, mounted and armed with Colt repeating rifles to act as skirmishers. Other small groups included the Life Guards, some ten or fifteen men, led by Kit Carson, who rode ahead to act as scouts, a company of California volunteers, two companies of "Carbineers" from the *Congress* and the *Portsmouth*, a small corps of sappers and miners to make repairs in progress, and some thirty-five or forty "Pike and Pistol men" from the U. S. S. *Cyane* who joined the expedition the morning of the march and had little discipline. Nearly three hundred other men were formed into the main body; all of these were sailors representing the ships in the harbor and they were divided into four companies of musketeers representing the *Congress, Portsmouth, Cyane,* and *Savannah.*[55]

Outside of Los Angeles the army met the last opposition offered by the Mexican forces in the two-day battles near the San Gabriel and Los Angeles Rivers. Stockton commanded between four and five hundred sailors, marines, troops and friendly Californians. Flores, the commander of the Mexican elements who had been released from jail, had approximately three hundred men when he attempted unsuccessfully to halt the advance of U. S. forces at the San Gabriel River on January 8, 1847. The Mexicans retreated and entrenched themselves on an elevated mesa near the Los Angeles River. The United States forces advanced in a square formation, with six cannon placed in strategic locations on the corners of the advancing troops. The Mexicans first cannonaded Stockton from atop their mesa, but the fire was ineffective at such a great range. The commander of the United States forces also recommended a technique which he called "dodging" enemy fire — when the flash of the enemy's cannon was seen, he told his men to fall down and not to get up until the ball whistled overhead — a practice he had pursued at San Gabriel.[56] This was followed by a half-hearted cavalry charge, which was easily dispersed by the American forces. Now Stockton took the offensive, ordering his cannon to fire on the hill. His forces then advanced and easily dislodged the enemy. In the two-day engagement of January 8-9, 1847, Stockton had one sailor killed and fourteen members of his force wounded. Flores had five killed and twenty-two wounded, but the remainder of his army had scattered and fled, never to reässemble again.[57]

Los Angeles was reöccupied on January 10 after Flores had fled to Sonora. Three days later Frémont, who was still en route to the town, met a small Mexican-Loyalist Californian force under Andrés Pico at an old ranch house a few miles from the recently-captured capital. Pico and Frémont signed the Capitulation of Cahuenga.[58] The Californians were pardoned for past hostilities and were free to go to their homes on giving up their weapons if they promised not to take up arms again during the war. They were guaranteed protection, with all the privileges of American citizens, without being required to take the oath of allegiance.[59] Frémont's battalion had not been an influential force, however, in bringing about the final capitulation, Joseph T. Downey of the *Portsmouth* wrote that:

> We knew that Col. Frémont and his party were on their route to cooperate in our attack, but where he was the Lord only knew. He had been some three months en route and as yet we had only heard of him

once, and then he was at Santa Barbara, some 300 [*sic*] miles from Los Angeles.[60]

California had now been repossessed in a much more costly and military manner than it had been during the summer months of 1846. With the Capitulation of Cahuenga resistance to United States occupying forces ceased. The naval squadron present on the Pacific Coast had made possible the annihilation of all effective enemy action. Without these vessels, Frémont could not have been supplied, the United States land forces would have been inferior to those maintained by Mexico in the province, Monterey and San Francisco probably could not have been held continuously after July, 1846, and General Kearny could not have been rescued. The reconquest would have been delayed until sufficient United States forces could have been dispatched to complete the occupation. Though there had been vacillation and errors throughout the early campaign, the presence of such large numbers of well-disciplined naval elements, immediate supplies with which to wage war, and a mobile, comparatively rapid means of transportation greatly influenced the course of the war and its ultimate results on the California Coast.

The Pacific Squadron had made possible the realization of President Polk's dream of "Manifest Destiny" and had taken possession of a vast land which would play an important part in the history of the Southwest. Within the next two years sufficient wealth would be taken from this domain to justify the entire military campaign and the purchase price of California combined.

CHAPTER 13

U. S. Military Forces in California

By D. E. Livingston-Little

THE COMPOSITION AND ACTIVITIES of the United States military forces in the Mexican War were various, as illustrated by the part the Navy played in the conquest. Oakah L. Jones, Jr., has clearly outlined the activities of the Navy, but no such study has been done recently to summarize all United States military movements in California during the war. D. E. Livingston-Little has provided information concerning "precisely what United States military units were in California, for how long, and where they were deployed." Very carefully and accurately the author details such actions as the capture of Monterey, the capture and difficulties in holding Los Angeles, and other important battles throughout California.

Likewise the arrival of the New York Volunteers was timely, for many of the earlier volunteers had completed their enlistments and were leaving for their homes in the East. These New York Volunteers served in many areas of California until October, 1848, whereupon many returned East; others would make their permanent homes in California. The author also examines the activities of the Mormon Battalion and concludes that it and the New York Volunteers have not received sufficient credit for their contributions to the war. This study thus provides some chronology as far as troop participation was concerned, and also it gives appropriate recognition to most of the principal players in the conquest of California.

This chapter originally appeared in JOURNAL of the WEST in April, 1972.

FOREWORD

AN ACCOUNT of the composition and activities of forces mentioned in the title may appear to be deceptively simple. Anyone with a reasonably good knowledge of the war, or of California history, is likely to feel himself capable of writing it, probably without additional research or study. However, he may be deceiving himself, as apparently many people have. The scope of the story to be reported, or the parameters, to use a popular modern term, may be variously defined, as follows: at the extreme of *over simplification*, one finds the few paragraphs in the ENCYCLOPEDIA BRITTANICA, and not much more in the standard texts on California history. At the other extreme one can find scores, if not hundreds, of monographic books and articles, each dealing with a single phase of the war in California. Often enough, each contains sweeping and frequently inaccurate generalization: two favorites are that the Cahuenga Capitulation ended the war, and that Kearny's march to California was the longest military march in our history (Doniphan, who accompanied the Kearny expedition to New Mexico, marched farther; Lewis and Clark, although not in wartime, marched twice as far).

The purpose of this paper is to offer a simple, accurate summary of the United States military movements in California from 1846 to 1848. We have been told that Commander Stockton's Naval forces, aided by Frémont's Volunteer Battalion, occupied California in a few weeks without any great opposition. Or, if we preferred, we could have read articles devoted to revealing exactly where Juan Flaco stopped and for how long on his ride for help. What seems to be lacking is a general account of precisely what United States military units were in California, for how long, and where they were deployed. This paper is an effort to supply that information.

THE MILITARY FORCES AND THEIR MISSIONS

First Lieutenant John C. Frémont was in or near California with his exploring party, including some Topographical Engineers, when the Mexican War began on April 24, 1846. The Bear Flag Revolution occurred between that date and the arrival of the Pacific Squadron, under command of Commodore John D. Sloat, on July 7. About three weeks prior to Sloat's occupation of Monterey, the Bear Flag party had declared California an independent republic. Although not directly involved in the fighting, Brevet Captain Frémont had thereafter assumed direction of the army of the Bear Flag Republic.

Upon Sloat's seizure of Monterey, Frémont marched his combined force of some one hundred sixty mounted riflemen to Monterey and offered their services to the United States. Sloat refused, being committed to a conciliatory policy, while Captain Frémont, his second in command, Lieutenant Archibald Gillespie, and the Bear Flag party in general had offended and alienated much of the Spanish-speaking population of California. However, on July 23, 1846, Sloat's successor, Commodore Robert F. Stockton arrived and relieved Sloat, who had asked to retire. Stockton proved less conciliatory, and enlisted Frémont's group as a Mounted Rifle Battalion to serve under Navy control. Frémont was commissioned as a major, Marine Lieutenant Archibald Gillespie as a captain. The California Battalion presumably had the status of a Marine battalion, certainly it was not an Army unit in spite of the fact that some of the men were Army troops.

Within thirty days thereafter, Stockton and Frémont had occupied San Diego and Los Angeles, and Stockton then announced his intention of leaving Frémont as military governor and returning to sea. Gillespie was left to garrison Los Angeles with a company of men, but enforced Sloat's directives so strictly that the local populace rose up under Juan Flores and expelled him, forcing his retreat to a ship in San Pedro Harbor. The legendary Juan Flaco had ridden five hundred miles to San Francisco in three days for help, which Stockton sent under Captain William Mervine aboard the frigate *Savannah*. Arriving at San Pedro on October 6, 1846, 299 sailors, marines and mounted riflemen disembarked the next day and set off to re-take Los Angeles. However, the force was driven back at the Battle of Domínguez Ranch by the "Old Woman's Gun" and General José Antonio Carrillo's mounted lancers. A week later,

Stockton moved his headquarters to San Diego, and was still there planning the reconquest of Los Angeles when General Kearny arrived at Warner's Ranch, east of San Diego, on December 2.

Brigadier General Stephen Watts Kearny had been ordered to lead an expedition to conquer New Mexico, and had left Independence, Missouri, in June, 1846. His command consisted of his own First Dragoons, Colonel Alexander W. Doniphan's First Regiment of Missouri Mounted Volunteers, some three or four companies of volunteer infantry, artillery and rangers and the Mormon Battalion, which departed later. After a relatively peaceful occupation of New Mexico, Kearny prepared to carry out the second part of his orders — to advance to California. Taking his Dragoons down the Río Grande, he met Kit Carson in the vicinity of present-day Socorro. Carson was carrying dispatches to Washington telling of the successful conquest of California. General Kearny sent most of his Dragoons back to Santa Fe, keeping with him only Company C and part of Company K, a total of about one hundred men in all. Kit Carson returned with Kearny as a guide. At the Colorado River, the Dragoons intercepted a messenger carrying dispatches to Mexico, and learned of the American defeat at Los Angeles in October. Greatly excited at the news, Kearny hurried on across the desert and before his men had adequately recuperated from the hard marches, they engaged General Andrés Pico's California Lancers at the Battle of San Pasqual, just southeast of present-day Escondido. The Dragoons were far short of fighting trim and their horses were in even worse condition. In addition, their powder was damp from rain, and they were probably out-numbered. In any case, the Dragoons suffered heavy casualties; twenty-one were killed or mortally wounded. Fourteen or sixteen others, including General Kearny, were also wounded. The Californios apparently suffered no fatalities, but after striking twice withdrew a short distance which allowed Kearny to send Kit Carson to Commodore Stockton for help. On December 12, four days after the Battle of San Pasqual, one hundred eighty men arrived from San Diego and escorted the Dragoons to safety.

Upon General Kearny's arrival in San Diego began the long and acrimonious debate with Stockton over who was the commander-in-chief, and, who, therefore, was the governor of California. At the moment, Stockton had all the forces, so Kearny could not insist, and he did not try until the Mormon Battalion arrived in California the following month.

During the next two weeks of December, Kearny and Stockton completed plans for a joint overland march to Los Angeles from San Diego. Setting out on December 29, 1846, the expedition numbered 604 men, including fifty-five of Kearny's Dragoons and about eighty of the Mounted Rifles in addition to Marines and Navy pikemen.

The one hundred forty-five-mile march took some ten days, and was essentially unopposed until the Stockton-Kearny forces approached the

San Gabriel River. At this point General José María Flores attempted to halt the Americans, but having inferior numbers and little artillery at his disposal he was forced to retreat towards the Los Angeles River. On the following day, January 9, 1847, the final battle was fought on a mesa between the two rivers in the vicinity of a site specifically located today by an historial marker near Downey Avenue and Forty-fourth Street in the City of Vernon. General Flores, who had asked for peace terms on January 4, and had been rejected because he had broken his parole, relinquished command of the Californios to General Andrés Pico, and left for Sonora. Pico took his force to San Fernando and, as Los Angeles was being occupied by the Stockton-Kearny forces, Pico was surrendering to Major Frémont at Cahuenga Rancho on January 13, 1847.

Both Kearny and Stockton were annoyed at Frémont's presumption and at his lenient terms, though in prospect of his becoming governor, Kearny felt clemency was doubtless more prudent than his and Stockton's previous harshness. Stockton, in any case, supported Frémont, and designated him as military governor in defiance of Kearny who marched his Dragoons back to San Diego. Stockton did likewise with his escort, sending the sailors and marines by sea from San Pedro on January 20.

The return journey took about a week, by which time Kearny had made contact with Lieutenant Colonel Philip St. George Cooke and the Mormon Battalion, directing them to meet him in San Diego, where they arrived on January 31. A power shift now began to take place as Kearny had not only his Dragoons but the Mormon Battalion as well, a total of something more than four hundred Army troops, while Stockton almost immediately departed San Diego with his squadron.

General Kearny also left San Diego immediately after ordering Lieutenant Colonel Cooke to move the Mormon Battalion fifty-three miles north to Mission San Luis Rey. Kearny arrived in Monterey aboard the *Cyane* to find Commodore William B. Shubrick in charge, and quite ready to acknowledge Kearny's right to command in California. In port, too, was the long-awaited artillery company commanded by Captain Tompkins: the First Lieutenants were E. O. C. Ord and William Tecumseh Sherman, while William Halleck of the Engineers was attached. There were some one hundred thirteen men and, in addition, some badly needed funds and extra uniforms.

While Kearny and Shubrick jointly tried to convince Frémont that he was not the supreme authority in California, Colonel Richard B. Mason arrived on February 12 with later and more specific orders directing that he should take over as governor and military commander, thereby releasing Kearny to return east as he had earlier requested to be allowed to do. Frémont was called to Monterey, ordered to disband his volunteers, which he belatedly did, though his repeated refusal to obey Colonel

Mason's orders brought about his court-martial and ultimate resignation from the service.

Lieutenant Colonel Cooke, who had earlier detached thirty men and an officer to garrison San Diego, in March moved the Dragoons plus the Mormon Battalion to Los Angeles, where they arrived on March 23. In the face of Indian attacks from the north, Cooke stationed a company of the Mormon Battalion at Cajon Pass on April 11. The remainder of the battalion encamped on the outskirts of Los Angeles, with the Dragoon company in the pueblo when it was not patrolling the surrounding area. By this date, mid-April, 1847, Frémont had disbanded his irregular volunteer battalion, and had surrendered the governorship to Colonel Mason, who maintained the capitol in Monterey. Colonel Jonathan Stevenson's First Regiment of New York Volunteers had just arrived in California, so that the military strength in April was about as follows:

First U. S. Dragoons — Co. C, part of Co. K	88 men
Third U. S. Artillery — Co. F	107 men
New York Volunteers — 10 companies	550 men
Mormon Battalion — 5 companies	304 men
Total U. S. Army Strength	1,059 men

The above figures do not include the members of the New York Volunteer Regiment who were still at sea, or the two hundred recruits who would arrive later.

The arrival of the New York Volunteer Regiment was very timely: the disbanding of Frémont's volunteers, and the dissention among the American leaders, seemed designed to encourage the still recalcitrant Californios to try again to drive out the invaders. There was much talk of General Anastasio Bustamente's invading California from Sonora with 1,500 men, and also of José Limantour's being in San Pedro with funds and commissions to raise forces against the Americans, when Colonel Stevenson arrived in Los Angeles on May 9 with two companies of the New York Volunteers to strengthen the force already there. Kearny had accompanied him and, when he left Los Angeles, Kearny ordered Frémont to accompany him back to Monterey, from whence they would both leave on the long march back to Missouri, *via* the California and Oregon Trails. Arriving in Monterey on May 27, they departed on May 31, 1847, together with their staffs, that of General Kearny included Lieutenant Colonel Cooke. His Mormon Battalion completed its year of service a short time later, and only enough men for one company re-enlisted. This separate company of Volunteers, known as Captain Davis' Company A, looked to Colonel Stevenson to represent them and lead them during the remaining nine months of their service in California.

To be more explicit about the activities of Colonel Stevenson's Regiment of New York Volunteers, they arrived in San Francisco aboard three transports: the *Thomas H. Perkins*, on March 7, with Companies K, F, G, and part of E, plus Stevenson and his staff and the regimental band. The *Susan Drew* arrived on March 19, with Companies D, I, H, and more of E. On the same day the *Loo Choo* put in carrying A, C, and more of K and E. The *Brutus* docked a month later with the remainder of the regiment. The *Sweden* and the *Isabella*, each carrying one hundred additional recruits, did not arrive until February, 1848, the month in which the treaty ending the war was signed.

On March 31, 1847, Companies A, B and F boarded the barque *Moscow* for Santa Barbara where they disembarked and camped upon the beach front. Company F was destined to remain in Santa Barbara "for the duration," but Companies A and B left on July 4 for La Paz, Baja California, on the United States Storeship *Lexington*. The two companies arrived there on July 21, 1847, and remained for fourteen months withstanding month-long sieges and numerous attacks by Mexican Army forces. In March, 1848, the *Isabella* arrived with Company D and, in addition, more than than one hundred recruits. Thus re-inforced, and commanded by Lieutenant Colonel Burton, the Americans marched into the interior, freed the American prisoners of war at San Antonio, dispersed the Mexican forces and embarked on the *Ohio* for Monterey on August 31, 1848.

Company C of the New York Volunteers, after debarking from the *Loo Choo*, moved to Sonoma in early April, 1847. About thirty-five of their number spent the summer and fall at Sutter's Fort, near Sacramento. Otherwise the company remained at Sonoma until May, 1848, when it was ordered to Baja California. That company got no further than Monterey, however, when plans were changed and it was ordered to return to Sonoma. Three months later, Company C exchanged posts with Company H, which had been at the Presidio of San Francisco since its arrival aboard the *Susan Drew*. Company H, incidentally, stayed at Sonoma only from August 5 to August 25, 1848, when it was returned to the Presidio of San Francisco and mustered out of the service.

Company D was one of the companies stationed at Monterey during most of its service. It arrived on the *Susan Drew*, was moved to Monterey on May 4 on the *Lexington* and there remained until March 5, 1848. During the year, Company D had been carrying out mounted patrols in the San Joaquín Valley and in the Sierra Nevada, an experience that probably recommended it for later service in Baja California. The company was sent to La Paz on the *Isabella*, along with the recruits, arriving there on March 19, 1848. Lieutenant Colonel Burton then utilized Companies A, B, and D to pursue the Mexican Army forces into the interior and defeat them at Todos Santos; Company D, immediately after that victory, was sent to relieve the Naval garrison at San José del Cabo, from which point it was evacuated by the *U. S. S. Ohio* (which had already picked up Companies A and B), on September 16, 1848. Company D was the last American unit to leave Mexican soil.

Companies E and G were the two headquarters companies that served in Los Angeles from the time of their arrival at San Pedro on the *Lexington* in early May, 1847, until their discharge on September 18, 1848. Company E was the divided unit, the last part of which arrived late on the *Brutus*. Company G was distinguished by having as its captain Matthew Stevenson, the son of the regimental commander. It was also the company which lost the life of a Sergeant Travers in the explosion of a powder magazine on December 9, 1847. A Private Andrew was also killed along with a Private Legare of E company in this unfortunate accident.

Company I arrived in San Francisco aboard the *Susan Drew*, then sailed to Monterey in early April where it did garrison duty until December, 1847, when it moved to San Diego, there to remain until discharged on September 25, 1848. Company I had the reputation of being the finest in the regiment: it was one of three recruited from up-state New York.

Company K, another of the up-state companies, arrived and remained on garrison duty at the Presidio of San Francisco until it was discharged on August 15, 1848. This represents the earliest date of discharge for Stevenson's New York Regiment: the last three companies were not released until October 23 and 24, 1848. By this date the California gold rush was under way and it was increasingly difficult to hold men on army pay (seven dollars a month). On the other hand, even the people who had criticised the soldiers, were beginning to regret the abolition of all authority in an increasingly lawless situation. Within a few months, therefore, by early 1849, plans were made for a constitutional convention to create a state government.

AFTERWORD

It is my hope that the above resumé of military activities in California during the Mexican War, 1846-1848, has clarified the roles of the principal participants. The reader may conclude, probably not without some justification, that the Mormon Battalion and Stevenson's Regiment of New York Volunteers played a rather more important role than that with which they are commonly credited. They certainly arrived at a crucial time and performed valuable peace-keeping duties. They also stayed longer, were numerically stronger and, for the military-minded, fought more and bloodier engagements than did any of Stockton's or Frémont's forces. But, finally, the value of this paper, if any, may be that of making certain that the entire cast gets presented, that some chronology is introduced, and that reasonably appropriate recognition is accorded all of the principal players in California's part in the Mexican War.

CHAPTER 14

The "All-Mexico" Movement

By Paul F. Lambert

WITHIN A YEAR after American troops arrived in Mexico territory, even while the American Navy was guarding against a new Mexican offensive, attitudes concerning the war began to change drastically in the United States. Prior to 1846 there were people in the United States who used their influence ineffectively to keep the country out of war. Once war was declared, these same people refused to serve in any capacity and even sought to create dissent among political parties in all sections of the United States.

Yet there also were individuals in the West and the South who supported the war completely and gladly fought in it. Many spoke of the potential for acquiring Mexican territory. However, a campaign to annex all of Mexico did not start with the war; rather it developed slowly in 1847. As the slavery issue declined slightly in the fall of 1847, the movement to take all of Mexico began to be accepted even by some Northerners who had become convinced that Mexico's lands were inhospitable to slavery. Yet most New Englanders remained hostile not only to the war, but also to the acquisition of all of Mexico.

Numerous arguments were used by the press and by politicians to rally support for the movement. Some argued that no hope existed for stability and progress in Mexico; therefore, the United States was obligated to act in behalf of the people of that backward Republic. Thus when the Treaty of Guadalupe Hidalgo was signed, many people favored rejecting the settlement, for it gave the United States only the territory originally desired. But as the American desire for peace grew stronger during treaty negotiations, the pressure for the acquisition of all Mexico lessened among even the most ardent supporters of the movement. Paul F. Lambert has skillfully recreated the mood of the American people during the Mexican War, the differing sectional attitudes, and the final abandonment of the movement by officials of the United States Government. Finally this movement may have been an extreme expression of Manifest Destiny, but analyzed in perspective it is obvious that many powerful factors made the success of such a movement impossible.

This chapter originally appeared in JOURNAL of the WEST in April, 1972.

WHEN THE UNITED STATES officially declared war on Mexico on May 13, 1846, few Americans seriously considered the possibility of acquiring all of Mexico. Yet by September, 1847, there was a significant movement afoot designed to achieve that end. During the war, the "All Mexico" campaign actually passed through three stages: an initial stage in which interest was light, a middle period in which the movement was hampered by the controversy over slavery, and a final span of growth which was abruptly halted by the Treaty of Guadalupe Hidalgo. Indeed, it has been asserted that the movement was gaining ground rapidly, and had the war continued much longer Mexican independence would have been subverted. The significance of the movement to acquire all of Mexico cannot be denied, but the assumption that this extreme expression of Manifest Destiny eventually would have triumphed is questionable.

John L. O'Sullivan coined the term "Manifest Destiny" in his newspaper, the *Democratic Review*, in 1845. Since 1839 he had been stressing the idea that American institutions ultimately would hold sway over the entire North American Continent.[1] At the outset of the Mexican War, the idealistic O'Sullivan opposed the acquisition of territory by force; rather he felt that annexation should wait until the Mexican people requested permission to enter the Union. O'Sullivan and his followers soon changed their view, and by August, 1846, he was advocating that the United States acquire both California and New Mexico as a basis for settling accounts with Mexico.[2] This view was commonly accepted by the Democratic party. As the war stretched out, however, so did the limits for indemnity; California and New Mexico had been viewed as satisfactory in anticipation of a short war.[3]

During the first few months of the war, however, there was little apparent interest in All Mexico. Expansionism was most evident in New York and in the West. The sentiments of Manifest Destiny were stimulated in the West by the war. The *Illinois State Register* exuberantly proclaimed the marvelous opportunity "for the prosecution of our glorious mission" which the Mexican War provided.[4] Indeed, Illinois remained the most expansionistic state in the West throughout the war.

Illinois' counterpart in the East was New York. Here, as in the West, Manifest Destiny was an important theme in the expansionist press. There were general assertions that the United States was destined to annex Mexico and that the Mexican War would probably hasten that event. Interest in Mexico also was excited by industrial and commercial considerations.[5] Before the movement to annex Mexico could gain widespread support, however, the troublesome question of slavery in the new territories would have to be faced.

This emotionally charged issue was raised early in the war by a rider to an appropriations bill — the Wilmot Proviso. It provided that slavery would be excluded from any territory acquired from Mexico, and it evoked a storm of emotion which almost wrecked the Union.[6] Southerners believed that the South had to maintain equality with the free states in the Senate to protect the "peculiar institution." Hence the Wilmot Proviso was a red flag in the face of pro-slavery Southern "bulls."

For a time, there was conflicting testimony before the public as to whether the Mexican lands would grow crops suitable to slave labor. Both Democrats and Whigs were split on this issue. Those Southerners who believed that these territories could not support slavery were unlikely to be ardent supporters of expansion, and in any case, they would not acquiesce to the Wilmot Proviso.[7] Conversely, many Northerners believed the infamous proviso was necessary to prevent the expansion of slavery. Certainly there was little chance for strong sentiments favoring the All Mexico movement to develop while the Wilmot Proviso remained to split the Democratic party in the face of a united Whig opposition.[8]

Despite the distracting salvery question, the campaign for the annexation of Mexico was formally inaugurated in May, 1847, when Moses Y. Beach of the *New York Sun* published an editorial entitled "Mexico Annexed to the United States." Raising the topic in reference to the controversy over slavery, Beach argued that the Wilmot Proviso was unnecessary because Mexican lands would never support slavery. And he asserted that "Mexico will be occupied and eventually annexed ...."[9] The public remained cool to the idea of acquiring Mexico during the summer months of 1847,[10] but by September the movement appeared to be gaining support. One factor which made this growth possible was the decline of the slavery question as an obstacle to All Mexico.

Beach's initial argument that Mexican lands could not support slavery was reiterated constantly by other Northern propagandists hoping to render the Wilmot Proviso inconsequential. Southern spokesmen opposing acquisition of Mexico on the ground that it would be prejudicial to slavery interests were quoted by Northerners to promote expansionism in their region.[11] By September, 1847, many Northerners were becoming convinced that neither Mexico nor her territories could support slavery. Indeed, politicians like Louis Cass, James Buchanan, and Robert J. Walker were stating publicly that the Wilmot Proviso was unnecessary. This made it easier for many people to accept the All Mexico concept. However, it should be noted that extremists both North and South were never satisfied.[12]

Another major factor aiding the growth of the All Mexico movement was Mexican obduracy. The Mexicans seemed unreasonable in their determination to continue fighting after they had been defeated soundly. John D. P. Fuller has asserted that "'the mere length of the war and the development of war psychology tended to make the American people more bombastic in expression and more impatient in feeling toward Mexico."[13] However, by late September news arrived that the Mexicans had refused to negotiate seriously with President James K. Polk's peace envoy, Nicholas P. Trist.[14] Hence with the abatement of the slavery issue in the North and with Mexican stubbornness, the movement for the acquisition of All Mexico was destined to grow stronger until scotched by the unexpected arrival in Washington of the Treaty of Guadalupe Hidalgo.

During this twilight period of the war, the various sections of the nation and the two major parties held different views toward the prospect of annexing Mexico. Generally, the Whigs were united in opposition to acquiring Mexico; many were against taking anything from Mexico save insisting that the Texas border be the Río Grande. The Democrats, however, were divided on the issue, with opinions ranging from firm opposition to ardent advocacy. Sentiments in the press and of politicians must be heavily relied upon in evaluating the strength of the movement in the several sections.

In surveying sectional attitudes, the Southeast must be considered apart from the Southwest. There were politicians in the Southeast who desired absorption of Mexico, but they were of less political stature than their Northern counterparts and thus were more infrequently quoted.[15] The more prominent of these men included Representative Louis Mc-Lane of Maryland, Senator Herschel V. Johnson of Georgia, Senator James D. Wescott of Florida, and Senators Dixon H. Lewis and A. P. Bagby of Alabama. They cited the dangers of a European power securing Mexico if that country were left weak and independent following the war. Manifest Destiny also was referred to as an authority for the acquisition of Mexico. These men were Democrats; Whigs favoring All Mexico were not to be found in the Southeast.[16]

Most Democratic politicians in the Southeast also looked upon the All Mexico movement with disfavor. The most outstanding Southern Democrat, John C. Calhoun, was firmly opposed to the movement. He had long viewed the war as immoral and unconstitutional, and as the war dragged on he came to fear the effect of extensive annexations on the peace of the Union. These potential territories would likely enter the Union eventually as free states, thus rendering the South a minority in the Senate.[17] Calhoun also was convinced that the Mexican population was inferior and to incorporate into the Union any but Caucasians would be disastrous to America's republican institutions. Indeed, Calhoun argued, not all people are capable of self-government. Calhoun spoke for the bulk of the Southeastern Democracy. Hence there was less support in the Southeast for the annexation of All Mexico than in any other area with the possible exception of New England.[18]

If New England was cool toward the Mexican War, it was frigid toward the All Mexico movement. This section was dominated by hostile Whigs, many of whom opposed the annexation of any Mexican territory. The belief that the war was the manifestation of a slavocracy plot to acquire more slave pens was still an important factor in this area.[19] Anti-slavery and partisan sentiments were not the only reasons that New Englanders were opposed to expansion. Some felt that as more territory was annexed, the less would be New England's influence in the Union. With each passing decade, its prominence in the Union seemed to decline. Hence Daniel Webster opposed any significant extension of territory whether slave or free.[20]

Notwithstanding the general attitude of adjacent New England, the North Atlantic seaboard area provided strong support for the campaign to absorb Mexico. In fact, Frederick Merk has referred to urban centers of this area as the "emotional, intellectual, political, and even diplomatic base" of the movement. The Democrats in these cities were very enthusiastic for All Mexico. The editors of the Democratically inclined "'penny press" were the "heart and mind and soul of the All Mexico crusade after the failure of the peace negotiation."[21]

Examples of these newspapers were the *Boston Times*, the *New York Sun*, the *New York Herald*, the *Philadelphia Public Ledger*, and the *Baltimore Sun*.[22] Manifest Destiny was a major theme of their editors; American institutions should be spread over the continent. Indeed they argued that the United States' mission was to regenerate the Mexican people by incorporating them into the Union. Exposure to American institutions would work a marvelous transformation in the Mexican character.[23] According to the *New York Sun*, it was absurd to speak of "our 'wronging the Mexicans' when we offer them a position infinitely above any they have occupied. . . . They may aim at the greatness and dignity of a truly republican and self-governing people."[24]

The notion of regeneration was used to make the conquest of Mexice more palatable. Annexing Mexico thus involved more than merely acquiring vast stretches of "'blessed and fruit bearing"[25] land for the use of Americans — Mexicans were to be uplifted. And as the desire for Mexico increased, the predicted time for regeneration seemed to grow smaller.[26] Most penny press editors were growingly confident that the Mexicans could easily be regenerated.[27]

In addition to Manifest Destiny, other arguments were used by the penny press and regional politicians to attract support for All Mexico. Some argued that because of the obduracy of the Mexicans there was no other way to obtain an honorable peace. Still others believed that absorption of Mexico was necessary to prevent that nation from falling into the hands of a European power following the war. Also appeal to American honor and self-respect was made in support of All Mexico. This would be the only dignified approach, the argument ran, as the Mexicans had forced the war on the United States, had been beaten soundly, and had stubbornly refused to surrender.[28]

There were also economic rationales voiced in favor of annexing Mexico. By the end of 1846, Mexico's rich silver mines were being mentioned frequently in the Eastern expansionist press. It was first noted in the *New York Herald* and later in the *Baltimore American* that Mexico exported fourteen million dollars in bullion annually to England. With the annexation of Mexico, that bullion would come to the United States and could be used to "pay every expense of the war . . . ."[29]

Another powerful economic inducement for All Mexico was the prospect of a future canal across the Isthmus of Tehuantepec, a project first recommended by the Spanish conqueror, Hernán Cortéz. The obvious benefits to be gained by such a canal were pictured in glowing terms; the commerce of the Eastern seaboard would acquire advantages that no European state could ever overcome. Indeed the proposed canal was deemed the key to the nation's future greatness. The effort to obtain transit rights across the Isthmus was abandoned only when the Mexicans informed Nicholas Trist that the rights were in the hands of British subjects.[30]   Thus economic arguments were certainly of considerable importance in Eastern support for All Mexico.

The Free West was also an ardent supporter for the acquisition of All Mexico, but economic justifications were not ascendant in that region.   The great motivator for expansionist passions in the West was a desire for land.   Indeed the West was more favorable toward annexing Mexico than any other section of the nation.[31]   In addition to the more common arguments centering around Manifest Destiny, it was widely asserted that expansion was desirable because as the number of states increased the stability of the Union would become more fixed.[32]

Nearly all Democratic newspapers in the region joined the All Mexico crusade, while many Democratic politicians, such as Senators Lewis Cass of Michigan and Stephen A. Douglas of Illinois, were active supporters.[33]   In fact, it was the Western Democratic members of Congress who formed the backbone of the All Mexico movement.   Prominent Whigs of the section were hostile to the movement, however, as the influential Henry Clay insisted that the United States should demand a proper boundary for Texas and nothing more.[34]   Yet Whigs in the West were woefully outnumbered on the question of expansion.

Of the Free Western states, Illinois provided the most ardent advocates for annexation of Mexico.   Indeed the state was considered the New York of the West.[35]   When Abraham Lincoln, a Whig member of the House of Representatives from Illinois, adhered to his party's viewpoint on the war and the annexation of Mexico, he was roundly condemned by his constituents and voted out of office.   Moreover, Illinois was the only state to have both senators vote against the Treaty of Guadalupe Hidalgo because they wanted more territory.[36]   Despite their glorification of Manifest Destiny, Westerners' thinking about the regeneration of the Mexican people generally were pessimistic.

Democratic editors of the trans-Allegheny West were much cooler toward All Mexico than their Eastern and Western colleagues.   They showed an acute bias against the colored and mixed-breed elements of southern Mexico.   While the most ardent Western expansionists did not declare that rapid regeneration was likely, individuals such as Cass and Senator Sidney Breese of Illinois did assert that the United States could absorb the Mexican population without resultant corruption of American institutions.   Regeneration, they argued, would be a long, arduous task; but it eventually could be accomplished.[37]

The issue of race was also an important factor in the Southwest where public opinion concerning annexation of Mexico was sharply divided. Here the people were torn between slave-holding interests, a desire for Mexican lands, strong frontier nationalism, and a revlusion for "inferior" Mexicans. Editors in this region tended to reflect public opinion quite closely, and the press was neither violently for nor against All Mexico. Some Democratic papers in the region favored taking some sparsely settled areas of Mexico, thus avoiding large numbers of Mexicans.[38]

Notwithstandng the inhibitions of racism and slavery there was considerable support among Southwesterners for the acquisition of all or at least a large part of Mexico. Even a Whig journal, the *New Orleans Picayune*, spoke favorably of acquiring Mexico. A railroad across Mexico and extensive territorial acquistions were believed to ensure the commercial future of New Orleans.[39] Furthermore, the area did produce some ardent expansionist politicians including Senators Sam Houston and Thomas S. Rusk of Texas and Senators Jefferson Davis and Henry S. Foote of Mississippi.[40] Nevertheless, the Southwest must be ranked behind the Free West and the Northeast in intensity of support for the acquisition of All Mexico.

In December, 1847, representatives and senators reflecting these varying sectional and party attitudes assembled in Washington for the tumultuous Thirtieth Congress. The administration's peace negotiator, Nicholas P. Trist, had been recalled and on December 7, President James K. Polk addressed Congress. He called for more troops to fight in Mexico, recommended a vigorous prosecution of the war, and hinted that continued Mexican obstinance might lead to prolonged occupation of that nation. The annexation of Mexico thus became a heated topic of debate in Congress during January and February of 1848.[41]

The opponents of All Mexico in the Thirtieth Congress were quite outspoken and were easily pinpointed. Virtually all Whigs spoke against the annexation of Mexico, asserting that American institutions faced ruin if Mexico entered the Union. The Whigs were joined in countering absorption by Calhoun's wing of the Democratic party. Calhoun himself was quickly recognized as the leader of the opposition forces in the Senate. Acquiescing in the absorption of New Mexico and California, the Calhounites staunchly opposed annexation of more of Mexico, for Calhoun feared the impact of Mexican territory on the South's "peculiar institution" and on the Union. Calhoun's opposition represented a formidable barrier for the expansionists.[42]

Determining those members of Congress who definitely favored the annexation of Mexico was more difficult than surveying the opposition. Most Democrats were expansionistic to some degree, but many were hesitant to commit themselves to All Mexico until they could be more certain of the drift of public opinion. However, there were twenty senators and congressmen who could be identified with the All Mexico movement. Fifteen of these men were from the West and Southwest, two were from New York, and three from the Southeast.[43] Although admitting that "not many Democrats openly advocated the absorption of Mexico . . . ," Fuller asserted that had the "war lasted much longer, perhaps all the Democrats except the Calhoun faction and a few New Englanders would have gradually become reconciled to the prospect of the absorption of Mexico."[44] Time was far shorter than the expansionists could have imagined, for the issue would soon be forced by the arrival from Mexico of the Treaty of Guadalupe Hidalgo.

President Polk's administration was subjected to similar pressures by All Mexico supporters as was Congress. In April, 1847, the President had sent Trist to negotiate a treaty of peace with Mexico. Trist was instructed to obtain Upper and Lower California, New Mexico, and rights of transit across the Isthmus of Tehuantepec. For all this he could offer as much as $30,000,000.[45] With Trists's apparent failure and the All Mexico movement growing stronger, several members of the administration began to demand increased cessions of territory.[46] The Secretary of the Treasury, Robert J. Walker of Mississippi, was the most enthusiastic supporter for the annexation of Mexico in the cabinet. In fact, he was considered by many to be the leader of those politicians who wanted to take all of Mexico.[47] Vice-President George M. Dallas of Pennsylvania was also converted: "Let us not shrink from subjugating implacable enemies, when we know that by so doing we shall advance the great objects of civilization . . . ."[48] Even Secretary of State James Buchanan, from Pennsylvania, also became an advocate of annexation after earlier advising moderation in territorial demands.[49]

But what was President Polk's attitude toward All Mexico? Fuller asserted that given more time, the expansionists in the cabinet might have been able "to secure the President who would probably be followed by the rest of the Cabinet."[50] Ray Allen Billington flatly stated that had Trist gone home when he was recalled, Polk would likely have sent new commissioners who would have insisted on complete annexation.[51] It seems apparent, however, that Polk never held much interest in acquiring more than California and New Mexico.[52] The President's bitterness toward Trist, who negotiated the Treaty of Guadalupe Hidalgo after he had been recalled, cannot be cited accurately as evidence that Polk had come to desire All Mexico. Norman A. Graebner demonstrated that Polk was harsh with Trist because of the diplomat's involvement with the Whig General Scott — not because the President had come to favor annexation of Mexico. "Trist's decision to remain in Mexico threw what was left of party rancor against him," Graebner continued, "for he appeared to be acting on the advice of Scott."[53]

Despite being disgusted with his envoy's insubordination, Polk was determined to evaluate Trist's treaty on its merits: "The treaty . . . should not be rejected on account of his bad conduct."[54] Polk accepted the treaty eagerly, but he never forgave the "impudent and unqualified scoundrel" who negotiated it.[55] The treaty contained everything Polk had wanted — California and New Mexico were to be ceded to the United States for fifteen million dollars.[56] The President's decision to submit the treaty to the Senate for ratification spelled doom for the All Mexico movement, and that august body ratified the Treaty of Guadalupe Hidalgo by a vote of thirty-eight to fourteen on March 10, 1848.

Several historians have asserted that the movement to acquire all of Mexico came extremely close to success. Albert K. Weinburg noted that the All Mexico movement fell short "only through a slight turn of events."[57] Fuller also attributed the failure of the All Mexico movement largely to the extraordinary behavior of Nicholas P. Trist, and Billington's views are noted above. Supporters of this view note that the *Puro* Party in Mexico were radical republicans who desired annexation to the United States to prevent anarchy and to foster republican institutions. They were a significant minority in Mexico. Had Trist left Mexico when he was recalled, these radicals might have gotten control of the government.[58] Also, if the situation in Mexico had degenerated to complete anarchy, as Trist believed it would when he departed,[59] then occupation would have been a necessity.[60]

It may also be argued that sentiment for annexation was growing rapidly and would have eventually overcome all opposition. Fuller asserted that while the people were not ready for All Mexico in November, 1847, "they would have been by the time of the next Presidential election had not the war ended in the meantime." Indeed, that the number of converts to annexation of Mexico was growing was evidenced by the support of the *National Whig* for absorption.[61] Furthermore, Weinburg noted that the notion of regeneration was becoming more and more acceptable in 1847 and 1848. This was important for Americans to overcome their racial bias against the inhabitants of Mexico and thus allow annexation.[62]

Historians such as Fuller, Weinburg, and Billington thus accepted the notion that the All Mexico movement would have been triumphant had Nicholas Trist refused to treat with the Mexicans after his recall. The rapidly growing annexation movement was nipped in the bud by the idealistic Trist, however. Proponents of this interpretation have tended to ignore a significant counter-movement that was taking place among the American people — the desire for peace. Although the terms of the Treaty of Guadalupe Hidalgo were kept from the public for several days, it became known at once that a treaty had been made and sent to the Senate. According to George L. Rives, "there was a unanimous expression of satisfaction that peace was at hand, and a universal chorus of advice to the Senate from newspapers all over the country to take the treaty whatever it might be."[63]   Thomas Hart Benton said that the treaty was a blessing for Polk, for "Great discontent was breaking out at home" over the war.[64]

Even the penny press responded favorably to the Treaty of Guadalupe Hidalgo. The *Boston Times* greeted the coming of peace happily and asserted that Mexico would eventaully "come to us, with or without a treaty."[65]   The editor of the *New York Herald* also believed that Mexico would eventually enter the Union, but "in the meantime we think the Senate has done right — the President has done right — Mr. Trist has done right . . . ."[66]   The strong public sentiment for peace probably was a factor in Polk's doing nothing to stop Trist's efforts at negotiation for a full month after rumors of his efforts began to flood the press. A shrewd politician, Polk desired peace.[67]

As the American public's demand for peace grew stronger, it was likely that the prolonged expense of completely crushing Mexican resistance and occupying that proud nation would have been prohibitive to the annexation of Mexico. Furthermore, it was also doubtful that Calhoun and his cohorts could have tolerated the annexation of all Mexico. For a Democratic administration to absorb Mexico would have meant destruction of the Democratic party and perhaps destruction of the Union. Moreover, the thought of a Whig administration implementing an All Mexico policy was absurd.

The movement for the acquisition of all of Mexico was an extreme expression of Manifest Destiny and is certainly an important historical phenomena. But it must be kept in proper perspective. There were powerful factors militating against the eventual fruition of the All Mexico movement; the Treaty of Guadalupe Hidalgo merely came at a propitious moment to accord the campaign for annexation of Mexico a peaceful death. It did not, as some have asserted, spare Mexico from total absorption by the United States.

CHAPTER 15

Nicholas P. Trist: *Treaty-Maker*

By Kenneth M. Johnson

THE UNITED STATES did not acquire all of Mexico for various reasons, some of which were explained in the previous chapter. However, just why the American acquisition of Baja California was not included in the Treaty of Guadalupe Hidalgo is the question to which Kenneth M. Johnson has directed his research. Having asked authorities in the field why Baja California escaped American grasp, the author usually was advised that Nicholas P. Trist violated his revised instructions. Yet his investigation revealed factors that had hindered the acquisition of Lower California and made the negotiation of the treaty very difficult. The author believes that Nicholas P. Trist has been unfairly blamed for the loss of Baja California. He concludes that no matter what Trist could have done, it would have been extremely difficult for the United States to pressure Mexicans into agreeing to the further fragmentation of their Republic. Thus Johnson contends that Trist was a good negotiator, for he had the essential qualities necessary: he knew when to stop negotiation and get a treaty signed.

This chapter originally appeared in JOURNAL *of the* WEST in April, 1972.

THIS STUDY is the result of two distinct but related matters. The first was a curiosity as to why Baja California was not ceded to the United States under the Treaty of Guadalupe Hidalgo. I knew in a general way that President Polk had stated that the cession of both Californias would be required in any settlement of the war. In discussing this with a rather well informed person in the field the answer was, "Baja California — Nicholas P. Trist gave it away when he negotiated the Treaty of Guadalupe Hidalgo." This led to an examination of Trist and his activities, and he turned out to be an unusual and interesting person. To complement a brief sketch of his life a few notes on the war with Mexico appeared advisable.

The second matter was the actual negotiation of the treaty. Negotiation is a subject that has long interested me. As a lawyer I have, over the years, acted many times as a negotiator or mediator, and as a result felt an empathy for Trist. The bargaining table, the long meetings, the return to the hotel, the before dinner drinks, and the after dinner discussions as to strategy all leave one bone-tired but matched with exhilaration when finally agreement is reached. The negotiator usually has two battles; the first with his counterpart on the other side, and then with his principal to convince him that what has been accomplished is the best that could be done. The latter is sometimes as difficult as the first.

THE WAR WITH MEXICO

President James K. Polk was an expansionist and he was most anxious to extend the United States to the Pacific through the acquisition of Oregon and California. To his credit both objectives were ac-

173

complished during his four-year term of office. While he hoped to avoid war as a method, nevertheless he would resort to war if necessary. For several years a dispute had existed between Texas and Mexico as to boundaries. The Texans claimed an area reaching to the Río Grande, while the Mexicans claimed that the border was the Nueces River. There is good reason to believe that Polk, through various emissaries, tried to persuade Texas to start a war over this matter which the United States would take over upon completion of annexation.[1] The Texans were not agreeable to this plan, and Polk then sent John Slidell to Mexico to negotiate the boundary question and to propose the purchase of California by the United States. Because of a political upheaval at the time the Mexican officials refused to see Slidell. Polk's next step was to send army units under General Zachary Taylor to the banks of the Río Grande. This, from the Mexican point of view, was an invasion by a foreign power. Clashes were inevitable and in May, 1846, the war was on. A most interesting and revealing statement of Polk's ideas about the war is found in his diary covering a cabinet meeting on May 13 and his discussions with James Buchanan, Secretary of State.

> Mr. Buchanan read the draft of a despatch which he had prepared to our Ministers at London, Paris, and other Foreign Courts, announcing the declaration of war against Mexico, with a statement of the causes and objects of the war, with a view that they should communicate its substance to the respective Governments to which they are accredited. Among other things Mr. Buchanan had stated that our object was not to dismember Mexico or to make conquests, and that the Del Norte was the boundary to which we claimed; or rather that in going to war we did not do so with a view to acquire either California or New Mexico or any other portion of the Mexican territory. I told Mr. Buchanan that I thought that such a declaration to Foreign Governments unnecessary and improper; that the causes of the war as set forth in my message to Congress and the accompanying documents were altogether satisfactory. I told him that though we had not gone to war for conquest, yet it was clear that in making peace we would if practicable obtain California and such other portion of the Mexican territory as would be sufficient to indemnify our claimants on Mexico, and to defray the expense of the war which that power by her long continued wrongs and injuries had forced us to wage. I told him it was well known that the Mexican Government had no other means of indemnifying us. Mr. Buchanan said if when Mr. McLane announced to Lord Aberdeen the existence of the war with Mexico the latter should demand of Mr. McLane to know if we intended to acquire California or any other part of the Mexican territory and no satisfactory answer was given, he thought it almost certain that both England and France would join with Mexico in the war against us. I told him that the war with Mexico was an affair with which neither England, France, or any other power had any concern; that such an inquiry would be insulting to our Government, and if made I would not answer it, even if the consequence should be a war with all of them. I told him I would not tie up my hands or make any pledge to any Foreign power as to the terms on which I would ultimately make peace with Mexico. I told him no Foreign [power] had any right to demand

any such assurance, and that I would make none such, let the consequences be what they might. Then, said Mr. Buchanan, you will have war with England as well as Mexico, and probably with France also, for neither of these powers will ever stand by and [see] California annexed to the U. S. I told him that before I would make the pledge which he proposed, I would meet the war which either England or France or all the Powers of Christendom might wage, and that I would stand and fight until the last man among us fell in the conflict. I told him that neither as a citizen nor as President would I permit or tolerate any intermeddling of any European Power on this Continent. Mr. Buchanan said if my views were carried out, we would not settle the Oregon question and we would have war with England. I told him there was no connection between the Oregon and Mexican question[s], and that sooner than give the pledge he proposed that if we could fairly and honourably acquire California or any other part of the Mexican Territory which we desired, I would let the war which he apprehended with England come and would take the whole responsibility. The Secretary of the Treasury engaged warmly and even in an excited manner against the proposition of Mr. Buchanan in his draft of his despatch. The Secretary of the Navy, The Atto. Gen'l, and the P. M. Gen'l in succession expressed similar opinions. Mr. Buchanan stood alone in the Cabinet, but was very earnest in expressing his views. . . . The discussion tonight was one of the most earnest and interesting which has ever occurred in my Cabinet.

The Cabinet adjourned about 11 o'clock p. m. and I retired to rest after a day of incessant application, anxiety, and labor.[2]

While the ostensible object of the war was the protection of the boundary claimed for Texas, it was clear from the start that the real purpose was territorial expansion. In view of the Cabinet discussions quoted above it is interesting to recall a portion of Polk's first annual message to Congress on December 2, 1845:

It is well known to the American people and to all nations that this Government has never interfered with the relations subsisting between other governments. We have never made ourselves parties to their wars or their alliances; we have not sought their territories by conquest.[3]

What Polk specifically desired out of the war was both Californias and New Mexico. (Alta California, of course, included the area now covered by the states of California, Nevada, Utah, and part of Colorado.) This is stated many times in his diary, and as late as his third annual message to Congress (December 7, 1847) we find him saying:

The cession to the United States by Mexico of the Provinces of New Mexico and the Californias, as proposed by the commissioner of the United States, it was believed would be more in accordance with the convenience and interests of both nations than any other cession of territory which it was probable Mexico could be induced to make.[4]

The war with Mexico saw the start of the war correspondent. This was the first war involving the United States that was followed by newspaper reporters in the field representing the major papers in Boston, New York and New Orleans. In fact the Treaty of Guadalupe Hidalgo was brought to Washington by James L. Freaner, correspondent for the *New Orleans Delta*. There was, of course, a time lag of from ten to fifteen days between the happening of an event and its being reported in domestic papers; however the public was well informed as to what was going on.

Another somewhat unique feature of the war is the small amount of literature that it produced. The first complete history was that of Justin H. Smith which did not appear until 1919, seventy-one years after the event. In examining catalogues of rare book dealers one will find dozens of items listed under The Civil War, or The Confederacy, but only two or three under the heading, "The War with Mexico." The standard histories of California make only a passing reference to it as a whole, limiting any detailed discussion to what happened in what is now the State of California. Perhaps this lack of writing was occasioned by a sense of guilt, present but not admitted. However, it now appears that a change is developing; beginning in about 1955 there has been an increasing number of diaries of participants and scholarly studies published. An example is, THE SIGN OF THE EAGLE, *A View of Mexico 1830-1855* (The Copley Press Inc., San Diego, California, 1970). This is composed of the letters of Lieutenant John James Peck, a soldier in the conflict with Mexico with added comment and annotations. The book is illustrated with contemporary colored illustrations extremely well reproduced.

The war was also notable for the unusually large number of conflicts, jealousies, and quarrels which developed. These were on three levels: first between President Polk and his two principal generals, Winfield Scott and Zachary Taylor; next between various generals including Scott and Taylor, and lastly between those of the regular army and the volunteers. Polk took every opportunity to disparage and express his distrust of both Scott and Taylor.

> The Cabinet fully discussed the conduct of Gen'l Taylor and were agreed that he was unfit for the chief command, that he had not the mind enough for the station, that he was a bitter political partisan and had no sympathies with the administration. . . . I stated what all the Cabinet knew, that I had never suffered politics to mingle with the conduct of this war; that I had promoted Gen'l Taylor and treated him very kindly and given him my confidence as chief in command of the army, but that I was compelled to believe that he had been weak enough to suffer himself to be controlled by political partisans, who had no command in the army, but who had attached themselves to it and had attended his camp for political purposes.[5]
>
> I have no great confidence in Gen'l Scott as a military commander . . . it is with reluctance that I assign him to this important command.[6]

The subsequent victories achieved by his generals did nothing to cause Polk to revise his opinion, and the diary continues to express his dislike and distrust. The fact that Polk was a Democrat and the two generals were Whigs did not help the situation.

As noted Scott and Taylor were both members of the Whig party; both were also politicians, and each hoped to be the party's candidate in the presidential election of 1848. Scott was jealous of Taylor because he was in the field first, and his victories in the north were giving him a great amount of favorable publicity. Taylor in turn became highly displeased with Scott when the latter diverted some of Taylor's troops to Vera Cruz and the Mexico City campaign, headed by Scott. In Scott's command quarrels and rivalries developed at an alarming rate. Again quoting from Polk's Diary for December 30, 1847:

> The Secretary of War called and handed me despatches which he had received by last night's mail from Gen'l Scott. Among them were charges preferred by Gen'l Scott against Major Gen'l Pillow, Brevet Maj'r Gen'l Worth and Brevet Col. Duncan of the U. S. Army. He left the despatches with me and I read them carefully. I deplore the unfortunate collusions which have arisen between the Gen'l officers in Mexico, as they must prove highly prejudicial to the public service. They have been produced as I have reason to believe, more by the vanity and tyrannical temper of General Scott and his want of prudence and common sense than from any other cause. . . . The whole difficulty has grown out of letters written from the army and published in the newspapers of the U. S., in which Gen'l S. is not made the exclusive hero of the War.[7]

A little later General William J. Worth filed charges against Scott and Scott was relieved of his command in January, 1848. It was true that various generals wrote to newspapers under a pseudonym criticizing their superiors, associates and the conduct of the war in general. It would appear that Scott had to battle with two sets of generals — those of Mexico and his own.

The last conflict was between those of the regular army and the volunteers; this existed at both the officer and enlisted levels. The officers of the volunteers considered those of the regular army to be snobbish, and the latter believed, that in the main, the former, many of whom were in office because of political reasons, were incompetent. Whenever there was a tough or dirty job to do, the volunteers felt that it was always assigned to them. Whenever there was a rape or an assault on civilians, and in Mexico City there was a good amount of this, if volunteers were involved this would always be noted; if the regular army was concerned the incident would be merely reported, without notation as to the class of participants. Hostility was mutual. In view of the disputes and conflicts within the American military forces it was a miracle that the war was won.

The war was far from having universal approval by the people as a whole; there were hawks and doves. The situation was similar to that now existing in the war with Vietnam. While the war was generally more favored by the Democratic Party the split was not really based on party lines. There were hawks and doves in both parties. Many in the north were suspicious of the war because in one way or another slavery might spread into the provinces acquired from Mexico by conquest. There were letters to editors and editorials *pro* and *con*. An example of the latter follows:

> We can easily defeat the armies of Mexico, slaughter them by the thousands, and pursue them perhaps to their capital; we can conquer and "annex" their territory; but what then? Have the histories of the ruin of Greek and Roman liberty consequent on such extensions of empire by the sword no lesson for us? Who believes that a score of victories over Mexico, the "annexation" of half her provinces, will give us more liberty, a purer Morality, a more prosperous Industry, than we now have? . . . Is not Life not miserable enough, comes not death soon enough, without resort to the hideous enginery of War?
>
> People of the United States! Your Rulers are precipitating you into a fathomless abyss of crime and calamity! Why sleep you thoughtless on its verge, as though this was not your business, or Murder could be hid from the sight of God by a few flimsy rags called banners. Awake and arrest the work of butchery ere it be too late to preserve your souls from the guilt of wholesale slaughter.[8]

In April, 1847, the Massachusetts Legislature passed a resolution condemning the war and said in part, "That such a war of conquest, so hateful in its objects, so wanton, unjust and unconstitutional in its origin and character, must be regarded as a war against freedom, against justice. . . ."[9] There was no question but that it was a country divided.

It is not the purpose of this article to tell the story of the Mexican War, or to outline in any detail the military activities in Baja California. The actions in the south end of the peninsula in a sense paralleled those in Upper California: no resistance to initial occupation, followed by an easily quashed revolt by the natives. In the La Paz area the majority of the citizens, on the theory that "if you can't beat them, join them," accepted the presence of the American forces and relations became rather friendly; officers were entertained and fishing parties arranged. When it was discovered that Baja California was to to be retained by Mexico these people suddenly became traitors and had to be removed for their own protection. I had always believed that the citizens were a little naïve in their assumption that the peninsula would remain under the jurisdiction of the United States. However it is true that rather definite assurance was given; in November, 1847, Commander Shubrick issued the following:

To the People of Lower California:

> The undersigned, commander in-chief of the Naval forces in the Pacific ocean, has learned that certain persons, unfriendly to the maintenance of the power of the United States in Lower California, have been

busy in encouraging disaffection, and under the plea of patriotic motives, are endeavoring to raise a party to serve their own selfish purposes. He is informed of the names of those who are thus busy in disturbing the peace, with a view only to take advantage of a state of misrule and disorder, to plunder their more peaceable fellow-citizens.

It will be in the power of the commander-in-chief, very soon, to turn his attention more particularly to Lower California. He, in the meantime, invites the well-disposed to stand fast in their fidelity, and he warns the evil-disposed that they will be sought wherever they may endeavor to conceal themselves, and when found, will be treated with severity.

The flag of the United State is destined to wave forever over the Californias. No contingency can be foreseen in which the United States will surrender or relinquish their possession of the Californias. . . .

W. Braford Shubrick,
Commander in Chief of the U.S. Naval Force in the Pacific Area.[10]

There was another unfortunate incident; Captain Henry M. Naglee of the New York Volunteers, and later a brigadier general in the Civil War and a prominent California business man and agriculturist, shot or caused to be shot, two Yaqui Indian prisoners who it was assumed were aiding the natives in revolt.

Viewing the war as objectively as possible it is difficult to quarrel with a statement from a Mexican source.

From the acts referred to, it has been clearly shown, that the real and effective cause of this was imposed upon us was the spirit of aggrandizement of the United States of the North, availing itself of its power to conquer us. Impartial history will someday clearly demonstrate that the conduct observed by that Republic was contrary to all laws divine and human, in an age that is called one of light, but which in fact is one of force and violence.[11]

A study of the spirit of the times in general, and of the Mexican War in particular, has led at least this writer to two conclusions. The first is that Mexico would have lost California and New Mexico even if the war had not been fought. Whatever it may be called, "manifest destiny" or "westward tilt," the movement for expansion to the West was an economic, social and political reality. If gold had not been discovered in California infiltration would have created another Texas situation. Assuming that there had not been a war the gold discovery would have speeded up the process. The acquisition of California by the United States was inevitable; the war was one method, but if there had been no war, another would have been found. The western migration which began in 1846 would surge ahead, war or no war, gold or no gold. It is perhaps significant that regardless of the unjust and unmoral nature of the war with Mexico no one has proposed that we give back any of the territory acquired. It has been said that the course of history is determined by the totality of conditions which make change inevitable, or by a willful man with power; the war with Mexico is an example of both.

The second conclusion is that the campaign of General Scott from Tampico, to Vera Cruz, to Mexico City, was one of the most brilliant military operations in history. With not enough troops, uncertain supplies, and disloyal subordinates he accomplished what from a theoretical military point of view would have been impossible. He was a great general even though his fame has not been completely recognized, clouded possibly by his admittedly irascible nature.

The Man

Nicholas Philip Trist was a member of the old time aristocracy of Virginia and was born in Charlottesville in that state on June 2, 1800.[12] He attended the United States Military Academy at West Point, but did not graduate, and commenced the study of law in the office of former President Thomas Jefferson. He was admitted to the bar of Virginia. Shortly thereafter he married the granddaughter of Jefferson, Virginia Jefferson Randolph. Jefferson became very fond of Trist and the latter, with his wife Virginia, resided at various times at Monticello, Jefferson's famous home. When Jefferson died in 1826 it was learned that Trist was one of three executors named in the will and was the one who accepted the laboring oar. Jefferson was completely bankrupt at the time of his death and the problems of the estate were many and complex. Trist appears to have done an excellent job of straightening out the complicated affairs of the estate. At about this time it became apparent that Trist's mother-in-law, Martha Jefferson Randolph, was also in deep financial difficulty and was being harrassed by creditors. Trist was earning very little, and to help Mrs. Randolph, Henry Clay, Secretary of State under John Quincy Adams, appointed Trist as a clerk in the State Department in 1828. The appointment was continued under the administration of Andrew Jackson and Trist became very friendly with him and at times acted as presidential secretary.

Trist was still lacking substantial income and managed to obtain, in April, 1833, a commission as United States Consul at Havana, Cuba. At this time consuls did not receive salaries but were compensated by retaining fees, and Havana was considered to be a very remunerative post. Trist's annual income in the State Department would have been about $1,600, while as consul he could expect something in the neighborhood of $5,000. While in Cuba Trist was able to buy a sugar plantation but in the end this resulted in a loss. The elite of Virginia were able in politics, but not so good in business. Trist suffered various difficulties while serving as consul; he was very strait-laced and if some American sailors got into a brawl and were jailed, and if Trist felt that they got what they deserved, his efforts to obtain their release would be less than spectacular. Also a consul was supposed to close his eyes to smuggling, or violations of import-export regulations by his countrymen; this Trist refused to do. This led to formal complaints by ships' captains and owners. The British Government also charged that Trist was hindering its officers engaged in slave-trade patrol operations. (Earlier England had abolished slavery and the slave-trade, and Trist was a slave-owner). While tempestuous is probably too strong a word to apply to Trist's term as consul it was certainly not serene. As a result of all of the complaints a Congressional hearing was held and Trist returned for a short time to the United States to attend the hearings which found no fault with his activities.[13] Trist continued as consul until July, 1841, when President John Tyler replaced him with someone else, not because of the complaints but as a result of the requirements of political patronage by a new President.

The period between 1841 and 1845 was difficult for Trist. He had, with his brother, an interest in a sugar plantation in Louisiana, but flooding and a fall in the price of sugar greatly reduced income from this source. He did some legal work and kept in close touch with his friends in national politics. One friend not in this class, and unusual for a man of Trist's background, was Robert Dale Owen, the social reformer and mystic of New Harmony, Indiana. In the Trist papers there is considerable correspondence between the two, and Trist sought Owen's advice on the education of his children. Later Owen was a very active abolitionist on the question of slavery, a position probably not favored by Trist.

In 1845 James K. Polk became President and named James Buchanan Secretary of State; Trist now again had friends in office and was soon brought back into the State Department with the title of chief clerk. This title does not indicate the importance of the position; Trist was "number two" man in the department and acted as Secretary of State in the absence of Buchanan. Today he would be called first undersecretary, or chief administrative officer. Trist thus assumed office at about the time of the start of the Mexican War and was in a position to know at first hand what was going on. In April, 1847, Trist was sent to Mexico on his famous mission, and then recalled, all of which will be treated a little later.

Polk was furious at the action of Trist in not obeying his recall, and when Trist returned to Washington in May, 1848, refused to see him, and also refused to pay Trist for his expenses and compensation after the recall. This amounted to something more than $13,000. While on his mission Trist was not a government employee, and was paid from an executive fund controlled by President Polk. As a matter of course Trist also lost his position in the State Department. He again returned to the practice of law, but not with very great success; one case took about a year of his time, and he had to sue for his fee. To help out, Mrs. Trist started a school for young ladies, but this also was not a success and did not last very long.   In order to provide a more regular income Trist worked during this period as a railway paymaster at a salary reported to be one hundred dollars per month.   He had an interest in husbandry and, in 1856, for the Farmers' Library, translated from the French a book by François Guenon entitled, A Treatise on Milch Cows.   Trist's middle years were certainly difficult from a financial viewpoint.   However, during the last years of his life financial security was assured.   In 1870 President Grant appointed Trist as postmaster at Alexandria, Virginia.   In those days the position was a sinecure, and a good postmaster was one who did not meddle with the every-day work of the service.   In 1871, twenty-three years after the event, Congress passed a special bill awarding Trist $14,599 for back pay and expenses in connection with the treaty mission.[14]   His last years appear to have been pleasant; as a friend of Presidents Jefferson, Madison and Jackson, and of General Scott he was regularly visited by those writing about the politics of the period and those prominent in it.   Trist died at Alexandria on February 11, 1874.

The Treaty

Expansionist-minded Senator Thomas Hart Benton of Missouri was a frequent visitor to President Polk and was the first to suggest to the President that it would be wise to have a commissioner authorized to conclude a treaty of peace, and that such commissioner should accompany General Scott.   Polk and Buchanan agreed that this proposal was desirable, and the problem then arose as to who should engage in this mission.   Generals Taylor and Scott were already running for the Presidency and Polk did not want anyone whose political ambitions might be advanced by the negotiation of a successful treaty.   Trist was soon selected for this post; he had several years of experience in the State Department, and because of the time spent in Cuba was perfectly at home in the Spanish language.   Trist was appointed on April 15, 1847, and shortly thereafter left for Mexico to join General Scott.   The entire operation was conducted in the deepest of secrecy.   Presumably only the President, his cabinet, and one clerk in the State Department had knowledge of the plan and all were charged to keep it top secret.   However, then as now, government secrets sometimes find their way out.   What happened can best be told in Polk's diary for April 21, 1847.

> My attention was called this morning to two letters purporting to have been written at this city and published in the *New York Herald*, in which the writer discloses with remarkable accuracy and particularity the fact of the departure of Mr. N. P. Trist, chief clerk in the Department of State, on a mission to Mexico.   The statement is so accurate and minute that the writer must have obtained information on the subject from someone who was entrusted with the secret.   It was a profound Cabinet secret, and was so expressly declared by me, and was communicated to no one else but to Mr. Trist himself and to Mr. Derrick, a clerk in the Department of State. . . .   In disclosing the fact of the mission of Mr.

Trist and its objects there has been treachery somewhere. I cannot believe any of my Cabinet have betrayed my confidence, and conclude, in the absence of further information on the subject, that the disclosure must have been made by Mr. Derrick, the clerk in the State Department recommended by Mr. Buchanan as worthy of all confidence, and who was employed in preparing the writing. I have not been more vexed or excited since I have been President than at this occurrence. The success of Mr. Trist's mission I knew in the beginning must depend mainly on keeping it a secret from that portion of the Federal press and leading men in the country who, since the commencement of the war with Mexico, have been giving "aid and comfort" to the enemy by their course. I do not doubt that there are men among them who would incur the expense of sending a courier to Mexico, and incur any other expense to discourage Mexico from making a peace, for the purpose of having the war continued, in the hope that the Democratic administration might be brought into disrepute by continuing it to a protracted length, and that they might gain some political advantage in the next Presidential election by it. . . . In the course of an hour after I had read the published letters in the *Herald,* Mr. Buchanan called on business. After it was transacted I called his attention to these letters. He had no knowledge how or through whom the matters disclosed in these letters had gained their way to the public. I told him that I strongly suspected Mr. Derrick, his Whig clerk in the State Department, who he had insisted should be trusted to aid in preparing the papers.[15]

Polk later called in Mr. Derrick who denied that he had released the information to any one. Polk was probably right in his suspicion that the leak had come from the State Department. All of the members of the Cabinet knew of Trist's mission; however there is no indication that they were informed of the details disclosed in the newspaper revelations. The question of how the leak occurred was never solved However, the event was the beginning of a certain coolness between the President and his Secretary of State. Thereafter in Polk's diary there are many remarks disparaging Buchanan.

During the foregoing commotion Trist was on his way to Mexico, sailing from New Orleans and arriving in Vera Cruz on May 6, 1847. Trist had with him his appointment and a letter from Buchanan to be delivered to the Mexican Minister of Exterior. With this letter was a draft of a proposed treaty which Buchanan, to bring in a little of the language of diplomacy, termed the *"Projet Treaty."* When Trist arrived in Vera Cruz General Scott was in Jalapa; as a result Trist sent the letter to Scott asking that it be sent to the Mexican Government. Scott, feeling that the Department of State was meddling in military matters, and that he was being used as a messenger boy became incensed, and several angry letters were exchanged. One from Scott to Trist from Puebla, dated May 27, indicates Scott's low boiling point and is a classic example of vituperation.

Sir: Your long studied letters of the 9th and 20th instant, making 30 pages, in reply to my short note of the 7th were handed to me, under one cover, at Jalapa, the morning of the 21st, when you knew, being on the spot, that I was about to march upon this place. Occupied, as I was, with business of much higher importance, I did not allow the seal of the package to be broken till the evening of the 22nd, which I took care to have done in the presence of many staff officers. One of them, at my instance, read a part, and reported to me the general character of the papers. I have not yet read them.

My first impulse was to return the farrago of insolence, conceit, and arrogance to the author; but, on reflection, I have determined to preserve the letters as a choice specimen of diplomatic literature and manners. The jacobin convention of France never sent to one of its armies in the field a more amiable and accomplished instrument. If you were armed with an ambulatory guillotine you would be the personification of Danton, Marat, and St. Just, all in one.

You tell me that you are authorized to negotiate a treaty of peace with the enemy, a declaration which, as it rests on your own word, I might well question; and you add that it was not intended at Washington that I should have anything to do with the negotiation. This I can well believe, and certainly have cause to be thankful to the President for not degrading me by placing me in any joint commission with you.

From the letter of the Secretary of War to me, of the 14th ultimo, I had supposed you to be simply authorized to propose, or concede to the enemy, the truce or armistice which usually precedes negotiations for a peace; and my letter to you was written on that supposition. If the terms of military conventions are left to me, the commander of this army, I have nothing more to desire or to demand for its safety.

In conclusion — for many persons here believe that the enemy, 20,000 strong, is about to attack this place — I have only time to ask you, in your future communications to me, to be brief and purely official; for, if you dare to use the style of orders or instructions again, or to indulge yourself in a single discourteous phrase, I shall throw back the communication with the contempt and scorn which you merit at my hands.[16]

Both Scott and Trist wrote angry letters complaining about each other to their superiors (W. L. Marcy, Secretary of War, and Buchanan, Secretary of State); however, a little later when they became better acquainted they also became very friendly and requested that their earlier caustic comments on each other be removed from the files. Scott to Marcy, July 25, 1847:

Although daily in expectation of something of special interest to communicate, nothing has occurred of that character, save a happy change in my relations, both official and private, with Mr. Trist. Since about the 26th ultimo, our intercourse has been frequent and cordial, and I have found him able, discreet, courteous, and amiable.[17]

Trist to Buchanan, July 23, 1847:

Justice — to say nothing of my own feelings toward a gentleman and public servant, [Scott] whose character I now believe that I had entirely misconceived — demands that I should embrace this early opportunity to say, that his whole conduct, in this regard, has been characterized by the purest public spirit, and a fidelity and devotion which could not be surpassed, to the views of the government, in regard to the restoration of peace. . . . Under these circumstances, it could not but be a cause of most serious regret on my part, if the correspondence between us, that took place shortly after my arrival in this country, should in any way be brought to the notice of the public; and consequently, if, in your judgment consistent with propriety, it would be highly gratifying to me to be permitted to withdraw it from the files of the department.[18]

During Scott's inexorable march from Vera Cruz to the central valley of Mexico the fluid and chaotic nature of the Mexican Government prevented Trist from having any meaningful negotiations as to a possible treaty. Antonio López de Santa Anna, a brilliant but unstable leader, was in and out of the Presidency. In April, 1847, the Mexican Congress adopted a decree reading in part as follows: "Every individual is declared a traitor, who either as a private individual, or as a public officer, either privately, or invested with official authority, or of revolutionary origin, shall treat with the government of the United States."[19] Certainly the time was not propitious for treaty negotiations. However, on August 22, 1847, when Scott was at the gates of Mexico City, Santa Anna proposed an armistice to provide for discussions which would lead to a treaty of peace. Commissioners were named to act for the government of Mexico, and within a few days meetings with Trist were arranged. Trist presented his draft treaty and the Mexicans came back with their proposed treaty; however, before anything could be determined, the armistice was terminated, both sides contending that the other had violated its terms. Fighting was recommenced and, on September 14, the capital was occupied. At this point there was, in effect, no Mexican Government with whom Trist could deal.

In the meantime back in Washington President Polk was becoming increasingly dissatisfied with Trist. He had been in Mexico for about six months and there was not even a suggestion of a treaty of peace. Polk appeared to have little knowledge or understanding of the realities in Mexico. In any event on October 6, 1847, Buchanan at the request of Polk sent a letter of recall to Trist. For some reason there was a delay and this letter did not reach Trist until November 16. This was just after the Mexicans had set up a provisional government at Queretaro and had advised Trist of a desire to open negotiations. After a good deal of soul-searching he decided to ignore his recall, and to attempt to form a treaty acceptable to himself and the Mexican commissioners. These were, José Bernado Couto, an able and prominent lawyer; Miguel Atristain, a former member of the Congress, and Luis Gonzago Cuevas, a former minister for foreign affairs of the republic. Couto and Atristain had served as commissioners during the earlier negotiations in August. Trist was strongly supported in his decision by

General Scott and the British legation which had acted as a go-between for Trist and the Mexican Government. In a sense the British had an ulterior motive to encourage an end to the war; a substantial portion of Mexican indebtedness was held in England and had been in default for some time. Peace might permit some payments. The Mexicans were, of course, informed of the termination of Trist's authority, but agreed to go ahead with the effort to reach agreement as to a treaty. Two principal facts led to Trist's determination to ignore his orders. The first was a feeling that the Mexicans were now in a mood favorable to peace and a treaty; a delay might prevent any treaty and a renewal of intensive warfare. Also the positions of the Americans at Monterrey and Mexico City were rather precarious; supply lines were long, and it was only a question of time when there would arise an able and bold guerrilla leader who could seriously imperil the position of the invaders.

In the Trist papers in the Library of Congress there is a letter from Trist to his wife dated December 4, 1847; it is a chatty, newsy letter of the type one would usually expect. However, it does contain a very interesting postscript reading as follows:

> In my last (28th ulto) I desired you to say to Mr. B. that I have had a final irrevocable farewell to all official employment, and to give him my very best regards and most heartfelt regret at parting with him. Procure the key to this cypher (your sagacity will tell you where) and decipher the following to be read to him most secretly. This determination, I came to this day, at 12 o'clock. It is altogether my own.
> Knowing it to be the very last chance, and impressed with the dreadful consequences to our country which cannot fail to attend the loss of that chance 75, 52, 39, 18, 65, 19, 1, 13, 3, 23, 58, 41, 10, 39, 29, 14, 27, 20, 61, 30, 7, 12, 45, 30, 9, 17, 29, 2, 3, 99, 23, 4, 41, 40, of, 6, 114, 5, 73, 3, 215, 50, 27, 200, 44, & across 61, 115, 32°, 21, 41, 200, 41, 20, 24, 15, 75, 26, besides the 3, 121, 4, 36, 23, 26, 73.

Mrs. Trist did have the sagacity to locate the key and the message decoded read, "I will make a treaty, if it can be done on the basis of up the Bravo and across by the 32°; giving 15 million besides the 3 million cash."

Two days later Trist apparently came to the conclusion that Buchanan should be more completely informed, and sent to the Secretary of State a sixty-one page letter, a typical example of Trist's extreme prolixity. Buchanan brought the letter to President Polk, and in the latter's diary under the date of January 15, 1848, he comments as follows:

> It [the letter] was dated on the 6th of Dec. last, and the most extraordinary document I have ever heard from a Diplomatic Representative. Though he had in a previous despatch acknowledged the receipt of his letter of recall from the Secretary of State, he announces that he had reopened negotiations with the Mexican authorities and had resolved to conclude a Treaty with them. His despatch is arrogant, impudent, and very insulting to his Government, and even personally offensive to the

President. He admits he is acting without authority and in violation of the positive order recalling him. It is manifest to me that he has become the tool of Gen'l Scott and his menial instrument, and that the paper was written at Scott's instance and dictation. I have never in my life felt so indignant. . . . If there was any legal provision for his punishment he ought to be severely handled. He has acted worse than any man in the public employ whom I have ever known. His despatch proves that he is destitute of honour or principle, and that he has proved himself to be a very base man.

The draft treaty that Trist carried to Mexico provided for the cession of both Californias to the United States in addition to New Mexico. This was in accord with all of the public statements as to the territory to be acquired; however, the instructions from Buchanan to Trist contained the following:

> While it is of the greatest importance to the United States to extend their boundaries over Lower California, as well as New Mexico and Upper California, you are not to consider this as a *sine qua non* to the conclusion of a treaty. You will, therefore, not break off the negotiation if New Mexico and Upper California can alone be acquired. In that event, however, you will not stipulate to pay more than twenty millions of dollars for these two provinces without the right of passage and transit across the isthmus of Tehuantepec.[20]

In the preliminary meetings in the latter part of August, 1847, Trist was probably surprised that the Mexican commissioners were absolutely adamant in their refusal of any suggestion that Lower California be ceded to the United States. However, there were five apparent reasons which consciously or otherwise motivated their thinking. (1) an exaggerated view of the value of the pearl fisheries on the east coast of the peninsula; (2) an expectation that in the mountains more or less opposite those in Sonora there would be valuable silver mines; (3) Baja California was well known and had a substantial literature — Venegas, Baegert, Clavijero, and Sales; (4) it was a face-saving gesture; the commissioners could say they did not give the United States everything it demanded, and (5) the commissioners had knowledge of Trist's instructions. There was a letter from Buchanan to Trist dated July 13, 1847, which contained a paragraph beginning with, "In case Lower California cannot be obtained . . ." This letter was hand-carried by Colonel Lewis D. Wilson who died in Vera Cruz on August 12, 1847. In some way the despatch came into Mexican hands for it was delivered to Trist, with the envelope opened, by a messenger acting for Luis de la Rosa, Minister of Foreign Relations. This matter is not of too much importance since Trist himself revealed that Lower California was not a *sine qua non*, during the negotiations in the latter part of August.[21]

Trist's description of the attitude of the Mexicans toward Lower California is of some interest and follows:

With respect to the lower part of Alta California, the commissioners had insisted upon the absolute necessity of their possessing an overland passage to Lower California; and although they were, I believe, struck with the truth which I pointed out to them, that their possessing the lower part of the Colorado would inevitably give rise in a short time to the old Mississippi question over again; yet they are so completely mastered by the *need of the moment,* (to part with the least possible amount of territory,) that it outweighs every consideration. . . . This I believe was the only reason for their catching up at once my remark, that my instructions did not require me to insist upon Lower California, and their setting down the abandonment of this part of our pretension as a settled point, regardless of the curtailment of the pecuniary compensation which I told them would necessarily result therefrom. In their hearts they were convinced of the truth of what I said (nay it was expressly assented to), that no benefit whatever resulted to Mexico from the possession of Lower California, whereas she would derive great advantage from the influences exercised over her sea coast opposite to the inner shore of that peninsula, by the flourishing commercial towns which would in a very short time spring up under the American flag. But this conviction had no influence, nor could it be expected to have any influence, over the determination of minds preoccupied by the one overwhelming consideration to which I have adverted.

Their retention of Lower California being decided upon, it followed (so they said) as a matter of course, that they must reserve also a land passage to that portion of their territory; though I believe that here also their real motive was to save appearances, more than anything else, and avoid exposing themselves, and the treaty into which they might enter, to the clamor that they had insulated Lower California, and by so doing had placed it at the mercy of our maritime power. That the possession of the land communication makes no practical difference whatever, under the existing circumstances and prospects of the two countries, is perfectly obvious.[22]

So, Baja California was lost. In the actual drafting of the treaty the leader for the Mexicans was Bernardo Couto, a well educated and highly respected lawyer whose blessing of the treaty was of material importance in its final acceptance by the Mexican Congress. Drafting a contract (and a treaty is a contract) in two languages so that each version means exactly the same is a delicate and difficult task. In a letter to Buchanan, Trist describes the drafting and redrafting of the various sections, and then goes on to say:

In this manner, modifications and remodifications succeeded each other, with reference to every topic the treaty contains; until finally its various stipulations were agreed upon, both as to substance and as to form. As this was done, the articles were written anew by me, translated by one of the commissioners (Senor Cuevas, who reads English very well, although he does not speak it or understand it when spoken) and then the phraseology changed in one or the other version, or in both, so that the idiom of both languages might be preserved, whilst at the same time the treaty should present in both a correspondence of expressions as well as a perfect identity of sense. In this I had to indulge the gentlemen on the other side (whose language is more peremptory than ours in its requirements for correct style) by allowing them to put into what they considered idiomatic Spanish the meaning of the articles drafted by me, varying the structure as far as they deemed necessary; and then myself writing the articles over again in English, so as to make them conform to the Spanish. As a result of this labor, the treaty, whilst it is in both English and Spanish, and not on either side a mere literal translation from the other, will be found to exhibit a correspondence in the two languages, which is by no means common in those which have come under my examination.[23]

Negotiations continued through the month of December and well into January, 1848. Nowhere in the record is there any suggestion that Trist had a secretary, or any staff other than a negro personal servant, presumedly a slave. As a result it was one against three, with the Mexicans stalling for time in the hope that something would happen to improve their position. Once it was decided that Lower California would remain in Mexican hands, then the question of where to draw the line arose. The Mexican commissioners attempted to persuade Trist that San Diego was really in Lower California.[24] The boundary question was the most important item on the agenda and various maps were examined including those of de Mofras. In the interpreting of the maps Trist was assisted by the very able captain of the Corps of Army Engineers, Robert E. Lee. At the eastern terminus of the line the famous Disturnell map was used, and this would later cause difficulty because the map mislocated El Paso. As far as the western terminus was concerned it was agreed that it would start

> . . . one marine league due south of the southernmost point of the port of San Diego, according to the plan of said port made in the year 1782 by Don Juan Pantoja, second sailing-master of the Spanish fleet, and published at Madrid in the year 1802, in the Atlas to the voyage of the schooners *Sutil* and *Mexicana*, of which plan a copy is hereunto added signed and sealed by the respective plenipotentiaries.[25]

Toward the end of January Trist's position hardened and he told the Mexican commissioners that the treaty was now in form acceptable to him, and that if the Mexicans did not sign within a few days all negotiations would end. On January 25, 1848, Trist wrote to Buchanan and said that he was sure that the treaty would shortly be signed; it was signed by all on February 2, 1848, and as already noted reached President Polk on February 19. Just two days after Trist had written to Buchanan, Polk sent a dispatch on January 27 to General William O. Butler (having already decided to relieve General Scott) directing that Trist be placed under arrest and sent back to the United States. Although Trist remained in Mexico for a while to testify at the Court of Inquiry concerning General Scott, he did become technically a military prisoner and was such when he returned home.

In remote Lower California the news of the treaty did not reach the American forces until the first part of April. As a result there was a minor engagement at Todos Santos on March 30; however, this was the last military action on the peninsula.

Back in Washington Polk, after the arrival of the treaty, faced serious problems. Those in opposition to the war were becoming more vocal and aggressive. Polk was having difficulty in persuading Congress to pass the required appropriations. Because of this background, Polk, in spite of his feelings of animosity toward Trist, decided to submit the treaty to the Senate, noting that, ". . . conforming, as it does substantially on the main questions of boundary and indemnity, to the terms which our commissioner when he left the United States . . . was authorized to offer . . ."[26] The treaty went before the Senate on February 23, 1848. The first act was a resolution by Senator Samuel Houston in which he referred to Trist as falsely representing his authority, acting contumaciously, and to the treaty as, "having been signed by a person falsely representing himself as a minister of this government while acting in violation of his instructions, the laws of the land, and the constitution of this Union, and to the great scandal of our national character."[27] With some modifications the treaty was ratified by the Senate on March 10 by a vote of thirty-eight to fourteen, by the Mexican Congress on May 25, and became fully effective on May 30, 1848.

One thing historians delight in doing is to recast popular conceptions as to some historical figure. To an extent this is happening to Trist. In the past he has been viewed as not brilliant but able; he had a job to do and he did it. He has been referred to as a diplomat with ideals (see note 12), and appeared to be a member of that very rare species, a bureaucrat who would accept responsibilities. However in a recent article Professor Jack Nortrup takes the position that Trist was a bungler and a dupe of the Mexican commissioners.[28] Terms such as "overinflated ego" and "inept" are applied to Trist. Nortrup indicates that Trist was unduly sympathetic to the Mexican position and states that Trist had announced, "that he would rather die than submit to the American terms if he were a Mexican." This is supported by a footnote to the diary of Inspector General Ethan Allen Hitchcock. However read in its context the remark loses a great deal of force and there is a certain amount of irony.

> I have often entered my protest against this war, and to-day I hear, from very good authority, that our commissioner has said that if he were a Mexican he would die before he would agree to the terms proposed by the United States. He ought, then to have refused the mission he has undertaken. A degrading proposition is alike dishonorable to him who proposes as to him to whom it is proposed.[29]

Another more recent work is also basically hostile to Trist.[30] There is one very strange statement in this book. On page 167 the authors deprecate Trist by stating that in the approximately sixty days between his decision to stay in Mexico, December 4, and make a treaty and its completion, the only communication by Trist with his government was by a coded postscript in a letter to his wife. In my copy of Senate Executive No. 52 (see note 20), I find letters from Trist to Buchanan dated December 6, 20, 26, 29, 1847, and January 12 and 25, 1848.

Trist may have lacked charisma, but in my opinion he was a notably successful negotiator. The territory acquired under the treaty contained what we now know as California, Arizona, New Mexico, Nevada, Utah, and portions of Wyoming, Colorado and Kansas. All of this for $15,000,000, less than the cost today of a Boeing 747. By the lowest estimates gold produced in California in 1848, 1849, and 1850 amounted to $51,669,767.[31] Inept or not, and even though Lower California was not obtained, the acts of Trist ended the war and caused the totality of the United States to reach from the Atlantic to the Pacific. Certainly he disobeyed orders; however in view of the results this becomes meaningless. An essential quality of a good negotiator is to know when to to give and when to stand firm; this Trist had. Thus I disagree with those who tend to denigrate Trist, and agree with Eugene K. Chamberlain (see note 21) who concludes his article with the statement that no blame attaches to Trist for the failure to acquire Lower California. I find only one fault with Trist, his extreme verbosity; if something could be said in ten words, he would use one hundred.

CHAPTER 16

Post-War Filibustering, 1850-1865

By Joseph A. Stout, Jr.

I N 1848 some Americans were chagrined that the United States had not insisted on the acquisition of more of Northern Mexico, especially Baja California and Sonora. To many people living in California, and those who went to the area later in the 1850s, it was only natural that these north Mexican areas should have become a part of the United States. This feeling, along with general frontier attitudes, provided the impetus for a number of filibustering intrusions into Northern Mexico with the ultimate aim of adding at least part of the territory to the continental United States. Six men led expeditions to Mexico; three lost their lives at the hands of Mexicans, and the remainder succeded only in getting out of Mexico with their lives. It is the contention of the author of this chapter that these participants in filibustering expeditions into Northwestern Mexico were not driven by the lofty ideology of Manifest Destiny, but rather that they were moved more by a spirit of adventure spawned on the frontier. These men represented "more the roily age in which they lived than any spirit of expansion."

This chapter originally appeared in JOURNAL *of the* WEST in April, 1972.

I N 1848 the Treaty of Guadalupe Hidalgo officially ended the war between the United States and Mexico, but several years would be required before Americans accepted the settlement. In fact, a particular group of men not only refused to accept the settlement, but for fifteen years after the war they attempted illegally to wrest away from Mexico even more territory. Further, it was almost natural that these *filibusteros* would invade Northwestern Mexico because that region was yet a frontier, and the frontier had always been a source of inspiration for those aspiring to a new start and new adventures. Moreover, the reminiscences and letters of participants in the war painted colorful pictures of the land to the south. It was a land of fascinating appeal: it was foreign, with a language strange to the Anglo and Saxon tongue; it was a distant, almost shimmering mirage; and it was badly governed by its ruling officials, torn by endless revolution, and subject to tyrannical dictators. Thus invasion of this territory carried with it a taste of flavorful adventure, a sense of lifting oppression from the shoulders of an inferior people, and a hope of quick wealth.

The decade and one-half following the end of the war saw six men making major attempts to wrest this territory (mainly Sonora and Baja California) away from its owner. These six men all came to the region ostensibly as colonizers, but in reality they saw themselves as presidents, sultans, or dukes creating new republics, dukedoms, or fiefs. Four of the men were from the Southern United States, while the other two were natives of France. Many Southerners and Frenchmen of this era were noted more for their romantic and quixotic visions than for any grasp of hard reality. Most of the filibusters were men who in one way or another had failed to win the fortune, high political office, and fame that they had sought through the usual channels and so turned to visions of themselves as rulers by self-proclamation and strength of arms rather than by election.

Inured to the boisterous, turbulent conditions on the frontier, those Americans who failed to find quick wealth in the gold fields sought prestige and riches by encouraging illegal filibustering expeditions into Northern Mexico. Many factors drove these reckless men. Some Southerners in California may have been interested in acquisition of territory for the expansion of slavery. Others merely wanted wealth and power.[1] In the United States the sectional conflict over expansion of slavery influenced most legislation in Congress to a greater or lesser degree — Northerners long had denounced attempts to annex new territory as part of the Southern slaveocracy conspiracy.

In Mexico conflict also existed, for although the war with the United States had begun with a degree of popular support and optimism, public opinion soon turned to apathy and discontent. Mexican governments rose and fell with dazzling rapidity. Nevertheless, one constant existed in Mexico — intense dislike and distrust of Americans. "Gringos" were hated or feared, and there were those who did not conceal their antipathy. Mexico had lost nearly one-half of its sovereign territory by the terms of the Treaty of Guadalupe Hidalgo — a humiliating experience for any patriotic and proud Mexican.[2]

Complicating the politics of Mexico was the centralist-federalist conflict which began anew during this period. The Catholic Church and the Army, along with other traditional oligarchs, supported the conservative centralists, while many elements, including the social reformers, supported the liberal federalists. Late in 1848 General José Joaquín de Herrera, a liberal, became president, but reconstruction, lack of credit, and racial war in Yucatan precluded any possibility of reform. In 1851 General Mariano Arista, also a liberal, assumed the presidency through one of the few peaceful elections the country had ever experienced. Attempts to establish a stable economy led to Arista's removal in 1853.[3] With the liberals out of office, the stage once again was set for the final act of one of Mexico's most infamous villains, Antonio López de Santa Anna. Mexico would permanently bear the scars of his rule, while the filibustering activities of the post-war period were partly a result of his misrule of the country.

Yet another major problem was the frontier which had always been plagued with scarcity of population. The Mexican Government was aware of this, and made several attempts at colonization.[4] Unfortunately, even those souls who were adventurous enough to attempt settlement were unwilling to remain in the path of hosile Indians. Moreover, with news of the gold strike in California, Mexicans as well as "gringos" raced for the gold fields, leaving their farms and homes in

193

Northern Mexico to the Indians. Gold had been discovered in California just nine days before the signing of the Treaty of Guadalupe Hidalgo. Shortly afterwards, ships jammed the harbors along the California Coast as hundreds of thousands headed for what they hoped would be easy riches.

As the gold fever abated, the disillusioned turned back to the cities, only to face harsh reality. The cities swelled with despondent men, many of whom were forced to turn to illegal activities to secure even a meager livelihood. San Francisco was typical of these new lawless cities. Cattle rustlers, horse thieves, murderers, and misplaced gold-seekers roamed the streets. The saloons were scenes of shoot-outs, stabbings, and other crimes of violence. Thus the gold rush had created a special kind of man accustomed to disorder and violence, one with little regard for the value of life, and property.[5] Such an environment quite naturally would spawn and encourage several vain ventures, and, because land represented the wherewithal, filibustering fever flourished on the Western frontier.

Joseph C. Morehead, scion of a prominent Kentucky governor, was first to lead a group of adventurers into Northern Mexico. In 1850, while quartermaster general of California, Morehead was ordered to aid General Joshua Bean, who was commissioned to lead militia in tracking and punishing Yuma Indians for raiding on the frontier.[6]

Until the Yuma expedition, Morehead's career apparently had been as respectable as possible in a frontier state of the 1850s. Morehead and Bean split forces and each fought battles with the Indians in the area. However, the quartermaster general remained in the field far past the time necessary to defeat the Indians, and California officials were suspicious. In fact, during this time Morehead was planning greater exploits. He spent much of this time gathering supplies from ranchers, miners, and others unfortunate enough to be in his path.[7] Morehead actually bought two boats and prepared to send three groups of men to Sonora and Baja California. One vessel was to land at La Paz and the other at Mazatlán, but before he could set out for Mexico, he discovered he had insufficient funds to secure all of the needed supplies. While securing these supplies at San Diego, many of Morehead's men became disillusioned with his wild schemes and deserted to return to San Francisco.[8] Despite wide-spread knowledge of his difficulties in California Mexicans were worried and began to prepare defenses to repel the expected intruders.

Thus when Morehead's sea expedition finally reached Mazatlán, Mexican authorities there were prepared to arrest any Americans who came to the port armed or in a large group. When the *Josephine*, one of the invasion ships, reached Mazatlán, the Mexican authorities stormed aboard to search for arms and ammunition, but found nothing to justify seizing the boat or arresting the Morehead party. The invaders escaped a Mexican dungeon by claiming to be miners seeking work. Still a mystery is what happened to Morehead and his party at Mazatlán, as no further information is to be had about the group. The other two parts of the expedition also met a similar fate. One disbanded before getting to La Paz, and another heading overland to Sonora was turned back shortly after reaching the Mexican boundary. All members were fortunate, for the Mexicans merely forced them to leave the country, warning them that if they persisted they would be shot.

Thus this first of the attempts to wrest additional territory away from Mexico ended almost before it began. Significantly, Joseph C. Morehead — politician, scoundrel, and adventurer — infused his band of followers with a desire for conquest, but the delay in San Diego and confusion in Mexico demonstrated his inability to direct their actions. Meanwhile, during 1850 and 1851, when Morehead's expedition was taking shape, others schemed to colonize Mexico — legally or illegally.

During 1848 to 1852 thousands of Frenchmen journeyed to California and Mexico to seek their fortunes. France was torn by poverty, revolution, and economic depression during these years. Suffering under extreme hardship in their own country, the emigrating sons of Gaul sought any means of escape. Many went only for gold; others sought adventure; still others left France for political reasons.[9] By 1851 nearly twenty thousand Frenchmen lived in California, mostly in the central and northern parts.

Charles de Pindray, according to French writers of the age, was eminently suited for the role of adventurer. While drifting through San Francisco in 1850, Pindray learned that the Mexican vice-consul at San Francisco, William Schleiden, wanted colonists to establish a settlement in Northern Mexico. He believed this his golden opportunity and quickly volunteered to lead the expedition.[10] Plans were formulated, and men were recruited easily. So much enthusiasm developed for the enterprise that Pindray charged each volunteer forty to fifty dollars to become a member of the company. This provided some financial assistance and material support when the group reached Guaymas. In addition, Mexican colonization laws were being considered which would legalize French colonization on the frontiers and provide more financial support.[11]

Pindray and eighty-eight Frenchmen sailed for Mexico aboard the bark *Cumberland* in November, 1851. Additional reinforcements were soon to follow, increasing the size of the expedition to one hundred fifty men. The first group arrived at Guaymas a month later, receiving a favorable welcome from the local citizens. In addition, the Sonoran government even granted the Frenchmen three leagues of land near Cocospera, a village in the valley of Río San Miguel, and that state looked upon the French as deliverers from the Apache ravages. Pindray and his men reached Cocospera in March and began limited agricultural projects. The French remained there until a few reinforcements arrived from California, and then they began searching for lost mines.[12] It was at this point that Mexican authorities turned against the French.

The reasons for the Mexican change of heart were many, but primarily it came as a result of information about Pindray's past. Don Manuel Robles Pezuela, Minister of War for Mexico, wrote to General Miguel Blanco, military commander in Sonora, on April 28, 1852, explaining the background of the French leader and warning the local government of potential danger. Robles told Blanco that Pindray should be watched carefully, for the Frenchman had committed several acts against the French Republic and had been forced to leave France quickly to save his life. As a result of this information, Blanco refused additional supplies to the French. And Pindray was warned that if he disobeyed any Mexican laws, his men would be driven out of the country while he would be imprisoned at Mazatlán.

With the Mexicans withholding support and equipment, the colony began to disintegrate. Pindray tenaciously argued for his right to remain in Sonora, and attempted to force the government to comply with the earlier agreements.[13] At this point some of the Frenchmen gave up and headed for California — in disgust. Pindray tried one final time to persuade the Mexican Government to support his expedition. With a few of his men, he made a special trip to Ures hoping to force supplies from the authorities. Of course, such a belligerent attitude only seemed to confirm previous Mexican suspicions about him. The Mexicans refused him aid, so he and his men began the trip back to Cocospera. They stopped for the night at Rayon, and there mysteriously he died — possibly from a Mexican bullet.[14] The *Daily Alta California* of August 15, 1852, suggested that Pindray "committed suicide by blowing out his brains . . . whilst laboring under a high fever, and in a fit of despair."[15] When news of his death reached those survivors at Cocospera, many of them quickly returned to California, some to join other groups gathering to colonize in Mexico, and others just to be free of entangling agreements that could cost them their lives. Yet, even as Pindray failed, another Frenchman planned a new "colonization" venture for Northern Mexico.

Count Gaston Raousset-Boulbon also attempted an agreement with Mexican authorities allowing him to establish French colonies in Mexico. In truth, this French nobleman had more than colonies in mind, for he had a grandiose dream of becoming the "Sultan of Sonora." Nevertheless, many Mexican citizens were optimistic about the French colonizers, hoping settlements would help to stabilize the frontier. According to an American living in Guaymas at the time, all the people who had met Raousset were "convinced that this expedition must have the best result."[16] On April 10, 1852, after a brief trip to Mexico, Raousset returned to San Francisco to recruit his California adventurers. He seemed fully convinced that Mexicans would support his activities. However, while he was back in the United States, quarrels in Mexico between state and central government authorities caused changes in Mexican attitudes toward the French.

Yet Raousset continued to organize his group, and he found recruiting a simple task among dissillusioned Frenchmen in and near San Francisco. Anglo-Americans were excluded from the venture, as Mexican law forbade them from colonizing in that land. Once the nearly two hundred men were recruited, arms, ammunition, and other supplies were purchased. With Raousset as supreme commander, the group was divided into sections of twenty men. Preparations and planning completed, the Raousset expedition sailed for Guaymas.

When the men arrived in Mexico, letters of recommendation were presented to all concerned Sonoran officials. In fact, Andre Levasseur, French Minister in Mexico, had given Raousset spotless recommendations. Thus the Frenchmen expected to be received cordially by Mexican citizens. However, state officials were unimpressed with the recommendations and were hostile because of disagreement with the central government. State officials insisted that Raousset follow the colonization rules closely and avoid any ostentatious display of military power.[17] The erstwhile French leader did not give Mexicans opportunity to support his efforts, for soon after arriving he carelessly referred to himself as the potential "Sultan of Sonora."[18] Consequently, considerable disagreement erupted between Raousset and Sonoran officials.

The Frenchmen traveled to several towns, failing to force the Mexicans to give them supplies that had been promised in earlier negotiations. However, the Mexicans by this time had become determined to stop the French at any cost. By September, 1852, Raousset seemingly abandoned all pretext of coming to Mexico for legal purposes. After defeating the Mexican state militia in a battle at Hermosillo, an occurrence of poor luck brought disaster to the French. Raousset and most of his officers grew ill with severe dysentery, rendering them incapable of carrying on the fight.[19] Soon thereafter the French put away their arms and accepted surrender terms. Most were sent back to the United States. Because of his illness, Raousset remained in Mexico for a while, but after his recovery he returned to California. Although his first attempt to conquer Mexico was a failure, the enterprising Frenchman was not discouraged, for early in 1853, health regained, he was back in San Francisco making plans for a second venture. However, even before he could get organized again, an American, William Walker, the "Grey-eyed man of destiny," announced that he would be president of the Republic of Lower California.[20]

During 1853 Walker and his major associate, Henry Watkins, planned an invasion of Baja California. In May, 1853, Walker began selling bonds for his "Republic," and he began recruiting men. By the end of September all preparations were completed, including chartering of the Brig *Arrow* to transport the group. However, on midnight September 30, the United States Army, learning of the planned invasion of Mexico, boarded the brig and officially detained it until an investigation could be launched to settle the question of legitimacy.[21] While the Army held the *Arrow* and while the court case over seizure was developing, Walker and several of his men slipped out of San Francisco aboard a smaller ship, the *Caroline*, a ship licensed in Mexico and owned by the son of the United States consul at Guaymas. With forty-five men on board, the ship sailed from San Francisco on October 16, headed for Cape San Lucas at the Southern tip of Baja California. There the party stopped briefly before proceeding to La Paz.[22]

On November 3, 1853, the *Caroline* and its party of filibusters sailed into La Paz harbor. There they took possession of the town and arrested Colonel Rafael Espinosa, the Mexican governor. Less than thirty minutes were required for them to capture the poorly defended city. When the Mexican flag was lowered, Walker declared the independence of Lower California. A new flag with two red stripes, a white stripe, and two stars was raised, and the "Republic of Lower California" was established.[23] Walker and his small group contemplated their situation in La Paz for three days. Finally, all agreed that they could neither hold La Paz with so few men nor could they invade Sonora, their real goal. Thus they contented themselves with plundering the area, disrupting the economy, and otherwise incurring the hatred of local Mexicans. Still no actual resistance was encountered until November 6, when the group was leaving.

The Walker party then sailed to Cape San Lucas, arriving there on November 8, 1853. The Americans were sorely disappointed, for the town was small, poor, indefensible, and still too far south. Moreover, a Mexican warship appeared on the horizon, causing Walker to fear that an attack was forthcoming. He decided to move much nearer to the United States border to await reinforcements, also knowing that a more northern base would facilitate his conquest of Sonora; thus the next day he sailed for Ensenada (Bahia) de Todos Santos. Headquartered at Ensenada, one hundred miles below San Diego, Walker awaited news and reinforcements before continuing his venture. And from there he sent his secretary of state, Frederick Emory, to California for supplies.[24]

Reinforcements arrived at Ensenada on December 28, almost two hundred men aboard the small brig *Anita*. By December 30, 1853, all appeared quiet at Ensenada, as Mexicans who had organized resistance to Walker were several miles south of his camp.[25] However, all was not well, for two thousand regulars of the Mexican Army formed near Guaymas, expecting to move into Baja California to engage the filibusters. On January 18, 1954, with his "Republic" tottering on the edge of political, financial, and moral bankruptcy, Walker grandiously annexed Sonora to Baja California and changed the name of the expanded county to the "Republic of Sonora," with Baja California and Sonora as the two states.[26]

On February 13, 1854, Walker had to move. His wounded were left to the care of sailors from an American ship, which had been cruising off the Mexican Coast, and he along with one hundred thirty of his men set out overland for Sonora. By the time Walker had reached the Colorado River, only twenty-five of his men had not deserted. These hardy souls retraced their steps to San Vicente in Baja California expecting to regroup for another attack on Sonora.[27] Mexicans quickly attacked the Americans, whereupon Walker and the survivors fled north toward the United States and safety. Finally, on May 8, 1854, after fighting several battles, Walker's group neared the border. There they found the Mexicans blocking their path to freedom. Nevertheless, Walker summoned his men to battle once again, and they charged the Mexican forces, thereby dispersing them long enough to reach safety. Thus, Walker, like those before him who had dreamed of empire in Mexico, failed to find his fortune. He returned to California and was greeted by Californians as a hero, but did not return to Mexico, for he learned upon arriving in California that the "Sultan of Sonora," Raousset-Boulbon was once again in Mexico hoping to gain control of the northwestern region.

Raousset-Boulbon had returned to San Francisco after his first failure. There he planned again to conquer Mexican territory, and this time luck seemed to favor him, for French Government officials and Antonio López de Santa Anna, dictator of Mexico, appeared receptive to a French colonization venture.[28] Despite objections from Mexican officials in Sonora, Santa Anna's government offered Raousset a contract to bring half-a-thousand Frenchmen to work in the mines of the state. However, the count was not satisfied with the agreement the Mexicans offered, and he broke off negotiations returning immediately to San Francisco. By July, 1854, he had organized a group of men and had journeyed to an area near Guaymas, where his men awaited an opportunity to participate in a revolution in the state.[29]

By July 13 the time for battle had arrived, for Raousset and his men had commandeered several buildings near the port, and were determined to fight Mexicans who were arriving in considerable number.

The Mexicans occupied barracks near the French, and both sides awaited an opportunity to attack. Raousset planned an attack that, if successful, would have resulted in the death of all Mexicans defending the area. In fact, Raousset ordered his men to use their bayonets when possible to conserve ammunition, and to instil fear into the hearts of the enemy.[30] After a vicious three-hour battle in which forty-eight Frenchmen were killed and twice as many wounded, the Mexicans succeeded in capturing the entire French party.

At last Raousset faced his fate at the hands of the angry Mexicans. He was court-martialed on August 9, 1854, convicted of conspiracy to overthrow the government, and sentenced to be shot. He faced a firing squad on August 12, 1854, after receiving last rites from a local priest.[31] Thus the final French attempt to colonize or to establish a foothold in Northwestern Mexico failed. Still others remained who had not heeded the warning Mexicans had given by putting the French leader to death, for even while the count died Henry Alexander Crabb, a prominent Californian, planned to "colonize" part of Mexico.

Crabb entered Mexico indicating that he had been invited by leading citizens of the state — including Ignacio Pesqueira, the potential governor of the state of Sonora. Crabb was married into a prominent California-Sonoran family, and with their assistance, he planned to colonize Sonora. Allegedly he and his family made critical connections in the state government which encouraged the colonization scheme. This may have precipitated a revolution in Northern Mexico, for conservative and liberal factions were already quarreling over who would control the state. By the summer of 1856 Crabb was making preparations to lead this colonization effort overland to Mexico. The Arizona Colonization Company, the formal title of Crabb's group, consisted partly of influential citizens of California, former state senators, and men of substantial backgrounds. Eventually the force was projected to total one thousand men; however, less than one hundred men actually made the trip. They sailed from San Francisco in January, 1857, and grouped near Los Angeles where they assembled supplies. From there, they journeyed to Yuma Crossing, where they remained for a short time before marching into Mexico.[32]

While the Americans marched into Mexico, Pesqueira, the commander of the state militia, prepared his defenses.[33] Mexicans were indignant over the invasion, but they were especially vehement in their condemnation of those Mexicans who may have invited Crabb to enter Mexico.[34] This attitude perhaps led to the death sentence later inflicted on the group of filibusters. In addition to Pesqueira's preparations, the Mexicans launched a maritime expedition on March 17, 1857, from Mazatlán destined to intercept any reinforcements coming to Crabb's rescue. Residents of the Mexican village of Caborca soon learned that

Crabb was approaching by land, and therefore they prepared to drive the Americans back to the United States.

On April 1, 1857, the first hostile contact was made when Mexicans ambushed the Americans as they neared the village. The intruders were unprepared for an attack, as they had no scouts in advance. As the party moved through a wheat field in disorderly formation, the Mexicans opened fire. After the initial volley, the Mexicans withdrew to the safety of the city. There they occupied a church building, and behind its thick walls determined to make a stand. Minor skirmishes took place for the next few days, but the Mexicans tenaciously held their positions. Then a superior Mexican force appeared and reinforced the village warriors.

On April 6 one of the Indians helping the local citizens shot a fire-tipped arrow into the thatched roof of Crabb's stronghold. Crabb attempted to blow the roof off with dynamite, but in the conflagration that followed several men were burned, and others were killed when the magazine exploded.[35] Reluctantly, the Americans asked the Mexicans for terms of surrender. In reply the Mexicans promised to treat the enemy as prisoners of war. Crabb and his men surrendered, but Mexican promises quickly proved worthless. The Americans immediately were bound and taken to a nearby corral where they were held until morning. At dawn the men were taken out in groups of five or ten and shot in the back — because, some said, the Mexicans could not look them in the face.[36] Thus Henry A. Crabb, like those before him who dreamed of conquest in Mexico, failed in his efforts, and he lost his life in the process. Only one man remained to promote a scheme to conquer Northern Mexico.

During the American Civil War, the last major expedition was planned by an American adventurer to gain territory that many believed should be in United States hands already. Between 1863 and 1865, ex-California Senator William McKendree Gwin promoted and planned, with the help of the French, who were intervening in Mexico, a colonization scheme with himself as the "Duke of Sonora." However, he received almost no support from the Mexicans and so little from Mexican Emperor Maximilian that his efforts, like those before him, failed miserably.

During the winter of 1862-1863, Gwin departed for France aboard the blockade runner, *Robert E. Lee*, which sailed from Wilmington, North Carolina.[37] In France through the Marquis de Montholon and Count Mercier, the French Minister of Foreign Affairs, Gwin met and visited briefly with Archduke Maximilian, newly appointed Emperor of Mexico. Maximilian was not friendly, but did not wish to anger the French Government upon whom the success of his crown in Mexico

201

depended. Finally in January, 1864, Gwin officially communicated his scheme to Napoleon III, and the French Emperor proved very interested in the plan, especially as financing was necessary if all of Mexico was to be occupied.[38]

In the summer of 1864, Gwin arrived in Mexico with the blessings of the French Emperor. Carrying letters legitimizing his activities, Gwin approached the French military commander of the area. Gwin soon learned, however, that the Mexicans were quite hostile toward his scheme, and even more significant, he learned that Maximilian, who was seeking Mexican support for his regime, would not support him.[39] In fact, Maximilian refused to see the ex-senator, and Gwin had no recourse but to complain to Napoleon III. As a last resort Gwin traveled to France to talk directly with the French Emperor. On January 19, 1865, he sailed from Vera Cruz. In a meeting with Napoleon, the hopeful American presented yet another plan, that of civilizing the Indians and converting Sonora into a highly productive region. Napoleon enthusiastically approved the plan, and he gave Gwin a letter which directed the French Army in Mexico to help implement the plans. However, once back in Mexico, Gwin found that his friend and only real supporter, Montholon, has been transferred to Washington. Moreover, the French military commander, Marshall Bazaine, then fifty-five years old, was deeply involved with the seventeen-year-old girl he was in the process of marrying. Thus the French commander wanted no part of an imbroligio that might cost him his love life.[40]

Gwin recognized defeat, for without support he would be wise to forget his schemes. Therefore, he requested a military escort to the United States — that the French would provide. Thus, the final American attempt to wrest territory illegally away from Mexico failed. Furthermore, the decade and one-half after the war between the United States and Mexico perhaps were the last years of Manifest Destiny, but the participants in these filibustering expeditions into Northwestern Mexico apparently were driven less by lofty ideology than by a spirit of adventure. They were opportunists whose desperation drove them into a hostile land whose people and whose fierce nationalism they little understood. These men represent more the roily age in which they lived than any spirit of expansion.

CHAPTER 17

Changing Interpretations of the Mexican War, 1846-1970

By Seymour V. Connor

THE STANDARD INTERPRETATION that James K. Polk was the instigator of the Mexican War has gone largely unchallenged in the annals of historical interpretation. Generations of students have read textbooks, heard lectures, and otherwise been told if Polk had been even partially willing to arbitrate, the war with Mexico would not have occurred.

While preparing a bibliography of this war, however, Seymour V. Connor compiled a quantitative analysis of attitudes and opinions as reflected in almost every book, pamphlet, and article published between 1846 and 1970. Nearly eight hundred sources were analyzed, even those printed in Mexico and Europe. After defining five types of publications and listing seven causal categories, Connor designed a program to make frequency and percentage counts of the various categories. Other types of information were also provided for in the program.

Significantly, one finding illustrated that there was no real "difference between Mexican imprints in causal and culpability factors." Moreover, just as in most historiographical studies, interpretations varied with the changing social, politcal, and cultural environment. Many other factors and characteristics were studied in pursuit of this investigation. And according to the author, this work demonstrated, "with the aid of the computer, that statistically there is no basis for the flagellation of Americans of the 1840s for the war with Mexico."

This chapter originally appeared in JOURNAL *of the* WEST in April, 1972.

EVERY READER OF TEXTBOOKS about the American experience *knows* that the United States was the instigator of the war with Mexico of 1846-1848, that James K. Polk deliberately plotted a conflict of aggression in order to acquire territory he coveted, and that a sense of guilt about this war is the legacy of every American. This interpretation of the war has literally dominated textbooks from college history books down to the elementary school level. The result has been unquestioning acceptance of this guilt, even by Southwestern college students who have been taught other interpretations in their state and regional history courses. And even some professional historians have swallowed this belief whole and have written their learned treatises more to reinforce their preconceived biases than to search for the truth.

Recently, while preparing a bibliography of the war between the United States and Mexico, one to serve as a beginning point for research on that conflict,[1] I decided to prepare a quantitative analysis of attitudes and opinions about this conflict as reflected in books, articles, and pamphlets published between 1846 and 1970. This study includes 766 works published about the war. It does not include the many federal documents, or fiction, or newspapers, but otherwise it is fairly complete.[2] Of these 766 items, approximately sixteen percent are Mexican imprints; two percent are European; and the remaining eighty-two percent were printed in the United States. These works were analyzed in the following categories: genre (or type); culpability for the war given by the source; specific cause of the war given by the source; and the three principal subjects treated by the source.

Five principal genres, classifications, or types of publications were used in this present study: (1) general accounts of the war, (2) special or topical studies, (3) reminiscences, memoirs, and letters, (4) biographies, and (5) special accounts indirectly related to the war, such as a history of the Marine Corps or diplomatic histories.

Seven culpability factors were used: (1) blame not indicated, (2) United States culpable because of expansionism, (3) United States to blame because of aggressive slaveocracy, (4) United States at fault, but reasons undifferentiated, (5) Mexico to blame because of hostility over the annexation of Texas, (6) Mexico to blame because of failure to negotiate, and (7) Mexico culpable, but reasons undifferentiated.

Seven specific causal categories were used: (1) ambiguous or not indicated, (2) the claims question, (3) American annexation of Texas, (4) the alleged Nueces boundary dispute, (5) California, either because of an American fear of British intervention or from a general American acquisitive desire for possession, (6) the machinations of President James K. Polk, and (7) the Mexican attack on Taylor north of the Río Grande.

These factors together with the principal subjects, the author, title, date, and place of publication were then coded for analysis by computer.[8] Here the author freely acknowledges that one cannot get objective results from subjective data no matter how verile the computer, and it is equally obvious that encoding the factors concerning culpability and cause is a subjective operation. Knowing this, I coded the ambiguous or not-indicated factor whenever there was any doubt at all, probably erring too far in this direction. A fairly complex program was then designed to make frequency and percentage counts of the various categories, as well as to make sorts by date of publication and subjects. This work done, it took the computer only 1.92 minutes to perform its work and less than five minutes to get the printouts, arranged alphabetically, arranged by date and subject, and tabulated for frequency.

The first meaningful finding was that there was no significant difference between Mexican imprints and American imprints in the causal and culpability factors. The second was that there have been cycles of interest in the Mexican War: about twenty-three percent of the works were published between 1846 and 1849; only fourteen percent were published from 1850 to 1899; the next half-century brought forty-four percent to light; and an amazing nineteen percent was published in the last two decades, 1950 to 1970. And several aspects of these cycles are interesting. For a few years after each subsequent American war, there has been renewed publication about the Mexican War. The 1880s and 1890s brought a rash of reminiscences from men who had fought both in the Mexican and Civil Wars. After 1850 the peak decades of publication were 1910-1919 and 1950-1959. It thus seems likely that the American involvement in Korea, Vietnam, and Southeast Asia may have sparked a renewed examination of the intervention in Mexico. Yet inexplicably the single year after 1850 with the largest number of publications about the Mexican War was 1928; nearly four percent of all imprints about it appeared that year.

Approximately seven percent of the 766 works may be classified as general histories of the war, dealing with origins, campaigns, and results. About forty percent are specialized or topical studies of some aspect of the conflict, many of these scholarly articles in academic journals. Reminiscenses and memoirs account for seventeen percent of the publications; biographies for thirteen percent; and miscellaneous items for the remaining fifteen percent.

On the interesting matter of culpability for the war, seventy-five percent of the works were ambiguous or did not attempt to affix blame. Sixteen percent found the United States at fault; nine percent faulted Mexico. The largest single category in this group was American expansionism or Manifest Destiny; 6.7 percent of the works singled this out as the primary element in the origin of the war. About one-third of the items blaming American expansionism for the war were published before 1850. This theme then submerged and did not reappear in publications until after the turn of the century. Beginning in 1903 one item approximately every third year through 1930 credited American expansionism as the real cause of the war. Curiously, from 1933 to 1943 there was a small outbreak of American flagellation comprising about twenty percent of all the items blaming the United States. Then American culpability was dormant as a separate theme until 1955. Since that time there have only been a few scattered works especially singling out American imperialism.

These data need rather cautious interpretation. In the first place, I only coded this factor for works which specifically emphasized it. Thus many works that considered expansionism as a partial cause of the war, but did not single it out as the major factor, as they were not coded for it. In the second place, overall, only a very small minority of the total works published — 6.7 percent — actually stressed this facor.

An even smaller percentage — 2.7 percent — focused on the aggressive slaveocracy or slavery expansion as the culprit. As might be expected, most of these were published at the time of the war and immediately thereafter. And most of these were abolitionist tracts. Only six works published after 1850 seriously considered slavery expansion to blame for the war.

The United States as provocateur, but with specific reasons undifferentiated, was emphasized in 6.6 percent of the works. Fifteen such items appeared between 1846 and 1850, principally political fulminations. A small scattering appeared in the 1880s, another handful were sprinkled in the first two decades of this century, one in the 1920s, and one in the 'thirties. Then, beginning in 1946 at the close of World War II, this interpretation — which was not really an interpretation but an anti-American polemic — began to surface again. Over a third of the total works emphasizing undifferentiated American culpability have been published since 1946.

Should this be regarded as some kind of revisionist trend? That is hardly likely inasmuch as these works offer no new data or new synthesis. Rather they rely on value words and adjectival excesses to scourge the United States.

It should be noted that 7.8 percent of the works found Mexico at fault for the war. One and one-half percent laid it to general hostility in Mexico over the annexation of Texas and nearly two percent blamed it on the failure of the various Mexican governments to negotiate.

Overall, through nearly a century and one-quarter of publication, most writers on the Mexican War appear to have taken a fairly moderate and objective position on national culpability. It is curious, therefore, that in so many survey texts on American history the United States emerges in students' minds as some sort of vicious and greedy imperialist. And it is even more curious that Robert Kennedy could say publicly that the Mexican War was a disgrace to the national honor and only a handful of historians, including Allan Nevins, challenged his statement.

As to specific causes, eighty-five percent of the works found multiple causes for the war. Almost all dealt with claims, annexation, California, and the so-called boundary dispute. It would have been too highly subjective to try to assess which of these factors received the greatest weight in works dealing with multiple causations. Thus here again, only works singling out and particularly emphasizing one cause were coded. This was just under fifteen percent of the total works and just more than 100 items. Approximately one-half of these, fifty-four to be exact, clearly pointed to the annexation of Texas as the single specific cause for the war. It is important to note that few of these works attached any sort of moral blame on either Texas or the United States for annexation.

The second largest group of works treating one specific cause centered on the machinations of the whipping boy, James K. Polk. It is in this group that one finds the images of evil master minds, sinister conspiracies and intrigues, and the other trappings of paranoia. Curiously, the works blaming Polk are limited to a few at the time of the war and the remainder after the turn of the century.

About two percent of the total works, but about fifteen percent of the works emphasizing specific causes, found that the actual cause of the war was the Mexican attack on Taylor. In other words, to these writers, none of the other causal factors was sufficient to cause war, and there would have been no war if Mexico had not attacked. As is to be expected, most of these were published prior to 1850, although a few came out in the period around World War I, reflecting perhaps opinions over the border raids of the Mexican Revolution and the Zimmerman Note.

Two popular ideas about the cause of the war, much bandied about in survey texts, are the alleged American desire for California and the so-called Nueces boundary question. Specifically, less than one percent of the total works emphasized these two factors to the exclusion of others, so numerically these are insigificant. But, almost every work in the big eighty-five percent group of multiple causes wove these two causes into the background for war. Thus, they have become important, not so much because they had anything to do with causing the war, but because people believe they did. The California question is usually linked with American expansionism and the machinations of President Polk. Almost nothing is said of the revolutionary divisiveness in California or British intervention on the West Coast and the situation in Oregon. Polk's interests and intrigues in California need a thorough reappraisal.

The Nueces controversy is somewhat different. The Texas claim to the Río Grande from its mouth to its source was so obviously preposterous that from the beginning of the war numerous people in the United States protested Taylor's occupation of the north bank of the river. These objections were brought out in Congress in the debate over the war message and were given quick currency in abolitionist tracts. However, objection to the occupation of the so-called disputed territory was not limited to abolitionists. One Virginia pastor published a small book in 1848 on the origins of the war and specifically found that Taylor's march to the Río Grande was the sole cause for the war. Others over the years have rather consistently placed this among the major factors in the origin of the war, although only one-half of one percent have singled it out as the exclusive cause.

This is no place to go into a lengthy discussion of the question, but what is worth noting bibliographically is that prior to hostilities, all of the arguments for the Nueces as the boundary were American. No Mexican imprint ever espoused the Nueces. Instead, the Mexican claim was consistently to the whole of Texas to the Sabine River — a claim as ridiculous as the Texas claim to New Mexico east of the Río Grande.

In summarizing this work, I noted a strong correlation between the culpability factors and the causal factors. Seventy-five percent of the works neither attempted to fix national culpability or found single causation. Slightly more than one percent did not assign blame, but did emphasize heavily one of the causal factors. On the 6.7 percent that saw the United States as imperialist aggressor, 2.3 percent found multiple causes, 2.4 percent emphasized the annexation of Texas, and 1.2 percent blamed Polk. Of the 6.6 percent that held the United States to blame in an undifferentiated way, nearly two percent viewed the annexation of Texas as the specific cause of the war. And of the 7.8 percent which blamed Mexico for the conflict, most did not find single specific causes, emphasizing instead Mexican political divisiveness, hostility over annexation, and failure to negotiate claims — all about equally. One percent of these did specifically give the Mexican attack as the cause of the war, however.

This bibliographic study thus demonstrates, with the aid of the computer, that statistically there is no basis for the flagellation of Americans of the 1840s for the war with Mexico. Granted a computer analysis of books, pamphlets, and articles is not always the way to truth, but this case study does make the student of history wonder why the few historians of recent years have found it so necessary to denigrate this one aspect of the American experience when previous students of the event so overwhelmingly failed to do so. The objective historian cannot answer this question. Perhaps it is a challenge that demands the attention of psychologists.

References

Chapter 1
California Ports: A Key to West Coast Diplomacy, 1820-1845

1. Anatole G. Mazour, "The Russian-American and Anglo-Russian Convention, 1824-1825, an Interpretation," *The Pacific Historical Review*, Vol. XIV (1945), p. 307.
2. Jaen Francois Galaup de La Pérouse, VOYAGE AROUND THE WORLD PERFORMED IN THE YEARS, 1785, 1786, 1787 AND 1788, BY THE BOUSSOLE AND ASTROLOBE (London, 1807), Vol. II, pp. 206-207.
3. See Charles Franklin Carter, "Duhaut-Cilly's Account of California in the Years 1827-1828," *The California Historical Society Quarterly*, Vol. VIII (1929), pp. 49-50.
4. See Rufus Kay Wyllys, "French Imperialists in California," *The California Historical Society Quarterly*, Vol. VIII (1929), pp. 116-117 and Abraham P. Nasatir, FRENCH ACTIVITIES IN CALIFORNIA (Stanford, 1945), p. 39.
5. *Ibid.*, pp. 16.
6. Quoted in Wyllys, "French Imperialists in California," p. 118. See also Eugene Duflot de Mofras, EXPLORATION DE L'OREGON, DES CALIFORNIES ET DE LA MER VERMEILLE, EXECUTEE PENDENT LES ANNEES, 1840, 1841 ET 1842 (Paris, 1844), 2 vols.
7. Rosamel was the captain of the French corvette, *Danaïde*, which had brought de Mofras to the coast.
8. Quoted in Wyllys, "French Imperialists in California," p. 118.
9. Quoted in Verne George Blue, "The Report of Captain LaPlace on His Voyage to the Northwest Coast and California," *California Historical Society Quarterly*, Vol. XVIII (1939), p. 317.
10. See Adele Ogden, THE CALIFORNIA SEA OTTER TRADE, 1784-1848, (Berkeley, 1941).
11. The East India Company monopoly ended in 1834. Since the China trade was opened to all British ships after this date, competition became much greater. Hallett Abend, TREATY PORTS (New York, 1944), p. 15.
12. See Adele Ogden, "Boston Hide Droughers Along California Shores," *The California Historical Society Quarterly*, Vol. VIII (1929), p. 289; Samuel Eliot Morison, THE MARITIME HISTORY OF MASSACHUSETTS (Boston, 1941), p. 266; Adele Ogden, "Hides and Tallow, McCullock, Hartnell and Company, 1833-1838," *The California Historical Society Quarterly*, Vol. VI (1927), p. 254; Herman J. Deutsch, "Economic Imperialism in the Early Pacific Northwest," *The Pacific Historical Review*, Vol. IX (1940), p. 388.
13. Thomas Randall, last vice-consul at Canton, to Alexander Hamilton, New York, August 14, 1791, INDUSTRIAL AND COMMERCIAL CORRESPONDENCE OF ALEXANDER HAMILTON, ed. by Arthur H. Cole and Edwin F. Gay (Chicago, 1928), p. 143.
14. Emory Johnson, HISTORY OF DOMESTIC AND FOREIGN COMMERCE OF THE UNITED STATES (Washington, 1915), Vol. II, p. 26. See also Foster Rhea Dulles, THE OLD CHINA TRADE (Boston, 1930), pp. 117-18; Tyler Dennett, AMERICANS IN EASTERN ASIA, (New York, 1941), p. 75; Ethel B. Nietrick, FAR EASTERN TRADE OF THE UNITED STATES (New York, 1940), p. 4.
15. See Sister Magdalen Coughlin, C. S. J., "The Entrance of the Massachusetts Merchant into the Pacific," *The Southern California Quarterly*, Vol. XLVIII (1966), pp. 327-352; "Boston Smugglers on the Coast (1797-1821): An Insight into the American Acquisition of California," *The California Historical Society Quarterly*, Vol. XLVI (1967), pp. 99-120; and "Commercial Foundations of Political Interest in the Opening Pacific," *The California Historical Society Quarterly*, Vol. XLX (1971), pp. 15-33.

    Although there were only ten American ships at Canton by 1718, between 1804 and 1809 there were 154 voyages to China under the American flag. Abend, *Treaty Ports*, p. 14; "Early Commerce in the North Pacific: List of Vessels and Masters, Chiefly from New England Ports, 1787-1807," Bancroft Library, University of California, Berkeley; "List of Private Trading Vessels Returning from the American Coast from 1745 to 1822," *Russian America*, Vol. III, Part 4. Transcript, Bancroft Library; William Dane Phelps, "Solid Men of Boston in the Northwest." Bancroft Library; "Record of Ships Arriving 1774 to 1847," William Heath Davis, SEVENTY-FIVE YEARS IN CALIFORNIA (San Francisco, 1929), Appendix B, p. 399.
16. November 16, 1819. John Quincy Adams, MEMOIRS OF JOHN QUINCY ADAMS, ed. by Charles F. Adams (Philadelphia, 1874-1877), Vol. IV, pp. 437-439.
17. *Ibid.* Vol. V, pp. 250-253. See also Stratford Canning to Lord Castlereagh, F. O. 5, Vol. 157, quoted in Katherine B. Judson, "The British Side of the Restoration of Fort Astoria," *The Oregon Historical Society Quarterly*, Vol. XX, pp. 328-329.

18. William R. Manning, EARLY DIPLOMATIC RELATIONS BETWEEN THE UNITED STATES AND MEXICO (Baltimore, 1916), p. 45; Jesse S. Reeves, AMERICAN DIPLOMACY UNDER TYLER AND POLK (Baltimore, 1907), pp. 60-65.
19. See especially Duff Green to Calhoun, Mexico, October 22, 1844. Quoted in J. Franklin Jameson (ed.) "Correspondence of John C. Calhoun," *American Historical Association, Annual Report* (2 Vols., Washington, 1899), Vol. II, p. 979.
20. Ashburton to Webster, April 28, 1844. Reeves, *American Diplomacy Under Tyler and Polk*, p. 105, n. 22.
21. Manning, *Early Diplomatic Relations Between the United States and Mexico*, pp. 31-49.
22. *Ibid.*, p. 56.
23. See especially Canning to Lord Liverpool (July 7, 1926). Quoted in Joseph Schaefer, "British Attitude toward the Oregon Compromise," *The American Historical Review*, Vol. XVI (1911), p. 292.
24. Poinsett to Clay, May 28, 1825, quoted in Manning, *Early Diplomatic Relations Between the United States and Mexico*, p. 52.
25. *Ibid.*, pp. 289-90.
26. Quoted in George Lockhart Rives, THE UNITED STATES AND MEXICO, 1821-1848 (New York, 1913), Vol. I, p. 244.
27. Quoted in Eugene Barker, "Jackson and the Texas Revolution," *The American Historical Review*, Vol. XII, p. 789.
28. Quoted in R. G. Cleland, THE EARLY SENTIMENT FOR THE ANNEXATION OF CALIFORNIA, *An Account of the Growth of Our Interest in California from 1835 to 1846* (Texas, n.d.), p. 15.
29. For an example of reflections of this rising and acknowledged interest see *Annals of Congress*, 18th Cong., 2nd sess., February 26, 1825, p. 691. See also James Morton Callahan, AMERICAN RELATIONS IN THE PACIFIC AND THE FAR EAST, 1784-1900 (Baltimore, 1901), p. 35.
30. The purpose, as stated in these instructions, was that the port of San Francisco would be most desirable for whaling vessels. Rives, THE UNITED STATES AND MEXICO, 1821-1848, Vol. I, pp. 259-260.
31. Forsyth to Butler, August 6, 1835. Quoted in Cleland, *The Early Sentiment for the Annexation of California*, p. 15, n. 44.
32. Quoted in *Ibid.*, p. 17. See also Robert Glass Cleland, FROM WILDERNESS TO EMPIRE (New York, 1944), p. 193.
33. See Lester G. Engelson, "Proposals for the Colonization of California by England in Connection with the Mexican Debt to British Bondholders, 1837-1844," *The California Historical Society Quarterly*, Vol. XVIII (1939), pp. 136-149. Also see Lauro de Rojas, "California in 1844 as Hartnell Saw It," *The California Historical Society Quarterly*, Vol. XVII (1938), p. 21.
34. Engelson, "Proposals for Colonization of California," pp. 136-137.
35. Rives, THE UNITED STATES AND MEXICO, 1821-1848, Vol. II, p. 47.
36. *London Times*, September 6, 1839. Quoted in Engelson, "Proposals for Colonization of California," p. 139.
37. Gertrude Cunningham, "The Significance of 1846 to the Pacific Coast," *The Washington Historical Quarterly*, Vol. XXI (1930), p. 50. See also, Cleland, *The Early Sentiment for the Annexation of California*, p. 22, n. 20.
38. Patrick Strauss, "Preparing the Wilkes Expedition: A Study in Disorganization," *The Pacific Historical Review*, Vol. XXVIII (1959), p. 227. His instructions, written in 1838 by the Secretary of the Navy, were to carefully examine "the territory of th United States on the seaboard." Richard Warner Van Alystyne, THE RISING AMERICAN EMPIRE (Stanford, 1947), p. 107.
39. Quoted in Rives, *The United States and Mexico, 1821-1848*, Vol. II, pp. 448-449.
40. Quoted by Aberdeen to Pakenham, December 15, 1841. *Ibid.*, Vol. II, p. 49.
41. Aberdeen to Pakenham, December 15, 1841. Quoted in Ephraim D. Adams, "English Interest in the Annexation of California," *The American Historical Review*, Vol. XIV (1909), p. 747.
42. August 4, 1842. Quoted in Frederick Merk, "British Party Politics and Oregon," *The American Historical Review*, Vol. XXXVII (1932), p. 663. See also, Ernest A. Wiltsee, "The British Vice Consul in California and the Events of 1846," *The California Historical Society Quarterly*, Vol. X (1931), p. 118.
43. Engelson, "Proposals for the Colonization of California," p. 140.
44. Van Alstyne, *The Rising American Empire*, p. 109.
45. Quoted in Rives, *The United States and Mexico, 1821-1848*, Vol. II, p. 46.
46. Reeves, *American Diplomacy Under Tyler and Polk*, pp. 102-103.
47. Tyler to his son, December, 1845. Quoted in Norman A. Graebner, "Maritime Factors in the Oregon Compromise," *The Pacific Historical Review*, Vol. XX (1951), pp. 338-339.

References

48. Everett to Calhoun, March 28, 1845. Rives, *The United States and Mexico, 1821-1848*, Vol. II, p. 46.
49. Jones to Upshur, September 13, 1842. Quoted in Reeves, *American Diplomacy Under Tyler and Polk*, p. 104.
50. Cleland, *The Early Sentiment for the Annexation of California*, p. 30, n. 47, n. 48.
51. See James Christy Bell, OPENING A HIGHWAY TO THE PACIFIC, 1838-1846 (New York, 1921), pp. 127-128; Reginald Charles McGrane, THE PANIC OF 1837 — *Some Financial Problems of the Jacksonian Era* (Chicago, 1924), p. 130. See also Lewis E. Atherton, "Western Mercantile Participation in the Indian Trade," *The Pacific Historical Review*, Vol. IX (1940).
52. Waddy Thompson to Daniel Webster, April 29, 1842. Quoted in Rives, *The United States and Mexico, 1821-1848*, Vol. II, p. 45.
53. Waddy Thompson to President Tyler, May 9, 1842. Quoted in *Ibid.*
54. Daniel Webster to Fletcher Webster, March 11, 1845, THE PRIVATE CORRESPONDENCE OF DANIEL WEBSTER, Fletcher Webster, ed. (Boston, 1903), Vol. II, p. 204.
55. Daniel Webster to Waddy Thompson, Washington, June 27, 1842, THE WRITINGS AND SPEECHES OF DANIEL WEBSTER, national edition, (Boston, 1903), Vol. IV, pp. 611-612.
56. Annis Heloise Abel, "Mexico as a Field for Systematic British Colonization, 1830," *The Southwestern Historical Quarterly*, Vol. XXX (1926), p. 64; James B. Winston, "The Annexation of Texas and the Mississippi Democrats," *The Southern Historical Quarterly*, Vol. XXV (1921), p. 9; and Rives, *The United States and Mexico, 1821-1848*, Vol. I, p. 200.
57. May 15, 1846. Quoted in Graebner, "Maritime Factors in the Oregon Compromise," p. 339.
58. Justin H. Smith, "The Mexican Recognition of Texas," *The American Historical Review*, Vol. XVI (1911), p. 38.
59. Quoted in R. A. McLemore, "The Influence of French Diplomatic Policy on the Annexation of Texas," *The Southwestern Historical Quarterly*, Vol. XLIII (1940), p. 344.
60. Rives, *The United States and Mexico, 1821-1848*, Vol. II, pp. 81-91.
61. Quoted in Smith, "The Mexican Negotiation of Texas," p. 50.
62. Quoted in Adams, "English Interest in the Annexation of California," p. 748.
63. Norman A. Graebner, EMPIRE ON THE PACIFIC (New York, 1955), p. 100. See also Van Alstyne, *The Rising American Empire*, pp. 135-138, and Nathanial W. Stephenson, TEXAS AND THE MEXICAN WAR: *A Chronicle of the Winning of the Southwest* (New Haven, 1931), p. 183.
64. Quoted in Richard R. Stenberg, "Polk and Frémont, 1845-1846," *The Pacific Historical Review*, Vol. VII (1938), p. 224.
65. *Baltimore American*, March, 1845. Quoted in Norman A. Graebner, "American Interest in California," *The Pacific Historical Review*, Vol. XX (1951), p. 14.
66. Quoted in Cleland, *The Early Sentiment for the Annexation of California*, p. 49.
67. Polk to Slidell, November 10, 1845. Quoted in Stenberg, "Polk and Frémont, 1845-1846," p. 217.
68. John Adams Hussey, "The Origins of the Gillespie Mission," *The California Historical Society Quarterly*, Vol. XIX (1940), pp. 47-48.
69. Quoted in Graebner, *Empire on the Pacific*, p. 118; Cleland, *The Early Sentiment for the Annexation of California*, p. 95, n. 56.
70. Quoted in Stenberg, "Polk and Frémont, 1845-1846," p. 217. Frémont was quoted as saying, "My private instructions were, if needed, to foil England by carrying the war now imminent with Mexico into the territory of California." Quoted in Richard Warner Van Alstyne, AMERICAN DIPLOMACY IN ACTION (Stanford, 1947), p. 576.
71. Quoted in Cleland, *The Early Sentiment for the Annexation of California*, p. 97.
72. Bankhead to Aberdeen, May 30, 1846. Quoted in Adams, "English Interest in the Annexation of California," p. 761.
73. Quoted in Engelson, "Proposals for the Colonization of California by England," p. 146.
74. Pico to Forbes, Santa Barbara, June 29, 1846. Quoted in Wiltsee, "The British Vice Consul in California and the Events in 1846." p. 115.
75. Samuel Hooper to George Bancroft, June 19, 1845, Bancroft Papers, Massachusetts Historical Society, Boston.
76. William Sturgis to George Bancroft, June 15, 1846, Bancroft Papers; Samuel Hooper to George Bancroft, June 15, 1846, Bancroft Papers.
77. Samuel Hooper to George Bancroft, Boston, June 25, 1846, Bancroft Papers.
78. Bancroft to Sloat, Washington, July 12, 1846, quoted in Hittell, "George Bancroft and His Services to California," California Historical Society *Papers*, Vol. I, pt. 4, p. 14.
79. Samuel Hooper to George Bancroft, New York, August 18, 1846, Bancroft Papers. Henry Mellus was a Bryant, Sturgis & Company agent who had gone out to the California Coast from Boston in the late 1830s.
80. Quoted in Dulles, *America in the Pacific*, p. 59.

References

Chapter 2

The Deterioration of Diplomatic Relations, 1833-1845

1. Justin H. Smith, THE WAR WITH MEXICO (New York, 1919), 2 vols., Vol. I, pp. 74-77, 425, 428.
2. *Ibid.*, pp. 75, 425.
3. AMERICAN STATE PAPERS, DOCUMENTS, FOREIGN RELATIONS, LEGISLATIVE AND EXECUTIVE OF THE UNITED STATES (Washington: Gales and Seaton, 1834), 6 vols., Vol. IV [cited hereinafter as *State Papers*]. *See also* James M. Callahan, AMERICAN FOREIGN POLICY IN MEXICAN RELATIONS (New York, 1932), pp. 16, 17.
4. Samuel Flagg Bemis, DIPLOMATIC HISTORY OF THE UNITED STATES (New York, 1955), 4th edition, p. 220.
5. William R. Manning, EARLY DIPLOMATIC RELATIONS BETWEEN THE UNITED STATES AND MEXICO (Baltimore: Johns Hopkins Press, 1916), pp. 46, 286. Extracts of Clay's instructions to Poinsett are in *State Papers*, Vol. V, p. 908, and Vol. VI, p. 578.
6. Bemis, *Diplomatic History*, p. 220.
7. *Ibid.* Poinsett finally was recalled as a result of his unpopularity.
8. "Treaty of Limits with the United Mexican States," in *State Papers*, Vol. VI, pp. 946-950. Signed on January 12, 1828, this treaty was not ratified and put into effect until April 5, 1832.
9. *See* Jesse S. Reeves, AMERICAN DIPLOMACY UNDER TYLER AND POLK (Baltimore: Johns Hopkins Press, 1907), pp. 64-65; actually the correspondence cited by Reeves is in the unpublished manucripts of the Archives, Vol. I, No. 30. These instructions, disseminated by Van Buren, were drafted by Jackson on August 13, 1829.
10. *Ibid*, p. 65; Bemis, *Diplomatic History*, p. 226; and Smith, *War With Mexico*, Vol. I, p. 62.
11. *House Executive Document* No. 351, 25th Cong., 2d Session, p. 317.
12. John Forsyth to Ellis, July 30, 1836, *House Executive Document*, No. 105, 24th Cong., 2d Session, p. 20.
13. Reeves, *American Diplomacy*, pp. 76-80. *See also* House of Representatives, *The Report of Committees*, Report No. 752, Vol. IV, 29th Cong., 1st Session, pp. 15-22.
14. William M. Malloy (comp.), TREATIES, CONVENTIONS, INTERNATIONAL ACTS, PROTOCOLS AND AGREEMENTS BETWEEN THE UNITED STATES OF AMERICA AND OTHER POWERS, 1776-1909 (Washington, 1910), 2 vols., Vol. I, pp. 1101-1105; *see also House Executive Document*, No. 252, 25th Cong., 3rd Session.
15. The most serious such violation was Commodore Thomas ap Catesby Jones' invasion of of Monterey, California. For details see *House Executive Document*, No. 166, 27th Cong., 3rd Session, pp. 3, 5, 70.
16. *House Executive Document*, No. 139, 24th Cong., 2d Session, p. 1. Congress never gave Jackson the authority he requested.
17. Reeves, *American Diplomacy*, p. 107.
18. *House Report of Committees*, No. 752, p. 25, and Smith, *War With Mexico*, Vol. I, pp. 81, 431.
19. Green to Bocanegra, United States Department of State, *Despatches from the U. S. Ministers to Mexico*, 1823-1906, RG 59, National Archives (microfilm publication). [Hereinafter cited as *Despatches*.]
20. Green to Bocanegra, March 30, 1844, *ibid*.
21. Green to Calhoun, April 8, 1844, *ibid*.
22. John B. Moore (ed.), THE WORKS OF JAMES BUCHANAN (New York, 1960), 12 vols., Vol. VI, pp. 294-306.
23. Green to Calhoun, April 25, 1844. *Despatches*.
24. Green to Bocanegra, May 23, 1844. *ibid. See also* Ficknor Curtis, LIFE OF JAMES BUCHANAN (New York, 1885), 2 vols., Vol. I, pp. 581-582.
25. *House Executive Document*, No. 351, 25th Cong., 2d Session, pp. 315-316.
26. Bocanegra to Green, May 30, 1844, *Despatches;* and *State Papers*, Vol. VI, pp. 946-950.
27. Green to Calhoun, June 7, 1844, *Despatches*.
28. Shannon to Calhoun. November 12, 1844, *ibid*.
29. Rejon to Shannon, October 31, 1844, *ibid*.
30. Shannon to Calhoun, December 9, 1844, *ibid*.
31. Shannon to Calhoun, January 9, 1845, *ibid*.
32. E. D. Adams. "English Interest in the Annexation of California," *American Historical Review*, Vol. XIV (April, 1909), pp. 744-763.
33. Milo M. Quife, (ed.), THE DIARY OF JAMES K. POLK DURING HIS PRESIDENCY, 1845 TO 1849 (Chicago: A. C. McClurg, 1910), 4 vols., Vol. I, pp. 34-35; Emith, *War With Mexico*, Vol. I, p. 95.
34. Cuevas to Shannon, March 28, 1845, *Despatches*.
35. Shannon to Cuevas, May 8, 1845, *ibid*.

36. Quaife, *Diary of James K. Polk*, Vol. I, p. 34.
37. Moore, *Works of James Buchanan*, Vol. VI, p. 300. *See also* Frederick Merck, MANIFEST DESTINY AND MISSSION IN AMERICAN HISTORY — *A Reinterpretation* (New York, 1963), pp. 84-85; and Bemis, *Diplomatic History*, p. 236.
38. Bemis, *Diplomatic History*, p. 237.
39. Quaife, *Diary of James K. Polk*, Vol. I, pp. 384-386. The claims issue was used as justification in the famous war message.

Chapter 3

A. Butler: What a Scamp!

1. Arthur Howard Noll, FROM EMPIRE TO REPUBLIC (Chicago: A. C. McClurg and Company, 1930), pp. 113-135.
2. *Ibid.*
3. Lucas Alamán was minister of foreign and domestic affairs under Bustamante and a staunch conservative; *see House Executive Document*, No. 351, 25th Cong., 2d Session, Vol. 12.
4. J. Fred Rippy, JOEL R. POINSETT, *Versatile American* (Durham: Duke University Press, 1935), pp. 106, 109, 11.
5. J. Fred Rippy, THE UNITED STATES AND MEXICO (New York, 1931), p. 6.
6. Charles Francis Adams, MEMOIRS OF JOHN QUINCY ADAMS (New York, 1970), Vol. XI, p. 359.
7. George Lockhart Rives, THE UNITED STATES AND MEXICO, 1821-1848 (New York, 1913), p. 236. *See also* William R. Manning, "Texas and the Boundary Issue, 1822-1829," *Southwestern Historical Quarterly*, Vol. XVII, (January, 1914), p. 22; William Graham Sumner, ANDREW JACKSON (Boston, 1910), p. 415; and John Spencer Bassett (ed.), CORRESPONDENCE OF ANDREW JACKSON (Washington, D. C., 1929), Vol. IV, p. 66.
8. Robert V. Remini, ANDREW JACKSON (New York, 1969), p. 178.
9. Van Buren to Butler, October 10, 1829. *House Executive Document*, No. 752, 25th Cong., 2d Session, pp. 3, 5-6.
10. Van Buren to Butler, October 10, 1829. *House Executive Document*, No. 351, 25th Cong., 2d Session, pp. 52-53.
11. Bassett (ed.), *Correspondence*, Vol. IV, p. 82.
12. *Ibid.*
13. *Ibid.*
14. Butler to Van Buren, January 10, 1829, *House Executive Document*, No. 351, 25th Cong., 2d Session, p. 310.
15. Translation of a paragraph in *El Sol* of January 9, referred to in Butler to Van Buren, January 10, 1830, in *ibid.*, p. 310.
16. Butler to Van Buren, March 9, 1830, *ibid.*, pp. 311-312.
17. *Ibid.*, p. 312.
18. Report of Lucas Alamán to the Congress of Mexico, March 10, 1830, *ibid.*, p. 314.
19. *Ibid.*, p. 322.
20. Seymour V. Connor, TEXAS: *A History* (New York, 1971), pp. 88-89.
21. Butler to Jackson, May 25, 1831, *ibid.* p. 381; Bassett, (ed.), *Correspondence*, Vol. IV, p. 335; Adams (ed.), *Memoirs*, Vol XI, pp. 358-359.
22. Van Buren to Butler, October 16, 1829, *House Executive Document*, No. 351, 25th Cong., 2d Session, pp. 52-53.
23. Coleman to Van Buren, December 10, 1829, *ibid.*, p. 57. *See also* Clayton C. Kohl, CLAIMS AS A CAUSE OF THE MEXICAN WAR (New York: New York University Press, 1914).
24. Butler to Alamán, January 17, 1832, *House Executive Document*, No. 351, 25th Cong., 2d Session, p. 428.
25. Alamán to Butler, February 3, 1832, *ibid.*, p. 432.
26. *Ibid.*, p. 434.
27. Butler to García, September 6, 1833, *ibid.*, p. 486.
28. Vasquez to García, September 28, 1833, *ibid.*, pp. 510-511.
29. Kohl, *Claims*, p. 3.
30. Juan Vera, Magistrate of Tehuantepec, to Ortiga, March 10, 1835, *House Executive Document*, No. 351, 25th Cong., 2d Session, pp. 558-561.
31. *Ibid.*, p. 558.
32. Martínez to Forsyth, May 17, 1838, *House Executive Document*, No. 752, 29th Cong., 2d Session, p. 763.
33. Butler to Forsyth, February 8, 1836, *House Executive Document*, No. 351, 25th Cong., 2d Session, pp. 581-582.
34. *Ibid.*, p. 582.
35. *Ibid.*, p. 581.

References

36. Address of Jackson to Congress, February 6, 1837, *House Executive Document*, No. 752, 29th Cong., 2d Session, pp. 6-7.
37. Jesse S. Reeves, AMERICAN DIPLOMACY UNDER TYLER AND POLK (Gloucester: Peter Smith, 1967), p. 73.
38. Butler to Jackson, December 23, 1831, *House Executive Document* No. 351, 25th Cong., 2d Session, pp. 410-411; Alamán to Butler, February 17, 1831, *ibid.*, p. 373.
39. Butler to Alamán, December 14, 1831, *ibid.*, p. 410.
40. Butler to Jackson, December 23, 1831, *ibid.*, p. 410.
41. Treaties with Mexico, May 1, 1832, *House Executive Document*, No. 22, 22nd Cong., 1st Session, pp. 1-27.
42. *Ibid.*, p. 3-4.
43. Reeves, *American Diplomacy*, p. 73; *House Executive Document*, No. 351, 25th Cong., 2d Session, p. 391.
44. Butler to Livingston, July 16, 1832, *ibid.*, p. 442.
45. Bassett (ed.), *Correspondence, Vol. IV*, p. 413.
46. *Ibid.*, p. 450
47. Minutes of conversation between Butler and Alamán, July 2, 1832, *House Executive Document*, No. 351, 25th Cong., 2d Session, pp. 442-443.
48. *Ibid.*, p. 443.
49. Minutes of second conversation between Alamán and Butler, *ibid.*, pp. 444-445.
50. *Ibid.*, p. 444.
51. *Ibid.*, p. 445.
52. Basset (ed.), *Correspondence*, Vol. IV, p. 463.
53. *Ibid.*, Vol. V, p. 2.
54. *Ibid.*, Vol. V, pp. 209-211; Eugene C. Baker, "Jackson and the Texas Revolution," *American Historical Review*, Vol. XII (July, 1907), pp. 788-809.
55. Bassett (ed.), *Correspondence*, Vol. V, p. 213.
56. *Ibid.*, Vol. V, p. 219. This man obviously was Santa Anna.
57. *Ibid.*
58. *Ibid.*, Vol. V, p. 229; Butler to Jackson, February 10, 1833, *House Executive Document*, No. 351, 25th Cong., 2d Session, pp. 446-447.
59. Bassett (ed.), *Correspondence*, Vol. V, pp. 17, 228.
60. Butler to Jackson, February 26, 1835, *House Executive Document*, No. 351, 25th Cong., 2d Session, p. 555.
61. Bassett (ed.), *Correspondence*, Vol. V, p. 251.
62. *Ibid.*, Vol. V, p. 252-253. There have been charges, mostly based on spurious evidence, that Jackson plotted to acquire Texas. *See* Richard R. Stenberg, "Jackson, Anthony Butler, and Texas," *Southwestern Social Science Quarterly*, Vol. XV (Autumn, 1934), pp. 229-250; and Bernard Mayo, "Apostle of Manifest Destiny," *American Mercury*, Vol. XVIII (1929), pp. 420-426.
63. Hernández to Butler, March 21, 1835, *House Executive Document*, No. 351, 25th Cong., 2d Session, p. 279.
64. *Ibid.*, p. 279.
65. Butler to Forsyth, November 28, 1835, *ibid.*, p. 564.
66. Monasterio to Butler, January 26, 1836, *ibid.*, pp. 576-579.
67. *Ibid.*, p. 572.
68. Butler to Forsyth, January 26, 1836, *ibid.*, pp. 576-579.
69. Butler to Forsyth, December 27, 1835, *ibid.*, p. 567.
70. Butler to Tornel, August 10, 1836, *ibid.*, p. 600; Adams (ed.), *Memoirs*, Vol. XI, p. 360.
71. Adams (ed.), *Memoirs*, Vol. XI, p. 360.
72. Butler to Tornel, August 10, 1836, *House Executive Document*, No. 351, 25th Cong., 2d Session, p. 600.
73. *Ibid.*
74. Tornel to Van Buren, August 13, 1830, *ibid.*, pp. 646.
75. Monasterio to Ellis, August 10, 1836, *ibid.*, p. 598.
76. Butler to Monasterio, September (no date) *ibid.*, p. 612.

Chapter 4

The Santangelo Case: A Controversial Claim

1. English-language copies of various documents pertaining to claimant's life in Europe in the case files for claimants, Orazio de Santangelo, the second of two volumes. (Records of the United States-Mexican Claims Commission, April 11, 1839-February 24, 1842, General Records of the Department of State, Record Group 76, National Archives), which document will be hereinafter cited as Santangelo Claimaint's File, NA. Santangelo's life in Europe has drawn the attention of an Italian historian, Nino Cortese,

References

"Le avventure italiane ed americane di un giacobino molisano, Orazio de Attelis," *Annuario del R. Istituto Superiore di Magistero di Messina*, Vol. XIII (1934-35).

2. Orazio de Santangelo, *Las cuatro primeras discusiones del Congreso de Panamá* (Mexico City, 1826), pp. 11, 13, 28, 41-43, 69-72; Orazio de Santangelo, *¿En donde estamos? en Méjico, ó en Constantinopla?* (Mexico City, 1826), p. 2.
3. Orazio de Attelis Santangelo, *Statement of Facts Relating to the Claim of Orazio de Attelis Santangelo* (Washington, 1841), pp. 7-9; Howard R. Marraro, "Pioneer Teachers of Italian in the United States," *Modern Language Journal*, Vol. XXVIII (November, 1944), pp. 555-582, especially pp. 558-559.
4. Santangelo, *Statement of Facts*, pp. 9-11.
5. J. M. Alpuche é Infante, *Satisfacción del Senador Alpuche* (Mexico City, 1826), p. 5; John Jordon, *Serious Actual Dangers of Foreigners and Foreign Commerce in the Mexican States* (Philadelphia, 1826), p. 23. Subsequently, Santangelo tried to minimize the significance of this by claiming that the Mexicans asked him to become a citizen, while he was willing to accept only honorary citizenship, Santangelo, *Statement of Facts*, p. 11.
6. *Las cuatro primeras discusiones*, pp. 79-162.
7. *Ibid.*, p. 165.
8. Santangelo, *Statement of Facts*, pp. 19-20.
9. Santangelo, *Statement of Facts*, pp. 35-40; Jordan, *Serious Actual Dangers*, pp. 1-39.
10. Marraro, "Pioneer Teachers," pp. 558-559; Santangelo, *Statement of Facts*, pp. 44-47.
11. Santangelo, *Statement of Facts*, p. 51.
12. *Ibid.*, pp. 48-54, 58-67, 69-85.
13. *Ibid.*, pp. 90-95.
14. *Ibid.*, pp. 97-119.
15. TREATIES, CONVENTIONS, INTERNATIONAL ACTS, PROTOCOLS AND AGREEMENTS BETWEEN THE UNITED STATES OF AMERICA AND OTHER NATIONS (Washington, 1910), 4 vols. Vol. 1, p. 1089.
16. David Vigness, "The Republic of the Río Grande: an Example of Separation in Northern Mexico" (unpublished Ph.D. dissertation, University of Texas at Austin) pp. 164-170.
17. THE PAPERS OF MIRABEAU BONAPARTE LAMAR (Austin, 1922), 6 vols., Vol. 55, pp. 143-152. Lamar, who knew Santangelo quite well, had the impression, *ibid.*, Vol. VI, pp. 270-271, that the land grant was not made. It actually was, *see infra*, note 38, but at the time the Texas legislature made the grant, in a rare error, it was not printed as a statute.
18. Orazio de Santangelo, *An Address Delivered by O. de A. Santangelo at a Public Meeting Held in New Orleans on 2d of February, 1839, by the Citizens of That Place, Having Claims against Mexico* (New Orleans, 1839) pp. 27-36.
19. *Joint Claims Commission Convention, April 11, 1839* (27th Congress 2d Sess., Document No. 1096).
20. As examples, John Bassett Moore, HISTORY AND DIGEST OF THE INTERNATIONAL ARBITRATIONS TO WHICH THE UNITED STATES HAS BEEN A PARTY (Washington, 1898) 6 vols., Vol. II, pp. 1234-1235, is sympathetic to Mexico's problems and efforts and H. H. Bancroft, THE WORKS OF H. H. BANCROFT (San Francisco, 1887), Vol XIII, pp. 314-317, is sharply critical of the United States Government's support of questionable claims, while Justin H. Smith, THE WAR WITH MEXICO (New York, 1919) 2 vols., Vol. I, pp. 74-81, 425-431, is severe toward Mexico and Seymour V. Cononor and Odie B. Faulk, NORTH AMERICA DIVIDED; THE MEXICAN WAR, 1846-1848 (New York, 1971), pp. 18-19, by implication take the American side. The most complete examination of the claims question by itself, Clayton C. Kohl, CLAIMS AS A CAUSE OF THE MEXICAN WAR (New York, 1914), pp. 33-43, 78-79, is mildly favorable to the claimants and their government.
21. Santangelo, *An Address Delivered . . . in New Orleans*, pp. 27-44; Orazio de Santangelo, *Protest Against the Convention of April 11, 1839, between the United States of America and the Republic of Mexico and against Both Said Governments: and Other Documents Relating to the Claims of Orazio de Attelis Santangelo, on the Government of Mexico* (Washington, 1842), pp. 9-51.
22. Santangelo, *Protest Against the Convention of April 11, 1839*, p. 17; Orazio de Santangelo, *Charges Preferred against Don Joaquín Velásquez de León and Don Pedro Fernández del Castillo* (Washington, 1841), *passim*.
23. Sitting of January 24, 1842, in Day Book 3, Minutes of the Proceedings of the Claims Commission (Records of the United States-Mexican Claims Commission, April 11, 1839-February 24, 1842, General Records of the Department of State, Record Group 76, National Archives); Santangelo, *Protest against the Convention of April 11, 1839*, p. 55. See also Orazio de Santangelo to Secretary of State Daniel Webster June 21 and 24, 1841, and to President Tyler, July 12, 1841, complaining about the State Department's handling of his case (27th Congress, 2d Sess., Senate Document No. 320), pp. 17-20.
24. Santangelo, *Statement of Facts*, pp. 131-157; Orazio de Santangelo, *The Honor of the United States of America under the Administration of Tyler, Webster & Co.* (New York, 1842), p. 42.

25. Santangelo, *The Honor of the U.S.A.*, p. 42.
26. Copy of the award decision signed by Henry Brackenridge, February 15, 1842, in Vol. II; Santangelo Claimant's File, NA.
27. Orazio de Santangelo's Claim, in the breakdown of claimants' cases into several financial estimates as to their worth (27th Congress, 2d Sess., House Document No. 291), p. 54. Because businesses and companies were involved, estimates to the number of claims vary. By one count there were 162. On this basis Santangelo asked for the sixth higest sum.
28. Such is the cautious conclusion drawn by Kohl, *Claims as a Cause of the Mexican War*, pp. 41-42.
29. Santangelo, *The Honor of the U.S.A.*, p. 8.
30. Orazio de Santangelo, *A Circular to the World. Is the Honorable McRoberts More Honorable that the Honorable Mitchell?* (New York, 1842), *passim*; Orazio de Santangelo, *Santangelo's Trial for Libel Against Samuel McRoberts, a Senator of the United States from Illinois, before the Court of General Sessions in the City of New York* (New York, 1842), *passim*; Santangelo, *The Honor of the U.S.A.*, p. 12.
31. Orazio de Santangelo, *Claimants on Mexico* (N.p., 1845), p. 2.
32. Orazio de Santangelo, *A Circular to Members of Congress* (New York, 1844), *passim*.
33. Santangelo, *Claimants on Mexico*, pp. 3, 8.
34. *Ibid.*, pp. 10-12.
35. Letters relating to the claim of Orazio de Santangelo for his 1826 expulsion from Mexico (Index to the Opinions of the Board of Commissioners, set up under the Act of Congress of March 30, 1849, pursuant to completion of Article XV of the Treaty of Guadalupe Hidalgo, February 2, 1848, General Records of the Department of State, Record Group 76, National Archives).
36. Marchese Santangelo de Attelis, *Un consiglio a Sua Maestà il Ré di Sardegna* (Genoa, 1848).
37. Mrs. Mary Santangelo to Charles Callaghan, April 17, 1850, in Vol. II, Santangelo Claimant's File, NA. Italics in the original.
38. Howard R. Marraro, ed., Diplomatic Relations Between the United States and the Kingdom of the Two Sicilies; *Instructions and Despatches, 1816-1861*, (New York, 1952), 2 vols., Vol. II, pp. 263-264, 266-269, 503-506. With regard to the Texas land, the patent was issued only on August 23, 1849, after the Santangelos had gone to Italy, Abstract of All Original Texas Land Titles Comprising Grants and Locations (Austin, 1942), 7 vols., Vol. IV, p. 1065. Mrs. Santangelo died in 1874. She had willed the land, located in present Zavala County, about eleven miles west of the Nueces River, to a Henry B. Thys. After several transferences, it fell to the Stuart family, the present owners, Georgia L. Price, County Clerk, Zavala County, Crystal City, Texas, to Lowell L. Blaisdell, n.d. September, 1971, a letter with accompanying documents, including a copy of the original patent specifying the exact location, and copies of others including the owners immediately following Henry B. Thys.
39. Decision in the case of Santangelo, March 19, 1851, (Opinions of the Board of Commissioners under the Act of Congress of March 30, 1849, General Records Department of State, Record Group 76, National Archives).
40. Seymour V. Connor, professor of history, Texas Tech University, gave to the writer the idea for this chapter, and offered leads as to how to obtain data on the Texas aspects of it.

Chapter 5

Sectionalism and Political Fragmentation

1. *Senate Document* No. 337, 29th Cong., 1st Session, Serial 476, p. 5.
2. *Senate Document* No. 22, 28th Cong., 2nd Session, Serial 450, p. 1.
3. *Appendix to the Congressional Globe*, 28th Cong., 2nd Session, p. 227.
4. *Congressional Globe*, 28th Cong., 2nd Session, p. 194.
5. *Appendix to the Congressional Globe*, 28th Cong., 2nd Session, p. 256.
6. *Congressional Globe*, 28th Cong., 2nd Session, p. 362.
7. *Senate Document* No. 337, 29th Cong., 1st Session, Serial 476, p. 2.
8. *Congressional Globe*, 29th Cong., 1st Session, p. 795.
9. *Ibid.*, p. 786.
10. *Ibid.*, p. 804.
11. *Senate Document* No. 395, 29th Cong., 1st Session, Serial 477, p. 4.
12. Justin H. Smith, The War With Mexico (New York: The Macmillan Company, 1919), Vol. II, p. 268.
13. Clayton S. Ellsworth, "American Churches and the Mexican War," *American Historical Review*, Vol. XLV (January, 1940), pp. 301-326.

14. Charles B. Going, DAVID WILMOT, *Free Soiler* (New York and London: D. Appleton and Company, 1924), p. 101.
15. *Congressional Globe*, 29th Cong., 2nd Session, p. 377.
16. *Ibid.*, p. 425.
17. *Ibid.*, p. 330.
18. *Ibid.*, p. 345.
19. *Ibid.*, p. 555.
20. *Ibid.*, p. 573.
21. Odie B. Faulk, LAND OF MANY FRONTIERS (New York: Oxford University Press, 1968), p. 137.
22. *Senate Executive Document* No. 52, 30th Cong., 1st Session, Serial 509, p. 36.
23. Justin H. Smith, THE WAR WITH MEXICO, Vol. II, p. 268.
24. *Congressional Globe*, 31st Cong., 1st Session, pt. II, p. 1589.
25. *Ibid.*
26. *Ibid.*, p. 1776.

Chapter 6

The Whig Abolitionists' Attitude

1. Edward L. Pierce, MEMOIR AND LETTERS OF CHARLES SUMNER (Boston, *Roberts Brothers*, 1893), 4 vols., Vol. III, p. 166.
2. Frank Otto Gatell, " 'Conscience and Jugdment': The Belt of Massachusetts Conscience Whigs," *The Historian*, Vol. XXI (November, 1958), p. 33.
3. David Donald, CHARLES SUMNER AND THE COMING CIVIL WAR (New York, Alfred A. Knopf, 1960), p. 110.
4. George Rawlings Poage, HENRY CLAY AND THE WHIG PARTY (Chapel Hill, The University of North Carolina Press, 1936), p. 14.
5. Arthur Charles Cole, THE WHIG PARTY IN THE SOUTH (Washington: American Historical Association), p. 116.
6. *Ibid.*, p. 110.
7. *Ibid.*, pp. 111-112.
8. *Ibid.*, p. 113.
9. In the House the vote was 120 to 98 and in the Senate it was 27 to 25.
10. Norman A. Graebner (ed.), MANIFEST DESTINY (Indianapolis: The Bobbs-Merrill Company, 1968), p. *xxxiii.*
11. *Congressional Globe*, 28th Cong., 1st Session, Appendix, pp. 704-705.
12. *Ibid.*
13. *The Liberator*, June 27, 1845, p. 101.
14. *Ibid.*, April 18, 1845, p. 69.
15. Pierce, *Memoir*, p. 99.
16. Frank Otto Gatell, JOHN GORHAM PALFREY AND THE NEW ENGLAND CONSCIENCE (Cambridge: Harvard University Press, 1963), p. 123.
17. *Ibid.*, p. 125.
18. *Ibid.*, p. 129.
19. Horace Greeley, THE AMERICAN CONFLICT (Hartford: O. D. Case and Company, 1885), Vol. I, p. 187.
20. Alfred Hoyt Bill, REHEARSAL FOR CONFLICT, *The War With Mexico, 1846-1848* (New York: Alfred A. Knopf, 1947), p. 106.
21. *Congressional Globe*, 28th Congress, 1st Session, p. 795.
22. Pierce, *Memoir*, p. 109.
23. *Daily National Intelligencer*, May 16, 1848, p. 3.
24. *Congressional Globe*, 28th Congress, 1st Session, pp. 543-544.
25. *Ibid.*, pp. 140-141.
26. *Ibid.*, 28th Congress, 2d Session, p. 58.
27. *Daily National Intelligencer*, May 16, 1846, p. 3.
28. *Ibid.*
29. Thomas Hart Benton and Abraham Lincoln doubted American territorial claims in Texas.
30. *Daily National Intelligencer*, May 16, 1846, p. 3.
31. *Congressional Globe*, 29th Congress, 2d Session, p. 58.
32. Pierce, *Memoir*, p. 114.
33. *Ibid.*
34. *Ibid.*, p. 115.
35. *Ibid.*, p. 117.
36. *Ibid.*, p. 118.

37. *Congressional Globe,* 30th Congress, 1st Session, p. 61.
38. Pierce, *Memoir,* p. 122.
39. *Ibid.,* p. 123.
40. *Ibid.*
41. Allen Nevins, POLK, *The Diary of a President, 1845-1849* (New York, Longmans, Green and Company, 1929), p. 186.
42. *The Liberator,* March 10, 1848, p. 38.
43. *Ibid.,* March 17, 1848, p. 42.
44. Cole, *The Whig Party,* pp. 125-126.
45. *Ibid.,* p. 126.
46. William Y. Thompson, ROBERT TOOMBS OF GEORGIA (Baton Rouge, Louisiana State University Press, 1966), p. 47.
47. *Ibid.*
48. Pierce, *Memoirs . . .,* p. 162.
49. Cattell, *John Gorham Palfrey . . .,* 160.
50. Pierce, *Memoirs . . .,* p. 168.
51. *Ibid.,* p. 169.
52. *Ibid.,* pp. 176-177.

Chapter 7

Jones at Monterey, 1842

1. A contemporary scholarly article is one by George M. Brooke, Jr., "The Vest Pocket War of Commodore Jones," *Pacific Historical Review* (August, 1962), pp. 217-233. The sources for this piece are letters, logs and other official documents, supplemented by newspaper accounts and excerpts from the polemics between Mexico and the United States. Curiously, one of the best accounts of Jones' fiasco, Hubert Howe Bancroft, HISTORY OF CALIFORNIA, Vol. IV, 298ff. (1886), is not cited. Charles Oscar Paullin, DIPLOMATIC NEGOTIATIONS OF AMERICAN NAVAL OFFICERS, 1778-1883 (Baltimore, 1912), describes some of Jones' behavior. Udolpho Theodore Bradley wrote a doctoral dissertation, "The Contentious Commodore: Thomas ape [*sic*] Catesby Jones of the Old Navy," Cornell University (1933). The essence of this appeared as an article, "Thomas ap Catesby Jones, a Personality of the Days of Sail," UNITED STATES NAVAL INSTITUTE PROCEEDINGS, Vol. LIX (August, 1933), pp. 1154-1156. A fairly recent doctoral dissertation dealing with Jones was produced by K. Jack Bauer, "United States Naval Operations During the Mexican War," Indiana University (1953) (University Microfilms, Ann Arbor, Michigan).

   The basic source materials for any study of the interesting and provocative experience of Commodore Jones are in a very few places. They have apparently been published for the most part, both as documents and in the form of commentaries. The largest collection of documents is to be found in President Tyler's Message on *Taking Possession of Monterey, Mexico,* 27th Congress, Third Session, House Document 166 (serial 422 in the Congressional Set). A selection of items, including a number of Jones' letters, appears in JOURNAL OF A CRUISE TO THE PACIFIC OCEAN, 1842-1844, IN THE FRIGATE UNITED STATES, edited by Charles Robert Anderson (Duke University Press, 1937). Jones' own version of the affair was published as "Commodore Thomas ap Catesby Jones' Narrative of his visit to Governor Micheltorena," *Historical Society of Southern California Quarterly* (1935-1936).

   In addition to the above mentioned sources, various letters, logs and reports may be found in other government publications and in a number of contemporary newspapers, such as the *New Orleans Advertiser* or those published in Mexico City. Bancroft was able to ferret out the main story, and he used all of the principal sources.
2. Major Edwin N. McClellan, "The Conquest of California," *Marine Corps Gazette* (September, 1923) upon whch is based the account of the Jones episode by Colonel Clyde H. Metcalf, A HISTORY OF THE UNITED STATES MARINE CORPS (Putnam, New York, 1939).
3. First Lieutenant George W. Robbins, U. S. M. C., who commanded the Marines ashore during the short occupation of Monterey, was appointed second lieutenant April 26, 1832, and was promoted to first lieutenant on December 11, 1836. He committed suicide by hanging on March 1, 1845. Professor H. Lockwood was one of twenty-two professors of mathematics serving with the Navy in 1842. Lockwood had been with the Navy since November 4, 1841, and retired on August 18, 1876. In 1842, he served as adjutant to the force that landed at Monterey.

References

Chapter 8

The Superiority of American Artillery

1. *House Executive Document*, No. 24, 31st Congress, 1st Session, Serial 576, pp. 22a, c, h, f. V. M. Porter, "A History of Battery 'A' of St. Louis," *Missouri Historical Society Collections*, Vol. II, No. 4 (March, 1905), pp. 1-48.
2. James Gilchrist Benton. A COURSE OF INSTRUCTION IN ORDNANCE AND GUNNERY: *Proposed for the Use of Cadets of the United States Military Academy* (New York: D. Van Norstrand, 1867), pp. 107, 166-167. William Gilham, MANUAL OF INSTRUCTION FOR THE VOLUNTEERS AND MILITIA OF THE UNITED STATES, *Combining as Much of the Systems of Cooper, Scott and Hardee, as is Recognized in the United States Army* (Philadelphia: Charles Desilver, 1861), pp.74-75.
3. Gilham, *Manual of Instruction*, p. 31.
4. David Lavender. CLIMAX AT BUENA VISTA: *The American Campaigns in Northeastern Mexico, 1846-1847* (New York: J. B. Lippincott Company, 1966), p. 227; Russell F. Weigley, HISTORY OF THE UNITED STATES ARMY (New York: Macmillan Company, 1967), pp. 171-172.
5. *House Executive Document*, No. 2, 29th Congress, 1st Session, Serial 480, pp. 220a, 220b.
6. *Ibid.*, p. 220f.
7. Maurice Matloff, (ed.), AMERICAN MILITARY HISTORY, *Army Historical Series* (Washington: U. S. Government Printing Office, 1969), p. 169; Lavender, *Climax at Buena Vista*, pp. 59-60.
8. Lavender, *Climax at Buena Vista*, p. 67; Benton, *A Course of Instruction in Ordnance and Gunnery*, p. 107.
9. Brevet Brigadier General Zachary Taylor, Report to Brevet Brigadier General R(oger) Jones, the Adjutant General of the Army, Camp near Matamors, May 16, 1846, in *House Executive Documents*, Nos. 20, 29, 29th Congress, 1st Session, Serial 486, p. 2 (hereinafter cited as H. E. D. 209)
10. Colonel David Emanuel Twiggs' Report to Taylor, May 11, 1846, *Ibid.*, pp. 13-14
11. Major Thomas Staniford Report to Twiggs, May 10, 1846, *Ibid.*, p. 19.
12. First Lieutenant Randolph Ridgeley Report to (Twiggs), May 10, 1846, *Ibid.*, pp. 13-14.
13. Taylor to Jones, *ibid.*, p. 3; Lieutenant Colonel William Goldsmith Belknap to Taylor, May 15, 1846, Camp near Matamors, *ibid.*, p. 24.
14. Belknap, *ibid.*, pp. 23-24.
15. Edward J. Nichols, ZACH TAYLOR'S LITTLE ARMY (Garden City: Doubleday and Company, Inc., 1963), pp. 78, 84.
16. Taylor to Jones, *H. E. D.*, 209, p. 6; Nichols *Zach Taylor's Little Army*, p. 77.
17. Holman Hamilton, ZACHARY TAYLOR: *Soldier of the Republic* (New York: Bobbs-Merrill Company, 1941), p. 187.
18. Taylor to Jones, *H. E. D.* 209, pp. 6-7.
20. Taylor to Jones, *ibid.*, p. 7; Twiggs to Taylor, *ibid.*, pp. 14-15.
19. Ridgely to (Twiggs), *ibid.*, pp. 20-21; Twiggs to Taylor, *ibid.*, pp. 14-15.
21. Weigley, *History of the United States Army*, p. 189.
22. Zachary Taylor, LETTERS OF ZACHARY TAYLOR FROM THE BATTLEFIELDS OF THE MEXICAN WAR (Rochester: Genessee Press, 1908), pp. 43-44.
23. Taylor, *H. E. D.*, 209, p. 76.
24. Taylor to Jones, Camp before Monterrey, September 22, 1846 ,*House Executive Document*, No. 4, 29th Congress, 2d Session, Serial 497, p. 76 (Hereinafter cited as *H. E. D.* 4).
25. Worth to Taylor, *H. E. D.* 4, pp. 103-104.
26. *Ibid.*, pp. 104-105.
27. Worth to Taylor, *H. E. D.* 4, p. 105.
28. Taylor, *Letters of Zachary Taylor*, p. 60.
29. Brigadier General David Emanuel Twiggs to Taylor, Camp near Monterrey, September 29, 1846, *H. E. D.* 4, p. 101.
30. Hamilton, *Zachary Taylor*, p. 214.
31. Taylor to R. Jones, *House Executive Document*, No. 8, 30th Congress, 1st Session, Serial 515, pp. 137-138, 142.
32. Arthur Douglas Howden Smith, OLD FUSS AND FEATHERS: *The Life and Exploits of General Winfield Scott* (et cetera, et cetera) (New York: Greystone Press, 1937), p. 273.
33. Taylor, *H. E. D.* 8, p. 142.
34. Brigadier General John Ellis Wool to Taylor, Camp Taylor, Aqua Nueva, Mexico, March 4, 1847, *H. E. D.* 8, p. 146.
35. Wool to Taylor, *ibid.*, p. 146.
36. Wool to Taylor, *ibid.*, pp. 147-148; Hamilton, *Zachary Taylor*, p. 236.
37. Captain John Paul Jones O'Brien to Captain John Macrae Washington, Camp on Battle Ground of Buena Vista, February 25, 1847, *H. E. D.* 8, p. 161; Nichols, *Zach Taylor's*

References

Little Army, p. 220; Francis B. Heitman, HISTORICAL REGISTER AND DICTIONARY OF THE UNITED STATES ARMY FROM ITS ORGANIZATION, SEPTEMBER 29, 1789, TO MARCH 2, 1903 (Washington: U. S. Government Printing Office, 1903), 2 vols., Vol. I, p. 1007.

38. Nichols, *Zach Taylor's Little Army*, p. 223.
39. Lavender, *Climax at Buena Vista*, p. 193.
40. Wool to Taylor, *H. E. D.* 8, pp. 148-149; Brevet Lieutenant Colonel Charles Augustus May to Taylor, Dragoon Camp, near Aqua Nueva, Mexico, March 3, 1847, pp. 198-199; Captain Braxton Bragg to (Taylor), March 2, 1847, *ibid.*, pp. 201-210.
41. *Ibid.*, p. 149.
42. O'Brien to Washington, *H. E. D.* 8, pp. 160-162.
43. Bragg to Taylor, *ibid.*, p. 202.
44. Washington to Wool, February 28, 1847, *ibid.*, p. 159.
45. Lieutenant Colonel William Weatherford to Wool, Camp San Juan de Buena Vista, February 26, 1847, *ibid.*, p. 175; Wool to Taylor, *ibid.*, p. 147.
46. Major Cary H. Fry to (Wool), Camp Taylor, March 3, 1847, *ibid.*, pp. 170-171.
47. Weatherford to (Wool), *ibid.*, p. 175.
48. Nichols, *Zach Taylor's Little Army*, pp. 231-232; Shover to Bragg, *H. E. D.* 8, pp. 208-209.
49. Taylor, *ibid.*, pp. 231-232.
50. Wool to Taylor, *ibid.*, p. 150.
51. Major General Winfield Scott to William L. Marcy, Secretary of War, Camp Washington, before Vera Cruz, Mexico, March 23, 1847, *ibid.*, pp. 224-225.
52. George Brinton McClellan, William Star Myers (ed.), THE MEXICAN WAR DIARY OF GEORGE B. McCLELLAN (Princeton: Princeton University Press, 1917), p. 72.
53. P. T. G. Beauregard, T. Harry Williams (ed.), WITH BEAUREGARD IN MEXICO: *The Mexican War Reminiscences of P. T. G. Beauregard* (Baton Rouge: Louisiana State University Press, 1956), p. 25.
54. Silas Bent McKinley and Silas Bent, OLD ROUGH AND READY, p. 192.
55. Brigadier General David E. Twiggs to (Scott), April 19, 1847, H. E. D. 8, p. 275.
56. Robert Anderson, AN ARTILLEY OFFICER IN THE MEXICAN WAR (New York: G. P. Putnam's Sons, 1911), pp. 138-140.
57. McKinley, *Old Rough and Ready*, p. 193.
58. McClellan, *The Mexican War Diary of George B. McClellan*, pp. 88-89.
59. Smith, *Old Fuss and Feathers*, p. 248.
60. Beauregard, *With Beauregard in Mexico*, p. 49.
61. Scott to Marcy, San Augustin, Acapulco Road, Mexico, August 19, 1847, *H. E. D.* 8, p. 304.
62. Major John Lind Smith to (General Scott), Tacubaya, August 27, 1847, *ibid.*, pp. 350-352.
63. Scott to Marcy, *ibid.*, p. 305.
64. Brevet Brigadier General Persifor E. Smith to (Scott), San Angel, near Mexico, August 23, 1847, *ibid.*, p. 326.
65. Major General Gideon Johnson Pillow to Scott, Mixcaca, Mexico, August 24, 1847, *ibid.*, p. 337; Beauregard, *With Beauregard in Mexico*, p. 55.
66. Brevet Major General William Jenkins Worth to Scott, Tacubaya, Mexico, August 23, 1847, *H. E. D.* 8, pp. 317-318.
67. Scott to Marcy, *ibid.*, p. 308; Captain Benjamin Huger to Worth, Tacubaya, Mexico, September 9, 1847, *ibid.*, p. 375.
68. Worth to Scott, Tacubaya, September 10, 1847, *ibid.*, p. 361; Huger to Worth, *ibid.*, pp. 374-375.
69. Worth to Scott, *ibid.*, pp. 363-364.
70. Major General John Anthony Quitman, Report to Scott, National Palace, Mexico, September 29, 1847, *ibid.*, pp. 410-411.
71. Pillow to Scott, *ibid.*, pp. 363-364.
72. Worth to Scott, September 16, 1847, *ibid.*, pp. 391-392.
73. Henry Wagen Halleck, ELEMENTS OF MILITARY ART AND SCIENCE: *A Course of Instruction in Strategy, Fortification, Tactics of Battle* (et cetera) (New York: D. Appleton and Company, 1861), pp. 290-292.

Chapter 9

Soldiering, Suffering, and Dying

1. Jefferson Davis, REPORT OF THE SECRETARY OF WAR, July 28, 1856, *Senate Executive Document*, No. 96, 34th Cong., 1st Session, Serial 827, pp. 605-606. [Hereinafter cited as *S. E. D.* 96.]
2. *Ibid.*
3. Stanhope Bayne-Jones, THE EVOLUTION OF PREVENTIVE MEDICINE IN THE UNITED STATES ARMY, 1607-1939 (Washington: U. S. Government Printing Office, 1968) p. 86.
4. *Ibid.*, pp. 86, 124; the cumulative mortality rate for the North in the Civil War, including

References

deaths from disease and killed in action was 98 per 1,000 per annum. The cumulative mortality rate for the Mexican War was 153.5 per 1,000 per annum.

5. Maurice Matloff, (ed.), AMERICAN MILITARY HISTORY, *Army Historical Series* (Washington: U. S. Government Printing Office, 1969), p. 465; of 10,420,000 soldiers who served in World War II, there were 235,000 battle deaths and 83,400 non-battle deaths for a total of 318,400 deaths.
6. William L. Marcy, Letter from the Secretary of War, May 4, 1848, *House Executive Document*, No. 62, 30th Cong., 1st Session, Serial 521, pp. 12-13; the effective strength of the army at the beginning of the war was 7,244 men, exclusive of the corps of engineers, topographical engineers, and ordnance.
7. Stanhope Bayne-Jones, *The Evolution of Preventive Medicine*, p. 186; the date for the beginning of the bacteriological era is 1876.
8. Edward J. Nichols, ZACH TAYLOR'S LITTLE ARMY (Garden City: Doubleday and Company, 1963), p. 115.
9. Otis A. Singletary, THE MEXICAN WAR (Chicago: University of Chicago Press, 1960), p. 144.
10. Lewis Wallace, LEW WALLACE: *An Autobiography* (New York: Harper and Brothers, 1906), 2 vols., Vol. I, pp. 124-125.
11. Justin H. Smith, THE WAR WITH MEXICO (Gloucester: Peter Smith, 1963), 2 vols., Vol. II, p. 73; soldiers indulged in fruits and sugar-cane brandy and this with the want of salt meats, among other factors, reportedly caused dysentery and ague.
12. Singletary, *The Mexican War*, p. 144.
13. Edward Hake Phillips, "The Texas Norther," *The Southwestern Historical Quarterly*, Vol. LIX (July, 1955), pp. 1-13; a "norther" is a severe cold front accompanied by high winds and usually heavy rains.
14. Darwin Payne, "Camp Life in the Army of Occupation: Corpus Christi, July, 1845, to March, 1846," *Southwestern Historical Quarterly*, Vol. LXXII), pp. 331-332.
    March, 1846," *Southwestern Historical Quarterly*, Vol. LXXII), pp. 331-332.
15. Payne, "Camp Life in the Army of Occupation," pp. 326, 335; by October 15, 1845, the army had increased to 3,860.
16. *Ibid.*, p. 332.
17. David Lavender, CLIMAX AT BUENA VISTA: *The American Campaigns in Northeastern Mexico, 1846-1847* (New York: J. B. Lippincott Company, 1966), pp. 59, 63; Taylor arriveed at Mattamors on March 28, 1846.
18. *Ibid.*, p. 88.
19. *New Orleans Times Picayune*, July 8, 1846, p. 2.
20. Lavender, *Climax at Buena Vista*, pp. 82-90.
21. Smith, *Zach Taylor's Little Army*, p. 128.
22. Lavender, *Climax at Buena Vista*, p. 89.
23. *Zach Taylor's Little Army*, p. 128.
24. William Starr Myers, GENERAL GEORGE BRINTON McCLELLAN (New York: Appleton-Century Company, Inc., 1934), p. 26.
25. Lew Wallace, Vol. I, p. 123.
26. *Ibid.*, pp. 123-124.
27. *Ibid.*, p. 125.
28. General Zachary Taylor to Brevet Brigadier General R[oger] Jones, The Adjutant General of the Army, Camp Camargo, October 15, 1846, *House Executive Document*, No. 60, 30th Cong., 1st Session, Serial 520, p. 352 [hereinafter cited as *H. E. D.* 60]. *See also* Taylor to R. Jones, September 2, 1846, Camp Camargo, *Ibid.*, p. 414.
29. *New Orleans Bee*, April 23, 1847, p. 2.
30. *Ibid.*, June 1, 1847, p. 2; June 12, 1847, p. 2.
31. Frank E. Vandiver, "The Mexican War Experience of Josiah Gorgas," *Journal of Southern History*, Vol. XIII (1947), p. 382.
32. Roswell S. Ripley, THE WAR WITH MEXICO (New York: Harper and Brothers, 1849), 2 vols., Vol. I, p. 13.
33. Winfield S. Scott to W. L. Marcy, Headquarters of the Army, Jalapa, April 282, 1847, *H. E. D.*, 60, pp. 944-945.
34. Scott to Brevet Colonel Wilson, Jalapa, April 23, 1847, *Ibid.*, p. 136.
35. Fayette Copeland, KENDALL OF THE PICAYUNE (Norman: University of Oklahoma Press, 1943), p. 190.
36. Scott to Marcy, Jalapa, April 28, 1847, *H. E. D.* 60, p. 944.
37. Smith, *The War with Mexico*, Vol. II, p. 46.
38. Robert Anderson, AN ARTILLERY OFFICER IN THE MEXICAN WAR, 1846-47 (New York: G. P. Putnam's Sons, 1911), p. 163.
39. Scott to Marcy, Headquarters of the Army, Puebla, June 4, 1847, *H. E. D.* 60, p. 993.
40. *Ibid.*; the troops were rationed salt-meats one day in nine in the elevated country.
41. Ethan Allen Hitchcock, W. A. Croffut (ed.), FIFTY YEARS IN CAMP AND FIELD (New York: G. P. Putnam's Sons, 1909), p. 269; Smith, *The War with Mexico*, Vol. II, p. 277.

References

42. Anderson, *An Aritllery Officer*, pp. 171-173.
43. Singletary, *The Mexican War*, p. 146; *see also* Scott's General Order, No. 101, Vera Cruz, April 19, 1847, *House Executive Document*, No. 56, 30th Cong., 1st Session, Serial 518, p. 125.
44. Smith, *The War with Mexico*, Vol. II, pp. 183-184.
45. Stanhope Bayne-Jones, *The Evolution of Preventive Medicine*, p. 86.
46. Smith, *The War with Mexico*, Vol. I, p. 518; a logistics blunder at Santa Fe caused the regiment to go on one-half rations for the remainder of its campaign.
47. *Ibid.*, p. 304.
48. *Ibid.*, p. 299.
49. D. D. Mitchell, letter to General Thomas Lawson, Surgeon General of the Army, St. Louis, September 9, 1847, *House Reports*, No. 404, 30th Cong., 1st Session, Serial 525, p. 13; Dr. A. Wislizenus, letters to Congress, St. Louis, August 19, 1847, *Ibid.*, p. 10; out of 920 members of Doniphan's regiment, 250 were sick with the disease.
50. John T. Hughes, DONIPHAN'S EXPEDITION: *An Account of the U. S. Army Operations in the Great American Southwest* (Chicago: The Rio Grande Press, Inc., 1962), p. 338.
51. General Dabney Herndon Maury, RECOLLECTIONS OF A VIRGINIAN (London: Sampson, Low, Marston and Company, 1894), p. 45.
52. The old establishment regulars were the professional soldiers who were in the army before the war. The new regulars were the hastily recruited personnel of the ten new regiments.
53. Jefferson Davis, Report of the Secretary of War, July 28, 1856, *Senate Executive Documents* 96, 35 Cong., 1 Sess., Serial 827, pp. 605-6, 610; hereinafter cited as *S. E. D.* 96; the mortality rate per 1,000 per annum was calculated from data obtained from the Secretary's Report.
54. James A. Huston, THE SINEWS OF WAR: *Army Logistics, 1775-1953, Army Historical Series* (Washington: U. S. Government Printing Office, 1966), p. 129; firearms models included Hall breech-loading rifles, Whitney rifles, Jencks carbines, and other percussion weapons. There was no question of the superiority of the rifles over muskets, except that it took longer to reload the muzzle-loading rifles.
55. Lynn Montross, WAR THROUGH THE AGES (New York: Harper and Brothers, 1960), p. 574. Only the base of the new "sugar-loaf" bullet came in contact with the bore, and the usual greased patch acted as a gas-top. A special ramrod with a cup-shaped head forced the projectile into position with ease and exactness. This new discovery increased the accuracy of the American weapon to approximately five hundred yards compared with riflemen of other nations who were still driving the ball into the bore with a ramrod and wooden mallet with accuracy of little more than one hundred yards.
56. Smith, *Zach Taylor's Little Army*, p. 85.
57. Ulysses S. Grant, PERSONAL MEMOIRS OF U. S. GRANT (New York: Charles L. Webster and Company, 1885), 2 vols. Vol. I, p. 95.
58. *Zach Taylor's Little Army*, p. 85.
59. Huston, *The Sinews of War*, p. 132. The regular infantry troops were outfitted in the standard "undress" blue uniform with matching short jacket, trousers and high loose crown cap. The bayonet was sheafed at the belt; and an oval waist belt-plate carried the initials of the Union in symmetry with the shoulder belt-plate bearing the image of the American eagle.
60. *Zach Taylor's Little Army*, p. 106.
61. Marcy to the Governors of the States calling for additional regiments, November 18, 1846, *H. E. D.* 60, p. 479-480; also travel pay to and from the war zone was fifty cents for every twenty miles.
62. Marcy, REPORT OF THE SECRETARY OF WAR, December 2, 1847, *Senate Executive Document*, No. 1, 30th Cong., 1st Session, Serial 503, p. 66. [Hereinafter cited as *S. E. D.* 1.]
63. George Winston Smith and Charles Judah, CHRONICLES OF THE GRINGOS: *The U. S. Army in the Mexican War*, 1846-1848 (Albuquerque: University of New Mexico Press, 1968), pp. 272, 289-290.
64. Jefferson Davis, *S. E. D.* 96, p. 610; the mortality rate is calculated from data obtained from this report.
65. Singletary, *The Mexican War*, pp. 144-146.
66. Marcy, REPORT OF THE SECRETARY OF WAR, May 4, 1848, *House Executive Document*, No. 62, 30th Cong., 1st Session, Serial 521, pp. 12-13.
67. Smith, *The War with Mexico*, Vol. I, p. 225.
68. Jefferson Davis, *S. E. D.* 96, p. 610; Leland D. Baldwin, THE STREAM OF AMERICAN HISTORY (New York: Richard R. Smith, Inc., 1952), 2 vols. Vol. I, p. 706. Baldwin reports that there were 6,750 deserters during the war; for an account of the famous San Patricio incident *see* Fairfax Downey, "The Tragic Story of the San Patricio Battalion," *American Heritage*, Vol. VI, No. 4 (June, 1955), pp. 20-24.
69. Samuel E. Chamberlain, MY CONFESSION (New York: Harper and Brothers, 1956), p. 226; *see also* Downey, "Tragic Story of the San Patricio Battalion," pp. 20-24.

References

70. Stanhope Bayne-Jones, *The Evolution of Preventive Medicine,* pp. 85, 184; the commanding officer is ultimately responsible for the sanitary conditions of the camp.
71. Taylor to Jones, Camp Camargo, September 2, 1846, *H. E. D.* 60, p. 414.
72. *Ibid.,* September 3, 1846, pp. 417-419.
73. Anderson, *An Artillery Officer,* p. 313.
74. Smith, *Zach Taylor's Little Army,* p. 119. For a comprehensive listing of the medicines carried by a medical doctor during the war, *see* "Claim of Dr. A. Wislizenus for medical supply payment," *House Reports,* No. 404, 30th Cong., 1st Session, Serial 525, pp. 3-4.
75. Stanhope Bayne-Jones, *The Evolution of Preventive Medicine,* p. 85.
76. Quoted in Roswell S. Ripley, *The War with Mexico,* Vol. I, p. 335.
77. Frederick Louis Huidekoper, THE MILITARY UNPREPAREDNESS OF THE UNITED STATES (New York: The Macmillan Company, 1915), p. 544.
78. Huston, *The Sinews of War,* p. 132.
79. *Ibid.,* p. 128; moreover, the telegraph was not used tactically during the war; David M. Pletcher, "The Building of the Mexican Railway," *Hispanic American Historical Review,* Vol. XXX, No. 1 (February, 1950), p. 126; it was January, 1873, before Mexico celebrated the inauguration of its first major railroad.
80. General H. L. Heiskell, Acting Surgeon General, Report of the Surgeon General, November 23, 1847, *S. E. D.* 1, p. 721.
81. *Ibid.,* W. L. Marcy, Report of the Secretary of War, December 2, 1847, p. 66.
82. Erna Risch, QUARTERMASTER SUPPORT OF THE ARMY: *A History of the Corps,* 1775-1939 (Washington: U. S. Government Printing Office, 1962), p. 254.
83. Thomas Lawson, Report of the Surgeon General, November 7, 1849, *Senate Executive Document,* No. 1, 31st Cong., 1st Session, Serial 549, p. 207; but of 7,228 cases of diarrhea and chronic dysentery, only 160 terminated fatally.
84. Stanhope Bayne-Jones, *The Evolution of Preventive Medicine,* pp. 97-98.

Chapter 10

Los Diablos Tejanos: The Texas Rangers

1. Hays, under authority of the governor, had recruited the regiment in the late spring of 1846. Before the outfit was fully organized, Hays permitted McCulloch's and R. A. Gillespie's companies, ready for battle before the rest, to report to Taylor for special scouting services on the understanding that they would rejoin him in August. The captains of the other eight companies in Hays' regiment were C. B. Acklin, S. L. S. Ballowe, Eli Chandler, F. S. Early, J. Gillespie, Tom Green, C. C. Herbert, and Jerome B. McCown. U. S. War Department Records Group No. 94 (National Archives, Washington, D. C.). *See also* James Kimmons Greer. COLONEL JACK HAYS: *Texas Frontier Leader and California Builder,* pp. 126-29. 285n.
2. Taylor to George T. Wood, July 7, 1846, Governors' Letters, 1846-60 (Archives, Texas State Library, Austin).
3. S. C. Reid, Jr., THE SCOUTING EXPEDITIONS OF MCCULLOCH'S TEXAS RANGERS. pp. 53, 61.
4. W. H. King, "The Texas Ranger Service and History of the Rangers, with Observations on Their Value as a Police Protection," in Dudley C. Wooten (ed.), A COMPREHENSIVE HISTORY OF TEXAS, Vol. II, p. 338.
5. John R. Kenly, MEMIORS OF A MARYLAND VOLUNTEER, WAR WITH MEXICO IN THE YEARS 1846-7-8, p. 53.
6. General Taylor and President Polk had been feuding since the war began. Not only were they personally antagonistic to each other, but they belonged to different political parties, too — Taylor was a Whig and Polk was a Democrat. The President feared that Taylor's victories were making him uncomfortably popular in the public eye, that continued success might make him a national hero in the mold of Andrew Jackson and thus a potential Presidential candidate. Polk would, therefore. take every advantage to disparage Taylor that he could find. See Otis A. Singletary, THE MEXICAN WAR, pp. 104-16.
7. Walter Prescott Webb, THE TEXAS RANGERS: *A Century of Frontier Defense,* pp. 95, 99.
8. Reid, *Scouting Expeditions of McCulloch's Texas Rangers,* pp. 108-109.
9. [Luther Giddings], SKETCHES OF THE CAMPAIGN IN NORTHERN MEXICO IN EIGHTEEN HUNDRED FORTY-SIX AND SEVEN BY AN OFFICER OF THE FIRST OHIO VOLUNTEERS, p. 143.
10. Unless otherwise cited. the account of the Texas Rangers at Monterrey is based on the following sources and books: Hays to General J. Pinckney Henderson, September 24(?), 1846, in THE PAPERS OF MIRABEAU BUONAPARTE LAMAR (ed. Charles A. Gulick), Vol. IV, pt. 1, p. 139; W. J. Worth's report, September 28, 1846, 29th Congress, Second Session, *House Executive Document No. 4,* pp. 102ff.; Reid, *Scouting Expeditions of McCulloch's Texas Rangers,* pp. 153-95; John S. Ford, "Truitt at Monterrey," in Ford, Memoirs (Archives,

References

University of Texas Library, Austin), Vol. IV, pp. 619-22; Webb, *Texas Rangers*, pp. 102-10; and Greer, *Colonel Jack Hays*, pp. 137-53.

11. T. W. Ridell to A. P. Murgotten, January 18, 1901, in the *Pioneer* (San Jose, California), February 15, 1901, as cited in Greer, *Colonel Jack Hays*, pp. 153, 387n.
12. Edward Bosque, MEMOIRS, p. 34 n.
13. Order No. 124, October 1, 1846, 30th Congress, First Session, *House Executive Document* No. 60, p. 508; Webb, *Texas Rangers*, p. 110.
14. Taylor to Adjutant General, June 8, 1847, 30th Congress, First Session, *House Executive Document* No. 60, p. 1176.
15. Reid, *Scouting Expeditions of McCulloch's Texas Rangers*, pp. 234-35.
16. Webb, *Texas Rangers*, p. 113.
17. Taylor to Adjutant General, June 16, 1847, 30th Congress, First Session, *House Executive Document* No. 60, p. 1178.
18. Originally Hays had raised a second regiment to protect Taylor's supply lines between Monterrey and the Río Grande, but then word came that the general would receive no troops for less than twelve months, and several of the companies disbanded. Within weeks, however, recruiters for Hays raised enough new companies to constitute a regiment of twelve-month volunteers. On July 10, in San Antonio, the outfit was mustered into federal service for twelve months or for the duration of the war. U. S. War Department, Records Group No. 94 (National Archives, Washington, D. C.); W. J. Hughes, REBELLIOUS RANGER: *Rip Ford and the Old Southwest*, pp. 22-23.
19. U. S. War Department, Records Group No. 94.
20. Ford, *Rip Ford's Texas*, p. 61.
21. Hughes, *Rebellious Ranger*, p. 24.
22. See Singletary, *The Mexican War*, pp. 71-101.
23. Greer, *Colonel Jack Hays*, pp. 168-70.
24. *New Orleans Picayune* October 10, 1847; *Niles National Register* (Baltimore), October 30, 1847.
25. Ford, *Rip Ford's Texas*, pp. 65-66.
26. *Ibid.*, p. 66.
27. *New Orleans Picayune*, October 29, 1847.
28. Ford, *Rip Ford's Texas*, pp. 66-68, 89.
29. *Ibid.*, pp. 75-77; *New Orleans Picayune*, December 9, 1847.
30. J. J. Oswandel. "Notes on the Mexican War, 1846-47-48," p. 38, *New Orleans Picayune*, December 9, 1847.
31. Justin H. Smith, THE WAR WITH MEXICO, Vol. II, p. 177.
32. Lane to Adjutant General, October 18, 1847, 30th Congress, First Session, *Senate Executive Document No. 1*, pp. 477-79; Oswandel, *Notes on the Mexican War*, pp. 171-77; Webb, *Texas Rangers*, pp. 115-16.
33. Lane to Adjutant General, December 1, 1847, 30th Congress, Second Session, *House Executive Document No. 1*, pp. 86-89.
34. Albert G. Brackett, GENERAL LANE'S BRIGADE IN CENTRAL MEXICO, pp. 173-74.
35. Ephraim M. Daggett, "Adventure with Guerrillas," in Isaac George, HEROES AND INCIDENTS OF THE MEXICAN WAR, p. 213.
36. Oran M. Roberts, "Texas," in CONFEDERATE MILITARY HISTORY (ed. Clement A. Evans), Vol. XI, p. 146.
37. Ford, *Rip Ford's Texas*, p. 81. "Hays' Rangers have come," General Ethan Allen Hitchcock recorded on the day they entered Mexico City, "their appearance never to be forgotten. Not in any sort of uniform, but well mounted and doubly well armed; each man has one or two Colt's revolvers besides ordinary pistols, a sword, and every man his rifle. ... The Mexicans are terribly afraid of them." Hitchcock, FIFTY YEARS IN CAMP AND FIELD (ed. W. A. Croffut), p. 310.
38. Ford, *Rip Ford's Texas*, pp. 81-82.
39. *Ibid.*, p. 82.
40. *Ibid.*, pp. 83-84.
41. Colonel Ebenezer Dumont's Letters, published in the *Indiana Register* and quoted in the *Democratic Telegraph and Texas Register* (Columbia), February 24, 1848.
42. Ford, *Rip Ford's Texas*, pp. 86ff.; Hughes, *Rebellious Ranger*, pp. 40ff.; Winfield Scott to W. L. Marcy, January 13, 1848, 30th Congress, First Session, *House Executive Document No. 60*, p. 1067.
43. Albert G. Brackett has a description of *guerrilleros*, their nature and their dress, in his reliable study, HISTORY OF THE UNITED STATES CAVALRY, FROM THE FORMATION OF THE FEDERAL GOVERNMENT TO THE 1ST OF JUNE, 1863, pp 210-13.
44. Ford, *Rip Ford's Texas*, pp. 86-89. See also the reports of Lane and Hays, 30th Congress, Second Session, *House Executive Document* No. 1, pp. 89-95, 98-100.
45. Ford, *Rip Ford's Texas*, pp. 101-104.
46. *New Orleans Delta*, April 24, 1848; U. S. War Department, Records Group No. 94.

References

47. Ford, *Rip Ford's Texas*, p. 72.
48. *Ibid.*, pp. 72-73.
49. For other views of the Texas Rangers in the Mexican War, I urge the reader to examine Webb, *Texas Rangers*, pp. 91-124; Hughes, *Rebellious Ranger*, pp. 22-56; and Greer, *Colonel Jack Hays*, pp. 126-213.

Chapter 11
Governor Armijo's Moment of Truth

1. Donaciano Vigil to Asamblea Departamental, June 18, 1846; Legislative, 1846. Proceedings, Mexican Archives of New Mexico (hereinafter cited as MANM).
2. See complaints of Albuquerque, Jemez, and Taos citizens to Armijo and Comandante Principal Juan Andrés Archuleta; Governor's Papers, 1846, communications sent and received and Letterbook, MANM. Ward Alan Minge, "Frontier Problems in New Mexico Preceding the Mexican War, 1840-1846," Ph. D. Diss., (University of New Mexico, 1965), p. 275.
3. Armijo to Ministro de Guerra y Marina, April 30, 1846. and reply July 20, 1846; Manuscript No. S-986, N. 421, New Mexico (prov.) Gobernador 1838-1845 (Armijo), Official Documents and Reports, Beinecke Rare Book and Manuscript Library, Yale University (hereinafter cited as Beinecke Papers).
4. Armijo to prefect of the nothern district, June 30, July 4, and July 6, 1846; Governor's Papers, 1846, Letterbook, MANM.
5. *Ibid.*, Armijo to the prefects, July 4 and 8, 1846.
6. Archuleta to Armijo and Agustín Durán to Archuleta, January 1 and 2, 1846; Governor's Papers, 1846, communications received by governor from within New Mexico, MANM.
7. Armijo to Ministro de Guerra y Marina, April 16. 1846. Beinecke Papers.
8. Military Records, 1846; Hacienda Records, 1846. MANM. Minge, "Frontier Problems," p. 296.
9. Armijo to Asamblea Departamental, August 10, 1846; Benjamin M. Read Papers, State of New Mexico Records Center. A note on page 420 of Read's ILLUSTRATED HISTORY OF NEW MEXICO (Santa Fe: New Mexico Printing Company. 1912), says that the Assembly authorized Armijo to raise 1000 pesos and then rescinded its resolution, leaving Armijo powerless to feed or provision his troops. *See* Lansing B. Bloom, "New Mexico Under Mexican Administration," OLD SANTA FE (April, 1915), pp. 364-5. The report of the Citizens of New Mexico to the President of Mexico, September 26. 1846, states that Armijo collected the money but did not reveal what he did with it; Max L. Moorhead (ed.), "Notes and Documents," *New Mexico Historical Review* (January, 1951), p. 72.
10. Minge, "Frontier Problems." p. 205. Bloom, "Mexican Administration," p. 360 in which the author quotes the *Minutes* of the Assembly, August 6, 1846.
11. Armijo's Proclamation. August 8. 1846. Read Papers.
12. Donaciano Vigil to the Asamblea Departamental, June 18, 1846; Legislative, 1846, MANM, in which Vigil discusses the disparity between *ricos* and *pobres* in New Mexico. For the Taos situation. *see* Manuel Alvarez Papers. 1833-1862, Bent, Charles *Correspondence*, 1839-1846, University of New Mexico. *See* also Consular Dispatches, Santa Fe, Manuel Alvarez. Memorial to Secretary of State Daniel Webster, Washington, February 2, 1846. vol. I, Naitonal Archives, Record Group No. 199.
13. Armijo to the Juez de Paz, Real del Oro, June 8. 1846; Governors's Papers, 1846. Letterbook. MANM. Julian Tenorio to Comandante Principal Juan Andrés Archuleta. March 28, 1846; Governor's Papers, 1846, communications received by Comandante Principal. Statistics on the presidial companies of Santa Fe and San Miguel del Bado can be found in Military Records, 1846. MANM.
14. Paredes to Armijo, March 25, 1846; Governor's Papers, 1846. communications received from Ministeria de Relaciones Exteriores, Gobernación y Policía, MANM. Archuleta to Armijo, February 26, 1846: Governor's Papers, 1846, communications received from within New Mexico. MANM. Armijo to the prefect of the third district, March 12, 1846; Governor's Papers, 1846, communications sent by governor, Letterbook. MANM. Circular to all prefects. June 4, 1846, Governor's Papers, 1846. Letterbook, MANM.
15. Information that the Fifth Division opposed the Plan of San Luis Potosi arrived in New Mexico January 1. 1846; Governor's Papers, 1846, communications received by comandante principal, MANM. Explanation of the change in command structure is reported in a communication from Ministario de Guerra y Marina to the archivero of the Secretaria de Guerra y Marina sometime after June 10, 1878, Beinecke Papers.

16. Governor's Proclamation, April 3, 1846, copy; Governor's Papers, 1846, communications sent by governor, proclamations, MANM. When the invasion of the Department was imminent, Armijo lowered the draft age to 15. *See* Ciruclar to the three prefects, July 18, 1846; Governor's Papers, 1846, Letterbook, MANM.
17. Armijo to the Ministro de Gerra y Marina, April 30, 1846, Beineke Papers. Armijo asked to have his friend Donaciano Vigil appointed Ayudanta Inspector to relieve his work load. It is likely that his real motive was to acquire the 3,000 pesos salary that accompanied this appointment.
18. Armijo to the Asamblea Departamental, May 11, 1846; Legislative, 1846, proceedings, MANM. Bloom, "Mexican Administration," p. 352.
19. Proclamation, June 6, 1846, as quoted in Bloom, "Mexican Administration," pp. 352-353.
20. Armijo to the Juez de Paz, San Miguel del Bado, June 23, 1846, Governor's Papers, 1846, Letterbook, MANM. Armijo to Coronel Don Pasqual Martinez, August 8, 1846; Governor's Papers, 1846, miscellaneous communications sent by governor, MANM.
21. In the Report of the Citizens of New Mexico, there is an allegation that Armijo was informed of U. S. invasion plans as early as May; Moorhead, "Notes and Documents," p. 70 note. Armijo's proclamations about the arrival of Texans or Americans can be found in Governor's Papers, 1846, Letterbook, MANM.
22. Armijo's report to the Ministro de Relaciones Exteriores, September 8, 1846; Moorhead, "Notes and Documents," p. 76. Armijo's faulty intelligence was due in part to the unusually large number of merchant caravans that accompanied Kearny's army.
23. Information on the Santa Fe citizens' meeting can be found in Bloom, "Mexican Administration," p. 363, and Read, *Illustrated History*, p. 417. Magoffin's report on the reaction of Armijo and Archuleta to his entreaties is expressed in correspondence with Secretary of War W. L. Marcy, August 26, 1846; Territorial Papers, 1846-1849, Magoffin Papers, State Records Center, Santa Fe. Testimony taken from Don Pio Sambrano on October 8, 1846, at El Paso, mentions Armijo's reluctance to assume command; Secretaría de la Defensa Nacional, Dirrecion de Archivo Militar, Operaciones Militares, California (hereinafter cited as Archivo Militar Records).
24. Armijo to the Juez de Paz of Las Vegas(?), July 3, 1846; Governor's Papers, 1846, Letterbook, MANM. Armijo may have known about a letter published in May in the *St. Louis* (Missouri) *Republican* from Thomas Hart Benton announcing that the Kearny expedition was being formed to protect the Santa Fe trade. George Winston Smith and Charles Judah (eds.), Chronicles of the Gringos (Albuquerque: University of New Mexico Press, 1968), p. 112.
25. There are a number of conflicting reports about the size of the Armijo-Speyer caravan and its arrival date. Two *guías* in the Mexican Archives of New Mexico indicate that the partners had paid their duties on this cargo by July 8, 1846, and the initials in the margins show that about one-third of the cargo belonged to Armijo; Aduana, *Guías* from New Mexico to Mexico. Hacienda Records, 1846, MANM. There are no documents supporting R. E. Twitchell's allegation that Armijo sold his share of the cargo to Speyer (Twitchell, *Old Santa Fe*, p. 250).
26. Armijo to Dan Manuel Armijo y Mestas, August 3, 1846; Governor's Papers, 1846, Letterbook, MANM.
27. Bloom, "Mexican Administration," pp. 370-1 note.
28. Magoffin Papers. Philip St. George Cooke, The Conquest of New Mexico and California (Albuquerque: Horn and Wallace, 1964), p. 31.
29. Testimony of Antonio José Apodaca, October 3, 1846, El Paso; Expediente Vol. XI 481.3/ 2199, Archivo Militar Records.
30. Donaciano Vigil was one of 105 Santa Feans who signed the Report of the Citizens of New Mexico, September 26, 1846; Moorhead, "Notes and Documents," p. 75.
31. Magoffin itemized his losses in 1849 when he appealed to the United States Government for reimbursement. Among his statements are references to bribes and payments to influential citizens. But by far the largest part of the $37,780 he claimed to have lost in out-of-pocket expenses resulted from a neglect of his mercantile business for two years and eight months; Magoffin Papers. One of the *guías* in the Mexican Archives of New Mexico shows a cargo valued at 21,601 pesos. This document is unsigned and undated. It is possible that these were the goods Armijo purchased and sent along to Chihuahua with Speyer; Aduana — *Guías* from New Mexico to Mexico, Hacienda Records, 1846, MANM.
32. Unreadable signature to Ministerio de Guerra y Marina, November 1, 1846; Expediente Vol. XI/481.3/2199, Archivo Militar Records. *See also* testimony of Santiago Magoffin, October 8, 1846, El Paso, in the same expediente.
33. Armijo to Ministro de Relaciones Exteriores, September 6, 1846, Moorhead, "Notes and Documents," pp. 76-8.
34. Ralph Paul Bieber, The Papers of James J. Webb, *Santa Fe Merchant*, 1844-1861 (Washington University Studies, Vol. XI, No. 2, 1924), p. 277.

References

35. Armijo to the Ministro de Guerra y Marina, March 30, 1847, and General Vicente Filisola to Armijo, April 9, 1847; Expediente Vol. XI/481.3/2588, Archivo Militar Records.
36. Report of Ministerio de Guerra y Marina, 1878, stating that on May 22, 1848, Armijo "fue dado de baja en el ejercito"; Beinecke Papers. Trias's letters to the Ministro de Guerra y Marina can be found in Expediente Vol . XI/481.3/3092, Archivo Militar Guerra y Marina can be found in Expediente Vol. XI/481.3/3092, Archivo Militar Records.
37. Trias to Ministro de Guerra y Marina, October 27, 1849, Expediente Vol. XI/481.3/3092, Archivo Militar Records in which it is noted that Armijo has been jailed in Chihuahua. Also in this expediente is found correspondence between the Ministro de Guerra y Marina and the Cámara which is concluded when the latter remarks that the indictment cannot be complete because of a lack of evidence. In 1854 inquiries were made about the conclusion of this investigation. Several government agencies were contacted, the final consensus being that the records had been misplaced when the American army occupied the palace at the end of the Mexican War; Expediente Vol. XI/481.3/4433, Archivo Militar Records.
38. Antonio Sandoval to Pedro García Conde, September 18, 1847; Expediente Vol. XI/481.3/3092, Archivo Militar Records.
39. Read, p. 432.
40. Twitchell, Old Santa Fe, p. 210.
41. Carlos María Bustamente, Gabinete Mexicano (Mexico: Jose M. Lara, 1842), Vol. II.
42. Armijo to Ministro de Guerra y Marina, January 12, 1846, Beinecke Papers.
43. Armijo refers to his one disgrace in letters to General Angel Trias, November 20, 1847, and to the Ministro de Guerra y Marina, March 30, 1847; see Expedientes Vol. XI/481.3/3092 and 2588, Archivo Militar Records. It is in the letter to Trias that Armijo says he does not want to reside where the enemy governs, so that when the war ends, he will be considered a loyal Mexican. The letter to Alvarez is dated April 6, 1849, a facsimile of which can be found in Read's Illustrated History, p. 364.
44. R. E. Twitchell said that Armijo had a motto by which he lived: "Vale mas estar tomado por valiente que serlo." Old Santa Fe, p. 253.

Chapter 12

The Pacific Squadron off California

1. The importance of these ports has been examined in Norman A. Graebner, EMPIRE ON THE PACIFIC: A Study in American Continental Expansion (New York: The Ronald Press, 1955).
2. George Bancroft to Commodore Sloat, June 24, 1845, in George L. Rives, THE UNITED STATES AND MEXICO, 1821-1848: A History of Relations Between the Two Countries from the Independence of Mexico to the Close of the War with the United States (2 Vols.; New York: Charles Scribner's Sons, 1912), Vol. II, p. 165. Hereafter cited as Rives, The U. S. and Mexico.
3. Ibid.
4. Joseph T. Downey, THE CRUISE OF THE PORTSMOUTH, 1845-1847: A Sailor's View of the Naval Conquest of California, Howard Lamar (ed.) (New Haven: Yale University Press, 1958), p. 237. Hubert H. Bancroft, HISTORY OF CALIFORNIA [The Works of Hubert Howe Bancroft, 39 volumes] (San Francisco: The History Company, 1886-1889), Vol. V, p. 199, states that the schooner Shark of twelve guns also was included in the Pacific Squadron. In addition Bancroft states that the frigates each carried fifty-four guns and the sloops twenty-four.
5. Rives, The U. S. and Mexico, Vol. II, p. 190.
6. Ibid.
7. Cadmus M. Wilcox, HISTORY OF THE MEXICAN WAR (Washington: The Church News Publishing Company, 1892), pp. 131-133.
8. Rives, The U. S. and Mexico, Vol. II, p. 190.
9. Bancroft, History of California, Vol. V, p. 206.
10. H. D. Barrows, "The Conquest of California," Historical Society of Southern California Annual Publications (Los Angeles: J. B. Walters Company, 1911), Vol. VIII (1909-1910), p. 78. Hereafter cited as Barrows, "The Conquest of California."
11. Bancroft, History of California, Vol. V, p. 230.
12. Thomas O. Larkin to Abel Stearns in George P. Hammond (ed.), THE LARKIN PAPERS: Personal Business and Official Correspondence of Thomas Oliver Larkin, Merchant and United States Consul in California (10 vols.; Berkeley: University of California Press, 1951-1964), Vol. V, p. 115. Hereafter cited as Hammond (ed.), Larkin Papers.

13. General Order of Commodore Sloat, July 7, 1846, in Hammond (ed.), *Larkin Papers*, Vol. V, pp. 107-108.
14. Wilcox, *History of the Mexican War*, p. 135.
15. Barrows, "The Conquest of California," p. 78.
16. Wilcox, *History of the Mexican War*, p. 133.
17. Larkin to Stearns in Hammond (ed.), *Larkin Papers*, Vol. V, p. 115.
18. Hammond (ed.), *Larkin Papers*, Vol. V, p. xvii.
19. Downey, *Cruise of the Portsmouth*, p. 127, says the ship anchored at Sausalito on June 3.
20. Wilcox, *History of the Mexican War*, pp. 125-126; Downey, Cruise of the Portsmouth, p. 128.
21. John Charles Frémont, Memoirs, Vol. I, p. 334, cited in Allan Nevins, Fremont: *Pathmaker of the West* (New York: D. Appleton-Century Company, 1939), p. 272.
22. Rives, *The U. S. and Mexico*, Vol. II, p. 187.
23. Downey, *Cruise of the Portsmouth*, p. 129.
24. Hammond (ed.), *Larkin Papers*, Vol. V, p. x.
25. Wilcox, *History of the Mexican War*, p. 135.
26. Downey, *Cruise of the Portsmouth*, p. 153.
27. Bancroft, *History of California*, Vol. V, pp. 238-240.
28. Robert W. Neeser, "The Navy's Part in the Acquisition of California," United States Naval Institute *Proceedings* (Annapolis: United States Naval Institute, 1908), Vol. XXXIV, p. 269.
29. Bancroft, *History of California*, Vol. V, p. 241.
30. Downey, *Cruise of the Portsmouth*, p. 131.
31. Neeser, "The Navy's Part in the Acquisition of California," p. 270.
32. *Ibid.*
33. Nevins, Fremont: *Pathmaker of the West*, p. 283.
34. Rives, *The U. S. and Mexico*, Vol. II, p. 194.
35. Justin H. Smith, War with Mexico (2 Vols.; New York: The MacMillan Company, 1919), Vol. I, p. 336. Frémont is referred to as a captain in the service of the United States and Gillespie as a lieutenant. After the California Battalion was organized on July 23, 1846, Frémont is cited as a major and Gillespie as a captain because of their status in that unit. These promotions were not effective in the Army of the United States. Smith's book remains the most authoritative and detailed concerning the campaigns of the War with Mexico.
36. Bancroft, *History of California*, Vol. V, p. 253.
37. *Ibid.*, p. 267.
38. Neeser, "The Navy's Part in the Acquisition of California," p. 272.
39. Edgar S. MacLay, A History of the United States Navy from 1775 to 1901 (3 Vols.; New York: D. Appleton and Company, 1906), Vol. II, p. 77.
40. Downey, *Cruise of the Portsmouth*, p. 143.
41. Smith, *War with Mexico*, Vol. I, p. 337.
42. S. F. DuPont, "The War with Mexico: The Cruise of the United States Ship *Cyane* During the Years 1845-48," United States Naval Institute *Proceedings* (Annapolis: United States Naval Institute, 1882), Vol. VIII, p. 420.
43. Bancroft, *History of California*, Vol. V, p. 281. The force was kept under arms at night because of an alarm created by two coyotes. Commodore Stockton maintains that the enemy was always in sight, threatening the flanks of the advancing American force, but this seems doubtful since the remaining Mexican troops had fled southward with Governor Pico and General Castro on August 10.
44. Nevins, Fremont: *Pathmaker of the West*, p. 292.
45. Thomas O. Larkin to James Buchanan, August 23, 1846, in Hammond (ed.), *Larkin Papers*, p. 215.
46. Smith, *War with Mexico*, Vol. I, p. 338.
47. Bancroft, *History of California*, Vol. V, 287.
48. Smith, *War with Mexico*, Vol. I, p. 340.
49. *Ibid.*
50. Accounts of General Kearny's westward march are readily available. I have utilized Ray Allen Billington's Westward Expansion: *A History of the American Frontier* (New York: The MacMillan Company, 1949), 579-581, for the basic outline of Kearny's principal activities and interspersed information from Smith's *War with Mexico*. For an account of his actions in New Mexico and prior to his arrival there, see Max L. Moorhead, New Mexico's Royal Road: *Trade and Travel on the Chihuahua Trail* (Norman: University of Oklahoma Press, 1958), pp. 153-164. Numerous personal memoirs are available, such as Ralph P. Bieber (ed.), Marching with the Army of the West (Glendale, California, 1936).
51. Downey, *Cruise of the Portsmouth*, pp. 166 and 169.
52. *Ibid.*, p. 169.

53. Nevins, FREMONT: *Pathmaker of the West*, p. 298.
54. Neeser, "The Navy's Part in the Acquisition of California," p. 274.
55. Downey, *Cruise of the Portsmouth*, pp. 182-185.
56. *Ibid.*, p. 212.
57. Smith, *War with Mexico*, Vol. I, pp. 342-344; Downey, *Cruise of the Portsmouth*, pp. 203-213.
58. Hammond (ed.), *Larkin Papers*, Vol. V, p. xvii.
59. Neeser, "The Navy's Part in the Acquisition of California," p. 275. The author erroneously refers to this agreement as the Treaty of Corvanga.
60. Downey, *Cruise of the Portsmouth*, p. 216. Frémont did not even enter Los Angeles until January 14, according to Downey. The naval elements left the town on January 20 and reëmbarked at San Pedro two days later, proceeding to San Diego where they rejoined their ships on June 24; see Downey, *Cruise of the Portsmouth*, pp. 222, 229-234.

Chapter 13

U. S. Military Forces in California

BIBLIOGRAPHY

Primary Sources

Executive Document, No. 8, REPORT OF THE SECRETARY OF WAR, December 2, 1847, pp. 77-78.
Senate Executive Document, 30th Cong., 1st Session, 1849. Maps of the battles of San Pasqual, San Gabriel and Los Angeles, with troop positions.
Record of Events Cards, Stevenson's New York Volunteer Seventh Regiment, during the Mexican War.
House Executive Document, No. 17, 31st Cong., 1st Session. Military Actions in California During the Mexican War.
National Archives Microfilm Publications, Microcopy No. 351. Compiled Service Records of Volunteer Soldiers Who Served During the Mexican War in Mormon Organizations. Roll No. 1: Mormon Battalion Volunteers, A-G; Roll No. 2: Mormon Battalion Volunteers, H-M; Roll No. 3: Mormon Battalion Volunteers, N-Z, and Captain Davis' Company A of Mormon Volunteers.
Microcopy No. 567 — Letters received by the Office of the Adjutant General (Main Series).
Microcopy No. T-135, 3 reels — *Selected Records of the General Accounting Office Relating to the Frémont Expeditions and the California Battalion, 1842-1890*.

Secondary Sources

Books

A BIOGRAPHICAL SKETCH OF THE LIFE OF WILLIAM B. IDE AND THE CONQUEST OF CALIFORNIA BY THE BEAR FLAG PARTY, by William B. Ide (Glorietta: Rio Grande Press, Inc., 1967).
THE CONQUEST OF NEW MEXICO AND CALIFORNIA — *An Historical and Personal Narrative*, by P. St. Geo. Cooke, Brigadier, Brevet Major General, U. S. A. (Albuquerque: Horn and Wallace, 1964).
Heitman, Francis B., HISTORICAL REGISTER AND DICTIONARY OF THE UNITED STATES ARMY (Washington: U. S. Government Printing Office, 1903), 2 vols.
MEXICO AND HER MILITARY CHIEFTAINS, by Fay Robinson (Glorietta: Rio Grande Press, Inc., 1970).
MILITARY GOVERNMENTS IN CALIFORNIA 1846-1850, by Theodore Grivas (Glendale: The Arthur H. Clarke Company, 1963).
THE NEW YORK VOLUNTEERS IN CALIFORNIA *including* WITH STEVENSON TO CALIFORNIA, by James Lynch, *and* STEVENSON'S REGIMENT IN CALIFORNIA, by Francis Clark, edited by D. E. Livingston-Little (Glorietta: The Rio Grande Press, Inc., 1970).
Nevins, Allan, ORDEAL OF THE UNION (New York: Charles Scribner's Sons, 1947) 2 vols.
Bill, Alfred Hoyt, REHEARSAL FOR CONFLICT (New York: Alfred A. Knopf, Inc., 1947).
Clarke, Dwight L., STEPHEN WATTS KEARNY, *Soldier of the West* (Norman: University of Oklahoma Press, 1961).
Smith, Justin H., THE WAR WITH MEXICO (Gloucester: Peter Smith, 1963) 2 vols.
Esposito, Colonel Vincent J., Editor-in-Chief, THE WEST POINT ATLAS OF AMERICAN WARS (New York: Frederick A. Praeger, 1959) Volume I, 1689-1900.

References

Periodicals

Theodore Grivas, "Alcalde Rule: The Nature of Local Government in Spanish and Mexican California," *California Historical Society Quarterly*, Volume XXXX (1961), pp. 411-432.

Remi Nadeau, "Baghdad on the Freeway," *American Heritage*, August, 1958, p. 821.

Peter Gerhard, "Baja California in the Mexican War, 1846-1848," *Pacific Historical Review*, Volume XV (1946), pp. 418-424.

James M. Jensen, "John Forster — A California Ranchero," *California Historical Society Quarterly*, Volume XLVIII (1969), pp. 219-241.

John Douglas Tanner, Jr., "Campaign for Los Angeles — December 29, 1846, to January 10, 1847," *California Historical Society Quarterly*, Volume XLVIII (1969), pp. 219-241.

Dwight L. Clarke and George Ruhlen, "The Final Roster of the Army of the West, 1846-1847," *California Historical Society Quarterly*, Volume XLIII (1964), pp. 37-44.

Les Driver, "Carrillo's Flying Artillery: The Battle of San Pedro," *California Historical Society Quarterly*, Volume XLVIII (1969), pp. 3335-349.

Dwight L. Clarke, "Soldiers Under Stephen Watts Kearny," *California Historical Society Quarterly*, Volume XLV (1966), pp. 133-148.

Chapter 14

The "All-Mexico" Movement

1. Julius W. Pratt, "John L. O'Sullivan and Manifest Destiny," *New York History*, Vol. XIV (July, 1933), pp. 221-222.
2. Frederick Merk, MANIFEST DESTINY AND MISSION IN AMERICAN HISTORY (New York, 1963), pp. 107-110.
3. *Ibid.*, p. 112.
4. *Illinois State Register*, July 17, 1846, in John D. P. Fuller, THE MOVEMENT FOR THE ACQUISITION OF ALL MEXICO, 1846-1848 (Baltimore: Johns Hopkins Press, 1936), p. 41. Hereinafter referred to as *All Mexico*.
5. *Ibid.*, p. 31.
6. Merk, *Manifest Destiny and Mission*, p. 166.
7. *Ibid.*, pp. 168-169.
8. Fuller, *All Mexico*, pp. 60-61.
9. *New York Sun*, May 27, 1847, in Merk, *Manifest Destiny and Mission*, p. 137.
10. *Ibid.*, p. 121.
11. Fuller, *All Mexico*, p. 74.
12. *Ibid.*, pp. 76-79.
13. *Ibid.*, p. 79.
14. Eugene I. McCormac, JAMES K. POLK: *A Political Biography* (New York, 1965), pp. 441-442.
15. Merk, *Manifest Destiny and Mission*, p. 152. John Hope Franklin also has demonstrated that there was a hard core of little-known Southern politicians who had contended strongly for the acquisition of all of Oregon in "'The Southern Expansionists of 1846," *Journal of Southern History*, Vol. XXV (August, 1959), pp. 323-338.
16. Merk, *Manifest Destiny and Mission*, p. 152.
17. Fuller, *All Mexico*, p. 86.
18. *Ibid.* Merk has noted that the South was virtually unified in view toward the Mexican population. Southerners tended to "fuse attitudes towards Mexicans and free Negroes . . . ." Merk, *Manifest Destiny and Mission*, pp. 161-163.
19. Fuller, *All Mexico*, p. 121.
20. *Ibid.*, p. 122.
21. Merk, *Manifest Destiny and Mission*, p. 122.
22. *Ibid.*, pp. 122-124.
23. Albert K. Weinburg, MANIFEST DESTINY (Baltimore: The Johns Hopkins Press, 1935), pp. 177-179.
24. *New York Sun*, November 20, 1847, in Merk, *Manifest Destiny and Mission*, p. 123. Merk also notes that William M. Swaim, editor of the *Philadelphia Public Ledger*, was one of the most inspired and steady supporters of the All Mexico movement. *Ibid.* See also, Fuller, *All Mexico*, p. 110.
25. *Boston Times*, January 28, 1848, in Merk, *Manifest Destiny and Mission*, p. 113.
26. Weinburg, *Manifest Destiny*, p. 177. Merk, *Manifest Destiny and Mission*, p. 164.
27. *Ibid.*, p. 158
28. Fuller, *All Mexico*, p. 110. Merk, *Manifest Destiny and Mission*, pp. 126-128.
29. *New York Herald*, January 7, 1848, in Fuller, *All Mexico*, p. 111. Merk, *Manifest Destiny and Mission*, p. 113.

30. *Ibid.*, pp. 128-130, 142-143.
31. William E. Dodd, "The West and the War With Mexico," *Journal of the Illinois State Historical Society*, Vol. V (July, 1912), in Ramon Eduardo Ruiz, ed., THE MEXICAN WAR: *Was It Manifest Destiny?* (New York, Holt, Rinehart, and Winston, 1963), pp. 40-41. Fuller, *All Mexico*, p. 115.
32. Dodd, "'The West and the War with Mexico," p. 41.
33. Merk, *Manifest Destiny and Mission*, p. 149.
34. Fuller, *All Mexico*, pp. 89-90. Merk, *Manifest Destiny and Mission*, p. 149.
35. The *Illinois State Register* was the state's outstanding spokesman for expansion. *Ibid.*, pp. 147-148.
36. Fuller, *All Mexico*, pp. 115-116.
37. Merk, *Manifest Destiny and Mission*, pp. 146, 159-160.
38. *Ibid.*, pp. 150-151. A Spanish scholar, Carlos Bosch Garcia, has implied that Americans, because of their racial bias, fulfilled their Manifest Destiny only in areas relatively devoid of foreign population. Carlos Bosch Garcia, HISTORIA DE LAS RELACIONES ENTRE MEXICO Y LOS ESTADOS UNIDOS, 1819-1848 (Mexico, 1969) in Ruiz, *The Mexican War*, pp. 62-64.
39. Fuller, *All Mexico*, p. 88. Merk has asserted that the *Picayune's* editor was inconsistent in his support of All Mexico, *Manifest Destiny and Mission*, p. 152.
40. *Ibid.*
41. Fuller, *All Mexico*, pp. 97-98, 128.
42. *Ibid.*, pp. 102-103, 128-129.
43. *Ibid.*, p. 130.
44. *Ibid.*, p. 134.
45. Milo M. Quaife, ed., THE DIARY OF JAMES K. POLK (Chicago: A. C. McClurg and Co., 1910), 4 vols., Vol. IV, pp. 471-470.
46. Fuller, *All Mexico*, p. 95.
47. McCormac, *James K. Polk*, p. 529, 88n.
48. *Niles Register*, Vol. LXXIIII, p. 392, in Fuller, *All Mexico*, p. 127.
49. *Ibid.*
50. *Ibid.*
51. Ray Billington, WESTERN EXPANSION: *A History of the American Frontier* (3rd. ed.; New York, 1967), p. 587.
52. McCormac, *James K. Polk*, p. 541.
53. Norman A. Graebner, "Party Politics and the Trist Mission," *Journal of Southern History*, Vol. XIX (May, 1963), pp. 149-154.
54. Quaife, ed., *Diary of Polk*, Vol. III, p. 313.
55. *Ibid.*, pp. 357-358.
56. Merk, *Manifest Destiny and Mission*, pp. 183-184.
57. Weinburg, *Manifest Destiny*, p. 160.
58. George L. Rives, THE UNITED STATES AND MEXICO, 1821-1848 (New York, 1913), 2 vols., Vol. II, pp. 643-644.
59. Merk, *Manifest Destiny and Mission*, pp. 180-182.
60. Justin H. Smith, THE WAR WITH MEXICO (New York: The McMillan Company, 1919), 2 vols., Vol. II, p. 309.
61. Fuller, *All Mexico*, pp. 84-85. It should be noted that the *National Whig* was a temporary journal dedicated to boosting Zachary Taylor for the Presidency and did not represent a wide range of Whiggish views.
62. Weinburg, *Manifest Destiny*, pp. 164, 176.
63. Rives, *The United States and Mexico*, Vol. II, p. 631.
64. Thomas Hart Benton, THIRTY YEARS' VIEW (New York: D. Appleton and Company, 1893), 2 vols., Vol. II, p. 710.
65. *Boston Times*, March 13, 1848, in Merk, *Manifest Destiny and Mission*, p. 189. Fuller, *All Mexico*, p. 157.
66. *New York Herald*, March 12, 1848, in *Ibid.*
67. Graebner, "Party Politics and the Trist Mission," p. 156.

Nicholas P. Trist: Treaty-Maker

Chapter 15

1. Price, Glenn W., ORIGIN OF THE WAR WITH MEXICO: *The Polk-Stockton Intrigue*, (Austin and London: University of Texas Press, 1967). Such an effort is the thesis of this book which tells a fascinating story supported by ample research and documentation.

References

2. THE DIARY OF JAMES K. POLK DURING HIS PRESIDENCY, 1845 to 1849, *Edited and annotated* by Milo M. Quaife (Chicago, 1910), Volume I, pp. 396-399. Polk's diary is a very interesting and valuable historical tool; while no doubt it was written with the thought that someday it would be published, it is more candid than would normally be expected. There is also another edition edited by Allen Nevins (1929).

3. MESSAGES AND PAPERS OF THE PRESIDENT, edited by James D. Richardson (1897), Volume V, p. 2248. There are at least two issues of the compilation. I have used one published by the Bureau of National Literature, New York; no date given.

4. *Idem*, Volume VI, p. 238.

5. *Polk's Diary*, Volume II, p. 236.

6. *Polk's Diary*, Volume II, p. 243.

7. *Polk's Diary*, Volume III, p. 260.

8. *New York Tribune*, May 12, 1846.

9. This is well covered in DISSENT IN THREE AMERICAN WARS, by Samuel Eliot Morison Frederick Merk, and Frank Freidel (Cambridge: Harvard University Press, 1970). Professor Merk treats of the Mexican War, and Professors Morison and Friedel consider the War of 1812, and the Spanish-American War respectively.

10. MESSAGE FROM THE PRESIDENT OF THE UNITED STATES TO THE TWO HOUSES OF CONGRESS, December 5, 1848: 30th Congress, 2nd Sess. *Executive Document* No. 1, Serial No. 537, p. 1084.

11. THE OTHER SIDE OR NOTES FOR THE HISTORY OF THE WAR BETWEEN MEXICO AND THE UNITED STATES, translated and edited by Albert C. Ramsay (New York, 1850), p. 32. Sometimes the work is cited under the name of Ramon Alcaraz whose name heads the list of Mexican editors who prepared the original in the Spanish language.

12. There is no full scale published biography of Trist; however in the Alderman Library of the University of Virginia there is a dissertation, in typescript and book length, covering his life, by Robert Arthur Brent. Brent was also the author of "Nicholas P. Trist and the Treaty of Guadalupe Hidalgo," *Southwestern Historical Quarterly*, Vol. LVII, No. 4 (April, 1954). Another article is, "Nicholas P. Trist, a Diplomat with Ideals," by Louis Martin Sears, *Mississippi Valley Historical Review*, (June, 1924). There is also a short note in the DICTIONARY OF AMERICAN BIOGRAPHY.

13. 26th Congress, 1st Ses. *House Report* No. 707, 1840, Serial No. 373.

14. UNITED STATES STATUTES AT LARGE, 42nd Congress, 1st Sess., p. 643.

15. *Polk's Diary*, Volume II, pp. 482, 483.

16. 30th Congress, 1st Sess., House of Representatives, *Executive Document*, No. 56, Serial No. 56, p. 186.

17. *Ibid.*, p. 201.

18. *Ibid.*, p. 21.

19. *Ibid.*, p. 142.

20. 30th Congress, 1st Sess., *Executive Document*, No. 52, Serial No. 509, p. 82. The draft treaty did provide for the granting by Mexico to the United States of a right of free passage over the Isthmus of Tehuantepec, but this also was not a *sine qua non*.

21. For more detail on possible knowledge by the Mexicans of treaty instructions, *see* Eugene Keith Chamberlain, "Nicholas Trist and Baja California," *Pacific Historical Review*, Vol. XXXII (1963), pp. 49-63.

22. *Senate Executive Document* No. 52, *supra*, p. 198, 199. The "Mississippi Question" refers to some problems as to navigation rights which arose after the Louisiana Purchase.

23. *Ibid.*, pp. 73-75.

24. A more detailed treatment of the San Diego problem is found in THE TREATY OF GUADALUPE HIDALGO, edited by George P. Hammond (Berkeley: University of California Press, 1949), pp. 73-75.

25. The quotation is from Article V of the treaty. The Atlas referred to accompanied a volume entitled, RELACION DEL VIAGE HECHO PER LOS GOLETAS SUTIL Y MEXICANA EN EL AÑO DE 1792 (Madrid, 1802). This book is extremely rare, and the atlas more so. There is a translation in English by Cecil Jane entitled, A VOYAGE TO VANCOUVER AND THE NORTHWEST COAST OF AMERICA (London, 1930). Unfortunately the atlas was not reproduced with the English translation.

26. *Senate Executive Document* No. 52, *supra*, p. 3.

27. *Ibid.*, p. 5.

28. Jack Nortrup, "Nicholas Trist's Mission to Mexico: a Reinterpretation," *Southwestern Historical Quarterly*, Vol. LXXI (1968), p. 321.

29. Ethan Allen Hitchcock, FIFTY YEARS IN CAMP AND FIELD, edited by W. A. Croffut (New York, 1909), p. 296.

30. Seymour V. Connor and Odie B. Faulk: NORTH AMERICA DIVIDED — *The Mexican War, 1846-1848* (New York: Oxford University Press, 1971).

31. Rodman, W. Paul, CALIFORNIA GOLD (Cambridge: Harvard University Press, 1947), pp. 345-348.

References

Chapter 16
Post-War Filibustering, 1850-1865

1. This idea is proposed in John Hope Franklin, THE MILITANT SOUTH (Cambridge, 1956), p. 117. For information about negotiations between the United States and Mexico concerning the Treaty of Guadalupe Hidalgo, *see* Joe A. Stout, Jr., "Nicholas P. Trist, Scoundrel or Patriot?" *Texas Military History*, Vol. III (No. 3, 1970), pp. 145-159.
2. *See House Executive Document 50*, 30 Cong., 2nd Sess., Serial 541, pp. 74-76
3. Numerous works are available. *See* Wilfrid H. Callcott, LIBERALISM IN MEXICO, 1857-1929 (Stanford, 1931), and Daniel Cosio Villegas, HISTORIA MODERNA DE MEXICO: *La Republica Restaurada*, 7 vols. (Mexico City, 1955-1965).
4. Patricia R. Herring, "A Plan for the Colonization of Sonora's Northern Frontier: The Paredes Proyestos of 1850," *The Journal of Arizona History*, Vol. X (Summer, 1969), pp. 103-114; and Odie B. Faulk (trans. and ed.), "Projected Mexican Colonies in the Borderlands, 1852," *The Journal of Arizona History*, Vol. X (Summer, 1969), pp. 115-128.
5. *Daily Alta California*, November 19, 1851. Examples of such violence can be found easily in this newspaper during the years 1851-1862.
6. *Ibid., January* 14, 1851.
7. *See* JOURNALS OF THE LEGISLATURE OF CALIFORNIA (Sacramento, 1851), pp. 104-105, 277, 452-479, 496-497; and *Daily Alta California*, January 14, 1851.
8. Ures, *El Sonorense*, May 30, 1851 (copy in Pinart Transcripts, Vol. IV, p. 312, the Bancroft Library). Other documents can be found in Alphonse Pinart, "Documents for the History of California" (Bancroft Library). See also H. H. Bancroft, HISTORY OF THE NORTH MEXICAN STATES AND TEXAS (San Francisco, 1886), 2 vols., Vol. II.
9. For the situation in France, *see* John Plamenatz, REVOLUTIONARY MOVEMENT IN FRANCE, 1815-1871 (London, 1952). For information on Raousset-Boulbon and Pindray, *see* Horacio Sobarzo, CRONICA DE LA AVENTURA DE RAOUSSET-BOULBON EN SONORA (Mexico, 1954).
10. Charles de Lambertie, LE DRAME DE LA SONORA, L'ETAT, DE SONORA, M. LE COMTE DE RAOUSSET-BOULBON ET M. CHARLES DE PINDRAY (Paris, 1855).
11. *Ibid.*, pp. 207-209 and chapter 2. *See also Daily Alta California*, October 5, 1852.
12. *Daily Alta California*, August 14, 15, 1852, and Ures, *El Sonorense*, May 14, 1852.
13. Sobarzo, *Cronica de la Aventura*, pp. 52-53. *See also Daily Alta California*, October 18, 1852.
14. Lambertie, *Le Drame de la Sonora*, pp. 256-257.
15. *Daily Alta California*, August 15, 1852.
16. *Ibid.*, August 28, 1852. *See also New York Daily Times*, August 6, 1852.
17. Lambertie, *Le Drame de la Sonora*, pp. 22-23. *See also*, Sobarzo, *Cronica de la Aventura*, pp. 91-92.
18. Cubillas to the State Congress of Sonora, Ures, September 23, 1852, Ures, *El Sonorense*, October 1, 1852.
19. *Daily Alta California*, December 18, 23, 1852.
20. Rufus K. Wyllys, THE FRENCH IN SONORA (Berkeley, 1932), p. 132. *See also Daily Alta California*, September 24, 1854, and December 18, 1852; and Lambertie, *Le Drame de la Sonora*, pp. 85 and 97.
21. W. A. Croffut. (ed.), FIFTY YEARS IN CAMP AND FIELD: *Diary of Ethan Allen Hitchcock*, U. S. A. (New York, 1909), pp. 400-403.
22. For many of the documents relating the Walker expedition *see*, Arthur H. Woodward, ed., THE REPUBLIC OF LOWER CALIFORNIA (Los Angeles, 1966). *See also Daily Alta California*, December 8, 1853, and Croffut, *Fifty Years in Camp and Field*, p. 403.
23. *San Diego Herald*, December 3, 1853.
24. Rufus K. Wyllys, "The Republic of Lower California, 1853-1854," *Pacific Historical Review*, Vol. II (June 1933), pp. 194-213.
25. *Daily Alta California*, January 10, 1854. *See also* William O. Scroggs, FILIBUSTERS AND FINANCERS: *William Walker and His Associates* (New York, 1916), p. 41.
26. *San Diego Herald*, January 28, 1854.
27. *Ibid.*, May 5, 1854.
28. A. De Lachapelle, LE COMITE DE RAOUSSET-BOULBON ET L'EXPEDITION DE LA SONORA (Paris, 1859), p. 138.
29. Lambertie, *Le Drame de la Sonora*, p. 105. The United States Government experienced diplomatic difficulties as a result of ths activities; *see*, James Gadsden to William Marcy, Mexico City, Ministeral Despatches, Department of State, RG 69, National Archives. (Microfilm publication).
30. José N. Yañez, "Detall y Algunes Documentos," Ures, *El Nacional*, August 25, 1854, pp. 243-246, in Pinart Transcripts, Sonora, V.

233

References

31. J. M. Yañez to Prefect, Guaymas, August 9, 1854, in *ibid.*, p. 148.
32. For the story of the Crabb expedition, *see* Joe A. Stout, Jr., "Henry A. Crabb: Filibuster or Colonizer?" *The American West*, Vol. VIII (May, 1971), pp. 4-9. *See also* Robert H. Forbes, CRABB'S EXPEDITION INTO SONORA (Tucson, 1952).
33. DATOS HISTORICOS SOBRE FILIBUSTEROS DE 1857, EN CABORCA, SON, (Caborca, Sonora, 1926), p. 10. *See also* J. Y. Ainsa, HISTORY OF THE CRABB EXPEDITION INTO N. SONORA (Phoenix, 1951).
34. For Mexican attitudes *see*, *Mexico City Estandarte Nacional*, April 24, 1857, Ministeral despatches. For a report of a participant of the expedition, *see* "Sworn Sttaement of Charles Edward Evans," in Correspondence, Charles B. Smith to John Forsyth, September 14, 1857, Mazatlan, in United States Congress *House Executive Document* No. 64, p. 65.
35. *Daily Alta California*, August 3, 1857.
36. *House Executive Document* No. 54, p. 74.
37. Evan J. Coleman, ed., "Senator Gwin's Plan for the Colonization of Sonora," *Overland Monthly*, second series, Vol. XVII, p. 606 (1891). All of the correspondence and documents relating to Gwin's Mexican plan were published during 1891 in the *Overland Monthly* (January-December).
38. See an interesting article concerning the French in Mexico and William Gwin in Lately Thomas, "The Operator and the Emperors," *American Heritage*, Vol. XV (April, 1964), pp. 4-23, 83-84.
39. Hallie M. McPherson, "The Plan of William McKendree Gwin for a Colony in North Mexico, 1863-1865," *Pacific Historical Review*, Vol. II (December, 1933), pp. 357-386.
40. William Gwin to Napoleon III, Mexico, July 3, 1865, *Overland Monthly*, Vol. XVII, second series, p. 596. For a complete biography of Gwin *see*, Lately Thomas, BETWEEN TWO EMPIRES: *The Life Story of California's First Senator, William McKendree Gwin* (Boston, 1969).

Chapter 17

Changing Interpretations of the Mexican War, 1846-1970

1. For the results of research, *see* Seymour V. Connor and Odie B. Faulk, NORTH AMERICA DIVIDED: *The Mexican War, 1846-1848* (New York: Oxford University Press, 1971).
2. All 766 items are included in the bibliography in *ibid.*, pp. 185-287.
3. Research funds for this project came from Texas Tech University, which I here gratefully acknowledge. Additionally, the research into the 766 items used in this study was made possible by a grant from the Henry E. Huntington Library and Art Gallery of San Marino, California.

Contributors

LOWELL L. BLAISDELL, professor of history, Texas Technological University, specializes in European history, which has led him into the early history of Mexico. His authorship of "The Santangelo Case: A Controversial Claim," is a natural outcome of his European studies. He also specializes in the themes of Revolution, its causes, circumstances, and personnel. Professor Blaisdell earned his Ph.D. degree at the University of Wisconsin in 1949 and has been a member of the history department at Texas Tech for the past fifteen years. He has published one monograph, THE DESERT REVOLUTION (1962), and various articles and book reviews in scholarly historical journals.

JOHN R. COLLINS, presently an assistant buyer for Neiman-Marcus Department Store in Dallas, Texas, is working toward his Ph.D. degree at Oklahoma State University. He received his B.A. degree at the University of Texas in 1969 and his M.A. at O. S. U. in 1971. He has authored several book reviews for JOURNAL of the WEST.

SEYMOUR V. CONNOR, a Fellow and past-president of the Texas State Historical Association, is a professor of history at Texas Technological University. He has published many articles on the history of the Southwest and a number of books, including THE PETERS COLONY OF TEXAS; TEXAS TREASURY PAPERS (3 vols.); A BIGGERS CHRONICLE; ADVENTURE IN GLORY; TEXAS: *A History;* NORTH AMERICA DIVIDED (with Odie B. Faulk); DEAR AMERICA; and other books.

SISTER MAGDALEN COUGHLIN, C. S. J., completed her undergraduate study at the College of St. Catherine in St. Paul, Minnesota, and did graduate study at the University of Nijmegen in The Netherlands, the University of Minnesota, Mount Saint Mary's College, Los Angeles, and the University of Southern California, where she earned her Ph.D. degree under Dr. Manuel Servín. She has been the recipient of a Fulbright Scholarship and of a Haynes Research Grant. Her special interest in Western history has been in the New England merchants' movement to the California Coast; four studies in this area have been published. She has also authored a number of book reviews. At the present time Sister Magdalen is dean for academic development at Mount Saint Mary's college in Los Angeles.

ODIE B. FAULK is professor of history at Oklahoma State University, Stillwater. He developed the inspiration for publishing this volume after he served as guest editor-in-chief for a topical number of JOURNAL of the WEST entitled "The Mexican War: *A Seminar Approach,*" which appeared in April, 1972. Professor Faulk is both a precise and a prolific historian. In 1972, he added volumes 18 and 19 to his list of published works. The two books, published by Oxford University Press, are (No. 19) TOMBSTONE: *Myth and Reality,* and, in co-authorship with Seymour V. Connor, NORTH AMERICA DIVIDED: *The Mexican War.* The last book mentioned earned the authors the Western Heritage Award for the best Western non-fiction book of 1971. Dr. Faulk earned his scholarly letters, B.S. (1958), M.A. (1960), and Ph.D. (1962), at Texas Technological College.

Contributors

JOE GIBSON received his B.A. degree at Texas Technological University. In 1970 he authored a chapter, "The History of the Legal Profession in Baylor County, 1879-1930," for THE HISTORY OF BAYLOR COUNTY. In addition to writing many analytical book reviews for JOURNAL of the WEST, and other publications, Gibson is presently teaching high school history at New Deal, Texas. He is completing his M.A. degree at Texas Tech.

CHERYL HAUN is currently a Ph.D. candidate at O. S. U. She earned her B.A. degree at Phillips University, Enid, Oklahoma, in 1969 and her M.A. degree at O. S. U. in 1972. She has been published as a book review author many times in JOURNAL of the WEST and other historical publications.

JAMES HIGH, a Ph.D. from the University of California, Berkeley (1951), is a retired lieutenant colonel, U.S. Marine Corps Reserve. His specialty is the history of civil affairs in Southeast Asia, where he is currently on sabbatical leave from California State University, San Jose. Dr. High has authored a textbook, TEACHING SECONDARY SCHOOL SOCIAL STUDIES (New York: John Wiley, 1962).

DONALD E. HOUSTON, a B.A. from Midwestern University, received his M.A. degree in 1971 at O. S. U. and is now a Ph.D. candidate at that institution. He has contributed many book reviews to JOURNAL of the WEST. His specialty in history treats upon the military phases of the advance of our history toward "Manifest Destiny."

THOMAS R. IREY earned his M.A. (1971) at O. S. U. and is now working on his Ph.D. at the University of Oklahoma. His particular field of interest is the history of science.

KENNETH M. JOHNSON is a San Francisco attorney-at-law and historian. He received his B.A. and J.D. degrees at Stanford University and practiced law in San Jose and San Francisco, where he was a member of the legal staff of the Bank of America. In 1968 he retired from the bank with the title of vice-president and counsel. Johnson is the author or editor of fifteen books on Western history. In 1966 he received an Award of Merit from the California Historical Society. His particular area of historical study centers on Baja California.

OAKAH L. JONES, JR., received his B.S. degree at the U. S. Naval Academy, Annapolis, Maryland, in 1953. In 1964 he earned his Ph.D. degree at the University of Oklahoma. He is now a professor of history at the U. S. Air Force Academy, in Colorado. Since the inception of JOURNAL of the WEST he has been a regular editorial staff member. His chapter in this book, which was published in JOURNAL of the WEST in April, 1966, led the editors to publish their first topical number, "The Conquest of California." Professor Jones has authored two books: PUEBLO WARRIORS AND SPANISH CONQUEST (1966) and SANTA ANNA (1968). In addition he has edited reprints of FEDERAL CONTROL OF WESTERN APACHES, by Ralph Ogle (1970), and MY ADVENTURES IN ZUNI, by Frank Hamilton Cushing (1970). He also served as guest editor-in-chief for the "Spanish Borderlands" topical number of JOURNAL of the WEST that appeared in January, 1969, and which he is now re-editing and developing into a textbook.

Contributors

PAUL F. LAMBERT is a Ph.D. candidate at O.S.U. He received his B.A. degree at East Central State College in 1968 and his M. A. degree at O. S. U. in 1971. He is a valued book reviewer for JOURNAL *of the* WEST.

D. E. LIVINGSTON-LITTLE, professor of history, Los Angeles Valley College, Van Nuys, California, like Professor Jones, has been a permanent member of the editorial staff of JOURNAL *of the* WEST since its inception in 1962. By his work with the editors of the Journal he has authored or edited three books on Western history. His first work, THE ECONOMIC HISTORY OF NORTH IDAHO, 1800-1900, ran serially in the Journal. His next book, which he edited, was entitled THE MEXICAN WAR DIARY OF THOMAS D. TENNERY (University of Oklahoma Press, 1970), and then came THE NEW YORK VOLUNTEERS IN CALIFORNIA: *With Stevenson in California* and *Stevenson's Regiment in California* (Río Grande Press, Inc., 1970). The professor is book review editor of JOURNAL *of the* WEST. He also served as guest editor-in-chief of one of the journal's topical numbers, "Indian Non-Military Intra-tribal and International Relations" in July, 1971.

STEPHEN B. OATES earned his Ph.D. degree at the University of Texas. He is a Fellow of the Texas State Historical Association and a contributing editor of *The American West*. He is presently a professor in the department of history at the University of Massachusetts, Amherst. He is the author of VISIONS OF GLORY: *Texans on the Southwestern Frontier* (1970) from which his chapter in this present work is taken, CONFEDERATE CAVALRY WEST OF THE RIVER (1961), THE REPUBLIC OF TEXAS (1968) and editor of RIP FORD'S TEXAS (1966). In addition he has written many articles on the Southwestern Frontier, the Mexican War, and the Civil War.

CURTIS R. REYNOLDS, a member of the history department, Tulsa Junior College, first appeared in print with book reviews for JOURNAL *of the* WEST. His first feature article for the Journal has been developed into the chapter he authored for this volume. He is a Ph.D. candidate at Oklahoma State University where he has earned his B.A. (1969) and his M.A. (1970.)

JOSEPH A. STOUT, JR., teaches history at Oklahoma State University and is director of the Will Rogers Research Project at the same institution. He earned his doctorate at O.S.U. and, aside from his many contributions of book reviews and feature articles to JOURNAL *of the* WEST, he has been published widely in his special field of historical interest: the filibustering expeditions by Americans and other foreigners into Mexico following the Mexican War.

DANIEL TYLER graduated from Harvard College in 1955. He then served in the U. S. Air Force as a jet fighter instructor. Upon leaving the military service he resumed his professional career, teaching high school history in Honolulu, Hawaii. He later received an M.A. degree at Colorado State University, Fort Collins, and pursued a doctorate in Western history at the University of New Mexico, under the direction of Donald C. Cutter. Tyler teaches Colorado and Southwest history at Colorado State University.

Index

E404 .F38 1973   c.1
Faulk, Odie B.   100105 000
The Mexican War, changing inte

3 9310 00031022 5
GOSHEN COLLEGE-GOOD LIBRARY